The Responsive Union

The European Union (EU) faces a serious crisis of democratic legitimacy. Citizens believe that the EU is run by distant and nonresponsive political elites. The EU's perceived lack of responsiveness to ordinary citizens poses a threat to its very survival. This timely book presents a comprehensive account of how EU governments signal responsiveness to the interests of their citizens over European policies. Schneider develops and tests a theoretical framework of the intergovernmental dimension of responsive governance in the EU, using evidence amassed over nearly ten years of multi-method research. The findings show that European cooperation in the Council of the EU takes place in the shadow of national elections. Governments signal responsiveness to their publics by taking positions that are in the interests of politically relevant voters at the national level, defending these positions throughout negotiations in the Council, and seeking appropriate policy outcomes at the EU level.

CHRISTINA J. SCHNEIDER is Associate Professor and Jean Monnet Chair of the EU at the University of California, San Diego. Professor Schneider is the author of *Conflict, Negotiation and European Union Enlargement*, published by Cambridge University Press in 2009. Her articles appear in the *American Journal of Political Science*, *British Journal of Political Science*, *International Organization*, and *International Studies Quarterly*, among others.

The Responsive Union
National Elections and European Governance

Christina J. Schneider
University of California

CAMBRIDGE
UNIVERSITY PRESS

CAMBRIDGE
UNIVERSITY PRESS

University Printing House, Cambridge CB2 8BS, United Kingdom

One Liberty Plaza, 20th Floor, New York, NY 10006, USA

477 Williamstown Road, Port Melbourne, VIC 3207, Australia

314–321, 3rd Floor, Plot 3, Splendor Forum, Jasola District Centre, New Delhi – 110025, India

79 Anson Road, #06-04/06, Singapore 079906

Cambridge University Press is part of the University of Cambridge.

It furthers the University's mission by disseminating knowledge in the pursuit of education, learning, and research at the highest international levels of excellence.

www.cambridge.org
Information on this title: www.cambridge.org/9781108472319
DOI: 10.1017/9781108589413

© Christina J. Schneider 2019

This publication is in copyright. Subject to statutory exception and to the provisions of relevant collective licensing agreements, no reproduction of any part may take place without the written permission of Cambridge University Press.

First published 2019

Printed and bound in Great Britain by Clays Ltd, Elcograf S.p.A.

A catalogue record for this publication is available from the British Library.

Library of Congress Cataloging-in-Publication Data
Names: Schneider, Christina J., author.
Title: The responsive union : national elections and European governance / Christina J. Schneider.
Description: New York : Cambridge University Press, 2018.
Identifiers: LCCN 2018022550 | ISBN 9781108472319 (hardback) | ISBN 9781108459259 (paperback)
Subjects: LCSH: Elections–European Union countries. | Political participation–European Union countries. | European Union.
Classification: LCC JN45 .S36 2018 | DDC 324.94–dc23
LC record available at https://lccn.loc.gov/2018022550

ISBN 978-1-108-47231-9 Hardback

Cambridge University Press has no responsibility for the persistence or accuracy of URLs for external or third-party internet websites referred to in this publication and does not guarantee that any content on such websites is, or will remain, accurate or appropriate.

To my family

Contents

List of Figures		*page* ix
List of Tables		xi
List of Acronyms		xii
Acknowledgments		xiv

1	Responsive Governance in the European Union	1
	1.1 The Argument in Brief	5
	1.2 Core Contributions	7
	1.3 Plan of the Book	10
2	The Politicization of European Cooperation	17
	2.1 Electoral Volatility and Prudential Motivations	19
	2.2 The Erosion of Domestic Electioneering	26
	2.3 The Politicization of the EU	31
	2.4 Conclusion	39
3	Signals of Responsiveness: A Theory	42
	3.1 Domestic Electoral Competition	43
	3.2 Bargaining over Policies in the European Union	48
	3.3 Signaling Political Responsiveness	56
	3.4 Principal Implications of the Theory	68
4	The EU-Aware Voter	72
	4.1 The Survey	73
	4.2 Variables and Model Specification	81
	4.3 Findings	83
	4.4 Conclusion	90
5	The EU Budget: Financially Trivial, Politically Substantial	93
	5.1 A Primer on the EU Budget	96
	5.2 The Salience of the Budget	101
	5.3 The Measure of Responsiveness: Budget Shares	106
	5.4 Signaling Responsiveness in Budget Negotiations	112
	5.5 The Fruit of Responsiveness: Public Approval	135
	5.6 Conclusion	141
6	Triumph and Agony in the 2007–2013 MFF Negotiations	146
	6.1 The Multiannual Financial Perspectives	151
	6.2 The Context: Four Fault Lines	157
	6.3 Negotiations under Predestination	165
	6.4 Summing Up	206

viii Contents

7 The Legislative Leviathan Marionette 212
   7.1 Why Focus on Position Defending? 215
   7.2 Data and Variables 218
   7.3 During Election Periods, Hold the Line 226
   7.4 The Unconditional Absence of Public Compromise 230
   7.5 Potential Costs Discourage Frivolous Defense 236
   7.6 Conclusion 245

8 The Waiting Game: *Après les élections, le déluge* 249
   8.1 Data and Variables 252
   8.2 With Elections Pending, Stall 257
   8.3 Time-Constrained or Electorally Motivated? 262
   8.4 The Potential for Conflict 263
   8.5 Conclusion 265

9 When the Music Stops: The German Politics of the Greek Bailout 267
   9.1 The Genesis of the Greek Crisis 270
   9.2 The *Schwäbische Hausfrau* Policy 276
   9.3 Fiddling While Rome Burns 281
   9.4 On the Road to Damascus 285
   9.5 The Wages of Defiance 290
   9.6 Conclusion 296

10 The European Republic 298

References 312
Index 334

Figures

1.1	Trust in the Council of the European Union	page 4
2.1	Electoral Volatility in Western Europe, 1950–2010	22
2.2	Government Approval Ratings in Western Europe, 1977–2002	24
2.3	Electoral Outcomes in Europe, 1970–2009	26
2.4	European Integration Index, 1955–2015	31
2.5	Public Interest in European Politics, 1975–1994	34
2.6	Politicization Index, 1990–2010	36
3.1	Political Responsiveness: Stages and Linkages	57
3.2	Analytical Framework for Political Responsiveness	63
4.1	German Attitudes toward Bailout and Immigration, 2016	76
4.2	Instructions for the Choice-Based Variant 1 Conjoint	80
4.3	Position Taking and Voter Support	84
4.4	Position Defending and Voter Support	86
4.5	Credit Claiming and Voter Support	88
4.6	Negotiation Competence and Voter Support	89
5.1	EU Budget Allocations by Heading, 2015	98
5.2	Google Trends of EU Budget, Foreign, and Immigration Policies, 2004–2016	106
5.3	Percentage EU Budget Shares, 1977–2013	108
5.4	Percentage EU Budget Shares by Member State, 1977–2013	110
5.5	Elections and Budget Shares for the Netherlands and Spain, 1977–2013	111
5.6	The Electoral Incentive Over Time	119
5.7	The Electoral Incentive and Unemployment Rates	121
5.8	The Electoral Incentive and Government Approval	123
5.9	The Electoral Incentive and Electoral Uncertainty	125
5.10	The Electoral Incentive and Formal Power	128
5.11	The Electoral Incentive and Ideological Divergence	130
5.12	The Electoral Incentive and Divergence in EU Support	132
5.13	The Electoral Incentive and Number of Claimants	134
5.14	Public Approval Levels of EU Governments, 1976–2002	137

List of Figures

7.1	Issues in CO_2 Emission Allowances for the Aviation Industry	221
7.2	Position Defense across Member States, 1998–2008	223
7.3	Position Defense in and out of Election Periods, 1998–2008	224
7.4	Salience of Legislative Issues in DEU II, 1998–2008	231
7.5	The Electoral Incentive, Position Defense, and Issue Salience	233
7.6	Electorally Motivated Unconditional Position Defending	235
7.7	Bargaining Success by Member State, 1998–2008	238
7.8	The Electoral Incentive, Bargaining Success, and Issue Salience	241
7.9	Electorally Motivated Non-Frivolous Position Defending	242
8.1	Duration of Legislative Negotiations, 1976–2009	254
9.1	Public Debt and Budget Deficits for Greece and the Eurozone, 2005–2012	271
9.2	Economic Indicators during the Eurozone Crisis	273
9.3	German Public Opinion during the Eurozone Crisis	285
9.4	Stuck between a Rock and a Hard Place	289

Tables

2.1	Delegation of Competences in the EU since 2009	page 29
2.2	Public Interest in European Affairs, 2015	35
3.1	Strategies to Signal Political Responsiveness	61
4.1	Demographics of the Survey Sample (in %)	74
4.2	Politician Attributes and Signals of Responsiveness	79
4.3	Choice-Based Variant 1 Conjoint (English)	81
5.1	Signals of Responsiveness in the EU Budget, 1977–2013	115
5.2	Signals of Responsiveness and Public Approval, 1977–2002	140
5.3	Summary of the Empirical Findings	142
6.1	Negotiating the Financial Perspectives, 1987–2014	154
6.2	Financing the UK Rebate	160
6.3	Context of the MFF 2007–2013 Negotiations, 2004	162
6.4	Preference Alignments in the MFF 2004–2013 Negotiations	167
6.5	Commission Proposal and Council Agreement, MFF 2007–2013	173
6.6	Proposals for the UK Rebate and Total Commitments, 2005	193
7.1	Position Defending in Legislative Negotiations, 1998–2008	227
7.2	Bargaining Success in Legislative Negotiations, 1998–2008	239
7.3	Revised Summary of the Empirical Findings	245
8.1	Elections and Legislative Delays	258
8.2	EU4 Elections and Legislative Delays	260
8.3	Time Constraint or Electoral Delay?	262

Acronyms

AR	Autoregressive
CAP	Common Agricultural Policies
CDU	Christlich Demokratische Partei Deutschlands/Christian Democratic Union
CEE	Central and Eastern European
CFSP	Common Foreign and Security Policy
COREPER	Committee of Permanent Representatives
CSDP	Common Security and Defense Policy
CSP	Common Structural Policies
CSU	Christlich-Soziale Union in Bayern/Christian Social Union in Bavaria
DEU	Decision-Making in the EU Dataset
EAGGF	European Agricultural Guidance and Guarantee Funds
EC	European Community
ECSC	European Coal and Steel Community
EC	European Community
ECU	European Currency Unit
EDC	European Defense Community
EDF	European Development Fund
EEA	European Economic Area
EFTA	European Free Trade Association
EMU	European Monetary Union
EP	European Parliament
ERDF	European Reconstruction and Development Funds
ESF	European Social Funds
ESIF	European Structural and Investment Funds
EU	European Union
EULO	European Union Legislative Output Dataset
EUR	Euro
FDP	Freie Demokratische Partei Deutschlands/Free Democratic Party
FYRM	Former Yugoslav Republic of Macedonia

List of Acronyms

GDP	Gross Domestic Product
GNI	Gross National Income
GNP	Gross National Product
GVA	Gross Value Added
IFOP	Institut Français D'Opinion Publique/French Institute of Public Opinion
IGC	Intergovernmental Conferences
IMF	International Monetary Fund
IMP	Integrated Mediterranean Programs
IQR	Interquartile Range
MFF	Multiannual Financial Framework
NHS	National Health Service
NATO	North Atlantic Treaty Organization
NRW	Nordrhein-Westfalen/North-Rhine Westfalia
OLS	Ordinary Least Squares
PPS	Purchasing Power Standards
QMV	Qualified Majority Vote
SEA	Single European Act
SGP	Stability and Growth Pact
SPD	Sozialdemokratische Partei Deutschlands/Social Democratic Party
SSI	Shapley–Shubik Index
TEU	Treaty on European Union
TFEU	Treaty on the Functioning of the European Union
TVC	Time-Varying Covariates
UK	United Kingdom
UKIP	United Kingdom Independence Party
UN	United Nations
VAT	Value-Added Tax
WEU	Western European Union
WTO	World Trade Organization

Acknowledgments

This book would not exist without the generous help and support from various directions. I would like to thank, first of all, my family and friends, for their enduring patience, encouragement, and good suggestions.

The seed of the idea to analyze the democratic politics of European cooperation was planted almost ten years ago when I was a postdoctoral fellow at the Niehaus Center for Globalization and Governance at Princeton University. Based on a discussion I had with the participants of the International Relations seminar, while I was presenting a paper on European cooperation, I became intrigued by the question of whether and how EU governments respond to national electoral pressures when cooperating at the European level. I especially want to thank Helen Milner for providing me with the opportunity to spend a year to develop the basic idea, and for her continued support over the past decade. For various fruitful conversations and suggestions during this period, I am also indebted to Andy Moravcsik, Christina Davis, Sophie Meunier, and my co-fellows at the Niehaus Center at Princeton.

From the basic idea to the finished book manuscript, it took almost a decade of theory development and refinement, data collection, and data analysis. I presented the manuscript at different stages of development at two book workshops. The first took place in January 2016 at UCSD, the second one almost one year later in January 2017 at the University of Konstanz. I am deeply indebted to Stefanie Bailer, Daniela Beyer, Christophe Crombez, Anastasia Ershova, Peter Gourevitch, Hakan Gunaydin, Emilie Hafner-Burton, Steph Haggard, Simon Hug, Daniela Kroll, David Lake, Dirk Leuffen, Helen Milner, Mark Pollack, Ken Scheve, Frank Schimmelfennig, Gerald Schneider, and Kaare Strøm for their participation in these workshops, the time that they spent reading and discussing the manuscript, and their constructive comments and suggestions. These discussions guided the substantive revisions of the book and improved it considerably.

Acknowledgments

I completed the book manuscript at the University of Konstanz, where I was an Alexander-von-Humboldt Experienced Fellow from March 2016 to August 2017, sitting in an office atop a hill facing the beautiful Lake Constance. I am grateful to the Alexander-von-Humboldt Foundation, which provided me with the financial and logistic support for this endeavor. Very special thanks go to Dirk Leuffen and Gerald Schneider, who were my hosts at the University of Konstanz and who provided me with the necessary support to complete the final draft of the book. In addition to the financial support from the Humboldt Foundation, I gratefully acknowledge financial support from the Lifelong Learning Programme of the European Union, the Graduate School of Decision Sciences at the University of Konstanz, and the UCSD Academic Senate.

The work has also gained from the fruitful discussions with colleagues and friends at various workshops and invited presentations. First of all, I would like to thank my colleagues at the political science department and the School of Global Policy & Strategy at UCSD. The intellectually vibrant and collegial atmosphere at UCSD provided vital support while I was writing this book. My colleagues were willing to provide comments and discuss issues pertaining to the main argument in the manuscript on multiple occasions, whether formally during workshop presentations or informally over coffee.

At UCSD and beyond, I received constructive suggestions from Marisa Abrajano, Christine Arnold, Jørgen Bølstad, Christian Breyer, Lawrence Broz, Marius Busemeyer, Tim Büthe, Eugenia da Conceicao-Heldt, Catherine de Vries, Pieter de Wilde, Antoaneta Dimitrova, Axel Dreher, Katjana Gattermann, Edgar Grande, Julia Gray, Markus Haverland, Seth Hill, Dan Honig, Leslie Johns, Dan Keleman, Matthias Matthijs, Heather McKibben, Maurits Meijers, Mareike Kleine, Yvette Peters, Thomas Plümper, Sven-Oliver Proksch, Anne Rasmussen, Christian Rauh, Berthold Rittberger, Molly Roberts, Branislav Slantchev, Jonathan Slapin, Art Stein, Robert Thomson, Johannes Urpelainen, David Wiens, Christopher Williams, Thomas Winzen, Christopher Wratil, Nikoleta Yordanova, and Asya Zhelyazkova. I am grateful to the participants of seminars at Princeton University (2008), University of California at Los Angeles (2015), Stanford University (2015), University of California at San Diego (2015), the Political Economy of International Organization Conference (2016, 2018), the Half-Baked Ideas Workshop at UCSD (2016), the University of Heidelberg (2016), the University of Konstanz (2016), the EU Centre of Excellence Speaker Series at McGill University (2016), the European Political Science Association Conference (2016), the University of Essex

(2017), the University of Munich (2017), the School of Advanced International Studies at Johns Hopkins (2017), and the Workshop on "Understanding Responsiveness in European Union Politics" at the Lorentz Center in Leiden, Netherlands (2018).

The analyses in the book rely on a number of different data sources. I am grateful to Dirk Leuffen, Frank Schimmelfennig, and Robert Thomson who were willing to share their data on legislative policies, the timing of legislative politics, and European integration with me. A special thank you goes to Michael Bechtel and Ken Scheve who provided guidance with the design of the conjoint experiment and incorporated my conjoint experiment into a larger survey they conducted in Germany. Roman Liesch provided expert help with setting up the online survey. The qualitative case study on the German politics on the Greek financial rescue package relies on a number of interviews with political and administrative elites in the German government and German opposition parties. Despite their hectic schedules, the interviewees gave an incredible amount of their time to answer my questions, and their insights were immeasurably valuable for the analysis. Abigail Vaughn provided invaluable research assistance and proofread various drafts of the book manuscript.

At Cambridge University Press, I would like to thank John Haslam, the commissioning editor of Social Sciences, as well as Tobias Ginsberg, the assistant editor, for their expert handling of my manuscript. I also owe an immense debt of gratitude to the anonymous reviewers for their excellent comments on the manuscript.

Most of all, I want to thank my husband Branislav. Our countless discussions and his supporting presence have immensely contributed to the success of the project. He was willing to engage in discussions about the book manuscript day and night. He always had my back so that I had the time to work on the project. And he pulled me away from my obsession with this manuscript to enjoy life and get perspective when I most needed it.

Unfortunately, I cannot thank everyone who has directly or indirectly contributed to the success of this work. My special thanks therefore go to everyone whom I did not mention and who inspired, motivated, and encouraged me in various stages of my project.

1 Responsive Governance in the European Union

> Every citizen shall have the right to participate in the democratic life of the Union. Decisions shall be taken as openly and as closely as possible to the citizen.
> – Treaty on European Union, Article 10.3

International organizations (IOs) have proliferated since the end of World War II, and they play a vital role in countries around the world. Governments have delegated significant decision-making powers to these organizations even in areas that directly affect their autonomy, because it is commonly believed that IO membership offers many benefits. With the increasing involvement of IOs in domestic affairs of member states, however, the criticism that they are elitist and technocratic has grown as well. Commentators assert that decisions are taken out of the voters' hands and transferred to unelected political elites. Since these bureaucrats and foreign actors are not accountable to domestic publics, decisions made in IOs are undemocratic and illegitimate.

According to the critics, IOs suffer from a "democratic deficit," which erodes both the ability and the willingness of governments to take policy positions and make decisions that represent the preferences of their citizens. The absence of domestic democratic scrutiny is said to give executives wide latitude to pursue their own goals, permit corporate groups to intervene in the policy process unchecked, and allow international bureaucrats to exploit their autonomy to tilt policies toward their organizational or parochial interests. Policies shaped by these influences might well conflict with broader societal preferences.

This crisis of legitimacy has afflicted many international integration projects around the world, including the European Union (EU), Mercosur, the North American Free Trade Agreement (NAFTA), the Association of Southeast Asian Nations (ASEAN), the World Trade Organization (WTO), the International Monetary Fund (IMF), and even the United Nations (UN).[1] With the ever-growing number of

---

[1] See, for example, Anderson (1999); Zweifel (2006); Malamud (2008); Joseph (2011); Zaum (2013); Dellmuth and Tallberg (2015); Colgan and Keohane (2017).

policies being made in these IOs, the pressure to "democratize" them has increased. For example, in its determination to improve the legitimacy and viability of IOs, the US State Department settled on their democratization as one of its main goals in the early 2000s.[2]

Nowhere has this debate been more salient than in the most ambitious project of regional integration in the world, the EU.[3] Dramatic setbacks in several policy areas over the past decade have only inflamed the charges against it. On the economic side, the Greek debt crisis of 2010 triggered a financial and political turmoil that brought the Eurozone to the verge of collapse. No sooner had the EU managed to stabilize its panicked markets than it confronted a security crisis when Russia annexed Crimea in the spring of 2014. This, and the civil war in Ukraine that followed, aggravated the already tense external security situation for the bloc. Doubts in the EU's ability to provide for its own security intensified in 2015 when it failed to thwart two major terrorist attacks in Paris and Brussels. The issue became even more complex and contentious when it merged with the problem of dealing with an unprecedented influx of refugees from the Middle East and North Africa. The disunity the EU showed in its failure to fashion a collective response to this mass migration was starkly underlined in June 2016 when a popular referendum in the United Kingdom decided to withdraw the country from the EU, precipitating a still-unfolding period of uncertainty and economic instability for the region.

The cumulative effect of these shocks has been to sharpen the EU's legitimacy crisis and to contribute to a rising wave of populism across Europe. Many Europeans have come to see the EU as being run by distant and unaccountable political elites who negotiate esoteric deals behind closed doors. Public perception of the institution took a nosedive in the 2010s, when for the first time since the early days of integration there were more Europeans who distrusted the EU than those who trusted it.[4]

---

[2] See the statements by Kim R. Holmes, Assistant Secretary for International Organizations Affairs in 2003 and 2004. Retrieved from https://2001-2009.state.gov/p/io/rls/rm/2003/26949.htm and https://2001-2009.state.gov/p/io/rls/rm/2004/39496.htm, accessed November 2016.

[3] The EU has changed its name several times since its inception: from the original "European Coal and Steel Community" in 1951 to "European Economic Community" in 1957, to "European Communities" in 1967, and to "European Union" in 1993. To avoid confusion of terms, I use the term "European Union" throughout this book even though it is anachronistic prior to 1993.

[4] Data from the Interactive Eurobarometer (http://ec.europa.eu/COMMFrontOffice/Public/index.cfm/Chart/index, accessed September 2016). The question was phrased as: "I would like to ask you a question about how much trust you have in certain institutions. For each of the following institutions, please tell me if you tend to trust it or

It is not merely faceless unelected bureaucrats in Brussels – like the ones who administer the European Commission – that citizens have come to suspect. Even the ministers from their own elected governments have lost the citizens' confidence when acting in their capacity as members of the Council of the European Union.[5] Trust in the Council, which is the EU's main intergovernmental legislative decision-making body, has been steadily eroding since the outbreak of the debt crisis (Figure 1.1). By 2013, only 33 percent of Europeans trusted the Council, while more than 44 percent did not. When it comes to European affairs, then, people do not seem to be inclined to trust even their own governments.[6] That much is evident in many of the pre-Brexit editorials, which excoriated the governments for being unresponsive to popular opinion when deciding European policies (and for doing so mainly behind closed doors). In 2008, fully 62 percent of citizens did not believe that their governments listened to them when it came to European issues, and those who perceive themselves to be voiceless on that matter have remained the majority as of 2017, the last year for which data are available.[7]

The idea that voters have lost influence over their own governments on European matters is superficially appealing (not the least because voters seem to believe it), but is it supported by the evidence? We know very little about the level of government responsiveness to domestic opinion when it comes to cooperation within the EU, which is surprising in

---

tend not to trust it?" Data are from the question asked about the EU. See Appendix A, available online at https://quote.ucsd.edu/cjschneider/books/, for a graph that illustrates the historical development of trust in the EU.

[5] The Council of the European Union is often called the Council of Ministers or just the Council and should not be confused with the European Council. I will use these terms interchangeably.

[6] Support for EU membership has generally remained steady around 50 to 60 percent since the 1990s, when it declined from an unprecedented high in the 1980s. This is on par with the levels during the 1970s. The share of the population that believe that EU membership is a bad thing has stayed well below 20 percent, suggesting that the legitimacy crisis has not yet become an existential one. See Appendix A for the evolution of popular support for EU membership from 1973 to 2015.

[7] The question specific to the national governments was only asked in 2008, where it was framed as: "Please tell me for each statement, whether you tend to agree or tend to disagree? On European issues, my voice is listened to by my government." Data from Eurobarometer 03/2008. The phrasing used since merely asks whether one believes their interests are being taken into account in the EU (61 percent reported a negative in 2008 on that version of the question). The findings are almost identical for the European Commission and the European Parliament. Appendix A provides historical results, which rely on the more general question of whether respondents felt that their interests were taken into account in the EU.

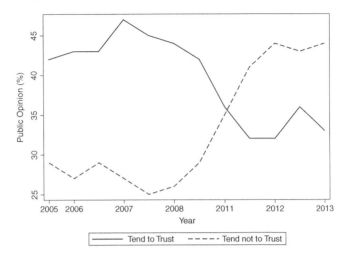

Figure 1.1 Trust in the Council of the European Union. Results of Eurobarometer surveys from 2005 to 2015 on the question "I would like to ask you a question about how much trust you have in certain institutions. For each of the following institutions, please tell me if you tend to trust it or tend not to trust it? – Council of the European Union." The respondents' answers ("tend to trust," "tend to distrust") are displayed in percentages.
Source: Eurobarometer (http://ec.europa.eu/COMMFrontOffice/PublicOpinion/index.cfm/Chart/index, accessed September 2016).

light of the EU's deepening and widening penetration into domestic policy. What incentives do governments have to represent the interests of their national publics in the EU? What does it mean for governments to be responsive in that context? And even if they are acting in the interest of their citizens, how can these governments demonstrate that fact when policies are decided at multiple levels of governance with the participation of a variety of institutional actors in the opaque and convoluted system of the EU? Since the Council of the European Union remains the most important legislative actor in the EU and because its members are ministers from the governments of member states, it provides a natural medium for responsiveness to domestic politics.[8]

[8] The other important legislative body is the European Parliament. The Parliament is directly accountable to European citizens via European elections, and its accountability has been studied elsewhere (Reif and Schmitt, 1980; Van der Eijk, Franklin, and Marsh, 1996; Schmitt and Thomassen, 1999, 2000). In this book, I focus on the responsiveness of governments to their citizens in the Council, which is another central but understudied (intergovernmental) source of democratic legitimacy in the EU. For studies of responsiveness in the supranational institutions of the EU, see, for example, Thomassen and Schmitt (1997), Proksch and Slapin (2010), and Rauh (2016).

If citizens could reward or sanction their national governments on the basis of their performance in European affairs, they could furnish the incentives for the governments to be responsive to their opinions even at the EU level.

Have electoral politics at the domestic level had any influence on government conduct at the EU level? How is that influence effected? What are the consequences for European cooperation and domestic politics? These are the questions I seek to answer in this book.

1.1 The Argument in Brief

The book presents a comprehensive account about how EU governments signal responsiveness to their citizens while cooperating at the European level. I develop and test a theoretical framework of the intergovernmental dimension of responsive governance in the EU using evidence amassed in nearly ten years of multi-method research. In a nutshell, I find that European cooperation in the Council of the European Union takes place in the shadow of national elections. EU governments are particularly responsive to their domestic constituencies before national elections (when they are most accountable). Surprisingly, they behave this way even when the issues are not politicized domestically. Governments signal responsiveness to their publics by taking positions that are in the interests of politically relevant voters at the national level, defending these positions throughout negotiations in the Council, and seeking appropriate policy outcomes at the EU level. When they anticipate unfavorable outcomes, they attempt to avoid blame and punishment by delaying negotiations until after national elections.

The argument can be briefly summarized as follows. The integration of policies in areas that affect everyday life has made the welfare of citizens more dependent on their governments' behavior at the EU level, which has politicized the EU. This is so despite the fact that many policies decided at that level are neither salient domestically nor even obviously electorally relevant. The problem for the governments is that they cannot reliably predict whether this will remain so. With the media, political parties, and interest groups increasingly subjecting European policies to public scrutiny, nobody can foresee what particular issue will catch on domestically. The governments hedge against appearing unresponsive in policy areas that become unexpectedly politicized during national elections by signaling their commitment to domestic interests at the European level whenever there is a chance that the policy might become electorally relevant.

The expansion of domestic electoral politics to encompass European affairs means that national elections affect both individual and collective bargaining behavior of governments of EU member states, and so influence policy in the EU. Governments that are willing and able to represent the interests of the relevant national electorate in EU legislative negotiations signal *political responsiveness* to their electorally relevant constituents. Governments wish to signal to domestic audiences that they are competent negotiators of their countries' interests and that they can attain outcomes that benefit their electorates; that is, that they govern responsively in the EU. They attempt to convey this impression by staking out and defending negotiation stances that can be interpreted as being in the national interest. They are particularly aggressive in this positioning during the electoral cycle, sometimes going against common European interests. Governments do not do this merely to burnish their populist credentials but to influence the European policy so that it more clearly favors their domestic constituencies, which allows them to claim credit for these policies. Failing this, they drag their feet as long as possible in order to delay the announcement of what they know will be an unpopular policy until it can no longer affect the votes of the electorate.

The strength of the motivation to choose such strategies varies with domestic political conditions and the government's ability to navigate the collective decision-making process in the EU. Governments are incentivized to signal responsiveness when national elections are competitive and when the issues are politicized domestically. For instance, poor economic performance could galvanize a strong opposition to charge the government with ineptitude, which could be countered by a competent performance in EU negotiations. The incentives are even stronger when the issues the government is negotiating are politicized domestically, so success could be expected to boost its approval ratings.

Even the most motivated government must engage the collective bargaining process in the EU to secure favorable policy outcomes. Whatever sovereignty it enjoys in setting its own foreign policy is drastically attenuated when it comes to EU policy, where it has to contend with 27 other member states and a motley assortment of supranational actors such as the European Commission and the European Parliament. The Council might be among the leanest EU institutions, but it still requires each minister to deal with 27 counterparts. In some policy areas decisions require unanimous consent, which at least in principle endows each government with the negative power to unilaterally block undesirable policies. Of course, it also severely weakens their positive power to obtain policies that they prefer.

In practice, though, there is not much difference between policy areas since most decisions in the Council are reached through cooperative consensus bargaining, which drastically limits an individual government's ability to set the terms or block them unilaterally. Even governments with great formal and informal bargaining power cannot simply secure their most preferred outcomes when other EU members coordinate their positions, something they might be quite willing to do in order to help each other appear responsive during election periods. As a result, electorally motivated short-term opportunistic behavior in the EU can have long-term effects on policies when it shifts those policies away from what they could have been had they been decided outside the shadow of national elections.

This argument assumes that voters – at least occasionally – want to take note of their government's responsiveness on European affairs when they go to the polls. I utilize observational and experimental evidence to analyze how a government's bargaining behavior in the Council (i.e., its attempt to signal responsiveness) and its perceived success in legislative negotiations affect public support for the incumbent. I show that both uncompromising and responsive negotiation stances as well as preferable policy outcomes are rewarded with significant increases in public support. Interestingly, on average this increase would not alter the incumbent's vote share enough to be decisive in the election by itself. One could interpret this to mean that governments generate "unnecessary" signals of responsiveness in the EU, but a more likely scenario is that this reflects prudential reasoning by governments that operate in a fluid domestic environment that makes it very difficult to forecast what issues might become salient and make a difference in competitive elections. The mere possibility that an EU policy might become electorally relevant domestically exports its politicking to the European level, a sort of politicization without foundation.

1.2 Core Contributions

A government's responsiveness to the will of the people is a key characteristic of democracy and indelibly linked to its legitimacy (Dahl, 1973, p. 1). Scholars who study democratic responsiveness have been mainly concerned with government conduct at the national or subnational level. This research has focused on the extent to which national politicians act in the best interest of their electorates by taking positions or making policy decisions that are representative of the preferences of domestic constituencies. Because these issues are so vital for our understanding of democracy, it is not surprising that they are the core of the academic study of democratic governance. This makes it all the more surprising to observe a large lacuna in our knowledge about governmental responsiveness within the EU.

Questions about the democratic responsiveness within the EU are of great academic and public interest. The EU's ability to contribute efficiently and effectively to the welfare of its citizens depends crucially on their perception of its democratic legitimacy, but the Union's widening reach has severely limited member governments' capacity for autonomous decisions. An ever-expanding scope of policies are now within the purview of the EU's collective decision-making apparatus. In all these policy areas, member governments must contend not only with domestic opposition parties and institutional veto players at the national level, but must navigate the byzantine EU bureaucracy as well. This drastically complicates governments' formulation of policies, potentially threatening the responsiveness to their publics.

One cannot hope to understand democratic governance in this complex system of multilevel delegation by studying responsiveness only at the national or subnational levels. And neither can one do so by focusing on the European superstructure alone, whether it is by treating the EU as a system or analyzing overall decision-making output. There is much to be gained by analyzing the responsiveness of member governments' behavior in intergovernmental negotiations at the EU level.

My study of the ability of EU governments to represent the views of their citizens builds on the extensive scholarly work on responsiveness within democratic countries and on the separate strand in the literature that studies the evolving institutions of the EU. By integrating and extending these approaches, I examine the challenges governments face when they need to appear responsive to policies at the European level and show how they can achieve that goal in the context of the EU's collective policymaking process. I argue that their behavior in these negotiations is an important ingredient of the democratic legitimacy of the EU. The intergovernmental view that I advance in this book fills a critical gap in the literature, contributes to the work on responsive governance in the EU, and gives us a novel way of thinking about its legitimacy crisis.

Consider, for instance, the Council of the European Union. Responsive behavior of governments in the Council is an important component of democratic governance, akin to the conduct of state governments when they represent their states' public interests in federal negotiations. For example, US senators are not expected to ignore their home states in Congress; the Senate would not be considered democratic if these representatives were not responsive to their constituencies. Transposing this to the EU means that a basic requirement for democratic legitimacy is that the member governments are responsive to their citizens when they cooperate in the EU. This is so even though EU governments are not accountable to all European citizens (such as, for instance, the European Parliament could be through European-wide elections), and even though the Council is only one of the intergovernmental institutions within the EU. The mechanism that can hold the governments accountable to their citizens even at the EU level is national elections. If electorates are concerned with policies decided in the Council, then these elections can provide ample incentives for their governments to act responsively there.

That domestic politics matter for European cooperation is, of course, well known. Far more interesting is the question of *how* domestic politics matter for European cooperation. My theory embeds models of national electoral politics into models of intergovernmental cooperation to study how governments signal responsiveness over EU-level policies to their home constituencies. By analyzing how domestic politics affect the way leaders negotiate within the EU, I provide the missing link between the work on the politicization of European affairs at the national level and the work on cooperation at the supranational level. The integration of the national and European dimension into a unified framework yields rich insights into the electoral dynamics of European cooperation. The combination of qualitative research – including archival work and interviews with political elites who were involved in the negotiations – with experimental and observational quantitative methods offers a unique opportunity to study the empirical implications of my theoretical argument from various angles, and to provide nuance to the proposed way of thinking about European cooperation in the shadow of national elections.

The findings speak directly to some of the central criticisms of democratic legitimacy in the EU. On the one hand, they corroborate the impression that in many cases European affairs have not attained the domestic salience they deserve. On the other hand, they also support the notion that European affairs have been politicized, especially so in the post-Maastricht era. European affairs have become an important factor in national electoral politics even though their importance varies across issues. In this, they have gone beyond the traditional impact of diffuse support for the EU on national elections. I show that it is not merely whether voters have warm feelings toward European integration that influence their electoral choices but also whether they perceive the incumbent government as having been responsive on specific policies at the EU level. In this, I bring the study of EU legitimacy closer to our standards for established democratic systems, where we typically use specific policy support as a benchmark for accountability.

1.3 Plan of the Book

I develop my theoretical argument about responsive European cooperation in the shadow of national elections in two parts. Chapter 2 provides a historical overview of the changing motives for EU governments to act responsively in EU negotiations. Employing a variety of different data sources at the national and the European levels, I demonstrate that incumbent governments have found themselves under increasing pressure to signal that their conduct in the EU is responsive to the preferences of their citizens. Domestic partisan dealignment and electoral volatility have magnified their uncertainty over the chances of winning reelection. Simultaneously, incumbents' ability to appear responsive by making certain policy choices nationally has become more constrained by the widening reach of the EU. The intensifying domestic politicization of European integration has made EU-level policies more salient electorally, which has enabled citizens to hold their governments accountable for negotiation behavior and policy outcomes they can achieve at that level.

Chapter 3 develops the main theoretical argument about signals of responsive governance in the EU. The first step is to understand how domestic elections affect the incentives and opportunities of governments to show themselves responsive through negotiations in the Council. I develop a domestic political economy model that links the competitiveness and timing of elections to a government's need to appear responsive at different stages of these intergovernmental negotiations. I adapt the typical definition of responsiveness in democratic system to fit the European context, and study both *input* and *output* responsiveness. The former refers to the government taking and defending positions that represent the interests of their national electorates. The latter refers to the government attaining policy outcomes that favor their national electorates. When governments are unable to signal responsiveness because they expect an unfavorable outcome, they might seek to delay these intergovernmental decisions until after national elections. Governments that face higher electoral uncertainty because of low public support or bad economic conditions, or who have to deal with European issues that have been politicized domestically have stronger incentives to signal responsiveness in EU negotiations.

To study how governments can convey such a signal, I embed the domestic political economy model into a model of intergovernmental negotiations that takes into account both formal procedures and informal rules in the EU. I argue that governments can use both individual and collective bargaining strategies to send signals about their responsiveness to the electorate. Governments can publicly stake out clear and unyielding positions that represent the prevailing opinion in the electorate, and they can keep defending these positions throughout the negotiation process. What outcomes these negotiations produce, of course, depends on the governments' competence in navigating the collective decision-making of the EU. They can use the leverage that the formal rules accord them and the influence that informal norms give to them to shape the policy in ways that move the outcomes closer to their preferences. They can also achieve informal understanding with other EU governments for mutually beneficial reciprocal cooperation that allows each electorally vulnerable government to signal responsiveness prior to national elections. I dub this behavior *hidden cooperation* by analogy to similar opportunistic behavior at the domestic level, and to reflect the fact that it is achieved behind closed doors.

The chapter concludes with a general discussion of the empirical implications of the theoretical model that will be analyzed in the second part of the book.

Before delving into this, I scrutinize one of the central assumptions of my theory – that voters are willing to hold their governments accountable over European policy issues. Chapter 4 describes a survey experiment designed to analyze how publics respond to different signals of responsiveness and to assess the internal validity of the demand side of the model. I conducted two conjoint experiments through an online survey of more than 2,500 Germans in the fall of 2016 over two salient European policy issues: the provision of another financial rescue package for Greece, and the admittance of more refugees and asylum seekers into the EU. I asked respondents about their approval for politicians who participate in EU-level negotiations over these issues. The politicians differed in several characteristics that affect approval (e.g., experience, party affiliation, gender), and I provided respondents with various signals of responsiveness that correspond to concepts in my theoretical model.

The results are consistent with the assumption that voters are more likely to approve of politicians who take the voters' preferred policy position, defend that position throughout the negotiations, and succeed in achieving the desired outcome. Voters are also apt to blame politicians for pursuing policies they disagree with and for failing to achieve outcomes voters like. These signals of responsiveness matter even when we account for partisan ideology – one of the strongest predictors of vote choice in Europe.

These findings, along with qualitative and quantitative evidence presented in subsequent chapters, underpin the causal mechanism and reveal the strong incentives for governments to signal responsiveness during EU-level negotiations. The rest of the book evaluates whether governments that face these incentives behave in ways consistent with the theoretical model and whether that signaling behavior has the expected effect on their domestic approval.

The first set of tests concerns the negotiations over the EU budget in the Council. These negotiations are particularly appropriate because the budget shares for individual member states are allocated annually under formal rules that provide a baseline expectation of what these shares should be. The regularity of the negotiations makes them especially useful for domestic electioneering, and the baseline allocations make it easy to observe when governments receive larger than expected shares.

In Chapter 5, I use a unique data set of all EU budget negotiations in the Council from 1970 to 2013 for a quantitative analysis of the size of allocations and its correlation with the need and ability to signal responsiveness. I find that EU governments with domestic elections in the near future receive significantly larger shares of the budget compared to those that do not have to face the voters. The effect has become more noticeable in the post-Maastricht era – when the EU became much more politicized – and is stronger when the upcoming elections are expected to be competitive because of a bad economy or low public approval for the incumbent government. The effect is also stronger when the electorally vulnerable government secures the hidden cooperation of the other members, and when the formal rules place them in a favorable bargaining position.

All of this evidence points to governments attempting to signal responsiveness over EU-level issues for domestic electoral purposes. But does it have the desired effect on the voters? I use aggregated Eurobarometer data to assess whether these signals are correlated with public approval of national governments. I find that public support for the governing coalitions increases when governments manage to secure larger budget shares in the annual negotiations. This result corroborates the experimental evidence presented in Chapter 4 and is consistent with the theoretical mechanism that grounds governments' behavior during EU-level negotiations in domestic political necessities.

The statistical correlations might be persuasive, but one still wishes to know whether they were produced by the mechanism specified by the theory. This requires a far more fine-grained analysis of specific negotiations. In Chapter 6, I present a detailed case study of the negotiations over the EU financial framework for 2007–2013. I use archival research and secondary sources to examine how various governments signaled responsiveness before elections: how they decided on the strategies to use and how their behavior shaped the policy outcomes. I consider the issues over which the member states were in conflict and examine the distribution of preferences among them. Since the principal

1.3 Plan of the Book

outlier was the United Kingdom, the narrative focuses on how the coming enlargement to Central and Eastern Europe (CEE) motivated a showdown over the UK budget rebate. I trace the evolution of negotiations from hidden cooperation with the UK government, which was facing national elections, to a deepening confrontation when opinion polls in France revealed that the proposed European constitution was in trouble, to outright conflict when the German government lost critical regional elections, and finally to the United Kingdom bowing to the inevitable after a last-ditch attempt to shift the costs of its rebate onto the new member states.

The analysis of this case also highlights the reasons governments might opt for different strategies. The negotiations held out little hope that the United Kingdom would obtain a favorable outcome on its budget rebate, whereas Germany and France expected a deal that the governments could promote as successful at home. Consequently, the Germans pushed for accelerating the negotiations to clinch that deal before their national elections, the French demanded tough terms to deal with the fallout of the failure of the constitutional referendum, and the British dragged their feet to delay what they knew would be an unpopular outcome, first until after their general election, and then in the hopes of a friendlier German government replacing the pro-French incumbent. These findings provide further support for the theoretical mechanism.

The good thing about budget allocations is that they are easy to observe, and the outcomes relatively straightforward to interpret for public consumption. This makes them prime targets for election-minded behavior by member governments, but also raises the question whether electioneering incentives arise in policy areas that are not as transparent. To answer this, I look at whether governments signal responsiveness over a large set of legislative issues. In Chapter 7, I use an extension of the massive DEU II data set, which includes not only the outcomes of various negotiations, but also the governments' positions on the legislative issues involved. I find that governments that face elections are much less likely to budge from their initial public commitments and more likely to achieve favorable policy outcomes. I further uncover an important difference in the conditions under which these signals occur. Since governments can unilaterally choose to defend their positions, the presence of elections should be sufficient to induce them to do so. On the other hand, since policy outcomes depend on collective decisions, the likelihood of obtaining favorable ones depends on whether other Council members consider the government especially vulnerable electorally. The analysis reveals that this is indeed so: while governments are just as likely to defend their positions irrespective of how competitive the elections are going to be, what their formal bargaining leverage in the Council is, and whether other members will cooperate with them, they are much more likely to obtain a favorable outcome when elections are close, they have a bargaining advantage, and the others are likely to engage in hidden cooperation. These statistical results corroborate the conclusion from the qualitative analysis in Chapter 6, which highlighted how crucially dependent policy outcomes are on the collective bargaining process.

Unlike budgets that have to be decided on within some time frame, negotiations over legislative acts can vary widely, and their duration depends on a number of factors over which individual governments might have little control. Consequently, the adoption of these acts does not conveniently synchronize with the rhythm of the electoral calendar. This makes it challenging to utilize favorable outcomes for electoral gain but somewhat easier to avoid unfavorable outcomes prior to elections. In other words, it might be difficult to speed up legislative negotiations in order to capitalize on a good outcome, but not so difficult to engage in delaying tactics to push a bad outcome until after national elections. When are such tactics likely?

In Chapter 8, I use data on the timing of all legislative proposals that were negotiated in the EU between 1977 and 2009 to analyze when EU members prolong negotiations in order to delay unfavorable outcomes until after elections. Since outcomes require the collective agreement of most Council members, any proposals that could be detrimental to some government would be less likely to secure such agreement when that government faces elections. Cooperation in the Council is much more likely when nobody must immediately answer to domestic constituencies for agreeing to a bad deal. The statistical analysis is consistent with this argument: proposals negotiated close to national elections are significantly less likely to be adopted than ones negotiated during non-election periods. Delays are particularly likely when issues generate a lot of distributional conflict and EU members expect unfavorable outcomes. When enough proposals come up for decision close to national elections, the resulting tactical delays create legislative tides in negotiations.

As I did with budget negotiations, I supplement the quantitative analysis of legislative delay with an in-depth case study of a particular instance of a government using that strategy. In Chapter 9, I draw on personal interviews with political and administrative elites, archival work, and secondary sources to examine the causes and consequences of the German delaying tactics during the negotiations that led to the first bailout of Greece in 2010. This case is particularly interesting because it involves an outcome that would normally appear as an unobserved counterfactual: the situation in which a government abandons its attempt to postpone a decision until after the elections. Since governments only engage in delays when they believe doing so would give them an electoral advantage and because they are usually good at dragging their feet, we can only infer indirectly what their disadvantage might have been had the unfavorable outcome materialized before elections. It is not often that a government is forced to change its strategy before the elections. Only some exigent circumstances that suddenly increase the costs of delay so much that they outweigh the electoral benefit of avoiding the outcome could compel them to reverse course and accept the punishment at the polls. The German government was subjected precisely to that sort of unexpected severe shock that derailed the original strategy and exposed the unfavorable deal before the elections. I provide evidence for the initial decision to delay, the surprise developments that forced a reevaluation of the strategy, and the electoral consequences of a late reversal expected by the theory. This, then, is the rare case that validates a government's fears of being punished by the electorate when it fails to signal responsiveness in its EU-level policy negotiations.

In Chapter 10, I pull together the evidence to assess the strengths and weaknesses of my theoretical argument and note how it can be applied beyond the EU. Circling back to the original motivation for the book, I then ask what these results tell us about the EU's current crisis of legitimacy, and possible ways of dealing with it. Since the crisis is essentially about the EU's perceived lack of responsiveness, the finding that member governments are, in fact, responsive when it comes to both budget and legislative policy suggests that part of the problem could be that the electorate is paying insufficient attention to European affairs or that there is insufficient transparency for them to assess the behavior of their governments when deciding how to vote. The politicizing of European cooperation and greater transparency of decision-making at the European level would increase the incentives for governments to behave responsively – making the EU more democratic and therefore legitimate – but these measures come at a price. The way governments become more responsive – by standing firm on domestically popular positions and attempting to redistribute policy benefits and costs so that they favor their publics – is likely to cause much more conflict among member governments. At the same time, relaxing the secrecy of the process will make it much harder to reach deals through hidden cooperation. Coupling this with more demanding and inflexible bargaining stances would lead to frequent breakdowns in policy cooperation. This would decrease the EU's effectiveness in contributing to its citizens' welfare, which in turn would undermine its legitimacy.

Proponents of a more democratic and politicized EU tend to assert that its institutional structure is strong and adaptable enough to cope with this conflict while retaining much of its usefulness. This optimism is unwarranted because it presupposes that Europeans will become more positively disposed toward the EU if it becomes more democratic, and this is not necessarily so. Without a true European *demos*, the largely cooperative nature of EU decision-making that works well behind closed doors would disintegrate in the harsh light of public opinion that would force governments to operate under the threat of voters' wrath at the polls. The resulting fear would inevitably impel governments to pander to their constituencies, and they would pull in different directions at the common bargaining table. With less being achieved at the EU level, citizens would rightly come to question the need for an "ever closer" Union, or any Union at all.

This is not to say that the EU should not strive for greater democratic legitimacy. Indeed, it is imperative that it does, especially now that it has succeeded beyond the expectations of its founders. But how does one preserve effective cooperation while making governance more responsive? I argue that there is no magic institutional arrangement that would solve what is, after all, a fundamental problem of governance inherent in any representative system: the tension between responsiveness to the short-term will of the voters and responsibility to craft effective long-term policies. Based on my findings, which indicate that governments are trying to signal responsiveness to their constituents but that the effectiveness of these signals is not very high, I suggest that the EU should actively seek to promote general awareness of its activities and its benefits. It cannot rely on the tender mercies of office-motivated national politicians whose incentives are to appropriate all the credit for successful collective policies and deflect any complicity in unpopular ones (usually by blaming the EU). It should strive for transparency but not for immediate politicization, and perhaps it should remind the European citizens why it came about and the role it has played in promoting both lasting peace and prosperity on the continent. The EU can be saved and enhanced, even if not in the pristine form its founders envisioned. Otherwise, many more will be in the unenviable position of the Britons, who are only belatedly beginning to discover what they had in their fractious membership in the European Union.

2   The Politicization of European Cooperation

> The giant is fast asleep because those who could wake it up generally have no incentive to do so and those who have an incentive cannot.
> – Green-Pedersen (2012, p. 115)

Do governments pay attention to what their domestic constituents want when they collaborate in the European Union (EU)? This is not an idle question. The EU was conceived as an elite-driven operation and was depoliticized on purpose (Schmidt, 2006; Mair, 2007). Its principal architect, Jean Monnet, designed the major institutions of the European Coal and Steel Community – the European Commission, the Council, and the European Court of Justice – without democratic mandates so that integration could proceed apace without being stalled by domestic politicization (Moravcsik, 1994). Monnet went so far as to engage in "information obstruction" by asking news agencies to *not* cover the Community because he was worried that public salience and scrutiny of the process would derail it (Meyer, 1999; Atikcan, 2015). As Pascal Lamy succinctly observed when he was the *chef de cabinet* of the European Commission in the 1980s:

> Europe has been built in a St. Simonian [i.e., technocratic] way from the beginning, this was Monnet's approach. The people weren't ready to agree to integration, so you had to get on without telling them too much about what was happening.[1]

This is a feature, not a bug, of EU institutions, but it has recently come under fire by critics who believe that it causes the EU to suffer from a democratic deficit.[2] With the EU penetrating more deeply and

---

[1] Cited by Ross (1995, p. 194), bracketed text added. Saint Simon was a Nineteenth century French technocratic utopian.

[2] The literature on the democratic deficit is large, and scholars have debated whether and to what extent a democratic deficit exists. See, for example, Scharpf (1992, 1999); Moravcsik (1994, 2008); Dahl (1999); Olsen, Sbragia, and Scharpf (2002); Rohrschneider (2002); Crombez (2003); Karp, Banducci, and Bowler (2003); Follesdal and Hix (2006); Schmidt (2006); König (2007); Hix (2008); Rohrschneider and Loveless (2010). Hix (2008) provides an overview of the debate.

widely into domestic policy, its insulation from domestic politics has become increasingly worrisome. The march of integration was neither influenced by nor a factor in national politics because it was not salient to voters, and most politicians had no interest in campaigning on it (Follesdal and Hix, 2006; Schmidt, 2006; Hix, 2008).

European affairs can only be politicized domestically through a "salient and polarised public debate among an expanding range of actors" (Hutter, Grande, and Kriesi, 2016, p. 8). But since European policy is not readily placeable along the prominent left–right ideological continuum, it did not provide a convenient platform for mainstream parties. Moreover, most of these parties had similarly positive views of European integration, which made them reluctant to play political football with it. Consequently, voters paid little attention to European matters. Even when it came to elections for the European Parliament, their votes were best explained by domestic issues rather than the performance of politicians at the EU level, at least until the last decade of the twentieth century.[3] By the same token, voter attitudes toward European integration did not enter their decision calculus in national elections either (Hobolt and de Vries, 2016).

With European affairs staunchly depoliticized, voters remained uninformed about them, and uninterested in learning more. The "diffuse feeling of approval" created a "permissive consensus" that permitted integration to proceed as originally intended (Lindberg and Scheingold, 1970). Even as this process has turned the EU's public into a "sleeping giant" (Van der Eijk and Franklin, 2004), domestic electoral considerations have remained quite peripheral to it, leading some to conclude that "expectations about the impending politicisation of European integration are misplaced" (Green-Pedersen, 2012, p. 115).

But is that so? The criticism of the EU's elitism rests on the notion that there is insufficient public interest in governments' behavior at the EU level. Without the constraint of domestic opinion, then, political elites have had a free pass to pursue European integration. And if the voters do not care, politicians have no reason to expose European negotiations to scrutiny. They do not have to worry whether their cooperation in the EU is responsive to domestic interests. Thus, the charge of a democratic deficit is fundamentally based on the absence of domestic politicization of European affairs, something that might have been true until the 1990s but has not been true since.

---

[3] Reif and Schmitt (1980); Van der Eijk and Franklin (1996); Van der Eijk, Franklin, and Marsh (1996); Van der Brug and Van der Eijk (2007).

Three interrelated developments have caused the politicization of European collaboration. The domestic partisan dealignment in several European countries increased electoral volatility. As incumbent governments became more uncertain about their chances of holding onto office, they became better motivated to appear responsive to their electorates.[4] This greater motivation to be responsive ran up against the increasingly tight embrace of the EU, whose growing reach over national policies sharply curtailed governments' ability to use their traditional electioneering tools. Just when governments needed these tools the most, they were denied them. Highly incentivized governments would, of course, look for alternatives, and the same process that denied them domestic autonomy would provide them with new opportunities. As the EU intruded into the domestic arena, interest groups that would normally focus on national policies became far more interested in decisions taken at the EU level. The countervailing pressure from different groups spilled the distributional conflicts into the public forum, and made European affairs far more salient among the voters. This has given governments reasons to electioneer on European policy platforms in ways that would have been unthinkable before the 1990s.

European collaboration now happens in the shadow of domestic elections. Before explaining how, I present some evidence for the three crucial developments that have made it possible.

2.1 Electoral Volatility and Prudential Motivations

Governments that cannot reliably estimate their chances of retaining office are highly motivated to signal that they are responsive to their electorate. That is, they want constituents to believe that government policies are consistent with their preferences (Stimson, MacKuen, and Erikson, 1995). Now, one might wonder whether public opinion matters at all to policymakers. After all, it is well-known that voters are uninformed and often uninterested in politics. As Berelson, Lazarsfeld, and McPhee (1954, p. 308) point out:

> The democratic citizen is expected to be well informed about political affairs. He is supposed to know what the issues are, what their history is, what the relevant facts are, what alternatives are proposed, what the party stands for, what the likely consequences are. By such standards the voter falls short.

---

[4] These developments are particularly problematic in countries with proportional representation, where parties often cannot obtain a majority vote by themselves and find themselves exposed to greater electoral pressure from competitors.

This held true in 1950s America and is just as true today across many Western democracies.[5]

If ignorance made voters politically irrelevant, this would be the end of the argument. But it does not. One early attempt to reconcile voter disinterest and the apparent influence of public opinion on policy makers argued that leaders formulate policy as they wish as long as they do not wake the "slumbering giant" of the public by venturing too far outside the boundaries set by its opinion (Rosenau, 1961).[6] This explanation, however, still begs the question of how voters can learn what they need to know, especially if they do not care to know it or know that they should care.

One prominent answer is that voters do not, in fact, need to know all that much to make reasonable choices. Instead of acquiring full information and going through an involved analysis of each and every issue, voters can form their political opinions with information shortcuts that provide them with the basic knowledge needed to identify a preferred candidate (McKelvey and Ordeshook, 1986; Wittman, 1989).[7] As Page and Shapiro (1992, pp. 387–388) put it:

> People probably do not need large amounts of information to make rational voting choices. Cues from like-minded citizens and groups (including cues related to demographic characteristics and party labels) may be sufficient, in an environment where accurate information is available, to permit voters to act as if they had all the available information.

Partisanship is a particularly influential information shortcut.[8] Voters rely on politicians' party affiliations to draw inferences about the policies they are likely to favor, the competence with which they are likely to be implemented, and the blame to be assigned when they fail. This information shortcut has connected party identification and voting choices so strongly that established parties have been able to deliver predictable numbers of votes to their candidates. The resulting regularity has contributed mightily to electoral stability, and has reduced the uncertainty about the security of political elites.

Partisanship, however, has been in decline throughout Europe, with citizens feeling less aligned with, and attached to, any particular party.[9]

---

[5] Magee, Brock, and Young (1989); Bartels (1996, 2008); Gabel (1998).
[6] The intellectual pedigree of the European publics being a sleeping giant is clearly traceable to the slumbering Americans.
[7] Gray (2009, 2013) and Gray and Hicks (2014) show that individuals can use IOs themselves as informational shortcuts for their opinions about countries.
[8] Robertson (1976); Fiorina (1981); Gabel (1998); Ray (2003); Gabel and Scheve (2007). As I will discuss below, retrospective evaluation of the economy and stances by organized interest groups are also quite important.
[9] Franklin, Mackie, and Valen (1992); Dalton and Wattenberg (2000); Dalton (2004); Mair (2008a); Kayser and Wlezien (2011); Rohrschneider and Whitefield (2012).

2.1 Electoral Volatility and Prudential Motivations

In nine European countries, the fraction of nonpartisans among the population went from 30 percent in 1976 to 40 percent in the 1990s (Dalton, 2000, pp. 25–28). The process has even accelerated in subsequent years:

> West European electorates, on average, now approach a point where almost half of the electorate (45 percent) does not identify with any party. This group is even larger in Central and Eastern Europe (CEE) where slightly over half of citizens evidently hold no long-term party loyalties (53.7 percent).[10]

The effect of this partisan de-alignment cannot be overstated in our context as it has made politicians much more vulnerable electorally. Whereas the weakening of the party identification force means fewer automatic votes for the opposition, it also means fewer votes for the incumbent. Moreover, it has made it easier for voters to cross party lines (or favor new parties) when their evaluations of a politician's responsiveness and competence shift. This has produced more electoral volatility and larger uncertainty over the voting outcomes.

Figure 2.1 shows the electoral volatility of 15 Western European countries from 1950 to 2010.[11] It uses data from Dassonneville and Hooghe (2017) to construct the Pedersen index of volatility (Pedersen, 1979). The index sums the absolute values of the differences in party votes between two elections, and divides it by two (since a win for one party implies a loss for another). It ranges between 0 and 100, with larger values corresponding to more electoral volatility.

Figure 2.1(a) plots average variation of all countries over five-year intervals. It clearly shows a jump to somewhat more volatile elections from the mid 1960s, a finding extensively documented elsewhere.[12] It also shows that even the extent of volatility itself became less predictable over the two decades on either side of the start of the twenty-first century. There is also the rather dramatic increase in volatility over the most recent period, from 2010 to 2014, likely a consequence of the financial crisis of 2008 (Dassonneville and Hooghe, 2017). The subsequent plunge into an economic recession soured voters on establishment parties, and provided fertile ground for populists of all stripes to make a play for a role in government (Cramme and Hobolt, 2015; Hutter, Grande, and Kriesi, 2016).

---

[10] Rohrschneider and Whitefield (2012, p. 26).
[11] The box plots convey information about the level (median), spread, and degree of symmetry about the median both within the central half of the data and beyond it. The box represents the interquartile range (IQR) – the set of values between the bottom and top quartiles. The bar in that box is the median. The whiskers include all data within 1.5 IQR of the bottom quartile and stop at the smallest such value. Any data points that exceed that range are shown individually as outliers.
[12] Franklin, Mackie, and Valen (1992); Dalton, McAllister, and Wattenberg (2000); Mair (2005, 2008b); Gallagher, Laver, and Mair (2011); Bischoff (2013).

22 The Politicization of European Cooperation

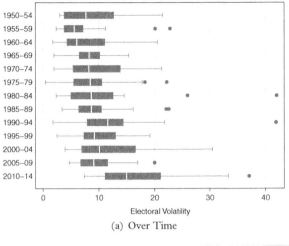

(a) Over Time

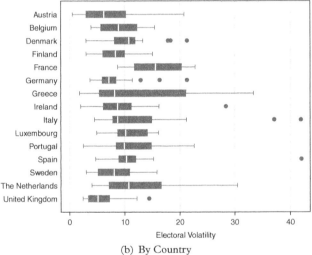

(b) By Country

Figure 2.1 Electoral Volatility in Western Europe, 1950–2010. Box plots of the Pedersen index of electoral volatility in 15 countries. Panel (a) shows the index during different time periods averaged for all countries. Panel (b) shows the index for individual countries averaged over the time period. Countries are listed alphabetically.
Source: Dassonneville and Hooghe (2017).

Figure 2.1(b) plots each country's average variation over time. It shows significant differences between relatively stable elections like the ones in the United Kingdom and the extremely volatile ones in France. Beyond that, it shows that most countries have experienced electoral volatility over time. Additional analysis reveals volatility has been quite high since the 1970s.[13]

Now, it is true that many established parties in Europe form relatively stable coalition governments and are often in power over several legislative periods. This gives them the appearance of electoral security but masks their fear that an unpredictable shift in public opinion might destroy their chances at the polls. King (1997, p. 50) uses an apt analogy to describe their predicament:

The probability of anything going seriously wrong with nuclear power stations may approach zero, but they tend nevertheless not to be built near the centers of large cities.

Consider, for instance, the German governing coalition under Angela Merkel. In the summer of 2015, Merkel had weathered the earlier dip in popularity occasioned by the Greek bailout. She enjoyed high levels of public approval and a largely disorganized weak opposition. Her position as chancellor seemed unassailable. And then the refugee crisis hit. When she famously declared that Germany could absorb the inflow ("Wir schaffen das!"),[14] her ratings plummeted. As she stayed the course against a rising tide of opposition to immigration throughout 2016, the political competition intensified, and observers noted the possibility that she might even lose the federal elections in 2017. She did not, but her party suffered one of the worst-ever federal election results, and the anti-immigrant and Eurosceptic right-wing Alternative für Deutschland (AfD) entered the Bundestag as the third-strongest party.

When even a government as popular as Merkel's had to run the electoral gauntlet and did not emerge unscathed, what should only an averagely popular incumbent expect? It will "run scared" (Jacobson, 1987). Or, perhaps more to the point, it will act *prudentially*. A government might believe that it is relatively safe but it knows that public opinion can change abruptly due to some unforeseen circumstances. It also knows that this change can have outsized electoral consequences when party identification is weak. A prudent government would therefore try to act responsively, principally before elections but especially when electoral volatility is high. When the incumbent government does not have a large reservoir of public good will, its incentives to act prudentially are correspondingly stronger.

To see the strength of that incentive, consider the "cushion" of public approval that incumbents have tended to have. Figure 2.2 shows

---

[13] See Appendix B, available online at https://quote.ucsd.edu/cjschneider/books/, for plots of the historical trends of electoral volatility within countries.
[14] "We can do this!"

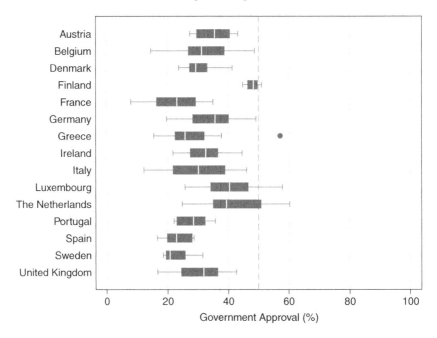

Figure 2.2 Government Approval Ratings in Western Europe, 1977–2002. Public approval ratings for the incumbent coalition governments. Ratings for each party calculated from the Sunday voting question in the Eurobarometer survey, and aggregated to obtain the rating for the governing coalition. The plot shows the coalition rating scores for the time period. Countries are listed alphabetically.
Source: Eurobarometer, Müller and Strøm (2000), and author calculations.

the approvals of the governing coalition for 15 Western European countries between 1977 and 2002.[15] The ratings represent the share of survey respondents who indicated that they would vote for one of the parties in the coalition government in any given year.[16] The plot

---

[15] Approval ratings are calculated using Eurobarometer survey data on voter intent. The European Commission created the public opinion surveys, called Eurobarometers, in 1973. They are conducted twice a year and involve about 1,000 face-to-face interviews in each country. The surveys focus on EU affairs and the economic situation in EU member states, but until 2002 they also asked about voter intent. The relevant question was, "If there was a 'general election' tomorrow (say if contact is under 18 years: "and you had a vote"), which party would you support?" Respondents received a list of political parties to choose from. In almost all cases, this list included all parties elected to the national parliament. Time-series data for this question are from Schmitt et al. (2005). More information is available on the Eurobarometer website http://ec.europa.eu/COMMFrontOffice/publicopinion/index.cfm, accessed May 2015.

[16] This approach considers the entire coalition as it was before an election and gives equal weight to each member. One alternative would be to identify the parties responsible for economic policies and weigh them more heavily (Anderson, 1995). The problem

2.1 Electoral Volatility and Prudential Motivations

shows how minimal this cushion is: with the exception of Finland, Luxembourg, and the Netherlands, the approval ratings are below 50 percent, and barely crack 40 percent (the average median is about 30 percent). These numbers would cause discomfort to any government, but they are particularly threatening to coalitions in countries with proportional representation. This electoral system forces parties to compete with many others, and often no party emerges as a majority winner. Government formation (and the appointment of a prime minister) then requires laborious negotiations before several parties can coalesce enough to form a coalition. Small fluctuations in vote shares could suddenly render previously viable coalition partners politically irrelevant and trigger searches for new ones, with unpredictable results.

These statistics are about intent, but what about actual votes? Figure 2.3 shows electoral results in European countries between 1970 and 2009 for the government (top panel) and the party of the prime minister (bottom panel).[17] At first blush, Figure 2.3(a) seems to indicate that while incumbent governments often fail to secure comfortable vote share margins, they should not be unduly worried. They perform reasonably well and obtain more than half of the votes most of the time. Recall, however, that these are coalitions, and in Europe these are often minority governments. The prime minister's party generally needs at least one coalition partner to govern. The extent of this problem can be clearly seen in Figure 2.3(b), which shows the vote share of the prime minister's party. It is exceptionally rare for this party to obtain more than 50 percent of the vote, indicating a need to rely on another party as a partner.

Of course, the relationship between a party's vote share and its ability to govern depends on the electoral system and the number of competitive parties. Still, the evidence indicates that incumbents tend to be vulnerable and that there is significant electoral volatility. Under these circumstances, a prudent government would hedge its bets by attempting to appear responsive to the electorate. The usual play in its signaling repertoire involves doing something voters would like (and give it credit for) in a domestically salient policy area. Unfortunately, this is precisely the play whose script the ever-more intrusive EU has yanked away from national governments.

---

with that approach, however, is that it would bias the results if voters cannot assign responsibility correctly. Data on the composition of coalition governments from Müller and Strøm (2000).

[17] Data availability varies by country. For many Central and Eastern European countries, there is no data available prior to the 1990s. The plots use all available data.

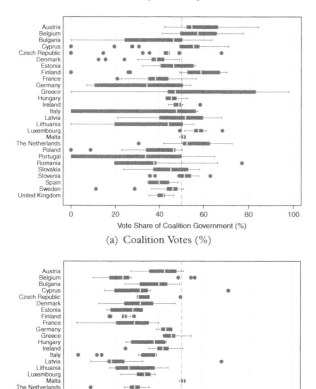

Figure 2.3 Electoral Outcomes in Europe, 1970–2009. Box plots of vote shares for all available years for each country. Panel (a) shows the vote share of the coalition government as the sum of the vote shares for each participating party. Panel (b) shows the vote share only of the prime minister's party. Countries are listed alphabetically.
Source: Döring and Manow (2015); Müller and Strøm (2000), and author calculations.

2.2 The Erosion of Domestic Electioneering

How does a government cope with an increasingly fickle (from its partisan perspective) electorate? By attempting to deliver something voters would approve of in an area they care about. One such area is

2.2 The Erosion of Domestic Electioneering

the economy: voting is strongly correlated with the incumbent's ability to demonstrate economic competence (Kayser and Wlezien, 2011; Dassonneville and Hooghe, 2017). This has provided governments with powerful incentives to improve voters' welfare before elections in the hopes that better economic conditions would induce them to retain the incumbent.[18] Public goods are visible and contribute to general welfare. Presumably, more competent governments can produce more public goods from the same fixed budget than less competent ones. If citizens were to observe a larger public goods provision prior to elections without a corresponding increase in the deficit, they could infer that the government is competent and reward it at the polls. Fiscal policy is well-suited for this kind of strategy (Franzese, 2002). It is not exactly transparent, and the size of the deficit tends to depend on a variety of other factors and often lags by months from the events that determine it. Governments could increase the deficit before elections and cut spending afterwards, and voters might be none the wiser.[19]

Public goods generate diffuse benefits, which might be good for the general public, but this tactic is not always the most effective way to induce politically relevant behavior in the electorate. Governments have strong incentives to target specific constituencies with policies that would deliver more concentrated benefits to them while dispersing the costs widely. For example, left-wing parties tend to favor trade policies that protect the income of workers who face competition from imports at the cost of higher consumer prices. Labor unions organize these interests and if they can deliver the votes, the parties that depend on these votes will listen. Conversely, right-wing parties tend to favor trade policies that encourage larger volumes of exchange that result in lower prices and larger corporate profits but drive down the wages in sectors that compete with imports. Business groups organize these interests, and if they can help a party garner the necessary votes, the party will listen (Milner and Judkins, 2004; Milner and Tingley, 2011).

Unfortunately for the governments, European integration has gradually eroded their ability to act autonomously, leading not only to sharp limits on what they can do with trade and monetary policies but

---

[18] The literature on domestic political business cycles is quite large. Drazen (2000a, 2000b) and Franzese (2002) provide excellent overviews. Somewhat surprisingly, the work on responsiveness to date has not made the connection to the fiscal and monetary strategies commonly discussed in the work on political business cycle. These strategies allow governments to influence voter perception of their ability to improve general welfare. As I argue in Chapter 3, we can interpret signals of "economic competence" as another dimension of responsiveness.

[19] The size of the deficit has other political uses, and some research has studied the conditions under which governments can openly inflate the deficit to provide more public goods (Alt and Lassen, 2006; Shi and Svensson, 2006).

placing serious constraints on what they can do unilaterally on a much wider policy spectrum. Table 2.1 gives an idea about the extent of EU penetration into national policymaking as of 2009. Article 5 of the Treaty on European Union (TEU, 2007) specifies the fundamental principle of EU law that the EU acts only within competences that member countries have conferred upon it in the treaties; any other competences remain with the member states. Article 2 of the Treaty on the Functioning of the EU (TFEU, 2007) defines three general categories of competence: exclusive (policy areas defined in Article 3), shared (policy areas defined in Article 4), and supporting (policy areas defined in Articles 5 and 6). In areas where the EU has exclusive competence, only the EU may legislate, and member states can do so only to implement the EU act. The customs union, competition, and commercial policies all fall in this category, and for the eurozone members, monetary policy as well. In the areas where the EU shares competence with the member states, both can act but the EU has precedence: states can legislate only to the extent that the EU has chosen not to. Internal market, social policies, and public health all fall into that category. In the areas where the EU has a supporting role, the EU can coordinate economic and employment policies, define and implement common foreign and security policies, and under certain conditions supersede the actions of the member states.

The implementation of policies where the EU is involved has placed significant bounds on what member governments can do to influence voter perceptions unilaterally. The integration of capital markets, fixed exchange rates, and an independent European central bank have rendered monetary policy largely ineffective. This has made it nearly impossible for governments to indulge in expansionary monetary policies and run higher deficits before elections (Clark and Hallerberg, 2000; Clark, 2002). The creation of the Common Market eliminated protective tariffs and quantitative restrictions on imports, and the Internal Market eliminated non-tariff barriers to trade, imposed tight controls on state subsidies and liberalized trade in services. Both processes led to an intensification of transnational competition in products but also to greater mobility of finance and investment capital, creating pressures to reduce tax rates and avoid regulations that could have negative effects for competition with other European countries. The European Monetary Union (EMU) eliminated devaluation as a policy instrument that could correct for a loss of international competitiveness; it imposed uniform interest rates that do not fit national economies with above-average and below-average rates of growth and inflation, and it constrained the fiscal policy responses of member governments by the deficit rules of the Stability and Growth Pact (Scharpf, 2003).

Table 2.1. *Delegation of Competences in the European Union since 2009.*

Exclusive Competence (Article 3 TFEU)	Shared Competence (Article 4 TFEU)	Supporting Competence (Article 6 TFEU)
Customs Union	Internal Market	Human Health
Competition Rules	Social Policies	Industry
Monetary Policy	Economic/Social/Territorial Cohesion	Culture
Conservation of Marine Biological Resources	Agriculture and Fisheries	Tourism
Common Commercial Policy	Environment	Education, Vocational Training
Concluding International Agreements	Consumer Protection	Youth and Sport
	Transport	Administrative Cooperation
	Trans-European Networks	Civil Protection
	Energy	
	Area of Freedom, Security and Justice	
	Public Health Safety	
	Research, Technological Development	
	Outer Space	
	Development Cooperation	
	Humanitarian Policies	
	Common Foreign and Security Policies	
	Common Security and Defense Policies	

This table presents policy areas where the EU has competence under the Treaty on the Functioning of the European Union. Exclusive competence means that only the EU can act. Shared competence means both the EU and member states can act but the latter can only do so if the EU has chosen not to act. Supporting competence means that the EU can coordinate, implement, and supplement actions of member states, and in some cases supersede their competence.

Source: EUR-Lex (http://eur-lex.europa.eu/legal-content/EN/TXT/?uri=uriserv%3Aai0020, accessed: September 27, 2016).

The increase in fiscal transparency and the sanctioning of excessive government deficits further diminished opportunities for incumbent governments to use fiscal instruments to appear economically competent before elections.[20] Eurozone members are now obligated to observe the Maastricht criteria and the Stability and Growth Pact. According to Article 121(1) of the European Community Treaty,[21] (i) the ratio of the annual government deficit to gross domestic product (GDP) must not exceed 3 percent at the end of the preceding fiscal year and (ii) the ratio of gross government debt to GDP must not exceed 60 percent at the end of the preceding fiscal year. As attested by the fact that even though violations of the Stability and Growth Pact are well publicized, they are exceptional, the Pact has curtailed governments' ability to manipulate deficits for electoral purposes.[22] European integration has affected all traditional levers of opportunistic policymaking.

The penetration of the EU into areas traditionally reserved for national policy-making is not only broad (evidenced by the distribution of policy areas across the three competence categories) and deep (evidenced by the extent of delegation of authority within policy areas), but also wide (as in the number of countries it affects). When newcomers accede to the EU they agree to be bound by the *acquis communautaire*, which automatically expands the EU's reach. But since these new members often bring diverse policy preferences to the negotiation table, it has become more difficult for individual governments to build the coalitions necessary to achieve policy outcomes they find favorable.

Figure 2.4 illustrates the dramatic acceleration of integration since the 1990s. It plots the European Integration index, which is a composite measure of the breadth, depth, and width of integration (Schimmelfennig, forthcoming).[23] This much-encompassing integration has largely disabled governments in policy areas that might be highly politicized domestically. National governments are no longer sovereign for many policies of interest to their constituents. Instead of doing something that can signal responsiveness to the electorate, governments have to negotiate with many others at the EU level or, worse, can do little if the EU has exclusive competence or has decided to act in an area of shared competence. Since voters often have no idea what the distribution

---

[20] Hallerberg, de Souza, and Clark (2002); Brender and Drazen (2005); Alt and Lassen (2006); Shi and Svensson (2006).
[21] Other criteria include targets for the inflation rate, the exchange rate, and long-term interest rates.
[22] de Haan and Sturm (2000); Gali and Perotti (2003); Dullien and Schwarzer (2009).
[23] See also Börzel (2005); Leuffen, Rittberger, and Schimmelfennig (2013).

2.3 The Politicization of the EU

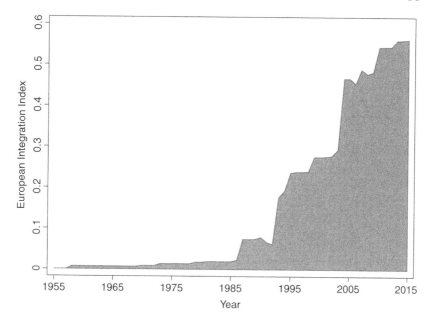

Figure 2.4 European Integration Index, 1955–2015. Index of European integration over time. The index is a multiplicative measure of the breadth (number of policies where EU has competence), depth (extent of delegation within policy areas), and width (number of actors affected) of integration. Source: Schimmelfennig (forthcoming).

of competences is, they end up blaming governments for unresponsive policies even though the governments are powerless to act in that area. This has produced "politics without policies" (Schmidt, 2006, p. 33). The double whammy of disability and blame has aggravated the citizens' dissatisfaction with their governments. Voters have been increasingly disengaging from traditional politics, and throwing their support behind protest movements or extremist parties (Mair, 2000).

2.3 The Politicization of the EU

What does a government do when the electorate is dissatisfied with its performance but its customary means of signaling responsiveness are out of reach? It casts about for new ways of influencing voter perceptions. It might find suitable domestic strategies.[24] However, even in these cases

---

[24] Schneider (2013); Schneider, Swalve, and Troeger (2016). This has led some scholars to argue that it is premature to speak about a decline in opportunistic domestic politics

the government would take note of the shrinking possibilities at the national level, and consider what it can accomplish internationally.

Ironically, what the EU taketh away in policy autonomy, it giveth in a new forum for politicking. The broader and deeper intrusion of EU competences has shifted policymaking to the EU level, and forced domestic interest groups to refocus their lobbying effort there as well. Since many of these policies have pronounced distributional effects, the competition among various interest groups has spilled out into the public forum. This has made European affairs much more salient domestically, and voters' attitudes toward the EU now affect their choices at home and for the European Parliament.

Consider first interest group politics. The EU might be deciding only a handful of issues of truly redistributive potential that are salient to voters (Moravcsik, 2002), but its competences cover a great many issues that are of intense interest to specific segments in the electorate. For example, Table 2.1 shows that the EU has shared competence over agriculture and fisheries. Recall that this means that member states can only act in these areas if the EU has chosen not to act. Given the significant redistributive effects of actions in these areas, the EU has tended to act. Consequently, the affected groups have intensely lobbied their governments to work toward agreements that guard their interests. Since these groups – farming, business, and labor – are crucial for mobilization of the vote, governments have often toed the line, which has led to intense conflicts in the Council (Hayes-Renshaw and Wallace, 2006; Bailer, Mattila, and Schneider, 2015).

Take, for instance, the negotiations over the Takeover Directive that regulates mergers and acquisitions of European companies: how long should bids stay open, who they are offered to, and what information must the company disclose to the public. The Council had evolved a common position when important German business groups (Volkswagen and BASF among them) lobbied the German government to abandon that position.[25] Gerhard Schröder, chancellor at the time, demanded extra allowances for company defenses against hostile bids.[26] The intervention was successful and the Directive was revised to accommodate German business interests (Hayes-Renshaw and Wallace, 2006, pp. 292f.).

(von Hagen, 2003; Mink and de Haan, 2005). This might be so, but even then the circumstances that permit those have drastically narrowed.

[25] "Takeover directive in danger?" *Euractive*, May 3, 2001. www.euractiv.com/section/all/news/takeover-directive-in-danger/, accessed February 5, 2018.

[26] "Germany isolated over takeover directive." *Euractive*, May 11, 2001. www.euractiv.com/section/all/news/germany-isolated-over-takeover-directive/, accessed February 5, 2018.

2.3 The Politicization of the EU

This is not an isolated incident. National interest groups frequently seek out officials in the relevant ministries to encourage them to take into account the groups' preferences when deciding on the positions the government would adopt in the Council (Hayes-Renshaw, 2009, p. 81).[27]

That conflicts over EU-level policies tended to deal with esoteric issues like hostile takeover bids can go a long way toward explaining why public opinion toward the EU has been so generic and uncertain (de Vries and Steenbergen, 2013). But as these decisions have increasingly impinged on the welfare of the public, the "sleeping giant" has stirred.[28]

As a first cut, consider the evolution of public interest in European politics between 1975 and 1994. Figure 2.5 presents the shares of survey respondents that indicated whether they were interested or not in matters related to the European Community.[29] Until 1986, no more than a quarter of European citizens reported any interest in European affairs. As integration accelerated, however, these affairs became more salient and correspondingly public interest increased, peaking at 54 percent in the late 1980s. Although it dropped down to about 40 percent during the following decade, it never returned to the previous state of apathy.

Of course, by themselves these numbers are not very meaningful. To understand how important they are, we need to compare them to public interest in domestic politics. We have a snapshot from the fall of 2006 when the Eurobarometer asked respondents about both European and domestic political affairs. In this survey, 58 percent of respondents indicated that they are at least somewhat interested in domestic politics, and 44 percent said the same about European affairs. This is consistent with the findings from a more recent Eurobarometer (fall 2015), which asked:

---

[27] That interest groups should pressure their government at the intergovernmental level is readily explicable by the composition of the relevant decision-making body, the Council (Greenwood, 1997; Klüver, 2013, p. 31). When the relevant body is supranational – the European Commission or the European Parliament – interest groups lobby its members directly. In this way, national lobbying also affects EU legislation (Schneider and Baltz, 2004). Klüver, Braun, and Beyers (2015) provide a concise overview of lobbying at the EU level.

[28] Mair (2000); Van der Eijk and Franklin (2004); Kriesi (2007); Kriesi, Tresch, and Jochum (2007); Van der Brug, Van der Eijk, and Franklin (2007); Kriesi et al. (2008, 2012); de Wilde and Zürn (2012); Risse (2015).

[29] Although the wording of the question changed somewhat, the common one was "As far as European politics are concerned, that is, matters related to the European Community, to what extent would you say that you are interested in them?" The possible answers were "Interested" and "Not interested." The Eurobarometer dropped that question after 1995. Alternative Eurobarometer questions provide largely consistent results. See Appendix B.

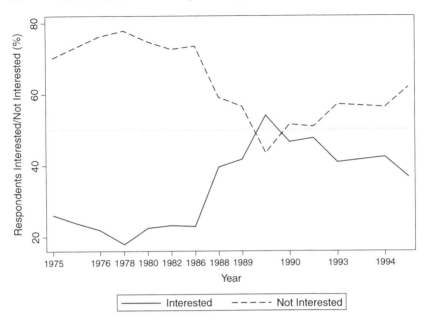

Figure 2.5 Public Interest in European Politics, 1975–1994. Share of respondents indicating that they are either "Interested" or "Not Interested" in response to the question "As far as European politics are concerned, that is, matters related to the European Community, to what extent would you say that you are interested in them?" Wider spacing of the yearly intervals indicates that the question was asked more than once during the year.
Source: Eurobarometer Interactive (http://ec.europa.eu/COMMFrontOffice/PublicOpinion/index.cfm/Chart/index, accessed June 2016).

When you get together with friends or relatives, would you say you discuss frequently, occasionally or never about ... [National Political Matters/Local Political Matters/European Political Matters]?

Table 2.2 shows the results. National and local political matters loom large in these responses, with, respectively, 78 percent and 74 percent of Europeans stating that they would at least occasionally discuss them. But so do European matters, with 66 percent of citizens indicating similar levels of interest. Only about a third never discuss European policies with anyone, a nearly complete inversion of the period between 1975 and 1986, when at most a quarter showed any interest in them.

Heightened public attention to European affairs has gone hand in hand with several other developments. Domestic debates about EU policy issues have become more common, and conflicts over integration have intensified, leading to an increase in polarization of opinions,

2.3 The Politicization of the EU

Table 2.2. *Public Interest in European Affairs, 2015.*

	Frequently	Occasionally	Never
	(% of Respondents)		
National Political Matters	24	54	22
Local Political Matters	20	54	25
European Political Matters	15	51	33

The table presents the share of respondents answering the question, "When you get together with friends or relatives, would you say you discuss frequently, occasionally or never about ... [National Political Matters/Local Political Matters/European Political Matters]"
Source: Eurobarometer 84 (Fall 2015).

interests, or values and the extent to which they are publicly advanced toward the process of policy formulation within the EU (de Wilde, 2011, pp. 566f.).

EU-level policies are now an integral part of "normal politics" domestically (Risse, 2015). Their salience has polarized public debates as even more political actors have gotten involved. European affairs and evaluations of the European project are now a staple of political discourse in many countries. The EU has become politicized.[30]

Figure 2.6 shows the extent of this politicization. The index takes into account the visibility of the EU (measured as the average share of EU-related newspaper articles), the polarization of political debates, and the extent of mobilization within the EU (measured as the average number of EU-related protest events) (Rauh, 2016). Politicization of the EU began in earnest with the signing of the Single European Act in 1986 (not on the graph). It created the Common Market, and extended the range of European competences to include policy areas like environmental protection, safety at work, and consumer protection (Scharpf, 2003, p. 6). The next spike was occasioned by the Maastricht Treaty of 1992, which broadened and deepened integration (Scharpf, 2003; Hooghe and Marks, 2009). The effects of the European debt crisis are discernible as well (Cramme and Hobolt, 2015; Kriesi and Grande, 2016).

Even though EU politicization varies in intensity depending on particular events, it has generally increased over time. The dashed line in

---

[30] Hutter, Grande, and Kriesi (2016, p. 8) define politicization as "an increasingly salient and polarised public debate among an expanding range of actors." Scholars disagree about the extent to which it has occurred along each of the three dimensions (visibility, range, and intensity), but there is significant consensus that European affairs have become very salient and polarizing.

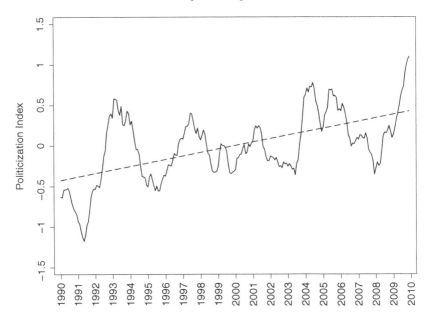

Figure 2.6 Politicization Index, 1990–2010. Six-months moving average of the additive index of politicization that accounts for the visibility of European affairs as well as the range and intensity of public debate. The dashed line is the trend fitted with OLS.
Source: Rauh (2016).

Figure 2.6 is the ordinary least squares (OLS) trend, which clearly shows an upward trajectory. This conclusion is corroborated by studies that use data on public debates, electoral campaigns, and domestic protests (Hutter, Grande, and Kriesi, 2016).

The consequences for domestic politics have been predictable. Voter attitudes toward European integration affect their choices, especially when political entrepreneurs succeed in making the EU electorally salient, and when the government confronts various dissenting groups in the media.[31] Mounting evidence suggests that the position parties take on European integration now influences their share of the vote in national elections.[32] This dimension used to be electorally irrelevant because it was largely orthogonal to the traditional left–right split that drove much of domestic politics. This is no longer so. Parties that advance Eurosceptic positions have managed to attract significant

---

[31] Coverage of EU issues in the national media has increased significantly since the 1990s (Trenz, 2005; Koopmans and Statham, 2010).
[32] Evans (1998, 2002); Tillman (2004, 2012); de Vries (2007, 2009, 2010).

2.3 The Politicization of the EU

voter support (de Vries and Hobolt, 2012). They have challenged the prevailing pro-European consensus of the mainstream parties and have contributed to the growth of internal divisions in centrist parties as well (Kriesi et al., 2012; Hutter, Grande, and Kriesi, 2016). This has forced the ruling parties on the defensive, and today it is the parties in the governing coalitions that tend to be most active in debates on European integration during election campaigns (Dolezal and Hellström, 2016).

The electoral effects are not limited to domestic politics. In elections for the European Parliament, voters tend to favor parties that represent their own attitudes toward European integration.[33] In general, voters do not seem to base their choices on the parties' specific policy positions, mainly because it is much more difficult to assign responsibility for decisions of the European Parliament to individual parties than it is domestically (Clark and Rohrschneider, 2009; Hobolt and Tilley, 2014). The effect is particularly strong for Eurosceptic voters, for whom anti-immigration attitudes contribute to a negative disposition toward the EU (Hobolt, Spoon, and Tilley, 2008; Treib, 2014; Hobolt, 2015).

The proliferation of referenda on EU matters, the rise of Eurosceptic parties, and the politicization of EU issues in national and European elections has moved public opinion from the "permissive consensus" of the early period to the "constraining dissensus" of today (Lindberg and Scheingold, 1970; Hooghe and Marks, 2009).[34]

But what do citizen attitudes toward the EU have to do with governments' responsiveness dilemmas? These attitudes are about the EU itself rather than about particular policies it pursues. In the language of Easton (1965), they indicate levels of *diffuse* rather than *specific* support and opposition. Of course, diffuse support for the European integration project is crucial if this process is to continue and succeed, and governments must be mindful of that. However, except for stridently Eurosceptic politicians who can campaign on generic anti-EU platforms, most political actors are much more concerned with levels of support for particular policies. In other words, for the vast majority of politicians, only specific support permits domestic electioneering, and so it should be more relevant for signaling responsiveness.[35]

---

[33] Clark and Rohrschneider (2009); de Vries et al. (2011); Hobolt and Spoon (2012); Hobolt and Tilley (2014).

[34] For the role of domestic politicization, see Franklin and Wlezien (1997); Gabel (2000); Schoen (2008); Hooghe and Marks (2009); de Vries (2010); de Vries et al. (2011).

[35] Studies of EU politicization mostly focus on the effects of diffuse support for EU integration on voter choices. The political consequence for such nonspecific attitudes has been for parties to clarify their positions on integration (Aspinwall, 2002, 2007; Koenig-Archibugi, 2004; König and Finke, 2007; Arnold, Sapir, and de Vries, 2012; Finke et al., 2012). This line of reasoning has been applied to the European Parliament

Generating specific support is more demanding of the voters – who must be induced to care about European policies – but far easier to target for mainstream politicians, who can place these policies on the familiar socio-economic left–right spectrum in ways they cannot do with the EU's existence (Börzel and Risse, 2009). Voters are more likely to be aware of generic ideas about EU integration than of the details of specific policies they might not even know are being decided at the EU level. It is up to the competing parties and elites to raise these awareness levels, and they do: national parties mobilize voters on both diffuse (constitutive) support and policy issues (Dolezal and Hellström, 2016).[36] Scholars find not only that political conflict over EU policy matters, but that governments are indeed trying to claim credit for EU policy outcomes that are favorable to their electorates (Schneider, 2013). They are also more likely to shift attention to issues that the public considers the most pressing problems in the European Council (Alexandrova, Rasmussen, and Toshkov, 2016), and they go against the majority in the Council when national parliaments have the formal powers to monitor and limit their government's positions (Hagemann, Bailer, and Herzog, 2016).

My shift to focusing on specific support is consistent with the common approach to the study of responsiveness within democratic states, in which diffuse support for the government rarely appears but voter attitudes toward particular policies often do. With European citizens becoming more attuned to European affairs, diffuse attitudes should turn more specific. Or, as Thomassen and Schmitt (1997, p. 169) put it:

> The more the European Union develops, the more we would expect political debates to be dominated by "normal" policy issues, like the problems of unemployment, or of organised crime, rather than by more constitutional issues.

This means that conflicts over policy issues rather than over the EU regime in general should come to be the main causes of politicization. There is some evidence that this is happening. Specific attitudes toward EU reform proposals shaped the EU's ability to reform (König and Finke, 2007). Governments with publics who were more skeptical about reform obtained better deals in the negotiations (Hug and Schulz, 2007).

---

and the Commission (Van der Eijk, Franklin, and Marsh, 1996; Thomassen and Schmitt, 1997; Williams and Spoon, 2015; Rauh, 2016; Spoon and Williams, 2017), the Council (Hagemann, Hobolt, and Wratil, 2016; Wratil, 2017), the EU's overall legislative output (Bølstadt, 2015; Toshkov, 2015), national parliamentary engagement in the EU's legislative process (Williams, 2016a), and the transposition of the EU's legislation (Williams, 2016b).

[36] de Bruycker (2017) further finds that politicization increases political elites' incentives to address public interests in the media (the effect is strongest for members of the European Parliament).

My point in this book is to show that issues of normal, everyday politics – rather than only constitutive ones – in the EU have become politicized, and that this is affecting how political elites behave within the EU.

2.4 Conclusion

Critics of the EU assert that the EU is run by unaccountable and distant political elites who decide behind closed doors without regard to domestic public opinion. Governments have no incentive to govern responsively because voters do not hold them accountable for their actions at the EU level. This view might have characterized the first decades of the EU's existence for the good reason that the institution was *designed* to be insulated from the hurly-burly of domestic politics. But this is no longer so.

In this chapter, I have argued that governments have stronger incentives to bring EU-level policies into their domestic public debates, and the EU's very success in achieving wider, deeper, and broader integration has provided them with the opportunities to do just that.

Party ideology that had produced strong alignment between party identification and voter choice no longer commands the same allegiance among the citizens. Voters have become more willing to cast their votes on specific issues, cross party lines when they do so, and even support political newcomers. The loss of partisan alignment has rendered parties far less capable of delivering predictable blocs of votes at the polls, and as a result electoral volatility has dramatically increased. This has injected incumbent governments with a heavy dose of uncertainty about their ability to stay in office. Prudential motivation impels them to attempt to persuade the volatile electorate that it should want them to remain in power. In other words, they have stronger incentives to signal responsiveness.

Under normal circumstances, governments that need to make themselves attractive to the voters reach for the traditional fiscal and monetary policy tools that enable them to provide more public goods or redistribute policy benefits and costs such that the benefits are concentrated among politically relevant groups while costs are either dispersed widely so they are less noticeable or imposed exclusively on political opponents.

Membership in the EU has rendered the governments' circumstances all but normal. Continuing integration has gradually taken these traditional tools out of the hands of national governments, and transferred them to the collective decision-making bodies of the EU. To make matters worse, citizens who are generally unaware of the extent to which authority has been delegated to the EU are apt to blame their national government for policies they dislike even when the government is powerless to do much of anything about these policies. This impels governments to attempt to persuade voters that they are doing everything they can to achieve favorable policy outcomes even when they have to navigate the maze of EU institutions to do so. In other words, they have stronger incentives to signal responsiveness specifically on EU-level policies.

Under normal circumstances, all government attempts to impress voters with their stances on EU-level policies would fall on deaf ears because Europeans had shown scant interest in the EU. Aside from a generically warm glow toward the EU that has allowed integration to proceed, citizen attitudes have been nonspecific and passive. In part this was by design: the image of a technocratic institution churning out esoteric policy memoranda was almost deliberately cultivated to put the average citizen to sleep. In part it was because for the first several decades, the EU's embrace was still fairly loose and the policies it decided did not impinge too obviously on the daily life of the average citizen. In a sense, Europeans did not know why they should care about EU policies.

The pace and scale of integration since the 1990s has rendered circumstances for EU members all but normal. As the EU has expanded its reach, the redistributive consequences of its policies have become more salient domestically. Interest groups have directed their lobbying efforts to influence the positions their government takes in EU negotiations. Competing interests have spilled their conflicts out into the public forum, igniting domestic debate and giving rise to Eurosceptic parties ready to challenge the sleepy consensus. Governments themselves had to delve in to defend their policy choices when challenged by opposition and protesters. Voters have become not merely more aware of the EU's existence but have taken note of specific EU-level policies that affect them. The sleeping giant has stirred. The EU has become politicized domestically at the policy level, which means that governments can speak to an alert audience. In other words, now governments have better opportunities to signal responsiveness specifically on EU-level policies.

To sum up, the past two decades have witnessed changes in the EU that have made it simultaneously imperative for member governments to signal responsiveness about EU-level policies and increased their ability to do so. Contrary to the assertions of critics of the democratic deficit, governments today should be quite willing to bring everyday politics to the EU, making it look a lot more like a normal democratic institution than an elite superstructure.

2.4 Conclusion

It is one thing to establish that something *should* happen and give some preliminary evidence that it does. It is quite another to develop an argument about *how* it happens and present systematic evidence that supports that particular argument. In the next chapter, I present the theory of government responsiveness within the EU, whose causal mechanism will be tested in the remainder of the book.

3 Signals of Responsiveness: A Theory

> A key characteristic of democracy is the continued responsiveness of the government to the preferences of the people.
> – Dahl (1973, p. 1)

> The single most important fact about politicians is that they are elected. The second [...] is that they usually seek reelection.
> – Tufte (1978, p. xi)

How can governments use negotiations at the EU level to signal that they are responsive to their domestic constituents? What strategies can they employ when collective decisions at that level might involve twenty-seven other governments, several supranational institutions, and layers of bureaucracy?

The punch line of the theory can be readily summarized. Governments can signal that they are responsive when they adopt policy positions close to the preferences of electorally relevant domestic groups, when they defend these positions throughout the negotiation process, and, most of all, when they achieve extraordinary success in these negotiations. Their ability to move from public posturing to claiming credit or disavowing blame for concrete outcomes depends on their bargaining leverage in the relevant decision-making EU institutions and on the willingness of the other members to engage in hidden cooperation to deliver particular outcomes.

The theory relies on two models: a political economy model of domestic electoral competition (Section 3.1), and a negotiation model of intergovernmental bargaining that accounts for the formal and informal institutional features of a specific EU decision-making body, the Council (Section 3.2). Putting these two models together allows me to define a *chain of responsiveness* as it pertains to European cooperation, identify classes of signaling strategies associated with that chain, and derive the corresponding strategies that pertain specifically to negotiations in the Council (Section 3.3). Collectively, these constitute my theory of political responsiveness in the context of the EU, and I will provide evidence for its empirical implications throughout the remainder of this book (Section 3.4).

3.1 Domestic Electoral Competition

Citizens wish to improve their welfare. To this end, they want politicians who are able and willing to represent their preferences in policymaking: citizens support politicians who appear competent and responsive, and oppose those who do not.[1] The primary medium through which this support and opposition are expressed is the regular and free election (Miller and Stokes, 1963; Powell, 2000). Voters could assess the performance of the incumbent government and form expectations about its likely future behavior when deciding whether to retain it (Alesina and Rosenthal, 1995; Duch and Stevenson, 2008). They could choose to reward the government they believe acted in their best interests, or to replace the one that they found unresponsive with an alternative that promises to be more to their liking (Manin, Przeworski, and Stokes, 1999). Elections have the potential to be an important tool to discipline governments, and the threat of electoral sanctions could be a powerful incentive for governments to behave responsively.

This is in theory. In practice, democracies can fall short of this ideal of accountability because voters often simply do not know enough or do not care enough to evaluate their government properly and so they cannot provide the appropriate incentives at the polls. In an environment where the right information is costly to acquire and difficult to verify, voters rationally resort to information shortcuts from sources they trust. They take their cues from elites who are presumably more knowledgeable, from media debates that frame the issues more accessibly, from organized groups that endorse policies in line with the interests of their members, and from party statements that convey the programmatic goals of the leadership. The more politicized the issue, the more likely voters are to be able to avail themselves of these information shortcuts.

Per Sir Francis Bacon, knowledge by itself is not power. However acquired, information can only influence the beliefs of the voters. For that influence to have practical political effects, voters must mobilize to act on their convictions. This is why interest groups are particularly potent in shaping policy (Grossman and Helpman, 2001). They collect, analyze, and disseminate information about policies of concern to their members and to the wider public. They are opinion leaders. But they

---

[1] Dahl (1956); Arrow (1963); Sen (1970); Page and Shapiro (1992); Stimson, MacKuen, and Erikson (1995); Wlezien (1995); Hobolt and Klemmensen (2005); Tausanovitch and Warshaw (2014).

can also coordinate the political activities of their members, affecting voter turnout and providing stable bases of political power for established parties (as, for example, the labor unions did for social democratic parties in Europe). Interest groups that mobilize more voters are better able to pressure governments to act responsively, at least in the relevant policy areas.

When it comes to this influence channel, interest groups rely on strength in numbers. But there are other ways to channel influence more directly. Campaign contributions and other financial support could tilt government policy toward directions favored by the interest group, but the interest group's main source of power is not so crass. It is lobbying, and the currency there is information and analysis, not money. The ability to provide vital information at all stages in the decision-making process, analyze technical aspects of the policies, estimate economic and political ramifications, and craft proposed solutions to problems are the main assets of interest groups. This influence peddling is very difficult to quantify, but while there are no good systematic data, there is considerable qualitative evidence of interest group impact on policy at both the national and EU levels.

In fact, consistent with my argument about the shifting locus of policymaking, interest groups have "Europeanized" and now often lobby at both levels simultaneously. However, in the EU they tend to have an easier time accessing the European Commission and the European Parliament than they do accessing the Council. When it comes to intergovernmental negotiations, interest groups still lobby mainly at the domestic level.[2] When it comes to estimating the effect interest group lobbying has on responsiveness, it all comes down to the degree of congruence between a group's preferences and those of the average citizen. Groups representing narrowly defined interests that seek to concentrate policy benefits on a small segment of the population while externalizing and shifting the costs onto others would be considered impediments to responsiveness. Groups representing the interests of broad swathes of the population would be considered more legitimate participants in the policy formulation process since their goal is to increase government responsiveness to the citizens.[3]

---

[2] Greenwood (1997) and Klüver (2013), who make an exceptional attempt to quantify them, summarize the various ways in which interest groups can exert influence. Coen and Richardson (2009) discuss influence at both levels, and Schneider and Baltz (2004) provide evidence that pressure from interest groups affects pre-negotiations on legislative proposals of the Commission.

[3] See Schattschneider (1960); Olson (1965); Giger and Klüver (2016) on the importance of the congruence between group-specific and general public interests.

3.1 Domestic Electoral Competition

This distinction further complicates any effort to analyze the relationship between lobbying activities and responsiveness. I will set aside the direct channels of influence but retain the indirect ones in my theorizing and empirical estimations. While this will doubtless understate the importance of interest groups for policymaking, it still allows us to uncover the relationship between domestic electioneering and EU-level policy formulation. To see this, note that lobbying groups pressure governments continuously whenever relevant policies are at stake, not merely during election years. In fact, because governments are more sensitive to public opinion during these years, groups representing parochial interests might have an incentive to scale back their lobbying. If the government listens to anyone before elections, it would be to groups that can shape public opinion and mobilize voters. These are the groups that help politicize the policy issues and that can claim broader representation. In other words, since lobbying happens during both election and non-election periods, any observable difference in government behavior between these periods can be attributed to the electoral factor, where it is the indirect influence of interest groups that matters. We might not be able to tell how important lobbying is, but we will be able to tell how important the need to signal responsiveness can be.

With this in mind, consider the incentives of the government during election periods. If it wishes to remain in office – and it invariably does – the government must appeal to voters. For this, the government must signal responsiveness in policy areas that these voters find important. But what are the policy positions that would do the trick? Political scientists and political economists tend to resort to the median voter theorem, which (roughly) states that parties should converge toward policies favored by the median voter (Downs, 1957). This result depends on elections being decided by majority rule and on voters having single-peaked preferences over policies arranged along a single dimension. Most of these assumptions are violated for many European elections, and none are satisfied for any. The theorem's powerful logic can, however, be applied if we disaggregate the electorate into politically relevant groups, as suggested by Rohrschneider and Whitefield (2012, p. 30).[4]

The simplest and most straightforward disaggregation is based on partisanship: we can divide the electorate into aligned partisans and independent voters. Aligned partisans tend to support a particular party because of custom or ideology, and even though this places some constraints on what policies the party would favor, the preferences are rarely policy specific. Independent (nonaligned) voters, on the other

---

[4] See Cox (1987); Bartels (2008) for general treatments.

hand, tend to make up their minds on the basis of party positions on policies they consider important. Because the pull of party identification is (by definition) strong for aligned partisans, parties will not waste resources competing for the votes of partisans aligned with opposing parties. Instead, they will focus on mobilizing their own partisans (core supporters) and appealing to independents (swing voters). This means that the "median voter" to whom a government must be responsive would vary with the composition of the ruling coalition. Each party in the coalition would have its own "median voter" to satisfy. While this would tend to give coalition governments an overall centrist flavor – parties cannot pull too far away from their coalition partners – it also means that when it comes to specific policy issues that are especially relevant to particular members of the coalition, the government would tend to be much more responsive. Interest groups that can mobilize supporters along policies relevant to these members – the agricultural lobby in France or the automobile lobby in Germany – can be particularly effective in getting the government to listen.

In sum, governments would tend to be responsive to the median voters of the parties in the ruling coalition.

Not all governments are created equal. The people who comprise them are dissimilar in how competent they are to deal with the issues of the day, how able they are to forge the internal bargains necessary to make policy, how good they are at "selling" the results of their work to the public, how beholden they feel to special interest group lobbies, and how long their time horizons are when they consider trade-offs between short term costs and benefits and long-term gains and losses. In other words, governments vary in how responsive to the politically relevant groups they can and want to be.[5]

Unfortunately, all governments have one thing in common: they want to stay in power. This would not be a problem if voters could unambiguously attribute any lack of responsiveness to incompetence or venality. They would simply throw the rascals out whenever the government slips in the delivery of outcomes voters want. But things are not so simple. Circumstances can generate unforeseen problems that governments are ill-equipped to handle. Some of these circumstances might well be beyond their control. Conflicts and economic downturns abroad can have serious domestic repercussions. The changing composition of foreign governments can alter the dynamics in intergovernmental EU institutions. Even the best laid plans sometimes come to grief.

---

[5] For example, Gray and Kucik (2014) show that new governments, beholden to new constituencies, tend to back-burner international trade commitments negotiated by their successors.

3.1 Domestic Electoral Competition

This presents voters with a problem: what are they to think when they observe outcomes they dislike? They cannot simply unconditionally sanction the government. This risks throwing the baby out with the bathwater: voters might end up replacing a perfectly reasonable government – one that they would have approved of if they had all the facts – with an untried and potentially far less responsive one. But they cannot simply unconditionally reward the government either. This risks putting the lunatics in charge of the asylum: voters might end up creating an environment where the government is corrupted by special interests but always has an excuse for its bad policies.

Voters would essentially have to adopt a decision rule that has an implicit threshold: they tolerate some misgivings about the incumbent as long as these remain below that threshold, and sanction the government if doubts exceed the threshold. Unfortunately, only individual voters know where their personal thresholds lie, which makes it exceedingly difficult to forecast just how much bad news the electorate would tolerate. In an environment characterized by such uncertainty, the government must be at pains to signal to voters that it is the type of government that they wish to retain despite evidence to the contrary. This need is especially pronounced when things have visibly gone bad and it is easy for the opposition to construct a narrative of incompetence or venality.

But what types of signals would the voters believe? No one has ever heard of a government that did not claim credit for popular or successful policies, but everyone knows that failure is an orphan. The government cannot just declare itself the reason for the good outcomes and disown the bad ones: cheap talk will convey no credible information under the circumstances. Instead, governments must have taken visible steps that signal a commitment to achieving policy outcomes that the politically relevant groups prefer, or, even better, actually deliver on these policies. Any government could potentially mimic the steps of a truly responsive one or luck out with the outcomes. However, governments that do not want these outcomes will find it much costlier to pursue them, and governments that are not competent enough to attain these outcomes except by accident will be far less likely to produce them. In other words, certain behaviors during policy formation as well as specific policy outcomes can serve as credible (albeit still noisy) signals to the voters that they should retain the incumbent government. Conversely, the absence of such behaviors and outcomes can be taken as evidence that they should replace it.

Which policies should the government target for signaling purposes? Ideally (for the government), it would only have to limit itself to policies that are of interest to its politically relevant groups. But in this, the government has a problem or, rather, a host of problems. With weaker partisanship and higher electoral volatility, governments cannot dependably identify the median voters relevant to the next governing coalition. They have to appeal increasingly to potential swing voters but do not know what issues animate them, and so have no idea where the "acceptability" thresholds are. This means that governments cannot easily forecast which issues will become politicized, so they cannot be certain that the policy they have selected for signaling responsiveness would be relevant. It further implies that when issues do become politicized, governments cannot reliably predict the course of public opinion (Mayhew, 1974, p. 57).

Because issue salience can sometimes change rapidly and unexpectedly, governments do not have the luxury to wait until the uncertainty is resolved. They must get ahead of the game with their signals of responsiveness. Prudential reasoning suggests that they would target any policy that is already politicized or has the potential to become so. While they should still favor policies that are relevant to interests represented in the governing coalition, they would also try to be responsive on policies that have a wider appeal, especially if that helps enmesh the swing voters.

To sum up, the domestic electoral model yields some straightforward conclusions. Governments will signal responsiveness to their constituents (core supporters and swing voters) in policies that deal with issues these constituents might care about (issues that have either become politicized or can conceivably become politicized). The signaling will consist of taking visible steps toward achieving policy outcomes these constituents favor and delivering these outcomes.

Of course, when it comes to EU-level policies, the outcomes depend not merely on the effort of any individual government but on the dynamics of collective decision-making. Let us now examine how intergovernmental bargaining occurs in the relevant institutional context.

3.2 Bargaining over Policies in the European Union

Since I am interested in how governments signal responsiveness in EU-level policies, the relevant institutional context is an EU decision-making body where governments participate directly in policy formulation. For reasons I explain shortly, this body is the Council of the European Union (Council), and in this section I examine the formal rules and informal norms that regulate its intergovernmental bargaining. The Council is not the only organ in the EU that participates in legislation: the European Commission and the European Parliament are also involved. Even though governments do not get to participate directly in these bodies, we cannot analyze policy outcomes in the Council without accounting for the interactions among them. As we shall see, over time the European Parliament in particular has come to exert a greater constraint on decisions in the Council.

The Enabling Institution: The Council of the European Union

There are two intergovernmental institutions in the EU: the European Council and the Council of the European Union. The latter is far more important for policymaking.

The European Council is a forum where the heads of state of all EU countries meet at least twice every six months.[6] It was created in 1974 but remained outside the European institutional framework until the Lisbon Treaty fully integrated it in 2009. The European Council sets the broad parameters for the grand strategy of European integration, and provides the long-term vision of where the EU is headed.[7]

The Council of the European Union (often called the Council of Ministers, or just the Council) is the principal intergovernmental decision-making body in the EU and one of its two legislative organs.[8] Its composition depends on the issues under review: there are different configurations tasked with policies in ten broad areas, and each has one representative from the government of every member state, usually the minister within whose purview the policy falls.[9] Discussions over policies usually begin in one of the Council's many working groups and the Committee of Permanent Representatives (Coreper), which comprises senior ambassadors. They try to work out an informal compromise before sending the issue to the Council Lewis (1998; 2003; 2005; Bostock 2002). The Council deals with everyday policymaking in the EU and provides governments with the occasion to state their positions on many policies, bargain over their specifics, and make collective decisions for EU legislation. If the European Council with its highly visible summits gets the lion's share of media attention, it is the mundane proceedings in the Council of the EU that decisively

---

[6] These meetings started in 1975 with three meetings a year. The number of meetings grew to four meetings per year since 1996. The average number of meetings between 2008 and 2015 was seven.

[7] For analyses of the European Council, see, for example, Moravcsik (1991, 1993, 1998); Schneider and Cederman (1994); Hug and König (2002); König and Slapin (2006); Slapin (2008); Tallberg (2008); Tallberg and Johansson (2008).

[8] When I refer to the Council in this book, it will be exclusively to mean the Council of the European Union.

[9] The Council configurations are (i) Agriculture and Fisheries, (ii) Competitiveness, (iii) Economic and Financial Affairs, (iv) Education, Youth, Culture and Sports, (v) Employment, Social Policy, Health and Consumer Affairs, (vi) Environment, (vii) General Affairs, (viii) Foreign Affairs, (ix) Justice and Home Affairs, (x) Transport, Telecommunications and Energy.

affect policy and the distribution of benefits of EU membership.[10] This makes the Council a particularly apt venue for signaling responsiveness domestically.

To understand what specific strategies a government might employ for this signaling, we need to understand how policy is made in the Council. As with any organization, the process is governed by both formal rules and informal norms.[11]

The Formal Rules of the Council For any policy, the first Council reading is the most important phase of the legislative process. It is during this reading that EU governments stake out their positions and negotiate to find a compromise formulation that they might have to defend in the second and third readings against interests represented in the European Parliament (Shackleton, 2000; Bostock, 2002). The primary sources of formal bargaining leverage for governments in these proceedings are the voting rules, which embody the structural power of their countries.

It is obviously important how votes translate into decisions.[12] The voting rules vary across issue areas and have changed over time. From the inception of the Council, some policies have required unanimity whereas others only qualified majority. The determination and assignment of voting weights for this qualification have also changed with the treaties. During the 1973 enlargement, the number of votes for the largest member states was increased from four to ten to give them more say against the larger combined total of smaller ones. The Nice Treaty strengthened this in 2003 by increasing the maximum number of votes to twenty-nine.[13] This proved a step too far, and the weighting scheme came under fire for introducing too much gridlock in the Council. The Lisbon Treaty, which became effective in November 2014, abandoned

---

[10] See Bueno de Mesquita and Stokman (1994), Thomson et al. (2006), and Thomson (2011) for insightful analyses of the Council.

[11] Tallberg (2008) provides an in-depth discussion of the different sources of bargaining leverage in the European Council. His theoretical approach applies equally well to the Council of the EU, and I examine the analogous sources of leverage in my analysis.

[12] There is a large amount of literature on intergovernmental negotiations in the EU that discusses the importance of voting rules. See, for instance, Carrubba (1997); Rodden (2002); Bailer (2004); Mattila (2004); Stokman and Thomson (2004); Tallberg (2006); Plümper and Schneider (2007); Schneider (2007); Schneider (2009, 2011, 2013, 2014); Aksoy (2010, 2012); Thomson (2011); McKibben (2013); Schneider and Tobin (2013); McKibben and Western (2014); Schneider and Urpelainen (2014). The Council has a rotating presidency, which confers additional leverage to the country that happens to hold it (Tallberg, 2006).

[13] Appendix C, available online at https://quote.ucsd.edu/cjschneider/books/, shows the distribution of votes under the Nice Treaty.

3.2 Bargaining over Policies in the European Union 51

the rough-and-ready weighting by assignment of different numbers of votes, and replaced it with two straightforward requirements. A proposal passes if (i) the majority of countries vote for it (55 percent if the proposal came either from the Commission or the High Representative, and 72 percent otherwise) and (ii) if the countries voting for it represent the majority of the EU population (at least 65 percent). To prevent the three most populous countries from vetoing decisions by the other twenty-five, a blocking minority requires at least four countries (if not all countries participate in the vote, the ones voting against must represent at least 35 percent of the EU population, plus one country). Because there are two criteria in which majorities must be obtained, and one of the criteria weighs member states differently, the system is somewhat confusingly called "double qualified majority." It used to be the case that many decisions were made by unanimity, but now unanimity is only required for issues that pertain to the Common Foreign and Security Policy, taxation, asylum, and immigration. For everything else, a double qualified majority is sufficient.[14]

The Lisbon rules were designed in part to break the gridlock in the Council and in part to implement the "one citizen, one vote" principle. The special rule for a blocking minority was introduced to alleviate the concern that small and medium-sized member states would not be able to have their voices heard in situations where the most populous ones disagreed with them. This concern, however, seems to derive from considering the voting arrangements solely in principle rather than in practice. Although officially the larger states could run roughshod over the smaller ones, the reality of decision-making in the Council has always been grounded on a very strong norm of compromise. Unofficially, the Council had developed a "culture of consensus" that studiously avoided the exercise of voting power to impose policies that did not command widespread support. Hayes-Renshaw, Aken, and Wallace (2006) show that even when qualified majority could be used to make collective decisions, the EU governments resorted to a vote in only 30 percent of the cases. For the rest, they opted to negotiate until they could construct a consensual deal. This pattern held even after the EU absorbed ten new countries from Central and Eastern Europe in 2004: between 2001 and 2006, only about 15 percent of legislative decisions in the Council were contested (Hagemann and De Clearck-Sachsse, 2007, p. 3). In the decade between 2004 and 2014, EU members abstained or voted against

---

[14] Detailed information can be found on the website of the European Union (www.consilium.europa.eu/en/council-eu/voting-system/qualified-majority/, accessed October 2016).

the majority in just 1.8 percent of cases (Hagemann, Bailer, and Herzog, 2016, p. 12).[15]

One would be hard-pressed to understand this absence of dissent, made all the more astounding by the formal voting rules and by the increasing divergence of preferences following the ascension of new members. Surely it is not that countries have always seen eye to eye that has enabled this culture of consensus to function.

The Informal Norms of the Council Consensus decision-making requires that dissenters are somehow persuaded to yield to the majority without being simply outvoted. They must be made whole for agreeing to go along with a policy about which they might not be happy, and this necessarily entails striking bargains over time and across issues while simultaneously reducing the costs of the disfavored policy. The structure of interactions within the Council facilitates negotiation and compensation that foster a culture of compromise so that decisions are cooperative rather than conflictual. At the most fundamental level, EU members do have an underlying common interest in making the EU work. The frequent meetings in the Council involve small numbers of people in authority, which makes it possible for them to create personal ties and long-term relationships that greatly augment the incentives to cooperate. Repeated interaction and a long shadow of the future open up opportunities for reciprocal behavior that rewards cooperation and punishes dissent (Axelrod and Keohane, 1985; Keohane, 1986). Council members are socialized to think in terms of problem-solving rather than policy imposition, as shown by Lewis (1998, p. 489):

There is a value in reaching agreement, in collectively solving problems, and understanding each others' domestic political constraints. [...] For example, a deputy of one of the large member states claimed, 'There is a higher sense of defending national interests and of leaving aside instructions, which is rooted in preserving the goodwill of my colleagues for the future. Without this, I won't have their respect and their help next time.'

This sort of reciprocity requires that Council members clarify their positions and identify points of agreement as well as areas of disagreement where some compromise needs to be crafted. It is exceedingly difficult to accomplish this in the harsh light of public opinion, where complexity and conditionality invariably lose to black-and-white

---

[15] For empirical evidence of the informal nature of Council negotiations, see Mattila and Lane (2001); Heisenberg (2005); Achen (2006); Hayes-Renshaw and Wallace (2006); Thomson et al. (2006).

3.2 Bargaining over Policies in the European Union 53

caricatures, and where issues that are linked might not be acceptable for the simple reason that those who stand to lose on one issue might not be the ones who stand to gain on the other. It should come as no surprise that intergovernmental negotiations in all sorts of settings – the Bretton Woods institutions and the World Trade Organization, to name a few of the most important ones – take place behind closed doors. Secretive elite cooperation characterizes bargaining in international organizations more generally.[16] The Council is no exception (Stasavage, 2004).

Secrecy in Council negotiations prevents domestic groups from mobilizing opposition to policies they dislike and permits governments to engage in cooperative bargaining. Governments can stake out their positions and strike bargains that induce them to change these positions and reach a consensual outcome. They can identify like-minded other members and build coalitions that can move the main policy beneficiaries to offer concessions or side payments to those that stand to gain less from it. This is where the large wealthy countries exercise their structural power: the greater resources their governments can bring into the negotiations to facilitate these kinds of deals (Moravcsik, 1998). Germany was long considered the paymaster of European integration because it was willing to spread its vast gains so that all EU members would benefit from deeper cooperation. By the same token, smaller countries are less likely to block decisions that favor the larger ones. It is this bargaining process, rather than the formal voting rules, that accounts for the fact that even though anywhere between 80 and 95 percent of all decisions are made by consensus, the outcomes track closely with what one would expect if they had been made by majority vote (Thomson et al., 2006; Schneider, 2009, 2011).

This is not to say that everyone is happy with the secrecy in the Council. There have been repeated efforts to lift the veil from intergovernmental negotiations. In Germany and France, domestic groups attempted to strengthen transparency rules to require the legislature and the public be informed about what their governments were doing in these negotiations. In both countries the rules were either ruled unconstitutional or simply ignored (Moravcsik, 1994, pp. 22–23). The European Parliament clamored for more transparency from the Council for years without effect (European Parliament, 2014). The British newspaper *The Guardian* took a different track: it sued the Council in

---

[16] Haas (1958); Putnam and Bayne (1984); Vaubel (1986); Putnam (1988); Moravcsik (1994); Sbragia (1994); Milner (1997); Lewis (1998, 2003, 2005); Elgström and Jönsen (2000); Bostock (2002); Bailer (2004); Stasavage (2004, 2005); Hayes-Renshaw and Wallace (2006); Svolik (2006); Dür and Gonzalez (2007).

the European Court of First Instance.[17] It even won when the Court ruled that the Council had failed to provide sufficient justification for holding back information, but to no avail: the Council went on meeting behind closed doors although it did spell out more explicitly the rationale for its rejection of transparency:

> The Council normally works through a process of negotiation and compromise, in the course of which its members freely express their national preoccupations and positions. If agreement is to be reached, they will frequently be called upon to move from those positions, perhaps to the extent of abandoning their national instructions on a particular point or points. This process, vital to the adoption of Community legislation, would be compromised if delegations were constantly mindful of the fact that the positions they were taking, as recorded in Council minutes, could at any time be made public through the granting of access to these documents, independently of a positive Council decision.[18]

Only the decline in democratic legitimacy of the EU in the late 1990s and early 2000s forced the Council to reconsider its stance. The optics of secrecy were so bad that the Council relented and granted the public access to its deliberations during their initial and final stages (when the Commission proposal is presented and when the final vote is taken). It also made some documents available, among them the voting records whenever decisions are put up to a vote.[19]

Although this has improved transparency somewhat, the Council remains far more opaque than national legislatures. Access to its documents is still tightly restricted, many decisions are not put up for a vote, and the public is excluded from the crucial stages of negotiations when bargains are struck and compromises made. Consequently, as long as governments wish to maintain confidentiality, the Council can continue its practice relatively unhampered by the public at large. Whatever direct constraints it has to operate under are imposed by two other European bodies: the Commission and the Parliament.

The Constraining Institutions: The European Commission and the European Parliament

The EU legislative process is quite elaborate and providing a holistic description is a formidable task that itself requires a book-length

---

[17] See Stasavage (2004, 2005) for this case.
[18] Council of the European Union, 1994, cited in Stasavage (2004, pp. 690f).
[19] The PreLex legislative tracking service of the EU provides the voting records (Hix, 2008, p. 149). VoteWatch Europe collects these data and presents them in easy-to-use format at www.votewatch.eu, accessed: January 2017.

3.2 Bargaining over Policies in the European Union

treatment.[20] The rules vary by policy area and have changed over time. I will account for the most significant changes in my empirical analyses. Here, I content myself with brief remarks about two collective EU bodies that play an important role in the legislative process and can influence what happens in the Council.[21]

The European Commission is the EU's supranational bureaucracy and has wide agenda-setting powers by virtue of its monopoly to propose new legislation. Although it often makes proposals upon request of the Council or the Parliament, it retains sole discretion as to the form the process will take, and it can force the Council to vote by unanimity. Under some circumstances, the Commission can even legislate on its own. Its members are supposed to act in the interest of European integration, without respect to national interests.[22] The European Parliament consists of politicians directly elected to the European level. It can exert an active role on legislation and influence through appointments to the Commission. Its members are supposed to represent the interests of all EU citizens.

The main process through which EU laws are made is the *ordinary legislative procedure*.[23] The Commission submits a proposal to Parliament and the Council. The Parliament decides its wording (first reading), and if the Council approves it, the act is adopted. If the Council disagrees, it sends back its own version to Parliament (second reading), and the Commission makes its position known. If Parliament approves the new wording or takes no action, the act is adopted, and if it rejects the new wording, the act fails. Parliament can also amend the proposal and send it back to the Council. At this point, the Commission can intervene again: if it rejects the amendments, the Council can only override its objections by a unanimous vote. If the Council approves the amended wording, the act is adopted. If it still disagrees, its members and an equal number of parliamentarians convene in a Conciliation Committee,

---

[20] Crombez (1996, 1997) and Crombez, Steunenberg, and Corbett (2000) provide excellent introductions to the legislative processes in the EU.

[21] For analyses of the European Commission and the Parliament, see Tsebelis (1994, 2002); Garrett and Tsebelis (1996, 2001); Garrett, Kelemen, and Schulz (1998); Hix and Lord (1997); Pollack (1997); Schulz and König (2000); König and Pöter (2001); Hix, Noury, and Roland (2006); König (2007, 2008); Warntjen, Hix, and Crombez (2008). The European Court of Justice is another important actor, but it is not as directly relevant to policymaking (Burley and Mattli, 1993; Mattli and Slaughter, 1998; Carrubba, Gabel, and Hankla, 2008).

[22] Of course, this does not always work as intended (Hug, 2003; Thomson, 2007; König and Junge, 2009).

[23] Formerly known as the *codecision procedure*, it was established in 1992 by the Maastricht Treaty, modified in 1997 by the Treaty of Amsterdam, and its scope expanded in 2001 by the Treaty of Nice. The current version is described in Article 294 of the TFEU.

where they have six weeks to compose a common text. If the time elapses without a common text, the act fails. Otherwise, the Council and Parliament vote on that text (third reading). Only if both approve it does the act become European law.

The Treaty of Lisbon extended the ordinary procedure, which accords a great deal of power to Parliament, to the vast majority of policy areas. Parliament has gradually clawed its way from a consultative body to a true legislative one nearly on par with the Council, and in doing so has immensely complicated the calculations of EU governments in the Council. There do remain some policy areas, where special legislative procedures are still used, and in these the Council tends to be dominant. Under the consultation procedure, the Council can adopt legislation proposed by the Commission on its own. The Council is required to consult with Parliament but is not bound by its position. The consent procedure, on the other hand, requires that Parliament consent affirmatively. In some limited circumstances, the Council does not need Parliamentary opinion at all, and can adopt unilaterally policies proposed by the Commission. The tendency, however, has been toward a greater role for Parliament, with attendant consequences for signaling responsiveness in the Council.

To sum up, the model of intergovernmental bargaining in the EU yields some straightforward conclusions. Although the collective decision-making and formal voting rules in the Council might make it seem that it is rather difficult for governments to obtain outcomes they prefer, the culture of consensus nourished under conditions of fairly limited transparency makes compromise bargains possible. But how can governments signal responsiveness when much of their behavior remains hidden by design, and when their ability to shape the outcome is constrained by another supranational actor?

3.3   Signaling Political Responsiveness

Governments are said to be responsive when they "form and implement policies that the citizens want" (Powell, 2004a, p. 91). Getting from citizen preferences to policies involves a series of intermediate steps, each of which has to function properly if the desired connection is to be achieved. Figure 3.1 illustrates the chain of causation that is necessary for political responsiveness to occur at the EU level.[24] Even though I focus on government behavior in the Council, I have also included

---

[24] This schematic is based on Powell (2004a) and adapted to the EU setting.

3.3 Signaling Political Responsiveness

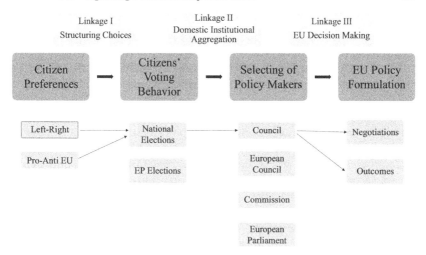

Figure 3.1 Political Responsiveness: Stages and Linkages in European Cooperation. Chain of responsiveness. The dashed black lines indicate the process of responsiveness on the intergovernmental dimension.
Source: Adapted from Powell (2004a).

the other relevant actors for the sake of completeness.[25] The linkages I am interested in are marked with dashed black arrows.

The chain of responsiveness begins with the preferences of the citizens, and the first link is between these preferences and the choices of the citizens at the voting booth. Scholars of American politics tend to study the connection between specific policy preferences of citizens and the corresponding policy positions of their representatives. In Europe, however, strong party discipline means that politicians that belong to the same party tend to adopt similar policy positions even if they represent different districts (Barnes, 1977, p. 119). In this context, citizens effectively choose among parties that offer alternative policy bundles, whose complexities are commonly reduced to an arraying along the left–right ideological spectrum.[26] Since the 1990s, the rising prominence of the EU has increasingly moved parties to adopt more explicit positions on the EU. Since these do not fit comfortably

---

[25] The responsiveness of these actors has been studied elsewhere. See, for example, Reif and Schmitt (1980); Van der Eijk, Franklin, and Marsh (1996); Thomassen and Schmitt (1997); Schmitt and Thomassen (1999, 2000); Proksch and Slapin (2010); Rauh (2016).

[26] See, *inter alia*, Irwin and Thomassen (1975); Barnes (1977); Dalton (1985); Thomassen (1994, 1999). Powell (2004b) summarizes the literature on "responsible party government."

along the left–right spectrum, they have added a second dimension to the voter choice, which now considers the pro–anti EU stance of parties in addition to everything else.[27]

The second link in the chain of responsiveness connects choices at the ballot box with the selection of policymakers who represent the interests of the citizens in European negotiations. Different electoral systems admit various degrees of voter control over government composition and thus over government-controlled appointments (Miller and Stokes, 1963; Powell, 2000). Moreover, the specifics of domestic legislative and executive institutions affect the policy-formulation process, and therefore determine the likelihood that official policy positions reflect the preferences of the citizens (Powell, 2004b). National elections have a direct effect on the memberships of the European Council (which comprises heads of state or government) and the Council of the European Union (which comprises relevant ministers), and a somewhat indirect one on the European Commission (which comprises government appointees).[28]

The third link in the chain of responsiveness connects the policy positions of member governments to the formulation of EU policy. Governments leverage whatever bargaining advantages they have under the formal voting rules and the informal culture of consensus to influence the negotiations over policies within the Council's secretive workings. Their task is further complicated by the fact that the final outcomes often reflect the influences of two actors with divergent collective preferences: the Commission (representing the EU itself) and the Parliament (representing European citizens at large).

This conceptualization of responsiveness in the EU context, despite its parsimoniousness, implies that it would be inappropriate to think of responsive governance in the EU from a systemic perspective. There are multiple channels through which citizen preferences might translate into policy outcomes, and they might represent different slices of the electorate. EU policy outputs might not be responsive to the European citizens taken as a whole (that is, assuming that such a European *demos* even exists), but this does not mean that individual governments have to be unresponsive to their constituents. They might be constrained by the institutional framework of the EU, but in a sense, this is analogous to the ways subnational governments might be limited when they cooperate nationally.

---

[27] Similar connections exist in elections for the European Parliament (Thomassen and Schmitt, 1997; Schmitt and Thomassen, 1999, 2000).
[28] Elections for the European Parliament influence the composition of the Commission as well since Parliament has to approve the entire college of proposed commissioners.

3.3 Signaling Political Responsiveness

The EU context, however, does present governments with a very specific problem. The intricacy of the policy-formulation process and its opaqueness make it extremely challenging for voters to assign credit and blame to governments for particular policy outcomes (Hobolt and Tilley, 2014). But if citizens do not know whether they should reward a government for an observed success or punish it for an observed failure, the chain of responsiveness will be broken at the first link. To restore some measure of accountability and endow this voting choice with meaning, it is necessary for citizens to form appropriate beliefs about the responsiveness of their governments not merely on the basis of observed outcomes but also on the steps governments take in their attempts to achieve them.[29] Consequently, the signaling strategies of the government must attend both to the "input" of the policy process (its actions during policy formulation) and to the "output" (the apportionment of credit and blame).

Strategies to Signal Responsiveness in the EU

Recall that the domestic electoral competition model indicates that governments would have strong incentives to *claim credit* for policies that benefit their politically relevant constituents (Section 3.1). The same is true at the EU level, where governments wish to take credit for any EU-level policies that are favorable to these constituents. Every government wants voters to believe that it has faithfully represented their preferences, strenuously exerted itself on their behalf, ably pursued their policy goals to their formalization, or deftly ensured that they were appropriately compensated for their concessions.[30] As problematic as it is to signal any of this credibly in a domestic context, it is considerably more challenging in the European one. Even if we ignore the Commission and Parliament, the determination of EU policies still involves negotiations among 28 member governments. As these take place behind closed doors, it is not possible to ascertain just how much effort any government has put in. The culture of consensus in the Council also means that voting records are not of much use since decisions tend to be unanimous.

---

[29] This applies to any setting where outcomes are only partially correlated with government preferences. See, for instance, Mayhew (1974); Tomz and Houweling (2008); Houweling and Tomz (2016a, 2016b); Grimmer, Messing, and Westwood (2012); Grimmer, Westwood, and Messing (2014); Cruz and Schneider (2017).

[30] Although the work on political business cycles and political responsiveness have not been explicitly connected, fiscal and monetary strategies before elections allow governments to signal to their constituents that they are capable of implementing policies that improve the voters' welfare. For an application to the EU context, see Schneider (2013).

The informal decision-making norms imply that governments are faced with formidable obstacles in claiming credit for any extraordinary policy achievements. They will, of course, still try.

As mightily as governments strain to take credit for success, their efforts in that regard pale in comparison with the diligence with which they strive to evade responsibility for failure. Domestically, a ruling government does not have much to fall back onto when confronted with bad outcomes. When circumstances permit, it could plead bad luck although such excuses might be seen as self-serving and so get instantly discounted. More profitably, governments could point fingers to someone else for their misfortunes: International organizations are convenient bugbears when it comes to policies that meet with considerable domestic disapproval (Vreeland, 1999; Przeworski and Vreeland, 2000).

In contrast, the EU provides a cornucopia of opportunities for what Weaver (1986) blandly calls *blame avoidance*. In addition to traditional finger-pointing to the EU itself, governments can shift blame onto other EU members.[31] Governments can also exploit the lack of transparency in the policy negotiation process to delay unfavorable but unavoidable outcomes until after national elections. The strong consensus norm can induce fellow member governments to go along with this for the sake of giving the appearance of unity. They might be especially likely to do so if the delaying government is generally cooperative and threatened electorally: losing a good partner can be most unwelcome. For instance, German Chancellors Helmut Kohl and Gerhard Schröder both delayed budget negotiations in the late 1990s in order to "defend German interests" before national elections. Conversely, an important member might use delay as an attrition strategy to obtain a more favorable deal, as British prime minister Margaret Thatcher did in the late 1970s and early 1980s to get the UK rebate.

Credit claiming and blame avoidance are the two main strategies for signaling output responsiveness (Table 3.1). From the government's perspective, each has an unpleasant flaw: credit claims are unlikely to stick, whereas blame avoidance is by definition trying to make the best of a bad situation. In other words, when it comes to output responsiveness the government does not have an effective strategy to send credible positive signals.

---

[31] Smith (1997); Tallberg (2002); Schmidt (2006); Novak (2013); Vasilopoulou, Halikiopoulou, and Exadaktylos (2014). The ready availability of other states allows governments to avoid blaming the EU when doing so would be counterproductive. See Hobolt and Tilley (2014) and Traber et al. (2016) for the lack of blame shifting toward the EU after the debt crisis.

3.3 Signaling Political Responsiveness

Table 3.1. *Strategies to Signal Political Responsiveness.*

Signals of Responsiveness Willingness/ability of a government to represent the interests of the politically relevant national electorate in the EU	
Input Responsiveness:	Position taking
	Position defending
Output Responsiveness:	Credit claiming
	Blame avoidance

In situations like this, signals of input responsiveness could become quite useful.[32] Consider any international negotiations. Governments can commit publicly to policy positions favored by the electorate even before entering these negotiations. *Position taking* is often portrayed as standing firm in the national interest, and since the definition of this interest depends on the ideological composition of the government, it is easily traced back to the electorally relevant constituents. Pre-negotiation public commitments are not costly in themselves, and the governments can engage in them unilaterally. However, they do increase the risks of bargaining failure and can become costly *ex post* if the government fails to secure the minimal terms it has committed to (Leventoğlu and Tarar, 2005). Position taking can provide the government with some bargaining leverage and shift the outcome toward its preferred position. The willingness to run the risk of breakdown can also serve as a credible signal to the electorate that the government is "fighting the good fight," i.e. that it is actively trying to be responsive.

Position taking can work in any international negotiations, but the EU context supplies governments with yet another strategy for signaling input responsiveness: they can stubbornly defend their initial positions throughout the negotiations. This would be of little consequence in traditional contexts where this sort of behavior is more or less expected and unexceptional. Not so in Council negotiations where the culture of consensus places a huge premium on compromise and so encourages governments to alter their positions to achieve it. *Position defending* in the Council breaks the European norm and can be quite costly for the government if it makes the other members less likely to cooperate on

---

[32] Mayhew (1974); Tomz and Houweling (2008); Houweling and Tomz (2016a, 2016b).

other issues. If the government is a repeat offender in that regard, these political costs can escalate as well. Since uncompromising negotiation tactics are not "business as usual" in the EU, they tend to receive a lot of media attention, which further enhances their value as signaling instruments.

Position taking and position defending are the two main strategies for signaling input responsiveness (Table 3.1). From a government's perspective, both strategies run some risk of causing Council negotiations to deadlock, which might trigger a qualified majority vote to impose the will of the majority on the recalcitrant member or provoke a failure of the legislative proposal altogether. Both strategies are also potentially costly, albeit for different reasons. Taking a public position and then failing to deliver increases the domestic political costs for a government that has revealed that it is not that competent. Defending a position in violation of the consensual norms in the Council increases the EU-level political costs for a government that has revealed that it is not that cooperative. The first cost might be expressed directly at the polls when voters punish the government that disillusioned them, and the second might do so indirectly when the government proves incapable of obtaining preferential treatment from its EU counterparts (the end result would still be punishment at the polls domestically). These risks and costs mean that only a government that is fairly dedicated to the position preferred by its constituents and reasonably certain of managing the intra-Council process successfully would opt for these strategies. This, in turn, provides a credible signal to the voters that their government is both willing and able to work on their behalf, which can induce them to reward the government with reelection.

It is worthwhile to summarize the analytical framework for political responsiveness in EU-level intergovernmental cooperation. Figure 3.2 shows the three principal stages in the policymaking process: (1) the formulation of each government's ideal policy position through the interaction of domestic interest groups and social pressures mediated by political institutions, (2) the statement and modification of these positions during the bargaining process among governments and other EU-level actors, and (3) the final legislative outcomes, if any, produced. The signaling strategies vary in the timing and context of their use. Governments can publicly commit to policy positions that are reasonably close to the ideal of their constituents even before negotiations begin. They can choose to defend these positions throughout the bargaining process, and occasionally pierce the veil of secrecy that shrouds them. If governments begin to suspect that their efforts to obtain a better deal are doomed to fail, they can engage in blame avoidance by stalling the

3.3 Signaling Political Responsiveness

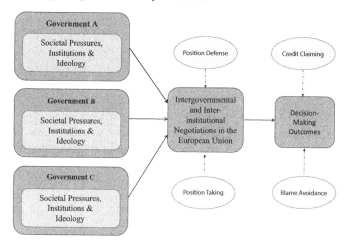

Figure 3.2 An Analytical Framework for Signaling Responsiveness in the European Union.

final decision until after its domestic electoral threat has passed or, if that proves impossible, by casting other EU members or the EU itself as the villains responsible for the bad outcome. If governments expect to succeed in obtaining a good deal, they will push for the outcome to be revealed in time to give them a boost at the polls, and they will claim credit for it.

Clearly, much of the contingent behavior of a government depends on how the negotiations are expected to unfold or, more precisely, on whether the government will be able to bargain its way into a better deal or at least postpone a worse one. To understand the factors that influence the likelihood of that happening, we need to take a closer look at what bargaining power looks like in the opaque Council negotiations.

Bargaining and Hidden Cooperation in Council Negotiations

In any negotiation there are certain objective structural factors that inevitably endow some actors with greater bargaining power than others. Among those are (i) the resources one can bring to the table, both to contribute toward the common goal and to compensate disaffected parties with side payments, (ii) the attractiveness of outside options – things one can achieve on one's own if negotiations fail, and (iii) the congruence of interests with potential coalition partners. In the EU setting, the main determinants of several of these factors are the size of the economy and the internal market (population). A country like Germany would naturally have more bargaining leverage than a country like Slovenia.

Invariably, these structural factors tend to be reflected in the formal structure of the institutions designed to facilitate cooperation. In particular, the larger and wealthier states tend to contribute more to the institution but also have a greater say in how it operates. The principle of no representation without taxation is commonly implemented by allocating larger vote shares to those states, or granting them veto powers or disproportionate influence on setting the agenda. In the Council, the qualified majority voting rules were explicitly designed to formalize the distribution of natural bargaining power among the members. The initial rough-and-ready allocation of certain number of votes was repeatedly modified as new members came in so as to ensure that the distribution of voting rights continued to mirror the distribution of power. As preferences began to diverge, qualified majority began to replace unanimity in more policy areas. After the last bout of expansion that brought into the fold numerous Central and Eastern European states, qualified majority was extended to almost everything. Formally, a country like Germany should tend to obtain more favorable EU deals than a country like Slovenia.

Recall, however, that the Council does not necessarily operate under the formal rules. There are still policy areas where unanimity is required, and it can always be triggered by the Commission during a second reading. Even in areas where qualified majority could be used, the strong culture of consensus tends to avoid formal votes in favor of crafting a mutually acceptable compromise. Formal and informal unanimity requirements endow less powerful members with disproportionate leverage in the bargaining process. The threat of exercising a veto can induce others to make policy concessions, as can the common desire to avoid imposing the collective will on a dissenting minority. There are, of course, limits to these kinds of strategies: veto threats do not make many friends, and a particularly recalcitrant member might find itself outvoted anyway. Thus, the informal norms suggest that while a country like Germany should still tend to obtain more favorable EU deals than a country like Slovenia, the disparity might not be as great as the inequality in structural and formal bargaining powers would imply.

The structural, formal, and informal factors determine the baseline deal each member should expect from Council negotiations. Think of them as the resources a government can deploy toward obtaining more favorable policy outcomes. Not all governments, however, are alike in their ability to make efficient use of these resources. Competent ones can

3.3 Signaling Political Responsiveness

go very far on a shoestring while incompetent ones can squander a king's ransom. Competence is multifaceted. It could manifest itself in lower costs of effort: the government might be better able to produce studies in support of its positions, which can help organize favorable coalitions in the Council. It could manifest itself in modest agency slippage: the government might be better able to exercise effective control over its domestic administrative apparatus and bureaucratic representatives in the EU, which can help ensure the delivery of a consistent policy position at all levels of governance. It might manifest itself in better selection of officials: the government might be able to rely on more skillful negotiators who can build the relationships necessary to maintain the networks of support that facilitate cooperation. Whatever form competence takes, it should enable a government to obtain deals that are more favorable relative to its baseline. In other words, a competent German government should not merely obtain a better deal than Slovenia, it should exceed the baseline expectations for any German government. Conversely, an incompetent German government might fail to secure even the baseline deal even if it still gets something better than Slovenia.

The reason we need to define a baseline and distinguish between governments that can punch above their weight (competent ones) and those that give away the farm (incompetent ones) is that these are the considerations that would affect the voting decisions of their constituents. Citizens should reward a government that meets or exceeds their expectations and punish one that performs below them. This is not merely for retrospective reasons: a competent government is likely to keep delivering better policy outcomes and is so worth keeping in office; an incompetent one is, of course, just the opposite.

These considerations have direct implications for the signals of responsiveness. Since a competent government faces lower risks of bargaining breakdown, lower political costs for playing a (reasoned) tough bargaining strategy and for building supporting coalitions, and expects to deliver better outcomes (and thus not only avoid domestic political costs but perhaps enjoy some gains), it has a much stronger incentive to use these strategies than an incompetent one, which might be actively deterred by the risks and costs it faces. This means that the signal of responsiveness is credible: if the competent government is much more likely to have sent it, then observing the signal must increase the voters' belief that the government is competent. This makes the voters more likely to retain the government. Conversely, a government's choice not to signal responsiveness can be interpreted as evidence of incompetence and, especially in conjunction with an unfavorable policy outcome, should spell electoral doom.

The logic of the model developed so far suggests that signaling responsiveness is a credible sign of competence because the costs and risks of the strategies put them beyond the reach of an incompetent government. This rationalizes the reward and punishment at the polls. But what if an incompetent government could somehow lower these costs and risks? What if it was somehow able to procure a favorable deal? It would then no longer be prevented from signaling responsiveness, which would render the signaling strategies uninformative. If both types of governments use the strategies, nothing can be learned from observing them. The strategies would have no electoral effects.

The secretive proceedings of the Council seem to provide an environment that is exceptionally conducive for just this problem to occur. Since interactions are repeated at frequent intervals, it is possible to engage in *hidden cooperation*: EU member states might agree to "scratch the back" of a government that faces reelection with the expectation that it would return the favor when some other member's political future is on the line. They could permit an electorally threatened government to effectively signal responsiveness in order to boost its chances of reelection. They could turn a blind eye when the recipient of this munificence presented itself as a tough negotiator defending its policy position. They could even agree to make the policy outcomes more congruent with the public opinion in that country.

The strategy of reciprocity that can be implemented behind closed doors makes it possible for incompetent governments to signal responsiveness and threatens to render the signaling mechanism inoperative. It also creates a logical conundrum. If voters became aware of the possibility of collusion, they could no longer interpret signals of responsiveness as evidence of competence and would have no reason to respond appropriately at the polls. Without the electoral reward, however, there would be no incentive for governments to help each other, and the collusive regime would collapse. But if voters expect that collusion does not occur, then signals of responsiveness become credible again and so get rewarded at the polls. This, of course, provides the electoral incentives for collusion to occur. The circle closes and we are back where we started. How are we to understand the effects of secrecy on the credibility of the signals of responsiveness?

Secrecy is clearly necessary for hidden cooperation: it cannot be sustained if voters observe it or realize that it is happening.[33] Voters

---

[33] Hidden cooperation is similar to hidden action in the domestic political arena. Governments that want to signal economic competence by providing more public goods before elections often secretly increase their budget deficits to do so. That they try to hide this action is clear: if voters observed that governments borrowed more

3.3 Signaling Political Responsiveness

would not be very impressed by a government walking on water if they find out that it is being propped up by the other EU members under the surface. They might be especially unhappy to learn that their government is secretly compromising to make the lives of other governments easier. They might even punish a government for trying to deceive them.[34]

Fortunately, secrecy is not sufficient for hidden cooperation. The essence of the reciprocal strategy requires that EU members sometimes forego the possibility of collusion. There are good practical reasons for them to do so, quite apart from strategic considerations. To see that even a fully secret reciprocal strategy cannot always help out a government before elections, suppose that it did. It would not take very long for observers to note how every government magically acquires the wherewithal to effect international deals that are especially pleasing to its voters just before these voters head to the polls. One would have to assume that either every such government is truly very responsive or, more realistically, that there is some behind-the-doors dealing going on. When this happens, the signaling effect would be eroded, decreasing the reward the voters would be expected to confer. For the reciprocal strategy to be effective, it must not produce a clear correlation between signals of responsiveness and impending elections. In other words, there must be times when EU members abandon an electorally threatened government to its own devices.

Of course, it is unlikely that governments strategically randomize to obfuscate the pattern of reciprocity, but it *is* likely that any government's willingness to cooperate with others varies with the electoral circumstances, the timing of elections, the ideological affinity to the government that needs assistance, and even with random idiosyncratic factors like personal relationships. For instance, governments with highly salient

---

to spend more, they would not interpret the increase in public goods as a signal of economic competence (Shi and Svensson, 2006). This also explains why increasing fiscal transparency reduces the ability of governments to use deficit spending (but not necessarily other spending) as an instrument to boost public good provision before elections (Alt and Lassen, 2006; Schneider, 2010; Schneider, Swalve, and Troeger, 2016).

[34] Stasavage (2004, 2005) shows that in the few cases when hidden cooperation became public knowledge, the public was outraged if their government had diverged from the public interest in the EU negotiations. For example, the Council allowed a Danish film crew to document Council negotiations in 2003 not knowing that these would be aired shortly thereafter. The documentary revealed, among other things, that the German foreign minister who had publicly supported Turkish membership (an extremely sensitive topic because of the large Turkish community in Germany) in fact expressed serious reservations about Turkish accession. This caused a tremendous public outcry throughout the EU and created an electoral backlash at home (Clare MacCarthy and George Marker. "Fury sweeps capitals of Europe as TV shows what summit leaders really said." *Financial Times*, April 19, 2003).

preferences tend to do better in Council negotiations (Thomson et al., 2006). Signaling responsiveness would be quite the salient preference for a government that finds itself in dire electoral peril. All else equal, the other governments would be more willing to shoulder some of the costs, so hidden cooperation would be more likely.

All else is, of course, not equal. Governments will be less willing to compromise if their own electoral fortunes are at stake or if there are too many elections coming up and so too many concessions to be made. They are also less likely to back a losing horse: if the government is almost certain to be thrown out of office, there is no reason to make costly concessions that would be of no avail. More to the point, governments might evince no desire to help out a distressed fellow government if they simply want it to lose the elections. This could happen if the majority in the Council wishes to see the opposition party in government because it is more closely ideologically aligned with them. Consequently, hidden cooperation would be less likely for EU members that are ideologically further apart from the Council median. Finally, good will could turn on a personal friendship, as famously exemplified by Helmut Kohl and Jacques Chirac. And so can animosity turn on general enmity, as exemplified by Jacques Chirac and Tony Blair in the early 2000s over reforms of the Common Agricultural Policy and the invasion of Iraq.[35]

In summary, hidden cooperation must be far more sporadic than the secrecy of the Council allows for. This limits the occasions in which incompetent governments can signal responsiveness, and so restores the credibility of the signaling strategies. In other words, even though collusion is sometimes possible, on average competent governments must still be more likely to signal responsiveness, and so reap the electoral benefits of these strategies.

3.4 Principal Implications of the Theory

The theory asserts that EU governments have incentives to use position taking, position defending, credit claiming, and blame avoidance strategies in Council negotiations to signal political responsiveness to their constituents. These incentives are particularly pronounced when governments are threatened electorally and when they expect to be held accountable for their actions in the Council. Their signals are more likely to be credible – and so rewarded at the polls – if they have greater

---

[35] See Chapter 6 for this case.

3.4 Principal Implications of the Theory

bargaining leverage (structural, formal, and informal) or if they secure the hidden cooperation of other EU members.

Although the derivation of explicit hypotheses must await the chapters in which they are tested, some general remarks about the empirical implications of the theory are in order.

There are two reasons *electoral distress* provides strong incentives to signal responsiveness. First, the government is obviously in desperate need to improve its standing with its politically relevant constituents. It must reassure the core supporters and appeal to the swing voters by providing some tangible evidence of its commitment to policies they care about, and some credible indication of its ability to deliver on these commitments. Second, a government at risk is much more likely to garner the collaboration of other EU members, both by its own intensified efforts to secure it and by the members' increased willingness to engage in hidden cooperation.

Governments can become electorally distressed for a variety of reasons. The most common culprit is an economy in the doldrums. A government presiding over a stagnant or deteriorating economy must persuade the voters that the tough times are not caused by its incompetence. The worse the domestic economic circumstances, the greater the urgency to signal political responsiveness in EU negotiations.

Some governments can get away with subpar economic performance because of their popular social policies or ideological stances. Public support, however, can wane for other reasons, such as a major scandal or an international failure. Low public approval ratings can sink a government even in the buoyant waters of a well-functioning economy. The lower the public support for the incumbent, the greater the urgency to signal political responsiveness in EU negotiations.

Finally, the absence of disapproval might not be evidence of approval. Governments should worry if opinion polls indicate that a significant fraction of the electorate is undecided. Since these voters are by definition not deeply committed to any particular ideology or party, they tend to be more concerned with economic benefits, which makes them a prime target for both the government and the opposition (Lindbeck and Weibull, 1987; Dixit and Londregan, 1998). The more uncommitted the voters, the larger the potential swing at the polls, the larger the government's benefit of persuading them to support it and the larger its cost of failing to do so. The larger the group of undecided voters, the greater the urgency to signal political responsiveness in EU negotiations.

No amount of signaling, credible or otherwise, would profit the government if voters do not know or care about it. Neither would its absence hurt the government. For the government to think itself potentially accountable for its behavior, it must believe that electoral decisions are affected by its conduct. And for this, the policy issues over which it is negotiating must be salient. That is, *electoral accountability* requires that EU policies be politicized domestically.

Politicization is a multiplier: it magnifies both the benefits of success and the costs of failure. It increases the force of commitments before negotiations (position taking) and decreases the desire to compromise during negotiations (position defending). It gives the government a powerful reason to delay any unfavorable realizations (blame avoidance) until after the election. The greater the politicization of EU policies domestically, the greater the urgency to signal political responsiveness in EU negotiations.

Structural bargaining advantages tend to be translated into formal voting power, making it easier for the larger and wealthier states to obtain more favorable deals. This can be especially evident when decisions are reached with a qualified majority vote, and somewhat less so when they have to be unanimous. The dominant informal norm of consensus mitigates this asymmetry somewhat and ensures that even the less advantaged can often obtain better terms than their bargaining power would predict.

The picture becomes more complicated when other EU institutions intrude in the policy-formation process. The Commission, with its agenda-setting powers, and Parliament, with its coequal legislative role under the ordinary procedure, are particularly relevant because their membership represents interests very different from those represented in the Council. They can, and will, constrain what the Council does, which greatly limits the opportunities for effective bargaining and hidden cooperation within it. This, in turn, makes it much less likely that the signaling strategies would succeed.[36] The more limited the influence of the supranational institutions in policymaking, the greater the urgency to signal political responsiveness in EU negotiations.

All of these implications are contingent on the logic of the theoretical mechanism, which rests on the built-in assumption that voters are cognizant of the government's behavior at the EU level and they use it to make inferences that affect their voting choices. Although I have explained how the mechanism works if this is the case, one might wonder

---

[36] Even so, neither the Commission nor the Parliament could view with equanimity the electoral loss of a pro-integration European government if the alternative is a Eurosceptic one. Both institutions might turn a blind eye to strategic negotiations in the Council in order to prevent an electoral loss that could endanger the integration process in the medium term and make it all the more difficult for them to fulfill their mandates more generally.

3.4 Principal Implications of the Theory

whether that assumption is justified. For all we know, voters might be reading tea leaves, flipping coins, or just looking at their pocketbooks when they go to the polls. Even if they care about EU-level policies (at least about the ones that become politicized), do they pay attention to the government's strategies of signaling responsiveness? Do they interpret position taking, position defending, credit claiming, and blame avoidance in ways consistent with the theory? These are questions I will turn to in the next chapter.

4 The EU-Aware Voter

This book is about responsive governance in the European Union, and consequently it focuses on the behavior of governments. The theory I developed in the previous chapter establishes the conditions under which governments would send signals of responsiveness during negotiations in the Council. Even after making allowances for voters being uninformed about EU-level policy matters (due to secrecy in the Council or the lack of politicization at home), the theory is premised on one major assumption: When voters care about EU-level policy – and so are willing to hold their government accountable for it – they will be attentive to the government's signaling strategy and interpret it in an electorally relevant manner. That is, it assumes that voters respond to the government's signals of responsiveness at least when European affairs are politicized. But do they?

To answer this question, I conducted a large-scale survey experiment about voter responses to different signals of political responsiveness in two salient policy areas. The survey was administered to 2,540 individuals in Germany during the fall of 2016. The two policies – providing another financial rescue package for Greece and admitting more refugees and asylum seekers – are highly politicized in Europe. They are especially salient in Germany as the country that has borne the largest share of the burden in the Greek bailouts and has accepted the largest number of immigrants in the European migrant crisis. I elicited each respondent's preferred policy positions in both areas, solicited their evaluations of various hypothetical politicians (of different genders, party affiliations, and political experience) who send different signals of responsiveness, and asked them how likely they were to vote for these politicians if elections were held next Sunday.

I find that respondents are more likely to vote for politicians who represent their favored policy positions, who defend these positions during negotiations, and who succeed in achieving the preferred policy outcomes. Conversely, voters blame politicians for adopting policy positions they disagree with, for sticking with them, and for failing to achieve preferred policy outcomes. Crucially, the assignment of credit and the attribution of blame depend on the disparity between the policies pursued by the politician and those preferred by the voter. There is no homogenous "national interest" that politicians can defend to maximize public support. As I have assumed throughout in the model, citizens reward politicians whose policy choices mirror their own preferences and punish those whose policy choices diverge. These findings hold even though I control for other important determinants of voting choice such as partisanship, gender, and political experience.

This experiment enhances the internal validity of the theory but its scope restricts its external validity. The results, however, are more than merely suggestive. They are corroborated by evidence that those governments that succeed in budget negotiations are rewarded with increased support domestically (Chapter 5 provides a quantitative analysis and Chapter 6 provides a qualitative analysis). Qualitative evidence shows that a government that fails to produce the EU policy demanded by the electorate is punished at the polls (Chapter 9). Thus, this book provides the first systematic evidence that voters respond to government responsiveness in European cooperation over issues that are politicized domestically.

4.1 The Survey

I designed an original choice-based conjoint online survey experiment that was conducted during the fall of 2016 in Germany. The survey received an internal review board (IRB) exemption at the University of California, San Diego, and was administered by *Respondi* on a sample of 2,540 adult Germans eligible to vote. All participants were informed that they were participating in an experiment and could not fill out the survey without giving their informed consent.

Although *Respondi* uses various techniques to generate a sample that resembles the underlying population, online samples are never true probability samples.[1] This particular sample skews toward younger and more educated male voters compared to the general voter population. To address this, I use entropy balancing to reweigh the data from the survey so that it matches the demographic margins from the voter population. In particular, I weigh on age groups, gender, and level of education. The sample is well-balanced geographically. Table 4.1 shows

---

[1] True probability samples are extremely difficult (if not impossible) to generate even with offline sampling methods. They come at considerable cost, and their benefits diminish with historically declining response rates.

Table 4.1. *Demographics of the Survey Sample (in %).*

Group	Voter Population	Online Sample (Raw)	Online Sample (Weighted)
Age 18–29	15.8	15.5	15.8
Age 30–39	13.5	11.8	13.5
Age 40–49	16.2	17.4	16.2
Age 50–59	19.6	18.9	19.6
Age 60+	34.8	36.5	34.9
Male	49	51	49
Low Level of Education	40.4	23.8	40.2
Medium Level of Education	29.4	39.5	29.6
High Level of Education	29.5	24.9	30.1

The table presents data on the demographic margins of the voter population, the raw online sample, and the weighted online sample. Data on the voter population are from the German statistical office (www.destatis.de) for the year 2015 (the most recent data available). Data on age groups are calculated for December 2015 based on the German census of 2011.

the demographic margins of the voter population, the raw online sample, and the weighted online sample.[2]

Policy Areas and Voter Preferences

The first step in the experiment was to elicit each respondent's ideal positions on the two policies.

Financial Bailout for Greece. The survey coincided with public discussions of another bailout for Greece.[3] The debt crisis had started in 2009, and the Greek government had received several financial aid packages from the EU and the International Monetary Fund (IMF).[4] These seemed to have resolved the crisis, but in the summer of 2016 the Greek economy plunged again and incited renewed talk about more financial aid.[5] Since contributions to these rescue packages were pegged

---

[2] The imbalances are relatively minor, and the results are robust when unweighted data are used. See Appendix D for the analyses using unweighted data.
[3] I use the terms "bailout," "financial rescue package," and "financial aid" interchangeably in the text, but the survey exclusively used "financial aid" (*Finanzhilfe*) because "bailout" tends to carry negative connotations, and "rescue package" sounds somewhat indeterminate as to its content.
[4] See Chapter 9 for analysis of the first bailout in May 2010.
[5] Smith, Helena. "A year after the crisis was declared over, Greece is still spiralling down." *The Guardian*, August 13, 2016. www.theguardian.com/business/2016/aug/13/greek-economy-still-spiralling-down-year-after-crisis-declared-over, accessed February 5, 2018.

4.1 The Survey 75

to the size of the economy, Germany always ended up with the lion's share of payments. In consequence, the discussions rapidly politicized the issue among German taxpayers (see also Chapter 9).

To elicit voter preferences regarding another Greek bailout, the question was phrased as follows:

We are now interested in your opinion about the debt crisis in Greece. Some believe that Greece should receive more financial aid from the European Union. Others believe that Greece should not receive more financial aid from the European Union. In general, how much do you support or oppose more financial aid for Greece?[6]

European Migrant Crisis. Starting in 2015, increasing numbers of people from Southwest Asia and Africa arrived in the European Union. Some were asylum seekers fleeing wars or persecution in their home countries, others were migrants seeking better economic prospects, and the majority were Muslim. More than three-quarters were from Syria, Afghanistan, and Iraq.[7] By the end of 2016, there were 2,582,780 first-time asylum applications in the EU, which exceeded the total for the previous seven years combined. Of these, Germany had received nearly half (1,221,665, or 47 percent). This was double its average share of the seven preceding years.[8] The German open door policy was made famous by Chancellor Angela Merkel who declared, "Wir schaffen das,"[9] with the predictable effect of gravely intensifying the politicization of the issue. Even setting aside the vocal xenophobic minority, critics asserted that the unprecedented influx of migrants would overburden the system, and that the costs of absorbing the immigrants were exorbitant. Indeed, by the end of 2016, the German government had already spent €20 billion on the refugees.[10]

---

[6] Wir sind nun an Ihrer Meinung zur Schuldenkrise in Griechenland interessiert. Manche sind der Auffassung, dass Griechenland von der Europäischen Union weitere Finanzhilfen erhalten sollte. Andere sind der Auffassung, dass Griechenland von der Europäischen Union keine weiteren Finanzhilfen erhalten sollte. Wie sehr sind Sie im Allgemeinen für oder gegen weitere Finanzhilfen für Griechenland?

[7] I use the terms "refugee," "immigrant," "migrant," and "asylum seeker" interchangeably in the text, but the survey exclusively used "immigrant" (*Einwanderer*) and "refugee" (*Flüchtling*) because these are the terms that the media tends to use and that are common in public debates. Technically, the terms refer to very different categories of people, and the concern tends to be about asylum seekers who enter the EU illegally.

[8] The EU received an average of 350,109 first-time asylum applications per year between 2008 and 2014. Over the same period, Germany received a total of 586,300, so about 81,185 on average per year, or about 23 percent of the EU average. Source: Eurostat, Asylum and first-time asylum applicants by citizenship, age, and sex, Annual aggregated data (rounded); http://ec.europa.eu/eurostat/en/web/products-datasets/-/MIGR_ASYAPPCTZA, accessed January 4, 2018.

[9] "We can do this."

[10] While Germany took the largest total number of refugees, Sweden and Hungary had more refugees relative to their populations.

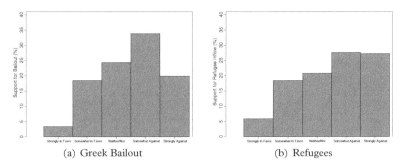

Figure 4.1 German Attitudes toward Bailout and Immigration, 2016. Histograms of responses in the online survey about respondents' attitudes toward (a) providing more financial aid to Greece, and (b) accepting more refugees in the EU.

To elicit voter preferences regarding the migrant crisis, the question was phrased as follows:

We are now interested in your opinion about the European refugee policies. Last year, more than one million people tried to enter the EU. Some believe that more immigrants should be accepted. Others believe that no more immigrants should be accepted. Are you for or against accepting more refugees in the European Union?[11]

For both questions, respondents could pick from the ordinal ranking "strongly in favor," "somewhat in favor," "neither in favor nor opposed," "somewhat opposed," and "strongly opposed."[12]

Figure 4.1 summarizes the respondents' attitudes toward (a) providing another financial aid package to Greece, and (b) accepting more refugees in the EU. The majority of surveyed Germans somewhat or strongly opposed both another bailout (54 percent) and more immigration (55 percent). The numbers of voters who have not formed an opinion on these issues were also similar across the policy areas: 24 percent (bailout) and 21 percent (immigration). The only difference was that Germans appear to remain resolved to accept more refugees than to help the Greeks (6 percent strongly in favor of more immigration versus 3 percent

---

[11] Jetzt sind wir an Ihrer Meinung zur europäischen Flüchtlingspolitik interessiert. Im vergangenen Jahr haben mehr als eine Millionen Menschen versucht, in die EU einzureisen. Manche sind der Auffassung, dass man weitere Einwanderer aufnehmen sollte. Andere hingegen sind der Auffassung, dass man keine weiteren Einwanderer aufnehmen sollte. Sind Sie eher für oder eher gegen die Aufnahme weiterer Flüchtlinge in der Europäischen Union?

[12] The ranking was randomly reversed to ensure that respondents were not just picking the first or the last answers.

4.1 The Survey

strongly in favor of more aid for Greece). Overall, there is significant variation in citizen preferences on both issues, and neither seems to offer anything close to a national consensus.

Both policy areas were highly politicized in Germany. Even though it might be interesting to see whether voters respond differently to policy issues that are not politicized, I chose not to do so for three reasons. First, it would be very difficult to model a non-politicized issue experimentally because by merely including such a policy area the experimenter would draw the respondent's attention to the issue in a way that would not happen in reality for non-politicized issues. This could elicit a response in the experiment even though there would have been no effect outside it. Second, the theoretical mechanism requires voter awareness of the issue, and the point of the experiment is to demonstrate that in this case voters make the hypothesized inferences and choices. For this, highly politicized issues are appropriate because they guarantee such awareness. If we were to discover no connection between signals of responsiveness and voter choices, then we would have fairly strong evidence that the mechanism has made implausible assumptions. Third, the common wisdom is that voters do not care about signals of responsiveness at the EU level even when the issues are politicized. Instead, voters are supposed to rely largely on the government's ideological stances to inform their electoral choices. The relevant setup here is to include ideological affinity as a control and see whether signals of responsiveness have a discernible effect anyway. As we shall see, this is exactly what the experiment does.

Political Scenarios

The second step in the experiment was to present respondents with the scenario for one of the policy areas. When participants were done answering questions for the first area, the survey returned to this step for the other area. The order of the policy areas was random. The scenario informed respondents that further positive action on the relevant policy would require more negotiations among EU members, and that German politicians would be involved. There were two variants of each scenario, which differed only in whether respondents were informed about the politician's final vote on the policy or about their negotiation competence (*Verhandlungsgeschick*). Half of the respondents were randomly selected to receive one variant, and the other half received the other variant.

In real life, of course, voters can only directly observe the behavior of a politician and would have to infer any intrinsic qualities such as competence. The first variant is designed to mirror that situation. With the experimental setup I can go a bit further and provide direct information about the intrinsic attribute (the second variant). This allows me to do two things. First, I can test directly the hypothesized causal mechanism that links voter evaluations of the politician's competence to their levels of support. Second, I can compare this to the indirect evaluation to check if voters are making the hypothesized inferences from the observed behavior of the politician.

The bailout scenario was framed as follows (the refugee one was analogous):

Further financial aid for Greece would require negotiations between EU members. These negotiations also involve German politicians. These politicians can represent different opinions and have more or less influence on the outcomes of the negotiations. We will now show you some examples of such a negotiation behavior. We will show you among other things:

- the position that the politician represented at the start of negotiations,
- [variant 1] the position for which the politician voted at the end of the negotiations, and
  [variant 2] the politician's negotiation competence, and
- the final policy outcome.

We will always show you two possible scenarios to compare. For each comparison, we would like to know which of the two politicians you would prefer if there was an election next Sunday. Even if you like or dislike both politicians, please let us know which one you would prefer to the other. In addition, we will ask you how likely is it that you would vote for each politician if there was an election next Sunday. There are neither correct nor incorrect responses for this question. *Please read the scenarios carefully before you make a decision.*

Respondents could not proceed to the next page without spending at least ten seconds on these instructions.

Politicians and Signals of Responsiveness

The third step in the experiment was to ask respondents to evaluate two sets of two hypothetical politicians who used different strategies to signal responsiveness in a policy area, choose which one they supported, and indicate how likely they would be to vote for each if elections were held next Sunday. Politicians were defined by three personal attributes (party affiliation, gender, and political experience), the initial position they took on the issue, either their final vote (variant 1) or negotiation competence (variant 2), and the negotiation outcome. Table 4.2 lists all possible values of the variables for each of the policy areas.

Each respondent was presented with a pair of hypothetical politicians (Politician A and Politician B) within a fully randomized choice-based conjoint framework, wherein each politician varied along the six

4.1 The Survey

Table 4.2. *Politician Attributes and Signals of Responsiveness.*

	Bailout	Refugees
	Personal Attributes	
Party Affiliation	CDU/CSU SPD FDP The Greens	CDU/CSU SPD FDP The Greens
Gender	Male Female	Male Female
Political Experience (years)	0 2 4 6 8 10	0 2 4 6 8 10
	Signals of Responsiveness	
Position Taken	Favors more aid Opposes more aid	Favors more refugees Opposes more refugees
Final Vote [variant 1]	Favors more aid Opposes more aid	Favors more refugees Opposes more refugees
Negotiation Outcome	More aid No more aid	More refugees No more refugees
	Intrinsic Quality	
Negotiation Competence [variant 2]	High Low	High Low

dimensions of each variant.[13] This design permits the identification of causal effects nonparametrically and so does not require one to make assumptions about the function that maps signals of responsiveness to levels of support.

Respondents were then asked to choose between the two politicians. They had to select one, and only one, of the two. The forced-choice design allows me to analyze the correspondence between the signals of responsiveness and what a voter might actually do at the ballot box. For a somewhat more fine-grained analysis, I also included a continuous

---

[13] See Hainmueller, Hopkins, and Yamamoto (2014) for this method. This design builds on previous experiments about political repositioning and voter behavior in American politics (Butler and Powell, 2014; Houweling and Tomz, 2016a, 2016b; Abrajano, Elmendorf, and Quinn, 2018). I adapted it for the European context and added the responsiveness dimensions.

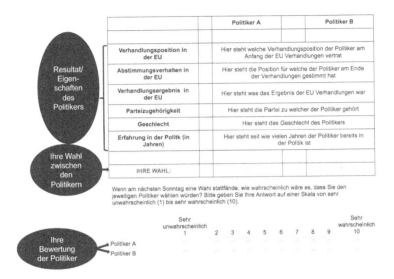

Figure 4.2 Instructions for the Choice-Based Variant 1 Conjoint.

measure of the intensity of voter preferences for both politicians. The respondents were asked,

If there was an election next Sunday how likely is it that you would vote for each of the politicians? Please give your answer on the following scale from highly unlikely (1) to highly likely (10).[14]

Half of the respondents were randomly chosen to receive the scale in this order, and the other half received it in reverse order, from highly likely (1) to highly unlikely (10).

When respondents were finished with their selections, they were presented with a second set of a different hypothetical pair, asked to choose between them, and to indicate the probability of voting for each (i.e., the step was repeated with two other randomly assigned politicians).

Figure 4.2 shows a screenshot of the instructions respondents received for variant 1 before being presented with the two sets of hypothetical politicians. It explains that they will be shown attributes and behaviors for two politicians, that they will have to choose between them, and that they will have to indicate the likelihood of voting for each.

[14] Wenn am nächsten Sonntag eine Wahl stattfände, wie wahrscheinlich wäre es, dass Sie den jeweiligen Politiker wählen würden? Bitte geben Sie Ihre Antwort auf einer Skala von sehr unwahrscheinlich (1) bis sehr wahrscheinlich (10).

4.2 Variables and Model Specification

Table 4.3. *Choice-Based Variant 1 Conjoint (English).*

	Politician A	Politician B
Negotiation Position in the EU	Opposes more aid	Supports more aid
Voting Behavior in the EU	Opposes more aid	Opposes more aid
Negotiation Outcome in the EU	More aid	No more aid
Party Affiliation	FDP	CDU/CSU
Gender	Male	Female
Political Experience (in years)	6	4
Your Choice	○	○

The row ordering of the variables and their values (in light gray) are merely examples. In the experiment both the order of the variables and their values were randomized.

Table 4.3 shows the basic layout of the choice-based variant 1 conjoint in English. Values for each dimension in each politician's profile were randomly assigned, and the ordering of the dimensions was also randomized. Each respondent was given two sets of these hypothetical politician pairs for each policy area, so they had to make a total of four forced choices. The analysis is based on the forced choices because these are what matters during elections. Estimations using the continuous measure of support intensity can be found in Appendix D, available online at https://quote.ucsd.edu/cjschneider/books/.[15]

4.2 Variables and Model Specification

The first set of explanatory variables measures how similar the politician's initial position and final vote are to the voter's preference on the issue, and how closely the outcome corresponds to the voter's ideal point. The voter's preference is measured on a 5-point scale ranging from 1 (strongly in favor) to 5 (strongly opposed), so I coded voters with values 1 through 3 as being in favor of the policy (more aid to Greece and more refugees to EU, respectively), and those with values from 4 through 5 as being opposed to it. The three measures of affinity are as follows:

> *Position Affinity*: An indicator variable that takes the value of 1 if the politician's initial policy position (in favor or against the policy) is the same as the voter's preferred position, and 0 otherwise.

[15] As expected, the estimated effects point in the same direction and the results are mostly significant but the uncertainty around the estimates increases.

Vote Affinity: An indicator variable that takes the value of 1 if the politician's final vote (in favor or against the policy) is the same as the voter's preferred position, and 0 otherwise.

Outcome Affinity: An indicator variable that takes the value of 1 if the policy is set to the position preferred by the voter, and 0 otherwise.

The second set of explanatory variables measures the politician's initial position, final vote, and the policy outcome without reference to the voter:

Position: An indicator variable that takes the value of 1 if the politician's initial policy position is in favor of the policy, and 0 otherwise.

Vote: An indicator variable that takes the value of 1 if the politician's final vote is in favor of the policy, and 0 otherwise.

Outcome: An indicator variable that takes the value of 1 if the outcome is in favor of the policy, and 0 otherwise.

Two variables are designed to measure the effects of position defending and credit claiming:

Defense: An indicator variable that takes the value of 1 if the politician's final vote is the same as the initial position, and 0 otherwise.

Success: An indicator variable that takes the value of 1 if the policy outcome is the same as the politician's final vote, and 0 otherwise.

One additional variable is designed to measure the effect of intrinsic competence of the politicians:

Competence: An indicator variable that takes the value of 1 if the politician's negotiation competence is high, and 0 otherwise.

All estimations share three controls:

Partisanship: An indicator variable that takes the value of 1 if the respondent and the politician affiliate with the same party, and 0 otherwise.

Gender: An indicator variable that takes the value of 1 if the respondent and the politician have the same gender, and 0 otherwise.[16]

Experience: A variable that measures the years of experience the politician has. It takes values from the set specified in Table 4.2.

---

[16] The results are robust if the politician's gender is used instead.

For the analysis, I estimate average marginal component-specific effects (Hainmueller, Hopkins, and Yamamoto, 2014). I regress the dependent variable, a binary measure of whether the respondent voted for a particular politician or not, on a set of indicator variables that capture the specific values that the given scenario takes for each of the attributes. For each dimension, I omit one of the attribute values and use it as the baseline category. The regression coefficient for each dummy variable indicates the average marginal component-specific effect of that value of the dimension relative to the omitted value of that dimension. I report standard errors for these estimates clustered by respondent to account for within-respondent correlations in responses.

I estimated separate ordinary least squares (OLS) models for each of the two policy fields. The results are robust (and even stronger) with a logit model, but since the interpretation of coefficients is more straightforward with OLS, I present them. I also estimated regressions that took into account the respondents' political knowledge and the respondents' attention during the survey.[17]

4.3 Findings

All results are presented graphically; the tabulations can be found in Appendix D. The figures consist of two panels, one for each policy. The panel on the left displays the results for the Greek bailout, and the panel on the right displays the results for the refugees. The independent variables are arrayed along the vertical axis, with the reference value omitted. The marginal effects are plotted on the horizontal axis. The estimated coefficients are denoted by either a dark-gray circle or a light-gray diamond (see the corresponding legend for their meanings), and their 90 percent confidence intervals are marked by bars of the same color.

Position Taking

The first signal of responsiveness is position taking, which in this experiment can occur twice: as the initial position the politician adopts (analogous to public precommitment) and the final vote the politician casts (considered without reference to the initial position). The sample is split into respondents who favor the policy (coefficient estimates marked with dark-gray circles), and those who oppose it (marked with light-gray

---

[17] Appendix D presents the results. In brief, the results for position taking, position defending, and credit claiming strategies are robust, although the uncertainty around the estimates increases slightly. The results for negotiation competence become insignificant.

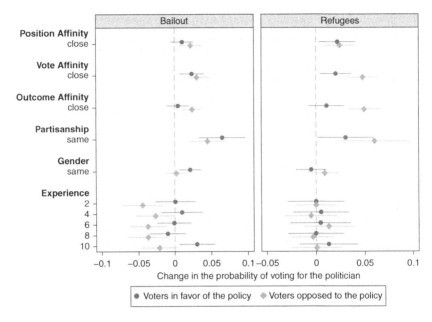

Figure 4.3 Position Taking and Voter Support. Marginal component-specific effects from a linear probability model. Bars denote 90 percent confidence intervals. Reference values for each variable omitted.

diamonds). The estimations use the affinity variables, and Figure 4.3 shows the results.

The theoretical model assumes that voters are more likely to favor politicians who take positions close to their ideal ones. The experimental evidence is consistent with that. If a politician takes a policy position similar to the one preferred by the voter, the voter is more likely to vote for that politician. The effect is even stronger if the politician votes for a policy similar to the one preferred by the voter. Consider, for example, voters who oppose accepting more refugees to the EU (light-gray diamonds, right panel). If the politician also opposes the policy, voter support increases by two percentage points over what it would be if the politician took a different position. If the politician actually votes against the policy, the increase in voter support doubles to four percentage points. Voters who support accepting more refugees to the EU (dark-gray circles, right panel) behave the same way. They are likely to reward politicians who take a similar position on immigration and even more likely to reward those who vote accordingly. The effects are slightly weaker compared to those for opponents but are statistically significant. The same pattern can be observed for the bailout policy

4.3 Findings 85

(left panel). The sole exception is that voters who favor giving more financial aid to Greece do not seem to read much into the initial policy position (the coefficient is in the right direction but is not statistically significant) although opponents still do. Both, however, are apt to reward politicians whose vote is in line with their preferences.

Note that these effects exist irrespective of whether the actual policy outcome is favored by the voter. Interestingly, voters who favor giving more aid to Greece and voters who favor accepting more refugees to the EU do not seem to reward the politician for participating in the collective decision-making that produced the policy outcome that corresponds to their preferred positions (in both cases the effects are not statistically significant). However, voters who oppose giving more aid to Greece and voters who oppose accepting more refugees to the EU are very likely to reward the politician when the policy outcome aligns with their preferences.[18]

Having the same party affiliation as the politician remains the strongest predictor of voting choice, just as the many studies of voting patterns in Europe would lead one to expect. However, it is worth emphasizing that position taking has a statistically discernible effect even when partisanship is taken into account.

Position Defending

The second signal of responsiveness is position defending. Since the experiment records both the initial position of the politicians and their final vote, the appropriate measure of defense is whether the vote was for the initial position. The sample is split into respondents whose ideal policy position is similar to the initial position of the politician (coefficient estimates marked with dark-gray circles) and those whose ideal policy position is different from the initial position of the politician (marked with light-gray diamonds). In addition to *Defense*, the estimations use the initial position taken by the politician, the policy they voted for, and the actual policy outcome. Figure 4.4 shows the results.

The theoretical model expects that voters are more likely to favor politicians whose behavior consistently signals that they are working on behalf of the voters (they take positions favored by the voters and defend them throughout the negotiations). It also expects that voters are very likely to view with disfavor politicians whose behavior consistently signals

---

[18] I speculate that this has something to do with inferences voters make about how decisive the politician might have been in the negotiations.

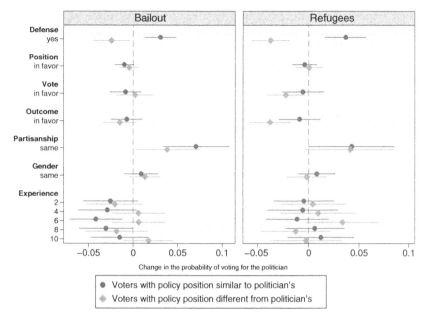

Figure 4.4 Position Defending and Voter Support. Marginal component-specific effects from a linear probability model. Bars denote 90 percent confidence intervals. Reference values for each variable omitted.

the opposite (they take positions the voters oppose and defend those positions throughout the negotiations).

The experimental evidence is consistent with these theoretical expectations. Across both issue areas, voters who agree with the politician's initial position are more likely to reward the politician for defending that position, and voters who disagree with the politician's initial position are more likely to punish the politician for defending that position. There is no reward for political consistency unless it is about policies voters agree with.

Interestingly, the inclusion of position defending all but wipes out the independent effect of position taking: the coefficients of initial position and final vote are mostly statistically indistinguishable from zero. The theory can readily explain that. Taken separately, the initial position and the final vote are weaker signals of responsiveness than the consistency between them. What is the voter to infer if a politician stakes out one position but then votes for another? One possibility is that the initial position was just cheap talk and the politician was never serious about it. Another possibility is that the politician meant it but was persuaded during the negotiations to change his or her mind. The first suggests that the politician might be a demagogue while the second suggests that the politician might not be that competent (since the initial position was apparently wrong). In either case the voter has little reason to reward the politician for inconsistency, and perhaps even a slight incentive to punish him or her for it. Consistency, on the other hand, signals both commitment and competence and is thus duly rewarded when the voter agrees with the policies the politician doggedly pursues and is just as duly punished when the voter disagrees.

The effect of position defending is statistically significant in all specifications even after accounting for partisanship (which remains a strong predictor of support).

Credit Claiming

The third signal of responsiveness is credit claiming. Since the experiment records the politician's final vote and the policy outcome, the politician can only claim credit for the outcome if the vote was for it. The sample is split into respondents whose ideal policy position is similar to the politician's final vote (coefficient estimates marked with dark-gray circles) and those whose ideal policy is different from that vote (marked with light-gray diamonds). In addition to *Success*, the estimations use the initial position taken by the politician, the policy they voted for, and the actual policy outcome. Figure 4.5 shows the results.

The theoretical model expects that voters should be more likely to reward a politician who manages to achieve policy outcomes they like. Conversely, a politician who votes for a policy voters dislike also owns the achievement when that policy becomes the outcome. Blame avoidance is not possible in a setting where voters get to observe the politician's actual voting record.

The experimental evidence is consistent with these theoretical expectations. Across both issue areas, voters who agree with the policy the politician votes for increase their support for the politician when that policy emerges as the negotiated outcome. Voters also tend to decrease their support for politicians who vote for policies they disagree with when those policies emerge as the negotiated outcome (although the effect in the bailout case is not statistically significant). There is no uniform reward for political success unless it involves policies voters agree with.

Interestingly, the effect of success (credit claiming) seems weaker than the effect of political consistency (position defending), both for rewards and punishments. I speculate that this might be due to voters' recognition that policy outcomes are the result of a collective choice

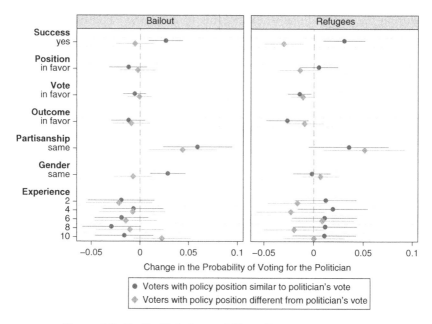

Figure 4.5 Credit Claiming and Voter Support. Marginal component-specific effects from a linear probability model. Bars denote 90 percent confidence intervals. Reference values for each variable omitted.

(and therefore more tenuously connected to the politician's commitment and competence) than the consistency between the initial position and the final vote (which are both matters of individual choice).

The effect of credit claiming is statistically significant in all specifications (except for the punishment for obtaining a bailout policy voters disagree with) even after accounting for partisanship (which remains a strong predictor of support).

Competence

The three signals of responsiveness whose effects we just analyzed have exact counterparts in the real world, which imparts value for the external validity of the experiment. The theory requires that voters observe these signals and make appropriate inferences about the competence of politicians, which in turn affects their electoral choices. This is all they can do in the real world where they do not get to observe that competence directly. After all, this is an intrinsic quality of the individual that even politicians sometimes do not know about themselves. The results thus far are fully consistent with voters making the required indirect evaluations

4.3 Findings

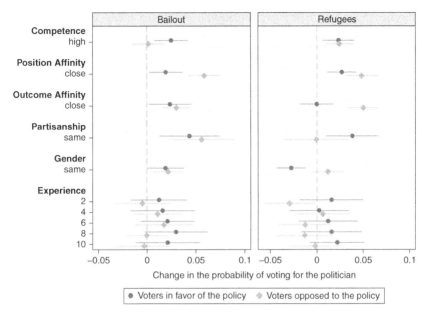

Figure 4.6 Negotiation Competence and Voter Support. Marginal component-specific effects from a linear probability model. Bars denote 90 percent confidence intervals. Reference values for each variable omitted.

of competence. The experiment allows us to take this one step further and check whether it is competence that matters to voters. There is no external validity to this exercise but it can give us confidence in the internal validity of the theory.[19]

The results in this section use the variant 2 scenarios, which provide respondents with information about the negotiation competence of the politicians instead of their final votes. The sample is split into respondents who favor the policy (coefficient estimates marked with dark-gray circles), and those who oppose it (marked with light-gray diamonds). In addition to *Competence*, the estimations use the affinity measures for the initial position taken by the politician and the actual policy outcome. Figure 4.6 shows the results.

The theoretical model expects that voters should be more likely to reward competent politicians irrespective of their policy positions.

---

[19] See Cruz and Schneider (2017) for evidence that perceptions of competence during negotiations allow governments to claim credit for outcomes. I also find that governments get credited for general competence to broker good outcomes in the EU (Chapter 6).

90   The EU-Aware Voter

Competence refers to the politician's ability to make efficient use of physical and human resources to achieve desired policy goals. Lack of competence implies not only that there is a lower probability of achieving these goals (which might not be a bad thing from the perspective of voters who disagree with the goals) but also that resources are being wasted in the process (of which all voters disapprove). The experimental evidence is largely consistent with these theoretical expectations. When voters support the policy, they are apt to reward politicians they perceive as competent negotiators. This is also the case for voters who oppose the refugee policy. The effect for voters who oppose the bailout policy is in the right direction but is not statistically significant.[20]

In the absence of information about the final vote (and thus, by extension of position defending), the initial position taking recovers its signaling importance. As we found previously, voters are more likely to reward a politician who takes positions similar to the ones they favor. Interestingly, they still reward competence even after controlling for the effect of position and partisanship affinity.[21] Partisanship remains a strong predictor of support (with the exception of respondents who are opposed to the refugee policy).

4.4   Conclusion

The evidence of the analysis of the conjoint survey experiment I conducted in Germany supports the assumptions and expectations of the theoretical mechanism outlined in Chapter 3. The results indicate that in a politicized context, voters will use the observed signals of responsiveness to make inferences that affect their electoral choices when they are provided with information about the behavior of politicians in EU-level negotiations and about the outcomes of these negotiations. The effects persist even when traditional determinants of these choices are included in the models.[22]

---

[20] These voters do reward competence if the politician takes the position they favor. Results available upon request.

[21] Note, however, that in contrast to the results on position-taking, position-defending, and credit-claiming strategies, the results on *Competence* are not robust to using the continuous vote choice as a dependent variable or to accounting for political knowledge and attention paid during the survey. The results are robust to using unweighted data. These results call for further analysis in future research on negotiation competence and voter approval.

[22] In related work, I show that voters also hold their governments accountable based on their own diffuse support for the EU regime (Schneider, 2017). For example, Eurosceptic respondents are more likely to hold governments accountable for policies on the European integration dimension than Europhile voters. Interestingly, the positive and negative effects are more prevalent for Eurosceptic voters, which is in line with

4.4 Conclusion

This is great news for the theory, and I can now proceed with the analysis of the hypothesized correlations between signals of responsiveness and electoral support knowing that voters do, in fact, respond to these signals appropriately (at least when the issues are politicized). Had I discovered that voters did not care about these signals – for example, if they made their electoral choices primarily based on partisanship – then there would have been no justification for politicians to signal responsiveness, and so their position-taking, position-defending, credit-claiming, and blame-avoidance behaviors would have had to be interpreted in some other way. The experimental results give me confidence that governments should expect that voters would hold them accountable for their conduct in European negotiations at least when issues are politicized. This expectation is all that is necessary to incentivize them to behave responsively before elections.

The experimental results have broader implications as well. First, they show that voters seem quite able and willing to reason inferentially from limited observables (position taking and position defending, for instance) to the desirability of supporting particular politicians. Against the widespread criticisms that impugn the average citizen's cognitive abilities, the respondents in this experiment clearly behave like reasoning voters.

Second, although the results confirm the common finding of European voting studies that partisanship – the ideological alignment between voters and politicians – is the strongest predictor of electoral support, they also show that responsiveness still matters. Signals of responsiveness influence voting choices in almost all circumstances, even after partisanship is taken into account. This suggests that politicians cannot take their constituents for granted even when they deal with EU-level policies. They must work diligently to retain the votes of their core supporters and attract the swing voters.

Third, the results show that the effects of political responsiveness are contingent on representation. That is, voters reward the politician who is responsive to their preferred policy positions but punish the politician who is responsive to policy positions they oppose. This rationalizes the assumption that politicians would seek to cater to their politically relevant groups and mostly abandon any hope of converting opposition voters. Moreover, as the preferences of core supporters and swing voters diverge, it will become increasingly difficult for governments to use signals of responsiveness to broaden their support. Being successful in

much of the literature on diffuse regime support and electoral accountability in the EU (Evans, 1998; Tillman, 2004, 2012; de Vries, 2007, 2010; de Vries and Hobolt, 2012).

the "wrong" policies might even backfire and push the swing voters into the opposing camp. To put it starkly, the "national interest" depends on who happens to be in office.

Now that I have been reassured by the experimental evidence that the responsive voter is not just a mythical theoretical construct (at least when EU issues are politicized), I can turn my attention to the empirical analysis of the political economy of responsiveness in the EU.

5 The EU Budget: Financially Trivial, Politically Substantial

> Politics is who gets what, when, where and how. — Lasswell (1936)

The European Community (EC) must have loved its farmers, at least if its extravagant expenditures on agriculture were any indication. It lavished them with subsidies that gobbled up 70 percent of the budget in 1985, and that had doubled in a mere six years, topping 59 billion European Currency Units (ECUs) in 1986 (Patterson, 1997).[1] This had distorted the price mechanism and encouraged significant overproduction. But annual spending hikes of 18 percent were obviously not sustainable. They were crowding out investments necessary to continue the integration in other areas. If the agricultural bounty was to continue at these rates, the EC would not be able to meet its obligations by 1988 (Moyer and Josling, 1990). To survive, the EC had to reform.

Germany and France had been among the most energetic drivers of integration. Their heads of state, Chancellor Helmut Kohl and President François Mitterrand, respectively, were not only among its avid supporters, they were keen on strengthening and improving the EC institutions. And yet it was Kohl and Mitterrand who dug in their heels on the common agricultural policy (CAP), and it was Kohl, "the strongest advocate of European Union and... a fervent promoter of institutional reform," who vetoed the British reform proposal in 1987 (Hendriks, 1991, p. 100). What happened?

The farmers happened. The reforms contained production ceilings to halt overexpansion and price cuts to move agricultural commodities closer to their market values. These threatened to drastically reduce the income of farmers, who quickly mobilized their lobbies and took to the streets (Hendriks, 1991; Patterson, 1997). They could not be ignored: in both Germany and France, the political survival of the government rested on its ability to please its rural constituents. Traditionally, the

---

[1] Since the ECU was approximately worth USD 0.982 at the time, this was the equivalent of nearly 60 billion of 1986 US dollars.

overwhelming majority of German farmers voted for Kohl's conservative Christlich Demokratische Union (CDU/CSU). If they were to jump ship, the government would be shattered at the polls. And it just so happened that elections were looming in both countries: a presidential one in France, and two critical state ones in Germany.

The final agreement on CAP was struck in February 1988, just a few months prior to these elections. There would be no savings for the EC budget. Although some limitations on agricultural spending made it into the policy, the budget would have remained in the red had it not been for a drastic infusion of money. Germany committed to boosting its contributions to the budget by more than 30 percent to pay for excess expenditures. As usual, tough negotiations about redistributing limited funds can be resolved miraculously to everyone's satisfaction by the *deus ex machina* of making more funds available:

> West Germany got credit for forging the agreement and could claim success for... minimizing the cuts in farmers' incomes. France could argue that the welfare of French farmers had been protected by the infusion of new funds into the CAP and that the potential damage of stabilizers had been limited. The UK and the Netherlands won limitations on agricultural spending plus price cuts for overproduction. The Mediterranean nations received large increases in regional, structural, and social funds. The Commission attained new revenues to keep the European Community solvent... [and] all the participants benefited in that the movement toward the single European market could proceed smoothly (Moyer and Josling, 1990, p. 97).

Everyone was politically happy except perhaps the German taxpayers who were funding all these blowout celebrations. Kohl ran the German government for another decade, and Mitterrand was to remain president for seven more years.

In this chapter, I show that this was not an isolated incident. The annual negotiations over the EU budget in the Council are riddled with electioneering, and governments threatened at the polls systematically tend to receive budget shares over and above what they would expect under normal circumstances.[2]

Applying the theory developed in Chapter 3 to EU budget negotiations is a good first cut for a test. The EU budget might be small relative to the overall wealth of the EU, but it is highly politicized at the national level. For governments, this creates political pressures that are quite out of proportion to the budget's modest size. Correspondingly, the urgency

---

[2] This analysis builds on my findings reported in Schneider (2013). The data set was expanded for the period 1977–2013 and to include the Central and Eastern European member states.

to signal responsiveness in these negotiations is very high. The budget is so politicized in part because the outcomes are so easy to understand: the more money, the better. There is no need to understand the arcane details of legislative acts that must be digested five times over before they are fit for public consumption. When the budget is fixed (which is most of the time), negotiations are purely redistributive: more for one country means less for others. This tends to get everyone fixated on comparing the relative sizes of budget receipts rather than considering economic efficiency or social desirability.

Ironically, this simplicity also provides governments with the opportunity to send signals of unusual clarity. Any government can expect that voters will understand when it performs well in negotiations (budget share sizes are an easy metric for measuring success), that they will make the appropriate inferences about its competence (zero-sum bargaining makes other governments loath to concede), and that they will reward it at the polls (hardly a citizen would clamor for less than a "fair share" of the budget). That the electoral repercussions will be forthcoming is also ensured by the fortuitous timing of spending negotiations, which are repeated every year, and which must be concluded by strict deadlines. Consequently, EU budget negotiations are exceptionally conducive for signaling responsiveness.[3]

The fact that these negotiations deal with something as well-defined as money also makes them convenient for study. Data on the annual EU budget stretch as far back as the 1970s and are readily available, which is something that cannot be said about the output of most any other negotiations.[4] This opens up possibilities for large-N quantitative analyses of the correlations between signals of responsiveness and elections that might simply be beyond reach for other types of negotiations due to data limitations.

Before getting into these analyses, it would be useful to explain how the budgetary negotiation procedures work (Section 5.1), substantiate the assertion that the EU budget is highly politicized despite its modest size (Section 5.2), and operationalize the dominant signal of responsiveness (Section 5.3). The analyses are themselves divided into two groups. The first set of results demonstrates that governments indeed tend to

---

[3] Many legislative negotiations happen only once for each policy, and the timing is endogenous to a variety of factors outside the Council's control. This makes it harder for governments to signal output responsiveness. See Chapter 7 for more on this.

[4] The analysis of electoral politics in other legislative areas requires information about the governments' policy positions at the beginning and the end of negotiations in addition to the outcomes. This sort of fine-grained detail can be obtained from in-depth interviews, a very laborious and costly process, which has permitted only a handful of the thousands of EU legislative acts to be coded systematically (Thomson et al., 2006, 2012).

systematically receive atypically large budget shares before elections, and that this tendency is stronger when they are more distressed about their chances of reelection, when they can leverage their formal and informal bargaining powers, and when they are not confounded by many other governments in electioneering mode (Section 5.4). The second set of results demonstrates that this signaling of responsiveness does have the expected consequences: larger budget shares tend to translate into higher domestic approval ratings of the governments (Section 5.5).

5.1 A Primer on the EU Budget

The budgetary procedures of the EU have changed with the evolution of the Union (European Commission, 2008). When the community was small and the drive for integration uniformly strong among the members, the budget was negotiated annually. As preferences diverged, these negotiations became increasingly acrimonious with states haggling over the appropriate allocation of the common financial resources (Laffan, 2000). With many veto players often having diametrically opposing interests, the budget became hostage to the most minimalist preferences, and the outcomes could only satisfy the lowest common denominator. Most EU members found this joint decision trap deplorable (Scharpf, 2006).

When gridlock became all too common in the 1980s, the EU finally stirred itself to reform. The budget process was split into multiannual financial frameworks (MFFs; also called *financial perspectives*) and annual spending plans. The MFFs are negotiated every seven years to establish political priorities and set the ceilings on total expenditures for each budget category. They are not designed to function as seven-year spending plans but to create a stable environment for financial programming. The actual allocations are decided every year and the total spending usually remains below MFFs ceilings to allow for unforeseeable events. It is the bargaining over these allocations that I will study in this chapter.[5]

The Annual Budget

The annual budget of the European Union lays down all revenue and expenditures for a single year. It must ensure that all EU policy areas

---

[5] See Chapter 6 for a case study that involves the 2007–2013 MFF negotiations. The MFFs are prepared by the General Affairs Council, which is mostly made up of the ministers for European Affairs from member states. The annual budget is prepared by the Economic and Financial Affairs Council, commonly known as the Ecofin Council, which is attended by the economics and finance ministers.

5.1 A Primer on the EU Budget

are adequately covered, and it must be balanced (the EU cannot incur deficits).[6]

The EU has several sources of revenue, some of which are raised on its behalf (e.g., customs duties on imports from outside the EU and sugar levies), and some of which it collects itself (e.g., deductions from EU staff salaries, interest, payments from non-EU countries, and surplus from previous budget). The combined income from these sources tends to be under 20 percent of the total. The rest comes from member state contributions calculated from their gross national incomes (GNIs), which comprise the vast majority of payments into the budget, and from their value added taxes (VATs).

The expenditures are divided into *commitments* (legal pledges to provide financing) and *payments* (cash or bank transfers to beneficiaries). Commitments might provide for immediate payments or for spending over several years. Multiyear projects are usually committed in the year they are decided but paid over the years as they get implemented. Thus, any given year's commitments might well exceed the payments. If projects terminate before planned completion, the total payments would be lower than the commitment. The EU refers to these multiyear financial schemes as "differentiated appropriations." Non-differentiated appropriations are for immediate disbursement and include administrative expenditures, direct payments, and, importantly, support for agricultural markets (that is, farmers always receive EU money in the year it is committed).

The annual budget is organized into categories that track the priorities set by the governing MFF. Figure 5.1 shows the commitments by policy area in 2015.[7] The largest budget heading is *Sustainable Growth: Natural Resources*, which takes up 39 percent of the budget and includes the Common Agricultural Policy (CAP). The bulk of CAP spending is consumed by direct payments to European farmers. The second largest heading is *Economic, Social, and Territorial Cohesion*, which takes up 37 percent of the budget and includes the structural development policies. Most of these policies are financed through European Structural and Investment Funds (ESIFs).[8] The bulk of ESIF spending is concentrated on less developed European countries and regions, and is

---

[6] The European Commission is empowered to borrow from international capital markets on behalf of the EU but cannot do so to finance the budget. All EU borrowing is to finance loans to countries, and the terms are almost exactly the same as those under which the funds were raised.

[7] Data are from the European Commission (http://ec.europa.eu/budget/annual/index_en.cfm?year=2015, accessed June 2016).

[8] The five funds are the Cohesion Fund, the European Agricultural Fund for Rural Development, the European Maritime and Fisheries Fund, the European Regional

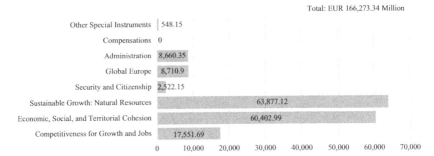

Figure 5.1 EU Budget Allocations by Heading, 2015 (in millions of euros). Total EU budget allocations for each policy area.
Source: European Commission (http://ec.europa.eu/budget/annual/index_en.cfm?year=2015, accessed June 2016).

designed to help them catch up and reduce their social and economic disparities to the rest of the EU.

Unlike policy areas that involve research, education, and health, which are managed by the European Commission, agricultural subsidies and structural funds are all managed by national and regional authorities. In fact, under the 2014–2020 MFF, the Commission was responsible for implementing only about 20 percent of the budget. The remaining funds were to be disbursed directly by the member states under the "shared management" procedure.[9] In this case, the total amount allocated to each country is designed to cover the needs of programs under the budget headings per previously set priorities. There are various eligibility criteria that affect which countries have access to certain fund allocations. Consider, for example, the European Regional Development Fund (ERDF) and the European Social Fund (ESF). To determine who can draw on these funds, all country regions are grouped according to their levels of economic development calculated from their gross domestic product (GDP) relative to the average EU GDP. Only regions in the poorest groups can usually rely on ERDF and ESF allocations. On the other hand, national agricultural production tends to play an important role for determining eligibility for CAP funds. Other requirements might also be factored in: since 2003, the EU has demanded that farmers

---

Development Fund, and the European Social Fund. They are mostly funded under the two largest headings.

[9] Only about 5 percent of the EU budget is spent on administration and salaries. For a concise summary of the EU budget under the 2014–2020 framework, see Druel et al. (2015).

respect standards for environmental protection, animal welfare, food safety, and land management.

As we shall see, the spending ceilings set by the MFFs and the eligibility criteria can explain much of the variation in annual budget allocations across EU members. They are not, however, deterministic, and there remains considerable wiggle room for governments to bargain for more funds.[10] They can shuffle allocations within and between spending categories when there are "unforeseen changes in expenditures," and the revision clauses of the MFFs allow modifications for up to 5 percent of the ceiling.[11] It is the ability of the governments to negotiate within these constraints that is of particular interest here. To understand the institutional constraints under which they must work, we must take a look at the formal procedure for allocating the budget shares.

The Formal Annual Budget Procedure

As with many other decisions in the EU, initially it was the Council that had exclusive budgetary authority, and Parliament acted only in a consultative role. In 1970, Parliament acquired final say on "non-compulsory" expenditure, which amounted to about 8 percent of the budget at the time, with the Council retaining full powers over all "compulsory" spending arising from international and EU treaty and act obligations. In 1975, Parliament acquired the right to reject the budget as a whole but could not amend it. The share of non-compulsory spending grew steadily and reached 58 percent in 2003 (Benedetto and Høyland, 2007). However, no further modifications to the procedure were made until the Treaty of Lisbon, which removed the distinction between the two types of expenditures, streamlined the process by limiting to a single reading in each institution, and put Parliament on equal footing with the Council, "budgetary co-decision" in EU-speak (Crombez and Høyland, 2015). These entered into force on December 1, 2009.

The co-decision procedure is set out in Article 314 of the Treaty on the Functioning of the European Union (TFEU), which specifies the stages and time limits for negotiating the budget. The process starts with the Commission preparing a draft budget under the guidelines laid down by Parliament and the Council. This draft is based on statements drawn up by various EU institutions, with each estimating its own needs arising from MFF obligations and legislative acts, among other

---

[10] Carrubba (1997); Rodden (2002); Mattila (2006); Aksoy (2010); Schneider (2011, 2013).
[11] See European Commission (1999, Part I, §19) and Puia (2010, p. 61) for more details.

items. For example, member states set prices for agricultural products in the Agriculture Council, which then forwards this information to the Commission for use in determining expected CAP spending. The Commission must submit the draft to both Parliament and the Council by September 1, which starts the formal negotiation period.[12]

The Council has until October 1 to adopt a position on the draft budget and submit it to Parliament. Although the adoption is officially by qualified majority vote, Council members try to negotiate a consensus position whenever possible. Aside from the strong governing norm for not imposing the will of the majority on minorities, there is another reason for seeking a unified stance: the Council must fully justify that position. Parliament then has 42 days to react. If it approves the Council's position or declines to make a decision, the budget is adopted. If a majority votes for amendments, then the new draft is referred back to the Council and the Commission, and the Conciliation Committee is immediately convened.

The Committee (with equal numbers of representatives from Parliament and the Council) has 21 days to agree on a common text, and this agreement is to be obtained by a qualified majority vote of the Council representatives and a majority vote of the parliamentarians. If the Committee produces a joint text, Parliament and Council have 14 days to approve it. If neither rejects the joint text, it is adopted as the budget. If Parliament rejects it or if Parliament takes no action but the Council rejects it, the Commission must prepare a new draft and the process restarts.[13] If the Council rejects it but Parliament acts positively, the outcome depends on what that action is. If Parliament confirms some or all of its previous amendments by a supermajority (60 percent of the

---

[12] In practice, Parliament and the Council often agree to a "pragmatic calendar." This moves up the due dates by four months so the Commission has to submit its draft by late April or early May. Politics can sometimes derail the pragmatic arrangements, however. For example, in 2016 the Commission delayed the submission of the draft budget until the end of June. It claimed that it needed more time to consider the costs of the migration crisis. Sources in Parliament, however, indicated that the move was an attempt to avoid public discussion of EU spending before the UK exit referendum of June 23, 2016. Since the "Brexit" campaign had emphasized alleged EU profligacy and regulatory overzealousness, this interpretation was widespread. (Ariès, Quentin. "Commission delays EU budget proposal until after Brexit vote." *Politico*, May 12, 2016. www.politico.eu/article/commission-delays-eu-budget-proposal-until-after-brexit-vote-britain-eu-budget/, accessed February 5, 2018).

[13] If no budget is adopted by the start of the financial year, there is a default system of "provisional twelfths" that becomes operational to keep the EU machinery afloat until an agreement can be reached. This allows the EU to fund each chapter of the budget up to one-twelfth of its preceding financial year's appropriation. Article 315 of the TFEU empowers the Council to authorize limited excess expenditures unless these get reduced by Parliament within 30 days.

total votes cast and a simple majority of its component members), then its version of the draft is adopted. If it fails to attain this supermajority, the outcome is taken to signify approval of the joint text, which is then adopted.

Despite some drawn-out debates, most budget negotiations conclude with agreements on schedule. Parliament vetoed the whole budget only twice before the Treaty of Lisbon (in 1979 and 1984), and the Committee has failed to agree on a joint text three times since (in 2011, 2013, and 2015), in which cases the new proposal drafted by the Commission was adopted (European Parliament, 2016, pp. 3–4).

5.2 The Salience of the Budget

The EU budget negotiations obey Sayre's law, which states that in any dispute the intensity of feeling is inversely proportional to the values of the issues at stake. The budget looks sizable in absolute terms (e.g., €143 billion in 2014), but is relatively trivial. It normally amounts to only about 1 percent of the GNI of the EU (the EU's own resources cannot exceed 1.23 percent of that GNI). As a frame of reference, the average national budget of an EU member state is about 48 percent of its GDP; the combined budgets of the twenty-eight EU countries are fifty times greater than the EU's. In its editorial about the blowups over the MFF for 2014–2020, *The Economist* put this in the proper perspective:

> The gap between the most austere and the most extravagant proposals that were on the table in Brussels was a lot smaller than this. At the end of the day, only a little over €30 billion a year separated the two—or about 0.05% of government spending, a margin that in the context of national budgets most political leaders would not even bother to debate.[14]

But one would not know this by the "screaming headlines" that generally turn the budget into one of the most hotly debated EU issues at the national level. The amorphous "national interest" quickly crystallizes around expected budget receipts, turning negotiations into "high decibel ones vested with considerable political drama and last-minute agreement" Laffan (2000, p. 725).[15] The grand-standing on behalf of the nation can become quite baroque without a deadline with reversion rules to reign in its more extravagant displays. It took nearly three years to hammer out the MFF for 2007–2013 (Chapter 6).

---

[14] "The European Union budget: Too timid by half." *The Economist*, December 1, 2012. www.economist.com/node/21567360/print, accessed April 2014.
[15] "Nothing like EU budget talks to bring out national interest." *Irish Times*, October 12, 1998.

Why is the financially trivial EU budget so significant politically?[16] In part, it is so because it happens to be EU's main instrument of redistribution that could overcome misgivings of its less integrationist members. Simply put, it is through the budget that member states interested in widening and deepening the EU can compensate the holdouts and coax them into agreement.[17] Germany agreed to put agricultural subsidies into the budget to mollify French farmers in return for France's support for the common market. Germany was also the main instigator behind doubling the structural funds in the 1980s to induce the poorer members to agree to the Single European Act (SEA) and the European Monetary Union (EMU). Politicians who need to "sell" these policies to reluctant publics fearful of being stuck with the bill can tout these compromises to argue that the extra benefits outweigh the costs.

It is this reasoning that explains why public discussions about the budget quickly zero in on how much one's own country gets relative to other EU members and relative to how much it pays into the budget. As Lindner (2006, p. 6) observes in his study of EU budgetary conflicts:

the relationship between national contributions to the EU budget and gains from it plays an important role within the national discourse over the costs and benefits of EU membership. This is particularly true for countries, the so-called net contributors, which contribute more than they gain [...]. The visibility of budgetary figures gives the net-contributions a high symbolic value that goes far beyond their financial importance.

With data about the budget easily available and numbers that can be crunched in every leading and misleading way imaginable, it is no wonder that proponents and opponents of EU-level policies would latch onto the budget figures as the principal clubs to wield in domestic debates. With each competing politician beating the nationalist drums louder than the next one, the parochial concerns of each member state would quickly come to dominate the centripetal force of common European interests in budget negotiations.[18]

The UK rebate is the archetypal example. When prime minister Margaret Thatcher rejected a proposed rebate in November 1979, she was quite explicit[19]:

---

[16] It is well-established that the budget is quite salient across the EU. See, *inter alia*, Mueller (2005); Zimmer, Schneider, and Dobbins (2005); Follesdal and Hix (2006); Lindner (2006).
[17] Moravcsik (1991, 1997); Carrubba (1997); Schneider (2011).
[18] Haas (1958); Sbragia (1994); Lewis (1998); Zimmer, Schneider, and Dobbins (2005).
[19] Statements by Margaret Thatcher at the "Press conference after Dublin European council." November 30, 1979. www.margaretthatcher.org/document/104180, accessed February 5, 2018.

5.2 The Salience of the Budget

We in Britain, together with Germany, are the financiers of the European Economic Community. We are a poor country. We are the seventh poorest out of the nine, whereas Germany is one of the wealthier ones. We, next year, will contribute more than Germany. We are saying we cannot go on financing the Community; we cannot go on putting money in the Community's coffers. We are giving notice of that and we want a very large proportion of our own money back, because we need it at home and we are having to cut expenditure at home. (...) [The proposed budget rebate] would still have left Britain with much much much too big a net contribution—a contribution next year of the same size as the German one and many many many times that of France. So, of course, I was not prepared to settle.

She eventually got what she wanted in 1984, and the United Kingdom began to get back two-thirds of any contributions it made in excess of its receipts. The size of that rebate was one of the most contentious European issues in the United Kingdom during the negotiations of the MFF for 2007–2013 even though its domestic impact was negligible (it was about 0.2 percent of the country's 2010 GDP). Naturally, when the UK government pushed for a larger rebate, the EU pushed back. And for good reasons: always deeply unpopular with other EU members, the UK rebate became grounds for other net contributors to clamor for their own rebates. The slogan in the EU soon became: We want our money back!

As each net contributor Member State has sought some of its contribution back, the EU budget has become much more political for governments who are keen to show their electorate that they are getting their "fair share" from the EU budget (McIver, 2008, p. 13).[20]

Eventually Denmark, Sweden, the Netherlands, and even Germany negotiated rebates for themselves, making France and Italy the largest net contributors.

It had been British Eurosceptics who needed to be paid off with the UK rebate. Ironically, it was British Eurosceptics who abruptly developed amnesia about it during Brexit debates in the run-up to the June 2016 referendum that would take the United Kingdom out of the EU. One of the most notorious slogans of the "Leave" campaign was the one plastered on its bus:

We send the EU £350 million a week. Let's fund our NHS instead.

But this ignored both the rebate and EU spending in the United Kingdom. When the rebate was accounted for, the weekly figure dropped to £248 million. When the money the EU sent back was accounted for,

---

[20] See also Le Cacheux (2008) and Laffan (1999, p. 10) for similar findings.

the weekly figure plunged to £136 million.[21] This was approximately £7 billion for the year. Was that a lot? The United Kingdom's national budget was £742.3 billion in 2015, so its net contribution to the EU was a measly 0.9 percent of what the government planned to spend. Would it have made a big difference to the National Health Service (NHS)? The national budget had allocated £141 billion on health, so spending the net contribution to the EU on health would have increased that allocation by a paltry 5 percent.[22] Since the net contribution goes toward financing all of the EU's activities worldwide, including its Common Foreign and Security Policy and most of its multilateral development and structural programs, it is arguable that the United Kingdom was getting a pretty good bang for its buck.

The United Kingdom, of course, had always been a reluctant partner in the schemes to deepen the EU. But it was no outlier in the politicization of the budget. For example, conservative members of the EU Parliament stalled the adoption of the 2000 annual budget to embarrass their left-wing national governments (Lindner, 2006, p. 104). And even the staunchly pro-EU Germans were not immune.

Chancellor Helmut Kohl had been broker and paymaster to many MFFs: Germany's net financial contributions to the budget had ballooned from 4 billion ECU in 1987 to 11.5 billion ECU in 1995. But in 1998, the negotiations over the MFF for 2000–2006 (the so-called Agenda 2000) ran aground. The EU was gearing to expand to the east, and the German public worried whether the new member states would be able to pay their fair shares of the budget. They had cause for concern: The reunification with East Germany was proving much more arduous and costlier than they had expected, and the country's wealth rank had

---

[21] Henley, Jon. "Why Vote Leave's £350m weekly EU cost claim is wrong." *The Guardian*, June 10, 2016. www.theguardian.com/politics/reality-check/2016/may/23/does-the-eu-really-cost-the-uk-350m-a-week, accessed February 5, 2018.

[22] Wallace, Tim. "Budget 2015 summary and highlights: Everything you need to know." *The Telegraph*, July 12, 2015. www.telegraph.co.uk/finance/budget/11724370/key-points-summer.html, accessed February 5, 2018. This is assuming that the future government would redirect the money to the NHS. The prominent Brexit leader Nigel Farage (associated with the Leave.EU campaign) disowned the promise within hours after the referendum results were announced. The official Vote Leave campaign, whose battle bus had sported the slogan, wiped its entire website soon thereafter (Stone, Jon. "Nigel Farage backtracks on Leave campaign's '£350m for the NHS' pledge hours after result: The UKIP leader said he had never made such a pledge." *The Independent*, June 24, 2016. www.independent.co.uk/news/uk/politics/eu-referendum-result-nigel-farage-nhs-pledge-disowns-350-million-pounds-a7099906.html, accessed February 5, 2018; Griffin, Andrew. "Brexit: Vote Leave wipes NHS £350m claim and rest of its website after EU referendum." *The Independent*, June 27, 2016. www.independent.co.uk/news/uk/home-news/brexit-vote-leave-wipes-nhs-350m-claim-and-rest-of-its-website-after-eu-referendum-a7105546.html, accessed February 5, 2018).

5.2 The Salience of the Budget

slipped. They were not unique: more than 83 percent of Europeans thought that new members would have to stand on their own, and this outweighed the desire to promote their economic development.[23] Kohl had become especially sensitive to the worries of the German public because of the general election in September (Laffan, 2000, p. 736). Since these fears concentrated on Germany receiving less than its fair share, it was quite possible that an increase in the total budget (and thus of Germany's contribution) would provoke an electoral backlash. And so it was that Kohl dragged his feet in the negotiations until the elections had safely passed.[24]

One could keep piling anecdotes to show that the EU budget is politicized way beyond the putative financial burdens it imposes on member states, but some more systematic evidence might be more persuasive. We could, for instance, consider how salient it is relative to other EU issues that are known to figure very prominently in the minds of the public. Immigration and foreign security are particularly apposite in that regard, especially in light of the crises over migrants and over Ukraine.

Figure 5.2 compares Google Trends on three EU policies: budget, immigration, and foreign policy from 2004 to 2016. Google Trends takes a subset of all internet search requests received by Google (in this case, 10 percent) over a certain period of time and analyzes how many of those were on a particular topic.[25] It is far from a perfect measure of salience – there are other search engines, not everyone gets their information online, and more obscure items might generate more searches – but it can at least give some indication about the frequency with which the more internet-savvy citizens look up information about the EU budget relative to information about EU foreign security and immigration policies. Since the absolute frequencies are not that relevant given the limitations of the sample, I have suppressed their labels to focus on the relative ones.

Searches for "EU budget" consistently outrank searches for "EU foreign policies" and generally track closely with searches for "EU immigration." In fact, aside from the spike in immigration searches

---

[23] See, for example, Eurobarometer 52, 1999. These concerns intensified as enlargements drew nearer. The German public had simply gotten "tired of paying when other Member States expect to keep receiving even when enlargement happens." (Judy Dempsey. "Paying for a bigger Europe: EU members are united over enlargement but divided over how it should be financed." *Financial Times*, February 11, 2002).

[24] Peel, Quentin. "Bonn's EU funding will soon be tested." *Financial Times*, September 1998.

[25] The analysis excludes repeated requests that come from the same IP address over a short period of time.

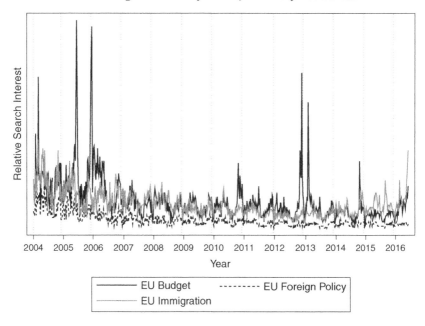

Figure 5.2 Google Trends of EU Budget, Foreign, and Immigration Policies, 2004–2016. Relative frequencies of searches for "EU budget," "EU foreign policies," and "EU immigration" in 10 percent of all Google searches from 2004 to 2016. Vertical dotted lines mark the adoption of annual budgets (December in each year). The MFF for 2007–2013 was adopted in February 2008, and the MFF for 2014–2020 was adopted in December 2013.
Source: Google Trends.

occasioned by the 2015 migrant crisis, budget searches very often generate considerably more interest than anything else. It is worth noting that these periods of intense salience do *not* coincide with negotiations over MFFs (the two MFFs during this period were adopted in February 2008 and December 2013), but map neatly to the adoptions of the annual budgets (indicated by the vertical dotted lines).

The annual EU budget appears to be relatively salient domestically, which implies that politicians should have incentives to signal responsiveness in these negotiations, especially prior to elections. Let us now turn to measuring how they do so.

5.3 The Measure of Responsiveness: Budget Shares

How would governments go about signaling responsiveness in budget negotiations? Since net contributions tend to provide the focal point

5.3 The Measure of Responsiveness: Budget Shares

for domestic debates, there seems to be a straightforward recipe for being perceived as responsive: pay less and receive more. The size of the contributions themselves are nearly impossible to change in annual budget negotiations because they are determined by formulas, and these can be altered by financial framework negotiations only.[26] This leaves the receipts, where everyone has an incentive to demand more. Because of the redistributive aspect of budget negotiations, the only credible signal of responsiveness is that one actually receives more. If everyone has incentives to bargain hard for their own shares, only highly competent governments would be able to get outcomes that exceed the baseline expectations. This would be true even if hidden cooperation is possible (and for these types of policies, cooperation often might not be possible because of the high domestic costs of making concessions to benefit other states). This, in turn, means that the government's inevitable credit claiming would resonate with voters whenever it is accompanied by larger receipts. In other words, the main dependent variable associated with the signal of responsiveness measures the size of budget receipts.

I assembled a data set of the budgetary receipts of all EU member states from 1977 to 2013. This includes all nine states that were members in 1977 (France, Germany, Italy, Denmark, the United Kingdom, Belgium, Luxembourg, Ireland, the Netherlands), and eighteen more as they acceded: Greece (1981), Spain and Portugal (1986), Austria, Finland, and Sweden (1995), Czech Republic, Estonia, Hungary, Latvia, Lithuania, Poland, Slovakia, Slovenia, Malta, and Cyprus (2004), and Bulgaria and Romania (2007).[27] The data come from the annual reports of the European Court of Auditors (1977–2006) and the European Commission (2000–2013).[28] To make the numbers comparable across periods and account for currency variations, everything was converted into constant 2012 euros.

Recall that the two largest budget headings include spending on CAP and ESIF. Because these have different eligibility criteria (which determine the baseline expectations about the shares a country "should" receive) and because they are especially contentious politically, I define three dependent variables:

---

[26] Consistent with this, I find that EU governments do not decrease their contributions prior to elections (results available upon request). In the next chapter, I show how they strategically use the size of their contributions during MFF negotiations.
[27] Croatia became a member of the EU in 2013 but not until July, so it is excluded from the data set.
[28] The Commission provides budget data on its webpage, http://ec.europa.eu/budget/figures/interactive/index_en.cfm, accessed June 2016. The data correlate very highly with information I obtained from other sources. The (small) differences are due to changing spending categories over time. The findings are robust if only data from the Court of Auditors are used (Schneider, 2013).

108   The EU Budget: Financially Trivial, Politically Substantial

Total Receipts: the percentage share of each EU member's total receipts from the overall budget commitments in each year.

CAP Receipts: the percentage share of each EU member's CAP allocation from the overall budget commitments in each year.

ESIF Receipts: the percentage share of each EU member's ESIF allocation from the overall budget commitments in each year.

To get some sense of the distribution of these variables, Figure 5.3 presents their scatter plots. It shows that there is a lot of variation in relative share sizes both across EU members and across time, with

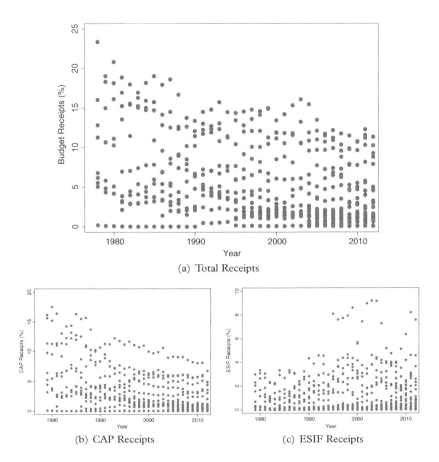

Figure 5.3 Percentage EU Budget Shares, 1977–2013. EU budget receipts (%), CAP receipts (%), and ESIF receipts (%) for EU member states between 1977 and 2013.
Sources: European Commission and Court of Auditors.

5.3 The Measure of Responsiveness: Budget Shares

the variance markedly decreasing after the twenty-first century enlargements. Figures 5.3(b) and (c) also show the shifting priorities of the EU, with CAP expenditures declining sharply (from about 73 percent in 1985 to 39 percent in 2015) and becoming more equitably distributed, and with ESIF expenditures going in the exact opposite direction (not surprising since the enlargements incorporated less developed countries).

For a closer look at how receipts vary for different member states, Figure 5.4 presents their box plots.[29] France, Spain, Germany, and Italy consistently rank among the top recipients of large EU budget shares, and while the small member states are also usually found near the bottom, some wealthy longtime members do not seem to have received large shares either (e.g., the Netherlands and Belgium). As one might have expected from the discussion of agricultural subsidies above, Germany and France have tended to get the largest CAP shares, whereas the largest ESIF shares are usually the preserve of the populous but lesser developed members like Italy, Poland, and Spain.

Spain, in fact, is the only state that is among the top three in all three measures. Some of this is because the country is in the somewhat unusual position of having a relatively large population, still relying on agriculture, and lagging in development compared to the EU core. This hits all the right buttons for formal eligibility, so Spain tends to qualify for a variety of EU funds. The budgetary advantage of formal eligibility can be starkly illustrated by comparing Spain with the Netherlands, a much wealthier and more developed member state that is far less dependent on agriculture. With Dutch GDP per capita consistently exceeding the EU average, and both unemployment and size of the agricultural sector significantly below their EU averages, the Netherlands qualifies for very few EU funds. In contrast, Spain's average unemployment rate of 14.4 percent is almost twice the EU average of 8.4 percent, and 11 percent of its workforce is employed in agriculture.

Figure 5.5 shows the strong effects of satisfying formal eligibility criteria. Before the Spanish accession in 1987, the Netherlands obtained relatively high shares of the budget. With the entry of Spain (and Portugal), however, its ability to qualify for funds declined precipitously. Being small and rich is not a blessing when it comes to distributions of the EU budget. The entrance of even poorer members from Central and Eastern Europe, many of which were also more populous than the Netherlands, kept the Dutch shares depressed. This also affected

---

[29] See fn. 11 in Chapter 2 for a description of this type of plot. Briefly, the boxes include observations between the first and third sample quartiles, and the bars inside them mark the median. Outliers are marked with circles.

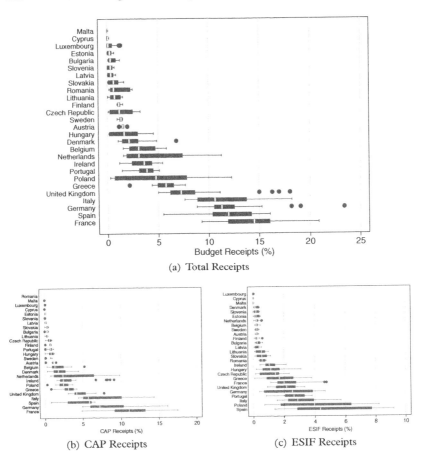

Figure 5.4 Percentage EU Budget Shares by Member State, 1977–2013. EU budget receipts (%), CAP receipts (%), and ESIF receipts (%) for individual EU member states between 1977 and 2013. Countries are listed by their median shares.
Sources: European Commission and Court of Auditors.

adversely Spain's ability to qualify: whereas its shares kept increasing over the last decades of the twentieth century, the entrance of even larger and even poorer countries (like Poland) reversed that trend in 2004.

Some of these redistributive changes were engineered quite deliberately. The SEA that went into effect on July 1, 1987, after a six-month delay so Ireland could sort out its constitutional rights to ratify the Act, aimed at harmonization among the states. Since the two new members were developmental laggards, an important strategy of achieving this goal

5.3 The Measure of Responsiveness: Budget Shares

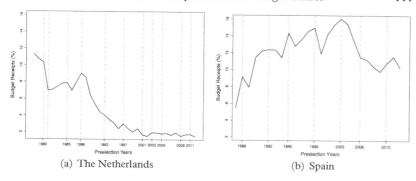

Figure 5.5 Elections and Budget Shares for the Netherlands and Spain, 1977–2013. Budget shares for the Netherlands and Spain between 1977 and 2013. The dashed lines indicate preelection years in each country.
Sources: European Commission, Court of Auditors, Döring and Manow (2015), and author calculations.

had to involve assistance that would help them catch up. Consequently, expenditures for structurally weaker members doubled and since the overall budget did not increase by much, the shares devoted to CAP began to decline. This accelerated the redistribution of the shares from countries like the Netherlands, whose major receipts were from CAP, to countries like Spain, whose major receipts came from the ESIF. On average, the Netherlands secured 4.6 percent of the budget compared to the 11.9 percent Spain managed to obtain. Since the Eastern European countries fared worse than Spain when they joined, the same logic drove the redistribution their way.

Overall, the patterns of budget receipts strongly suggest that the main driving force are formal eligibility criteria, and that this is intentional. So what of responsiveness signaling? Figure 5.5 is indicative in that regard as well. The dashed vertical lines mark each year that preceded one in which a major election was held. It is in these *preelection* years that credit claiming would have to occur, and therefore these are the years where the budget shares should show distinct increases over the trend. The pattern here is plain to see: both governments tended to receive larger shares during these years and, in a tendency that is even more likely to implicate electioneering, these increases did not persist. Indeed, the percentage allocations often dropped back almost immediately to the trend line established by structural factors. The plots also demonstrate that if hidden cooperation does transpire, it is not consistent. There are preelection years in which no increases occur (e.g., 1992 for Spain and 2005 for the Netherlands), and preelection years in which receipts actually decline (e.g., 1981 for the Netherlands). All of this is consistent with the theoretical model.

Of course, these plots are merely suggestive. It could be that the same factors drive both receipts and elections independently of each other. For instance, it could be that a bad economy forces the government to hold elections while simultaneously making the other EU members more generous in their allocations to help out the economy of a fellow member state. We would observe the same pattern but it would have nothing to do with signaling responsiveness. To disentangle the effects, we need to control for these potential alternative causes. We would also like to establish a bit more precisely the expected baseline receipts that are determined by structural factors. We would also like not to hang everything on the rough-and-ready gauge of possible electioneering incentives: preelection years might well be appropriate if elections were held early in the following year, but for elections in, say, late fall, it could be that the early budget resolutions under the pragmatic schedule in the same year are more relevant. Finally, we would like to know whether these patterns hold for other EU member states as well. For all of this, more systematic analysis is needed.

5.4 Signaling Responsiveness in Budget Negotiations

I now turn to a series of quantitative analyses of EU budget negotiations between 1977 and 2013 to see whether governments signal responsiveness by obtaining unexpectedly larger shares of the budget before national elections. The results are quite robust to a variety of model specifications, inclusion of different control variables, and accounting for potential data problems.[30]

I expect to find evidence of larger shares in the total budget, but also in CAP and ESIF allocations, and I expect that there will be systematic differences between the latter. Not only are the qualification rules for the funds different, but the CAP funds would have to be more politicized, for three reasons. First, ESIF funds are usually allocated for specific projects, and this can happen throughout the budget cycle. Of course,

---

[30] See Appendix E, available online at https://quote.ucsd.edu/cjschneider/books/, for the specification of the model and for all robustness checks. The results persist in models with year-fixed effects or with random effects. They are not driven by the largest EU member states. They are essentially the same if I specifically account for the compositional nature of the dependent variable (the fact that the shares have to sum up to 1). I have also conducted extensive checks on the earlier, and somewhat smaller, data set (Schneider, 2013). The results held up to alternative model specifications and inclusion of other control variables. They are not caused by the endogenous timing of elections.

governments can still claim credit for the total allocation, but the distributions (and so, actual money) do not occur until later in the fiscal year; visibility might be more limited since the projects might be unrelated. In contrast, CAP funds are disbursed immediately to their direct beneficiaries, the farmers. Second, since projects are geographically dispersed and temporarily scattered, potential beneficiaries do not have much in common, making it hard to organize into effective interest groups. In contrast, farmers tend to form a well-identifiable group that shares common interests, and they organize into effective lobbies. Third, the Council was more autonomous for CAP-related spending than for non-compulsory ESIF spending, at least until 2009, when Parliament acquired greater say over both. In other words, I expect the effect for CAP to be stronger.

Common Explanatory Variables

My principal explanatory variable is designed to measure whether electioneering incentives are likely to motivate the government at the annual budget negotiations table. Since these negotiations are typically concluded by late fall, the outcome is most likely to influence elections held in the following year. Since the pragmatic schedule can sometimes move up the calendar, the outcome could also influence elections that occur subsequently in the same year. Consequently, I assume that electoral incentives might exist both in years that precede elections and years in which elections occur. The results do not change if I use more precise measures that take into account the specific month of the election or if I use two separate variables for preelection and election years (Schneider, 2013). Thus,

> *Election Period*: an indicator variable for each EU member that takes the value of 1 in the year in which national elections for government in that state are held, as well as in the preceding year, and the value of 0 otherwise. Data from Döring and Manow (2015).

The battery of control variables is used to establish the baseline expectations about the shares and thus include factors that influence formal eligibility, the capacity to take advantage of funds, and one's potential for informal clout. The first set of variables accounts for structural characteristics that commonly enter the various eligibility criteria and for the government's formal bargaining power. The size of the agricultural sector is crucial for determining CAP subsidies, the level of development is a key qualifier for ESIF funds, and the overall wealth of the country largely determines both contributions and receipts.

Agricultural Sector (ln, $t-1$): measures the size of the agricultural sector in previous year. It is the log of the number of employees in that sector (in thousands of work units). Data from Eurostat.

GDP per Capita (ln, $t-1$): measures the level of development in the previous year. It is the log of the country's GDP per capita. Data from Eurostat.

GDP (ln, $t-1$): measures the overall size of the economy in the previous year. It is the log of the country's GDP. Data from Eurostat.

Voting Power (%): the Shapley–Shubik index (SSI) of formal bargaining power, which measures the frequency with which a state's membership in a coalition is pivotal when all voting coalitions are equally likely. Data from Bräuninger and König (2005).

The second set of variables accounts for non-electoral incentives to obtain larger receipts in the budget negotiations:

Unemployment ($t-1$): the national unemployment rate in the previous year, measured in percentage points. Data from Eurostat.

Public Support for EU: the percentage of citizens who believe that "EU membership is a good thing" minus the percentage of those believing that "EU membership is a bad thing." Data from the Eurobarometer.

Finally, the third set of variables accounts for other constraints that limit the ability to obtain larger shares. New member states typically lack the administrative capacity to absorb new funds and have neither the experienced personnel nor the longer periods of interaction of older members to have much clout in negotiations. Moreover, since the budget did not increase in proportion to the size of new entrants, enlargement has made it harder to redistribute funds.

New Member State: an indicator variable that takes the value of 1 for each new member state in all years from its accession to the next enlargement, and 0 otherwise.

EU Membership Size: the number of EU member states in each year. (This variable also controls for the stepwise increase in sample size.)

Summary statistics can be found in Appendix E.

5.4 Signaling Responsiveness in Budget Negotiations

Table 5.1. *Signals of Responsiveness in the EU Budget, 1977–2013.*

	Budget Share (%)		
	Total Receipts	CAP Receipts	ESIF Receipts
Election Period	0.112**	0.096**	0.060
	(0.046)	(0.032)	(0.037)
Agricultural Sector (ln, $t-1$)	1.271**	2.129**	−0.751**
	(0.368)	(0.277)	(0.264)
GDP (ln, $t-1$)	−3.893**	−3.914**	0.076
	(1.163)	(0.813)	(1.134)
GDP per Capita (ln, $t-1$)	4.757**	5.193**	−0.647
	(1.170)	(0.788)	(1.228)
Unemployment ($t-1$)	0.023	0.018	−0.024
	(0.024)	(0.014)	(0.016)
Voting Power (%)	0.676**	0.597**	−0.055
	(0.067)	(0.054)	(0.054)
Public Support for EU	−1.202**	−0.148	−0.630**
	(0.407)	(0.260)	(0.319)
New Member State	−1.066**	−0.475**	−0.688**
	(0.147)	(0.092)	(0.121)
EU Membership Size	0.058**	0.061**	−0.022
	(0.027)	(0.015)	(0.019)
Constant	59.917**	55.718**	1.432
	(18.550)	(13.132)	(18.309)
Country Fixed Effects	Yes	Yes	Yes
Observations	553	538	544
R^2	0.879	0.806	0.531
Wald χ^2	369172**	160238**	526390**

Note: ** $p < 0.05$.
OLS models with unbalanced panels, country fixed effects, panel-corrected standard errors, and panel-specific Prais–Winsten transformation of the error terms (AR1).

The Basics: Impending Elections Mean Larger Shares

Table 5.1 reports the estimation results of unbalanced panel models with country fixed effects. Overall, the models fit the data very well. The high R^2 values and the robustly significant Wald tests suggest that the variables together explain a large amount of the variation in the dependent variable, and that they are jointly significantly different from zero.

If the hypothesis that governments obtain unexpectedly larger budget shares prior to elections is valid, the *Election Period* variable should have a positive and statistically significant estimated coefficient in the presence of other variables that could account for the receipts. This is precisely what we find for shares of the total budget (which increase by 0.11 percent), and for shares of CAP allocations (which increase by 0.10 percent). The ESIF shares also go up, and the increase of 0.06 percent is smaller than the CAP increase, both as expected. The effect, however, is not statistically significant. We already expected that the effect should be weaker for ESIF than for CAP, and it is. As we shall see, it will also turn significant once we account for potential conditioning.[31]

That the substantive effect is small is not particularly troubling – we already knew that the budget is financially trivial – it is its political value that matters. Voters generally know neither the monetary value of their national budget share nor its size relative to those of other members and so are unlikely to be impressed with such figures in the abstract. However, they might care if they are told that whatever the share is, it is *larger* than the country's usual one. To this end, the credit-claiming signal is to demonstrate an increase in the share, and here even trivial differences can be packaged to sound more impressive. For instance, the average CAP share is 4.47 percent, so boosting this by another 0.1 percent of the budget to a 4.57 percent share can be claimed as a 2 percent increase, effectively making it appear as if the effect is 20 times larger. Recalling that this represents something that the government managed to obtain despite restrictive rules that operate with set eligibility formulas (which makes the negotiable "surplus" small) and in a context where the outcome depends on negotiations with many other states (a lot of claimants for parts of that "surplus") makes it even more politically valuable.

In fact, the small substantive effects lend credence to the argument that governments negotiate hard for these tiny increases entirely for political purposes, often to impress rather specific relevant constituencies, rather than deliver some economic value on the national level. What is trivial for the average citizen can be far from negligible for the average farmer. Contrast this with domestic political budget cycles caused by governments trying to enhance their appeal by delivering more public goods prior to elections. This strategy requires actual outlays of real money: government spending increases by about 0.5 percent of the country's GDP (Shi and Svensson, 2006). In election periods, the budget surplus can decrease by up to 0.5 percent of the country's GDP.[32] These fluctuations are quite large, and nothing at the EU level

---

[31] See Figure 5.8, for example.
[32] Persson and Tabellini (2002); Brender and Drazen (2005); Alt and Lassen (2006); Shi and Svensson (2006).

5.4 Signaling Responsiveness in Budget Negotiations

can even remotely approach them. Since the increases in budget shares are unlikely to be useful for altering the state of the economy, their value has to be indirect, and so political. That is, they are signals of responsiveness.

Of course, not everything can be explained by politics, especially in the technocratic EU. The results clearly show that the eligibility criteria are the most important determinants of the distribution of shares. All four relevant variables are significant and have very large substantive effects. A 1 percent increase of the number of people employed in a state's agricultural sector is correlated with a 0.013 percent increase in its budget share.[33] A 1 percent increase in GDP per capita boosts the country's budget share by another 0.05 percent of the budget. Wealthy members tend to do rather well when it comes to the budget. This is not only because they are also the ones with a lot of formal influence (as the voting power variable indicates) but also because income is among the most important factors for eligibility.

In this context, however, the finding that average income is unrelated to ESIF funds is anomalous; after all, these are specifically earmarked to help with economic development so there should be a strong negative correlation between wealth and receiving ESIF funds. Indeed, this is precisely what I found in previous research with budget negotiations from 1977 to 2004: larger GDP per capita meant larger total shares and CAP shares but lower ESIF shares (Schneider, 2013, p. 471). That data set ended in 2004, just before the accession of 12 relatively underdeveloped Central and Eastern European (CEE) countries. One explanation for the anomalous insignificance in the larger data set that includes these countries is political. While all newcomers were eligible for ESIF funds, they were not immediately given access but transitioned gradually so that existing beneficiaries could adjust (Schneider, 2009). In fact, as the negative and significant coefficients on *New Member State* indicates, newcomers were getting much less of everything across the board. This meant that over a number of years several older members continued to receive ESIF funds even though they were wealthier than the new members. This interpretation is supported by the fact that excluding the CEE member countries restores statistical significance to the negative coefficient on GDP per capita (see Appendix E).

---

[33] The effect on the CAP share is even more pronounced, as one would expect. The effect on ESIF, on the other hand, is to decrease the share. Since the effect is positive and significant in the random effects models, the cause of this reversal is the inclusion of country fixed effects. Results available upon request.

118 The EU Budget: Financially Trivial, Politically Substantial

Consistent with previous work, I also found that governments with populations more supportive of the EU tend to receive smaller shares of the budget. If countries where the EU is less popular also happen to be laggards in integration, this could be interpreted as support for the argument that the budget can be used to persuade governments to agree to further integration measures (Carrubba, 1997, 2001). More directly related to my theory, however, it could also mean that governments whose populations are more skeptical of the EU have greater incentives to show that they are negotiating in the national interest. They signal responsiveness by getting larger budget shares.

This suggests that perhaps the strength of the electoral motivation to send these signals should vary with the degree of politicization of the EU more generally. We know that this politicization has increased considerably over time, especially since the ratification of the Maastricht Treaty in 1992.[34] Thus, it should be the case that the effect of the principal explanatory variable should become stronger over time.

To test this hypothesis, I estimated the model with total shares of the budget, and this time interacted *Election Period* with the year. The regression coefficients are reported in Appendix E. I present them here in a more easily digestible form.[35] Figure 5.6 shows the marginal effect of being in an election period and its 90 percent confidence interval as they change over time.

The solid line that represents the strength of the electoral incentive (the marginal effect of *Election Period* conditional on the year) shows an upward trend over time. Moreover, the effect becomes statistically significant in the early 1990s. Since politicization accelerated over that period (see Chapter 2), this evidence is consistent with the hypothesis that governments have become more willing to signal responsiveness in budget negotiations during electoral periods, especially since they also found their ability to signal it by other means heavily restricted by the Maastricht Treaty of 1992.

Even though politicization appears relevant, it is a rather diffuse motivator for governments. More immediate concerns should provide them with even stronger (and therefore more detectable) incentives to

---

[34] Mair (2000); Van der Eijk and Franklin (2004); Van der Brug, Van der Eijk, and Franklin (2007); Hooghe and Marks (2009).
[35] I adapted the Stata program GRINTER provided by Frederick Boehmke (http://myweb.uiowa.edu/fboehmke/methods.html, accessed October 2016). I do not include interaction effects on the CAP and ESIF funds because these funds have experienced drastic changes over time. This confounds the electoral effect and makes the interpretation of results very challenging.

5.4 Signaling Responsiveness in Budget Negotiations

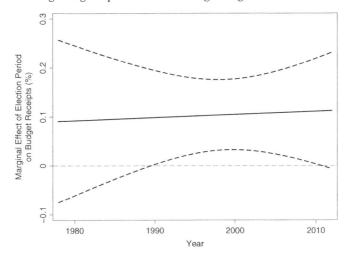

Figure 5.6 The Electoral Incentive Over Time. OLS estimation of models as described in Table 5.1 for total receipts but with *Election Period* interacted with the year. Estimated coefficient (solid line) and 90 percent confidence intervals (dashed lines) plotted over years in the sample.

signal responsiveness. I now turn to a closer look at some situations that might give them just these kinds of concerns.

Stronger Motivator: Electoral Distress

The more objective factors suggest that the more incompetent or unwilling a government is to deliver on policies that citizens prefer, the stronger its incentive is to persuade voters that they should allow the government to remain in power. Electoral distress could be related to adverse economic circumstances, to low public approval ratings (perhaps due to failure of important noneconomic policies), or to larger uncertainty about the electoral outcome.

Bad Economic Times Few scholars doubt that the state of the economy matters for voting choices.[36] One widely used measure of troubled economic circumstances is unemployment, and it is particularly appropriate for my case because people who find themselves out of work are both upset and have lower opportunity costs to do something about it. That is, they are much more likely to translate their inability to find

---

[36] Van der Brug, Van der Eijk, and Franklin (2007).

a job into a statement at the polls. The government would have to strive mightily to suggest that their plight was caused by forces beyond its control. In order to do this, signaling competence in anything related – such as EU budget negotiations, for instance – is key. In other words, when unemployment is high, governments should receive even larger shares of the budget when they are facing elections.

To test this hypothesis, I estimated the three original models with an added interaction term between *Unemployment* and *Election Period*.[37] Figure 5.7 shows how the marginal electoral effect varies with the level of unemployment, and the uncertainty of its estimation (the 90 percent confidence interval indicated by the dashed lines). The plots also display the kernel density estimate of the conditioning variable (indicated by the short-dashed line), which gives us an idea where most observations for *Unemployment* are in the sample, and its mean (the vertical solid line).

The results provide strong support for my hypothesis. The higher the unemployment rate, the stronger the electoral effect: the more governments fear an unsettled labor force, the more motivated they are to signal responsiveness to its concerns by obtaining larger shares of the budget, and therefore, the larger their receipts are as fraction of the total budget [panel 5.7(a)]. The prospect of elections is associated with receiving an extra 0.1 percent of the budget when unemployment is held at the sample mean, as seen in panel 5.7(a) at the vertical line. If unemployment were to rise to 14 percent, which is the 90th percentile in the sample, the strength of the effect triples: governments are now expected to get an extra 0.3 percent of the budget. A further indicator that the signal is driven by electoral distress is that the effect is not statistically significant until unemployment gets close to the mean and then increases in significance as unemployment climbs. In other words, only abnormal rates of unemployment cause anxiety for the government, and it gets discernably more anxious when they become exceptional.

The exact same pattern can be seen when it comes to ESIF [panel 5.7(c)]. This plot also reveals that while the effect reported in Table 5.1 was just below the customary levels of significance at a hypothetical zero unemployment, it becomes immediately significant when unemployment exceeds the mean. Since the poorer countries are also the ones with high unemployment, this suggests that when it comes to structural development funds they can punch above their wealth.

---

[37] All results are reported in Appendix E.

5.4 Signaling Responsiveness in Budget Negotiations

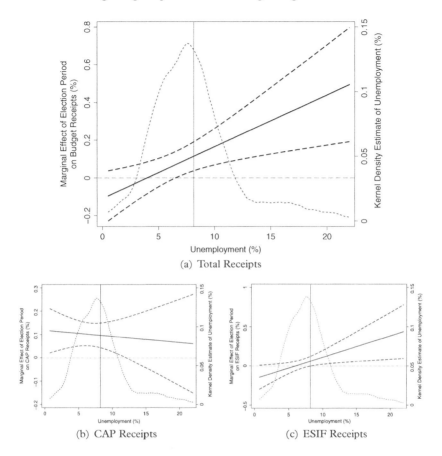

Figure 5.7 The Electoral Incentive and Unemployment Rates. OLS estimation of models as described in Table 5.1 for budget shares (%) but with *Election Period* interacted with *Unemployment*. Estimated coefficient (solid line) and 90 percent confidence intervals (dashed lines) plotted over rates of *Unemployment* in the sample. Kernel density estimate of *Unemployment* (short-dashed line) and its mean (vertical light solid line) also shown.

The pattern for CAP, on the other hand, is almost an exact mirror image of the other two [panel 5.7(b)]. While the electoral incentive still produces larger CAP shares (it is positive everywhere), its strength declines as unemployment goes up, and it is only statistically significant at low to moderate levels of unemployment (below 12 percent). This can readily be accounted for by recalling that while CAP benefits are concentrated in the politically powerful farmer lobbies, high unemployment rates mean that the costs are widely borne. With everybody suffering, it is more difficult for a smaller interest group to exert pressure for particularistic benefits and imperative that the government finds a way to signal to a wider audience. Both of these weaken incentives to signal responsiveness by obtaining larger CAP shares.

Disapproval of the Government A bad economy is not the only thing that can sink a government. An unpopular foreign policy, a corruption scandal, a controversial domestic decision – all could erode support for the incumbent. All strengthen the government's incentive to signal responsiveness. There are so many potential reasons a government could find itself in trouble, and they could be so idiosyncratic that it could be quite a challenge to code all of them. They all have one thing in common: they all decrease public approval for the government. Since governments obsessively track their approval rates, we also have fairly good data. My conditioning variable is defined as:

> *Government Approval* $(t-1)$: the percentage of citizens who would vote for the incumbent government coalition in the previous year.[38]

To test the hypothesis that the strength of the electoral incentive depends on public approval, I estimated the three original models, adding *Incumbent Support* and interacting it with *Election Period*. Figure 5.8 shows how the marginal electoral effect varies with levels of approval for the government, and the 90 percent confidence levels of its magnitude, along with the distribution of the conditioning variable and its mean.

The results support the hypothesis. The lower the government approval, the stronger the electoral effect: governments faced with failing approval ratings are quite motivated to signal responsiveness in the hopes of improving their chances at the polls, and so they tend to obtain even larger shares of the budget [panel 5.8(a)]. Popular governments (with approval ratings that exceed approximately 35 percent), on the other

---

[38] This variable is described in fn. 15 on page 24. An alternative way to measure the electoral threat is with the margin of victory for the government in the previous elections, but there are two problems with this. First, since governments are likely to react to narrow margins of victory by attempting to widen their appeal, this measure would seriously overestimate the competitiveness of the next election when their strategy succeeds. Second, the margin of victory is appropriate for winner-take-all majoritarian two-party systems but not for those with proportional representation where the government is often coalitional. These issues are widely acknowledged, but scholars still use the margin of victory because they often do not have high-quality periodic public approval data as we do here (Gelman and King, 1993; Meirowitz, 2005; Kleine and Minaudier, 2018). For the sake of checking the robustness of the results to this alternative operationalization, however, Appendix E presents results from estimations using the margin of victory as well.

5.4 Signaling Responsiveness in Budget Negotiations   123

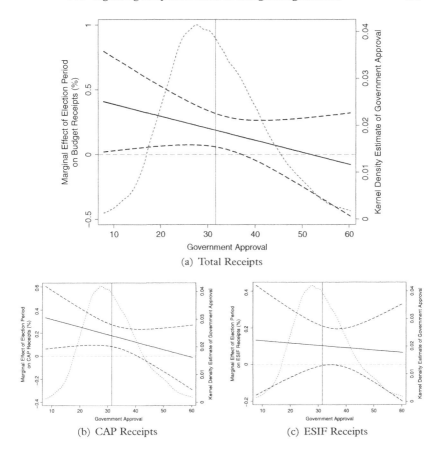

Figure 5.8 The Electoral Incentive and Government Approval. OLS estimation of models as described in Table 5.1 for budget shares (%) but with *Government Approval* ($t-1$) added and interacted with *Election Period*. The estimated coefficient (solid line) and 90 percent confidence intervals (dashed lines) are plotted over rates of *Government Approval* in the sample. The kernel density estimate of *Government Approval* (short-dashed line) and its mean (vertical light solid line) are also shown.

hand, do not seem to feel much urgency, and the effect loses statistical significance (the uncertainty of the estimates at the very low end is due to few governments that have such abysmal approval levels). The glare of public disapproval is catalytic on government performance: dropping from the 32 percent mean approval by 20 percent (two standard deviations) doubles the size of the effect from about 0.2 percent, and the budget share will be augmented by more than 0.4 percent.

The same pattern can be seen in CAP allocations [panel 5.8(b)]. Since the estimations control for the level of unemployment, this figure shows the conditional effect of the electoral incentive when the unemployment is held at zero. This implies that the disapproval is perhaps not related to bad economic times, which push a government to find more general signals of responsiveness. Instead, a government can seek to burnish its tarnished image by appealing to well-organized interest groups, such as the agricultural lobby. Popular governments do not need to electioneer with particularistic benefits when the economy is at full employment, as evidenced by the disappearance of the effect above 40 percent approval rates.

This hypothetical zero unemployment rate is probably also the reason the effect is not significant for ESIF receipts [panel 5.8(c)]. Since these are meant for countries with structural problems, which are usually the ones that are underdeveloped compared to the EU average, it is very likely that these will have unemployment rates well above that average as well. The plot represents an extraordinary scenario of an underdeveloped economy working at full employment, and so it is not surprising to see that governments would not put much effort into signaling that they can get even more development funds.

Volatile Swing Voters Voters who have not committed to supporting some party can be politically relevant if they constitute a large fraction of the electorate. They might throw in their lot with the incumbent government if they deem it responsive, or they might opt to vote for the opposition instead. This is why they are called "swing voters."[39] The potential for a swing in the electoral outcome grows with the number of undecided voters, and it becomes progressively harder to forecast what will happen at the polls. This uncertainty strengthens the incumbent government's incentive to signal to the uncommitted that it is responsive to their concerns. My conditioning variable is defined as:

> *Undecided Voters*: the percentage of voters who do not know whom they would vote for if elections were held "next Sunday."[40]

To test my hypothesis, I estimated the three original models, adding *Undecided Voters* and interacting it with *Election Period*. Figure 5.9 shows

---

[39] Cox (1987); Jacobson (1987); Bartels (2008).
[40] See fn. 15 on page 24 for the wording of this question in the relevant surveys.

5.4 Signaling Responsiveness in Budget Negotiations

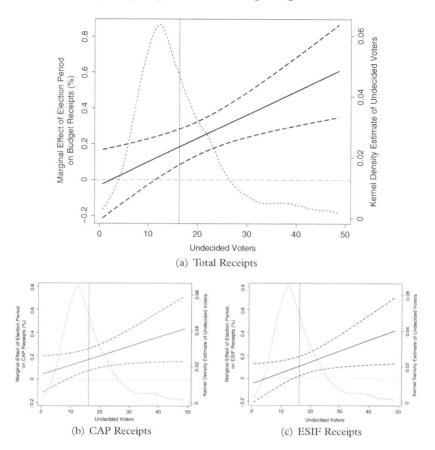

Figure 5.9 The Electoral Incentive and Electoral Uncertainty. OLS estimation of models as described in Table 5.1 for budget shares (%) but with *Undecided Voters* added and interacted with *Election Period*. The estimated coefficient (solid line) and 90 percent confidence intervals (dashed lines) are plotted over rates of *Undecided Voters* in the sample. The kernel density estimate of *Undecided Voters* (short-dashed line) and its mean (vertical light solid line) are also shown.

how the marginal electoral effect varies with the level of uncertainty in the electorate as described by the fraction of swing voters.

The results provide strong support for the hypothesis. The more undecided voters, the stronger the electoral effect: governments faced with potentially volatile electorates are highly motivated to signal responsiveness in the hopes of getting the swing voters on their side and so they obtain even larger shares of the budget [panel 5.9(a)]. This incentive gains traction when the undecided voters represent as little as 12 percent of the electorate, and the corresponding increase becomes even more significant as uncertainty goes up. Increasing the fraction of uncommitted voters from the mean of 16 percent to 25 percent (one standard deviation) boosts the extra share of the budget by almost 30 percent (to 0.23 percent). Increasing that fraction to 35 percent more than doubles the extra share. Conversely, if most voters are committed one way or the other, the government has little incentive to signal anything and so the electoral effect is statistically insignificant.

When it comes to electoral volatility, the exact same pattern can be observed with both CAP [panel 5.9(b)] and ESIF [panel 5.9(c)] receipts. Governments who are fairly confident in their electoral forecasts do not receive larger allocations of either agricultural or structural funds. They quickly step up their game, however, when they have to compete for many swing voters.

In sum, my analyses using three distinct ways of conceptualizing electoral distress all point to the same conclusion: the more a government is worried about its prospects at the polls, the larger the increase in its share of the budget before elections. It is self-evident why a government at risk domestically should be highly motivated to signal responsiveness by obtaining exceptionally attractive budget deals. What is less obvious is how it is able to achieve that goal in negotiations with many other governments. After all, one country's uncommonly large budget share is another country's abnormally small one. Only governments with some advantages in the Council are likely to secure deals for which they can claim credit at home, as are the ones who manage to persuade fellow EU members to help them out with temporary concessions. Power and hidden cooperation are the enablers of credit-claiming governments. I turn to analyzing them next.

Enablers: Structural and Informal Powers

Whether even a motivated government can nudge budget negotiations to an outcome for which it can claim credit depends on how well it can manage a process that involves twenty-seven other governments, many of which might prefer that gains accrue to themselves. Despite the strong norm of non-adversarial decision-making designed to culminate in a consensus budget, more powerful countries tend to enjoy distinct advantages, some of which, such as voting rights, will be formalized institutionally. The norm, however, allows for deviations from this pattern, especially when a government can persuade fellow Council members to engage in hidden cooperation that enables it to deliver an electorally beneficial outcome.

5.4 Signaling Responsiveness in Budget Negotiations 127

Greater Formal Power in the Council When collective decisions are put up to a vote, those who control more votes have disproportionate influence on the outcome. Even an informal consensus norm operates in the shadow of a final vote: any exceptionally recalcitrant minority could be brought to heel by submitting the decision to a formal vote. The desire to uphold the norm would make the majority more amenable to compromise and the holdouts less inclined to obstruct it. States with more structural power are better positioned to strike such deals. They often have more experienced personnel and larger administrative staff, which provide them with informational and expertise advantages. They dispose of more resources, which makes them more effective coalition builders. They can often ensure that a consistent "national" position is presented at various levels of governance simply because they exercise tighter control over their bureaucracies. Since structural power is formalized in the Council through the voting rules, it is the governments with more formal power that should receive even larger shares of the budget when they are facing elections.

To test this hypothesis, I estimated the three original models with an added interaction term between *Voting Power* and *Election Period*. Figure 5.10 shows how the marginal electoral effect varies with the formal influence of the state in the Council.

The results provide strong support for the hypothesis. The more influential the government's position in the Council, the stronger the electoral effect: governments that enjoy built-in formal advantages under the voting rules are better able to obtain the larger shares of the total budget for which they can claim credit [panel 5.10(a)]. Moreover, the results are indicative of the limits of motive without capacity. Whereas every government is motivated to increase its receipts before elections, only the more powerful among them can do so consistently enough to be detectable by the estimations. A decline in voting power of less than one standard deviation wipes out the statistical significance of the electoral effect. Conversely, a rise of one standard deviation not only keeps the effect statistically significant, it nearly doubles its size.

An analogous pattern can be seen for CAP allocations, where the effect is even stronger [panel 5.10(b)]. This is not surprising considering that many of the countries formally privileged by the voting rules also happen to have sizeable agricultural sectors. That they also tend not to be eligible for many ESIF funds helps explain why the effect is not statistically significant in that case [panel 5.10(c)]. Criteria for access to development funds invariably tend to disqualify the wealthier states, leaving them with very little to bargain for in ESIF allocations. On top of that, the distribution of these funds was subject to meddling by

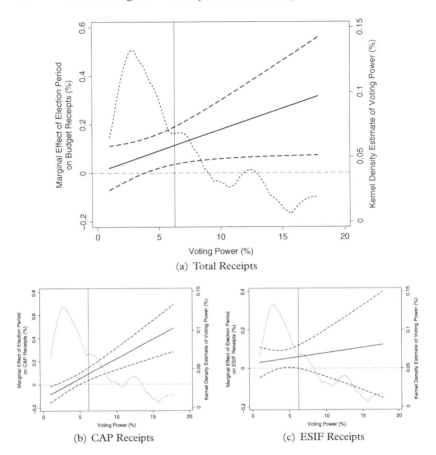

Figure 5.10 The Electoral Incentive and Formal Power. OLS estimation of models as described in Table 5.1 for budget shares (%) but with *Election Period* interacted with *Voting Power*. The estimated coefficient (solid line) and 90 percent confidence intervals (dashed lines) are plotted over rates of *Voting Power* in the sample. The kernel density estimate of *Voting Power* (short-dashed line) and its mean (vertical light solid line) are also shown.

Parliament even before it was put on an equal footing with the Council. This makes it even harder for governments to turn their formal power in the Council into real bargaining leverage. In other words, they should not expect to be able to use ESIF allocations to signal responsiveness. And they do not.

Beneficiary of Hidden Cooperation The powerful states tend to be the ones more likely to get the collective to produce an outcome to their liking. Even then, their ability to do so is constrained by formal eligibility

5.4 Signaling Responsiveness in Budget Negotiations

criteria. But this is not the only factor that might enable a government to receive at least a temporarily larger than usual budget allocation; it could rely on the reciprocal help of the others. This cooperation must be hidden, since by definition the larger share could not be a signal if it was granted by others precisely to make it look like the government was more competent than it really was. The closed-door negotiations make it possible, and they also make it nearly impossible to measure the extent of such cooperation. We must resort to indirect measures that might be correlated with it.

One such potential correlate is partisan heterogeneity. We know that the observable level of cooperation declines when the Council becomes ideologically more heterogenous (Schneider and Urpelainen, 2014). Governments that are more ideologically distant from the majority in the Council might find it harder to organize a supporting coalition on their behalf and so they could be less able to secure larger shares before elections relative to governments that are closer to the majority. The conditioning variable is:

> *Ideological Divergence*: the absolute distance between a government's ideology and the Council average. A government's ideological score is composed of the positions that the parties in the governing coalition occupy on the left–right spectrum, weighted by their numbers of ministers in the cabinet. A party position is from the Comparative Manifesto Project, with negative values indicating that it leans left, and with positive values indicating that it leans right (Warntjen, Hix, and Crombez, 2008). Since for the hypothesis the distance matters but not the direction, this variable takes on positive values irrespective of whether the outlier government is more left wing or more right wing than the Council average. For a perfectly aligned government, this variable will take the value of 0.

To test my hypothesis, I estimated the three original models, adding *Ideological Divergence* and interacting it with *Election Period*. Figure 5.11 shows how the marginal electoral effect varies with the government's ideological distance from the Council's core. Note the kernel density estimate, which shows that the vast majority of governments are fairly close ideologically, and although there is some divergence, it quickly falls off, with true extremists being few and far between. The mean distance is 2.5, and the standard deviation is 2.3, which means that 95 percent of observations in the sample will have an ideological distance of less than 7.1, which accounts for the enormous uncertainty of the estimates for values that exceed that.

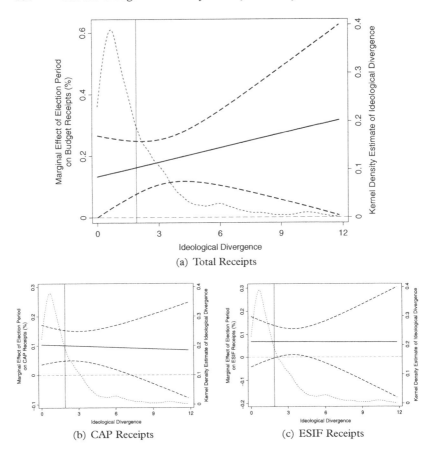

Figure 5.11 The Electoral Incentive and Ideological Divergence. OLS estimation of models as described in Table 5.1 for budget shares (%) but with *Ideological Divergence* added and interacted with *Election Period*. The estimated coefficient (solid line) and 90 percent confidence intervals (dashed lines) are plotted over rates of *Ideological Divergence* in the sample. The kernel density estimate of *Ideological Divergence* (short-dashed line) and its mean (vertical light solid line) are also shown.

The results are mixed at best, and contrary to the hypothesis at worst. On one hand, there is evidence that governments whose ideology diverges from the Council mean obtain smaller increases in their CAP shares [panel 5.11(b)]. The effect is statistically significant for almost all observations in the sample but is substantively quite weak (the line of the estimated coefficient is nearly flat). The effect barely registers either statistically or substantively for ESIF receipts [panel 5.11(c)].

When it comes to total receipts, the effect is significant, substantively more pronounced, and in the wrong direction [panel 5.11(a)]. For instance, while a government in perfect ideological synchrony with the Council could expect an increase of about 0.13 percent in its share of the total budget, an outlier two standard deviations away can expect an increase almost double that.

This might mean that ideological distance measured along the traditional left–right spectrum is not a good proxy for the reluctance of other EU members to cooperate. Consider, for instance, the attitude of the German CDU to the victory of the British Labour party over the Conservatives in 1997. Both the CDU and the Tories were conservative, so ideologically aligned on the left–right spectrum, and both were distant from the left-leaning Labour Party (even in its New Labour centrist incarnation). According to the *Ideological Divergence* measure, the CDU should have been far more likely to cooperate with the Tories, but in fact the CDU was quite relieved when they lost. The problem was that the Tories had grown increasingly Eurosceptic while Labour was moving in the opposite direction. The Tories even quit the center–right European People's Party (EPP) – the largest party in the European Parliament since 1999 and the one to which the CDU also belonged – in 2009. This made it very difficult for the pro-EU Germans to align with them on European matters.

This suggests that we need to be more precise about measuring divergence: it has to be along a dimension that would be highly correlated with willingness to cooperate on European policies. The British example above hints that a government's stance on the EU might be a more appropriate proxy for how disposed core EU members would be to help it out. I therefore propose another conditioning variable, this one defined as:

> *Divergence in EU Support*: the absolute distance between a government's position on the EU and the Council average. Calculated analogously to *Ideological Divergence* except that the Comparative Manifesto Project was used to create the individual party scores along an anti–pro European integration spectrum. Data from Warntjen, Hix, and Crombez (2008).

I estimated the three original models, adding *Divergence in EU Support* and interacting it with *Election Period*. Figure 5.12 shows how the marginal electoral effect varies as the government's position on EU integration diverges from the Council mean. As with ideological distance, the kernel density estimate shows that in the bulk of observations the

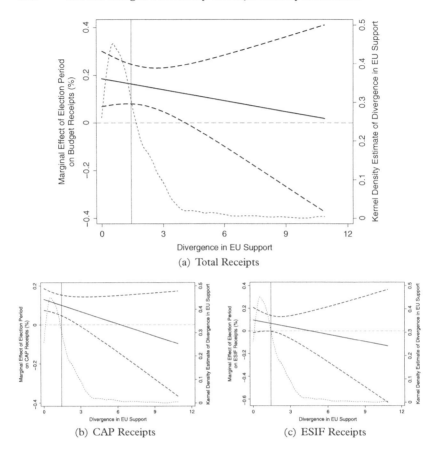

Figure 5.12 The Electoral Incentive and Divergence in EU Support. OLS estimation of models as described in Table 5.1 for budget shares (%) but with *Divergence in EU Support* added and interacted with *Election Period*. The estimated coefficient (solid line) and 90 percent confidence intervals (dashed lines) are plotted over rates of *Divergence in EU Support* in the sample. The kernel density estimate of *Divergence in EU Support* (short-dashed line) and its mean (vertical light solid line) are also shown.

divergence in EU support is significantly smaller than the mean. The mean distance and the standard deviation here are both 1.4, and thus more than 95 percent of the observations in the sample have divergence in EU support that is less than 4.2. This accounts for the rather large uncertainty of the estimates for values that exceed that.

The results provide consistent, albeit not very strong, support of the hypothesis. The farther out a government is on EU integration

5.4 Signaling Responsiveness in Budget Negotiations

relative to the Council mean, the smaller the increase in its share of the budget before elections, both for total receipts [panel 5.12(a)] and CAP allocations [panel 5.12(b)], where the effect is statistically significant for almost all observations in the sample, but not substantively large. The effect cannot be reliably detected when it comes to ESIF allocations [panel 5.12(c)].

Overall, these results indicate tentative support for the hypothesis that hidden cooperation might help tide some governments over the occasional election, provided these governments are sufficiently close to the majority on EU matters. There is little evidence that such hidden cooperation is pervasive and systematic. This tepid correlation is what the theory led us to expect: a readily detectable pattern would expose the collusion and negate its intended effects. The differences between Figure 5.11 and Figure 5.12 further indicate that when it comes to the Council, a conflict over the desirability of European integration matters much more for a government's ability to signal responsiveness than a disagreement along the traditional left–right dimension.

The Constraint: Many Claimants

Even the most perfectly aligned government would find its appeals falling on deaf ears if there were others clamoring for the same kind of concessions. With twenty-eight governments in the Council, it is not unusual to have multiple administrations facing imminent elections. In fact, at least six of them would be doing so during an average budget year. Since budget negotiations are essentially redistributive, the more governments that vie for increased shares of an already tightly chopped-up pie, the less of a concession each of them should expect. In other words, the electoral effect should get weaker as the number of upcoming elections increases. The conditioning variable is simply:

> *Number of Elections*: the number of governments facing national elections during the coming budget year.

I estimated the three original models, adding *Number of Elections* and interacting it with *Election Period*. Figure 5.13 shows how the marginal electoral effect varies when more governments have to face the voters at the polls.

The results provide fairly strong support for the hypothesis that signaling responsiveness by obtaining larger budget shares becomes rather difficult when there are more governments trying to do the same thing. The extra receipts a government can expect before an election fall rather spectacularly as more governments become interested in securing

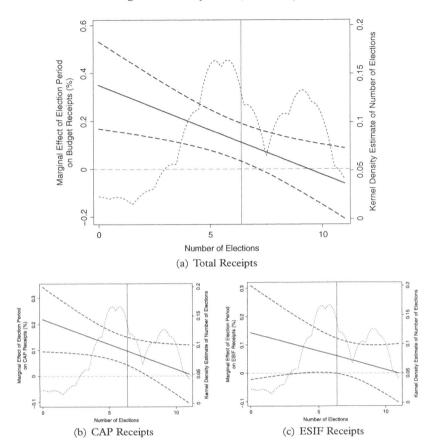

Figure 5.13 The Electoral Incentive and Number of Claimants. OLS estimation of models as described in Table 5.1 for budget shares (%) but with *Number of Elections* added and interacted with *Election Period*. The estimated coefficient (solid line) and 90 percent confidence intervals (dashed lines) are plotted over rates of *Number of Elections* in the sample. The kernel density estimate of *Number of Elections* (short-dashed line) and its mean (vertical light solid line) are also shown.

larger shares for themselves (or avoiding the appearance of having made concessions) for the same reason [panel 5.13(a)]. Whereas a government could count on more than 0.35 percent pre-electoral bump in its share of the total budget, this benefit drops by about 15 percent when another government has to face its voters. It is more than halved when there are six more elections, as there would be in an average year.

An analogous, albeit a slightly weaker substantively, dynamic can be observed in the CAP allocations [5.13(b)]. When it comes to ESIF receipts, the trend is there but the statistical significance generally is not [panel 5.13(c)]. This difference might be attributable to a government's ability to negotiate an electorally motivated redistribution of agricultural funds rather than structural ones, given that Parliament has had a say in the latter, even before it had acquired a say in the former.

That the decline in the size of the electoral bump is caused by the mutually constraining demands of an increasing number of claimants can be inferred from the fact that the effect becomes statistically indistinguishable from zero when more than seven governments expect elections. With so many mouths to feed, there are no leftovers to redistribute. That the estimation fails to uncover the electoral effect despite the rather significant number of observations with forthcoming elections in that range (as evidenced by the kernel density) is further evidence that the effect simply does not exist there. Not only do more claimants strain the redistributive mechanism, they can easily overwhelm it.

In sum, the results strongly support the hypothesis that EU governments signal responsiveness in negotiations over the EU annual budget. They systematically receive larger shares during election periods and so can claim credit for success at the EU level. This effect exists even when a variety of factors that affect eligibility for funds are taken into account. It is stronger when governments find themselves threatened at the polls. It is especially pronounced for countries with structural or informal advantages, although a limited degree of hidden cooperation could assist the occasional government with the occasional election. The ability to signal with abnormally large budget receipts is heavily dependent on this fact – that there are not too many other governments trying to do the same thing. This limit is inherent in the redistributive nature of these negotiations.

The findings so far demonstrate that governments do the signaling dance before elections. But what if they are dancing in front of blind audiences? Do voters reward incumbents for being responsive in EU budget negotiations?

5.5 The Fruit of Responsiveness: Public Approval

We have now found that governments facing national elections tend to receive atypically large shares of the EU budget and that these increases tend to be more pronounced when the governments are worried about their prospects of remaining in office. This is consistent with the theoretical mechanism, which explains these augmentations as being electorally motivated: governments seek to signal responsiveness to the relevant political constituencies in the hopes of improving their chances of reelection. But do these signals have the desired effect? Do they, in fact, boost the incumbent's performance at the polls?

Answering this question is quite challenging because it requires that we construct an estimate for the outcome of the hypothetical election that would have occurred without the government signaling. We can, however, ask a closely related question instead: Do the signals make citizens more likely to vote for the government? In the experiment reported in Chapter 4, I was able to construct the appropriate hypotheticals and analyze how voting intentions changed as the signals varied. For obvious reasons, this is not possible in the real world, where neither the treatment nor the timing of surveys is properly controlled.

Fortunately, the theory does not require us to figure out whether the governments are *correct* in their forecasts about the potential effects of their signaling strategies. It only requires that the governments *believe* that they would be helpful. For this we only need to consider the types of indicators that the governments themselves tend to use to determine whether their behavior sits well with the voters or does not. The dominant barometer for gauging electoral prospects is the level of public approval for the government. Governments are almost compulsive in collecting and sifting through public opinion polls, so it is not unreasonable to expect that they would base some political decisions on their potential impact on the moods of the public. Moreover, they might be especially prone to doing so when elections loom. Public moods might be fleeting and inconstant, but they do not turn on a dime. The closer the opportunity to act on the mood, the more likely it is to affect the decision. Consequently, governments have a strong incentive to ensure that the public is positively disposed toward them when elections are near. This, of course, is precisely why they want to claim credit for larger budgetary receipts.

For these reasons, my dependent variable is defined as:

> *Government Approval*: the percentage of citizens who would vote for the incumbent government coalition.[41]

Public support for EU governments varies quite a bit. Figure 5.14 shows a histogram of approval levels for all EU members between 1976 and 2002. The mean is about 32 percent, but approval could go as low as 8 percent and as high as 60 percent. Some of that variance is accounted for by differences over time and across governments (Figure 2.2 in Chapter 2). Some of it can be accounted for by the electoral system

---

[41] This variable is described in fn. 15 on page 24.

5.5 The Fruit of Responsiveness: Public Approval

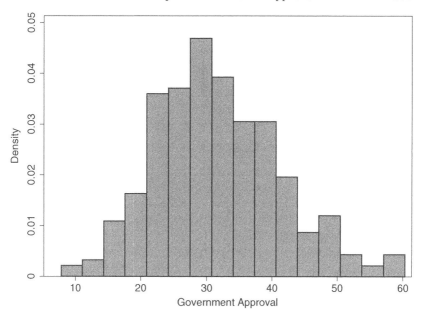

Figure 5.14 Public Approval Levels of EU Governments, 1976–2002.
Histogram of *Government Approval*, bins of approximately 3.25 percent.
Sources: Müller and Strøm (2000), Eurostat, and author calculations.

and the number of competitive parties. For instance, approval rates for coalitions of the Italian government have ranged from 12 percent to 46 percent over the sample period.

Since we want to know whether higher budget receipts (the signals) are associated with higher levels of public approval (the effect), my three principal explanatory variables are the shares of the budget received in the previous year; that is, *Total Receipts*, *CAP Receipts*, and *ESIF Receipts* lagged by one year. One might be concerned with reverse causation here. After all, it was the variation in the current values of these variables that I explained previously, and in one of the models I used (the lagged value of) *Government Approval* to explain that variation (p. 122). Previously, I said that the level of approval determines the size of the shares, and now I state that the size of the shares determines the level of approval. The effect, in fact, goes both ways, which is why the variables are lagged differently in the two estimations. The results are robust to using instrumental variable regressions as well (Appendix E).

Of course, public approval also depends on a host of other factors.[42] The first set of control variables are potentially relevant economic indicators. In addition to *Agricultural Sector* and *Unemployment*, I use:

> *GDP Growth per Capita*: the annual GDP growth divided by the total population. Data from Eurostat.
>
> *Inflation (%)*: the annual inflation rate. Data from Eurostat and World Development Indicators.

The second set of control variables are potentially relevant political factors:

> *Minority Government*: an indicator variable that takes the value of 1 if the governing coalition controls less than 50 percent of the seats in Parliament, and 0 otherwise. Data from *Parties and Elections in Europe*.
>
> *Coalition Size*: the number of parties in the governing coalition. Data from Schmitt et al. (2005) and Müller and Strøm (2000).

I also use *Election Period*, although the inclusion of this variable here must be treated with caution because the direction of the effect might be indeterminate and its statistical significance undetectable because of confounders. On one hand, the government has an incentive to work hard to improve its image. If it succeeds, the approval levels should rise. On the other hand, the opposition has an incentive to go into overdrive trying to paint the government in a negative light. If it succeeds, the approval levels should fall. It is not possible to say *a priori* which of these contrary effects would be dominant. It could be that they cancel each other out. Moreover, if the government is using budget receipts to burnish its image for electoral purposes, then these receipts would be higher in election years (as we have already established). But then one of the positive effects of being in an election period would be already accounted for through the inclusion of these receipts. This makes it more likely that we would not detect an independent statistically significant effect of *Election Period*.

The third set of control variables are EU-level indicators that might well influence the public mood in any given country. In addition to *New Member State*, I use:

> *Contributions to EU Budget (%)*: the government's share of the total annual financial contributions to the EU budget. Data from the European Court of Auditor's Annual Reports.

---

[42] See Appendix E for details about operationalization, summary statistics, and data sources.

5.5 The Fruit of Responsiveness: Public Approval

Cohesion Country: an indicator variable that takes the value of 1 if the country's GDP per capita is below 75 percent of the EU average, and 0 otherwise. Data from Eurostat.

Exports to the EU (log): the log of the government's annual exports to the European Union. Data from the IMF.

To account for idiosyncratic reasons that public approval rates might systematically vary across countries, all estimations include country fixed effects.

Table 5.2 reports the estimation results of unbalanced panel models. The models fit the data quite well. The high R^2 values and the Wald tests suggest that together the variables explain a large amount of the variation in approval, and that their joint effects are statistically significant.

If the hypothesis that receiving larger budget shares should be associated with higher public approval levels is correct, then the estimated coefficients of the principal explanatory variables should be positive and significant. The evidence supports the hypothesis for *Total Receipts* (strongly so) and for *CAP Receipts*: a 1 percent increase in the budget share is associated with 0.5 percent and 0.6 percent increase in public approval for the incumbent, respectively.

How big are these effects? To gain some intuition about their magnitude, it is useful to place them in context by comparing them to the electoral effects of commonly used economic indicators. In the United States, a 1 percent decline in real per capita household income results in a 0.5 percent decline in the House vote share for the incumbent party (Kramer, 1971), whereas a 1 percent increase in GNP growth increases the vote share for the governing party by 1.8 percent (Lewis-Beck and Stegmaier, 2000). More directly, a 1 percent increase in the growth rate of real disposable income generates six more seats for the president's party in the Senate (Lewis-Beck and Rice, 1992).[43] In Europe, economic factors are also important, although somewhat less so. One standard deviation improvement in the general economic situation increases the intended vote share for the incumbent government by about 2 percent (Nadeau, Niemi, and Yoshinaka, 2002), whereas a 1 percent increase in unemployment above the international average decreases the vote share for the government by 0.6 percent (Powell and Whitten, 1993). These magnitudes compare favorably with the sizes of the statistically significant signaling effects reported in Table 5.2.

There is no evidence that signaling with ESIF funds leads to higher approval ratings. This might be because ESIF receipts are not very

---

[43] Lewis-Beck and Stegmaier (2000) provide an extensive overview of the large body of literature on this issue.

Table 5.2. *Signals of Responsiveness and Public Approval, 1977–2002.*

	Government Approval (%)		
	Total Receipts	CAP Receipts	ESIF Receipts
Total Receipts ($t - 1$)	0.526** (0.232)		
CAP Receipts ($t - 1$)		0.628* (0.356)	
ESIF Receipts ($t - 1$)			−0.064 (0.439)
Contributions to EU Budget (%)	−0.352 (0.270)	−0.235 (0.288)	−0.100 (0.285)
GDP Growth per Capita (%)	385.724 (242.400)	405.166* (245.001)	417.156* (240.801)
Minority Government	−2.397 (1.583)	−2.184 (1.614)	−2.196 (1.605)
Coalition Size	6.678** (0.724)	6.614** (0.761)	6.379** (0.755)
Unemployment (%)	−0.630** (0.274)	−0.580** (0.292)	−0.595** (0.269)
Inflation (%)	−0.167 (0.178)	−0.147 (0.182)	−0.127 (0.185)
Election Period	0.431 (0.779)	0.135 (0.805)	0.198 (0.828)
New Member State	1.286 (1.961)	0.217 (2.062)	−0.180 (2.080)
Exports to the EU (log)	0.148 (0.112)	0.195* (0.117)	0.185 (0.118)
Agricultural Sector (ln)	11.249** (3.471)	10.313** (3.947)	12.141** (3.847)
Cohesion Country	3.866 (3.023)	3.144 (3.472)	3.139 (3.499)
Constant	−46.961** (15.324)	−43.992** (17.150)	−50.053** (17.258)
Country Fixed Effects	Yes	Yes	Yes
Observations	238	229	229
R^2	0.773	0.776	0.771
Wald χ^2	1520**	2307**	361**

Note: *$p < 0.10$, **$p < 0.05$.
OLS models with unbalanced panels, country fixed effects, panel-corrected standard errors, and panel-specific Prais–Winsten transformation of the error terms (AR1).

salient to domestic audiences in many countries, coupled with the absence of well-organized lobby groups that could pressure the government on behalf of constituents who rely on these funds. This is in contrast to CAP funds that go to politically active farmers. (Note, in particular, the statistically significant effect of *Agricultural Sector*.) It could also be due to the overriding importance of eligibility criteria for the distribution of structural funds, which sharply limits governments' ability to redistribute these funds. And it could also be due to Parliament having consistently had greater say over these funds, leaving the Council with less room for maneuver.

Among the other control variables, *Unemployment* and *Coalition Size* stand out as significant, and *GDP Growth per Capita* somewhat less consistently so. To nobody's surprise, when unemployment goes up, public approval for the government goes down. The effect is substantively large too: a 5 percent increase in unemployment is associated with a 3 percent drop in support for the incumbent. It also seems that when it comes to the number of parties in the governing coalition, the more the merrier. Adding just one more party boosts the government's approval rating by about 6.5 percent. This is probably because larger governing coalitions tend to represent a larger slice of the electorate, leaving a smaller share of voters to flock to the opposition. (This interpretation is supported by the unpopularity of minority governments – the coefficient for *Minority Government* is negative albeit not statistically significant.) The support for the idea that growth makes for more popular governments is weaker and statistically detectable in the CAP and ESIF models, but not (barely) in the one for total receipts.

Finally, it seems that the principal explanatory variables and the controls have left no discernible independent effect of impending elections on public approval. *Election Period* is nowhere close to being statistically significant in any of the models. Whether this is because this effect is mostly mediated through the variables that are already in the model or because of the endogenous efforts of the government and the opposition to smear each other remains a question.

5.6 Conclusion

The preponderance of evidence presented in this chapter establishes that domestic electoral politics matter for the distribution of the annual EU budget. Governments systematically receive significantly larger shares of the budget when they come up against national elections. This correlation holds even when we account for a variety of non-electoral factors that affect the sizes of these receipts. Moreover, the atypical increases are even greater when governments expect trouble at the polls, have the wherewithal to negotiate the relevant concessions in the Council, and do not have to contend with similarly motivated fellow EU members. Governments have solid reasons for sending these signals because public approval of a government is positively associated with it

Table 5.3. *Summary of the Empirical Findings.*

	Signals of Responsiveness		
	Total Receipts	CAP Receipts	ESIF Receipts
The Fundamental Result			
Impending Elections	✓	✓	✗
Politicization over Time	yes		
Electoral Distress			
Bad Economic Times	yes	weak	yes
Disapproval of the Government	yes	yes	no
Volatile Swing Voters	yes	yes	yes
Structural and Informal Powers			
Voting Power in the Council	yes	yes	no
Ideological Divergence	weak	no	no
Divergence in EU Support	yes	yes	no
Constraining Factors			
Number of Claimants	yes	yes	no

For all conditioning variables, "yes" means that the size of the electoral effect depends on the variable and is significant; "weak" means that the relationship is tenuous; "no" means that there is no evidence that the effect depends on the variable. Empty cells mean that the relationship was not tested.

securing larger shares of the budget. Taken together, these results lend considerable support to the argument that these increases in EU budget receipts are instances of the credit-claiming signal of responsiveness.

We can, in fact, go beyond this general conclusion. The analyses of how the size of the electoral effect depends on circumstance and structure provide further insights and reveal interesting nuance. Table 5.3 provides a summary of these findings.

At its most rudimentary, for the signal to matter, citizens must be at least vaguely aware of what goes on at the EU level. As we have seen, that used to be difficult, but over time the EU has intruded ever more widely and more deeply into the daily lives of Europeans, who therefore have become more aware of events at the EU level. This has furnished political entrepreneurs with opportunities to exploit and amplify the concomitant policy disagreements, with the end result that the EU has become increasingly politicized over time. This has made EU-level policymaking a much more conducive environment for domestic electioneering, and

5.6 Conclusion

governments have taken advantage of that. The size of the electoral effect is conditional on the degree of politicization of the EU in the member states.

The incentives to work strenuously for voter approval rise and fall with the circumstances. If they favor the incumbent, reelection is likely and the marginal benefit of yet another signal of responsiveness is fairly small. If, on the other hand, the situation is perilous and the government is tottering on the edge of defeat or is highly uncertain about its prospects, there is much to be gained by persuading voters to stay the course with the incumbent. I looked at various measures of electoral distress and invariably found the same story: governments with a greater need to appeal to voters consistently send stronger signals of responsiveness. Whether it is the unemployment rate, the level of disapproval for the government, or the number of uncommitted voters, any worsening with respect to the sample baseline (mean) triggers efforts by the government to secure a larger budget share. The steeper the deterioration, the more intensive these efforts are.

The need to appear responsive to voters in times of electoral distress is so great that the signals even show up in the least likely places: negotiations over ESIF allocations. Unlike total receipts and CAP allocations, where the atypically large shares are readily detectable, there is no unconditional effect of impending elections on structural funds. The contrast with CAP suggests several potential reasons. Unlike the farmers who receive direct subsidies under CAP, whose numbers are great, and who are organized in powerful political interest groups, the potential beneficiaries of ESIF funds suffer from crippling disadvantages. They do not share readily identifiable common interests, their numbers are few, and they have no lobby to channel their demands. Since it is unlikely that their vote, as a group, would depend on their receipt of ESIF funds, it does not generally pay to target them as a group with signals of responsiveness.

It can, however, pay to do so in specific circumstances. For instance, when unemployment is very high, any measure that can bring down that particular statistic before elections would be used. Similarly, when electoral uncertainty is rampant because of large numbers of undecided voters, anything that could tilt some of them toward favoring the government would be attempted. Obtaining more ESIF funds can help in these circumstances and it could also signal that the government is serious about development (which presumably should reduce unemployment and swing the uncommitted toward support for the incumbent).

Beyond domestic political realities, there are two other reasons why CAP could be very different from ESIF when it comes to redistribution of budget allocations. The first is that Parliament has always had greater say over the "non-compulsory" structural funds than over the highly salient agricultural ones. This was explicitly so before the distinction was abolished and the co-decision procedure was introduced. However, it remains so to this day. This generally made it difficult for governments to alter the ESIF allocations in the Council. Moreover, access to ESIF funds tends to be restricted by eligibility criteria calculated through formulas that essentially rule out many of the wealthier member states. Some EU members simply do not qualify for ESIF funds and so cannot use them for electoral signaling.

That it is this "policy by formula" that explains why ESIF receipts do not show up as signals of responsiveness in most cases can be inferred from the fact that even powerful countries with every structural and informal advantage at the bargaining table cannot obtain larger ESIF allocations. When there is any room for maneuver, these countries can deploy their formidable institutional and resource strengths and secure redistributions for which their governments can claim credit. This is exactly what we see when it comes to total receipts and CAP allocations.

The informal norm of consensual decision-making in the Council ensures that not every victory is to the strong. Sometimes EU members can cooperate to help a less influential government obtain larger receipts before elections. Of course, they can only do so behind closed doors and when they retain sufficient control of the negotiation process (i.e., not with ESIF funds). And they are not likely to favor a government that diverges too much from the average preferences in the Council. As it turns out, it really matters what preferences are being considered here. Partisan ideology, along the traditional left–right dimension, does not seem to be the deciding factor. Attitudes toward EU integration, on the other hand, seem to matter a lot. Thus, governments that do not drift too far either for or, more commonly, against EU integration could be beneficiaries of hidden cooperation in the Council.

Whether by power, skill, or luck, a government's ability to increase its share of budget receipts is limited by the redistributive aspect of the negotiations. More for one means less for others, so if there are more governments vying for larger shares, the likelihood that any one of them would be able to secure the desired enlargement would quickly plummet. Thus, when there are more governments facing impending elections, the signals of responsiveness become weaker both for total receipts and CAP allocations (as usual, there is no discernible effect for ESIF funds). This is yet another piece of evidence for the theoretical mechanism, where the larger number of coming elections translates into more claimants on a fixed budget.

5.6 Conclusion

With all these findings, we can be reasonably confident that governments deliberately seek to increase their budget shares before elections. I also found evidence that they do this because they can expect voters to respond favorably: public approval for the incumbent increases when the total share and the CAP allocation for the country go up. As with almost everything else, nothing happens with ESIF shares. Presumably, since governments cannot strategically redistribute these funds, they do not use them for signaling, and therefore voters pay no attention to them. When the effects exist, their substantive impact is in line with what one could expect from other economic indicators. In other words, the signals work.

The strength of these quantitative analyses is that they help detect whether the patterns the theory leads us to expect in the data really do exist. But their weakness is that this is also the most they can tell us. Now we know that governments increase their budget receipts before elections and that larger receipts result in more favorable public approval rates. We should still want to know more. For example, we have seen the credit-claiming strategy in action. Given the formal rules and deadlines that govern negotiations over the annual budget, this is the only signal of responsiveness one could expect governments to use here. But the theory is more general than that, and it specifies at least three other strategies that could be viable in other policy-making and legislative contexts. It would be beneficial to expand the scope of analysis beyond the annual budget negotiations. It would be even better if there was some more direct evidence for the theoretical mechanism itself – as in governments taking into account the likely electoral consequences of various outcomes and adjusting their negotiation strategies accordingly. To find this kind of evidence, however, a different method of analysis is called for.

The next chapter does both: it shifts to a different context – negotiations over the multiannual financial framework for 2007–2013, and it employs a different method – process tracing the behavior of key governments in the shadow of national elections.

6 Triumph and Agony in the 2007–2013 MFF Negotiations

> I can't believe that these leaders spend so much time arguing over such small sums.
> — A bemused US diplomatic observer
> Berlin summit, 1999

Once upon a time, the EU budget was negotiated every year. But what worked when parties to the bargain were few and their warrants for discord were modest could not survive the growth of the European Union. As the EU's ever-widening reach brought in new members and penetrated more deeply into areas where nations were once considered sovereign, policy preferences diverged and the occasions for conflict became recurrent. The once harmonious budget negotiations turned into protracted fights over who should get how much and what the money should be spent on. And whenever the negotiations deadlocked, there was the risk that the impasse would turn into a failure to approve a budget for the coming year. By the early 1980s, the EU faced the very real possibility that it would not be able to continue to function unless its members found a way to avoid that risk. It had to reform or collapse, and so reform it did.

The reforms turned budget negotiations from months-long annual convulsions into biennial agonies every five years.[1] EU members would now craft multiannual financial frameworks (MFFs) that would set the overall spending limits and priorities over a seven-year period. In the annual budget negotiations, redistributions and other changes would be permissible only if they met the guidelines of the governing MFF. The major conflict would now be concentrated on setting the MFF.

---

[1] The Commission started the process with a proposal that became the Delors I Package in 1988 and continued it with the Delors II Package in 1992. These expanded and stabilized the EU's budget by creating its fourth "own resource" with contributions based on the GNP of the member states but limiting the combined total of its resources to a little over 1 percent of the EU's GNP. The reforms also introduced the "financial perspectives" that would enforce budgetary discipline by setting priorities and spending ceilings every five years (Delors I) and then at least every five years [Delors II (in practice seven years)]. The financial perspectives eventually became the multiannual frameworks.

This would greatly expand the time to agreement, but seven years gave the EU enough time to accomplish the task. In contrast, the discipline imposed on the budgets during that period would streamline the annual negotiations and minimize the risk of breakdown. The arrangement provided for a stable and predictable fiscal environment over a longer period while allowing for enough flexibility so it did not prejudice future growth or adjustments as the EU evolved.

The EU expanded twice more before the twentieth century came to an end: informally with the reunification of Germany in 1990, and formally with the 1995 accession of Austria, Finland, and Sweden. Although the Federal Republic of Germany (West Germany) had trouble incorporating the former German Democratic Republic (East Germany), these enlargements were not onerous. The three new members were wealthy and already quite integrated economically with the EU. Only their neutrality during the Cold War had kept them from formalizing these ties.[2]

The first real test of the MFF system came in 2003 when the EU was about to embark on an unprecedented expansion with ten Central and Eastern European (CEE) countries.[3] Eight of the so-called A10 newcomers had been members of the former Soviet bloc and were still undergoing painful economic, political, legal, and social reforms. They were all underdeveloped, quite a bit poorer compared to existing members, but populous as a group.[4] They had participated informally during the negotiations of the financial perspective for 2000–2006 (Agenda 2000), but because the accession had been uncertain, they had only managed to eke out pre-accession assistance of about €3 billion per year, and a total commitment of about €12 billion per year for 2002–2006 if they became members (as seen later in Table 6.2). At 3 percent of the EU-15 budget for pre-accession aid and 8 percent of the projected EU-21 budget for post-accession commitments, these amounts were not great, and even they were pushing the budgets to the limits given projected revenues. The EU-15 had already anticipated that enlargement would require rethinking the financial perspective during the next MFF negotiations.

---

[2] Norway, a NATO member, and neutral Switzerland were in similar positions, and both applied to join the EU. Norway even signed the treaty, but it was vetoed by a national referendum in 1994. Switzerland withdrew its application after a national referendum in 1992 revealed insufficient public support for membership.

[3] The A10 that joined the EU in 2004 were Cyprus, Czech Republic, Estonia, Hungary, Latvia, Lithuania, Malta, Poland, Slovakia, Slovenia. Bulgaria and Romania joined in 2007, and Croatia followed suit in 2013.

[4] The wealthiest, Slovenia, was at about 65 percent of EU-15 average GDP per capita in 1999, with Bulgaria trailing at less than 20 percent.

By 2003 it was clear that the A10 would be joining the EU, and from 2004 they would no longer be candidates who could only shout from the sidelines. They would be members with voting rights. For the wealthy existing members, the enlargement was a great opportunity to gain free access to large markets, and a promise to open the door for lucrative investments. But for this potential to be realized, the newcomers had to be brought up to par. They would need structural funds for development over many years, and could be hardly expected to make large contributions to the EU budget during that time. Someone else would have to pay. It took almost three years to figure out that this someone would be (mostly) the United Kingdom.

This delay was long and the outcome bitterly contested. Both are puzzling because, as we shall see, the essential characteristics of the outcome had been predictable from the outset: the British rebate would be reduced, the Common Agricultural Policy (CAP) would remain unchanged, the structural development funds would continue to be spread across all member states, and the revenue ceiling would remain roughly where it had been. All that the intense bargaining and the sharp rhetoric amounted to was tinkering at the margins, some relief to net contributors, and ensuring that the newcomers would not get shafted. Hardly the stuff of high drama. And yet, in October 2005, the president of the European Parliament was warning publicly that

The EU is facing a crisis, and one of the clearest signs of this is the failure to reach agreement on the new financial perspective.[5]

Why did that happen? The breakthrough deal that clinched agreement on the financial perspectives did not slash the most important expenditures all that much (as seen later in Table 6.5). It reduced the CAP commitments from the Commission's original proposal by 3 percent, from €301 billion to €293 billion, a difference of less than 1 percent of the proposed total. It reduced the structural development funds by 11 percent: from €345 billion to €308 billion, a difference of 4 percent of the proposed total. And while it is true that the total commitments were reduced by 13 percent from €1,025 billion to €862 billion, the cuts came from areas where little disagreement had been registered.[6]

---

[5] European Union Committee of the Regions. "Josep Borrell, President of the European Parliament: 'A sound agreement on the financial perspective is vital for funding the Community's economic and social cohesion policies'." Brussels, 19 October 2005, COR/05/111. http://europa.eu/rapid/press-release_COR-05-111_en.htm, accessed January 17, 2018.

[6] The headings that saw the deepest cuts were Competitiveness (1a), with €61 billion, The EU as a Global Partner (4), with €46 billion, and Natural Resources (2), excluding CAP, with €25 billion.

Even the reduction of the total budget was foreseeable since the net contributors had announced that they would keep expenditures down.

In this chapter, I suggest that the delay was almost entirely driven by signals of responsiveness by the governments of the United Kingdom, Germany, and to a lesser extent, Poland and Spain, and that the negotiations continuously pivoted around the unmovable French position on CAP. The argument can be briefly summarized as follows.

The first 18 months were taken by Britain's Tony Blair pretending that the fate of the rebate was not negotiable, and with Germany and France playing along in the hopes that the United Kingdom would reverse its position once the general election in May 2005 was over. Although Blair's position immediately moderated after the elections, he sought a radical reform of CAP. Neither France nor Germany had been prepared for this, especially because the EU had just negotiated a settlement that would keep CAP unchanged until 2013. Even worse for Germany's chancellor, Gerhard Schröder, his party (Sozialdemokratische Partei Deutschlands, SPD) suffered a humiliating defeat in the important state of Nordrhein-Westfalen. He lost a vote of confidence and was now facing federal elections in September. As a result, the European Council summit in June 2005 failed to produce an agreement. Although the SPD lost the election, its defeat was not decisive and the Christlich Demokratische Union/Christlich-Soziale Union (CDU/CSU) did not gain a parliamentary majority in the federal parliament (Bundestag). It took until early October to negotiate a grand coalition with Angela Merkel replacing Schröder as chancellor. Although the Franco-German friendship was still strong, Merkel was far more evenhanded, which undermined French President Jacques Chirac's uncompromising stance; France agreed to a review of CAP in 2008. In December, Merkel brokered the deal that halved the United Kingdom's rebate so it would have to contribute €10.5 billion more over the MFF period and restored funding to the CEE countries (which had been about to pay for most of the cuts). The last five months of the process were taken up with readings in Parliament, which ended with adding about €4 billion to the total.[7]

This episode shows instances of position taking, position defending (with hidden cooperation to permit it), blame avoidance (through delay), and, of course, credit claiming. This should come as no surprise. The political environment in many countries was volatile: over the course of negotiations, five incumbent governments would be thrown out (Spain, Portugal, Bulgaria, Germany, and Poland), one would enter a

---

[7] The budget table makes it look like less than €2 billion were added, but this is because certain funds were excluded (European Commission, 2014, note to table 6.2, p. 84).

crisis it would lose (Italy), and three governments would win reelection (Denmark, the United Kingdom, and Hungary). As usual, local and national issues dominated the campaigns, but new governments pursued their EU-related goals with fresh vigor (e.g., the Socialists of Spain). Even the winning incumbents had to tread carefully after losing seats (e.g., Labour in Britain).

The EU was also particularly politicized because some governments had decided to put the new European Constitution up for a referendum vote by their citizens. The public mood on the EU varied: the 2005 referenda approved the Constitution in two countries (Spain and Luxembourg), but rejected it in two others (the Netherlands and France). The latter would have contrary effects on the budget negotiations. The EU budget hawks in the Netherlands could claim that the negative vote showed that the Dutch public was getting tired of being a large net contributor, and they could insist their demands about restraining the budget and reforming CAP be heard. French President Chirac, on the other hand, could see the negative vote in his country as a warning to preserve the existing CAP payments to France and to ensure that regional development benefits continued to flow. This weakened any commitment to drastic budget reductions and ensured a stance nearly diametrically opposed to the Dutch. "Nearly" because both still agreed that the British rebate had to go.

The MFF 2007–2013 negotiations provide us with a glimpse of how these strategies for signaling responsiveness work, especially because it is possible to document the reasons that made them necessary in the eyes of many governments. This case also shows how governments might be unable to exploit structural advantages effectively when domestic opinion does not favor their positions, and how they can engage in hidden cooperation to allow another government to avoid taking the blame for a bad outcome right before elections. It also shows how the formal bargaining power of the (far from unified) net contributors was felt in reducing the total size of the budget. Finally, it demonstrates how the informal norms give even the weaker member states a voice in shaping the final outcome and avoid glaringly unfair distributions of the benefits.

Before delving into the interplay between member state negotiations and their domestic politics, I provide some context on how the MFFs are negotiated and how fiscal discipline is enforced (Section 6.1). I then summarize the preferences of the most important actors regarding four critical fault lines – budget size, UK rebate, CAP reform, and cohesion policies – and outline the major groups that coalesced in defense of various positions (Section 6.2). I use pathway analysis to trace the negotiations from the opening proposal of the Commission in February 2004 to the agreement at the European Council summit in December 2005 to analyze the reasons governments took certain positions, defended them, and, in some cases, made concessions (Section 6.3).[8] To keep the narrative from getting bogged down in excessive detail, I will focus on two key players, the United Kingdom and Germany, and the elections there, although I will bring in other important actors, such as France and Poland, when their behavior is relevant.

6.1 The Multiannual Financial Perspectives

In 1988, the Commission proposed to reform the budgetary process by introducing two major innovations (Delors I Package).[9] The first was to set the revenue on sound financial footing by augmenting the EU's "own resources" with contributions by member states. To induce the states to agree, the Commission capped the total EU budget to a little over 1 percent of the EU's gross national product (GNP). These payments would eventually become the largest source of income for the EU budget.

The second innovation was to split the annual negotiations over the composition of the budget into two components: determining the budget headings (priorities) with their overall expenditures, and deciding on the precise distribution of allocations within these preset limits. The negotiations over priorities and their caps had been by far the most divisive part of the process, so now these were to take place no more than once every five years.[10] These "financial perspectives" (later, MFFs) would give states a stable environment with enough time to reach an agreement without holding the budget hostage every year. Since nobody could predict exactly what needs the EU might have over the period covered by a financial perspective, the Commission proposed to continue

---

[8] See Gerring (2008) for methods for choosing cases. The pathway analysis relies on a large number of archival resources, including technical reports, memoirs, secondary sources, speeches, official government announcements, and newspaper articles. I searched for newspaper sources in two steps. First, I retrieved newspapers using systematic keyword searches on the relevant topics. Second, I searched for further articles on specific questions that became relevant for the line of argumentation. For the newspaper articles, I added the author names and website addresses whenever available. Since many newspaper articles were retrieved from newspaper data bases and archives in the United States and Germany, they often do not contain information on either author names or web links (I used accessible online versions whenever possible). All newspaper articles, speeches, letters, and reports cited in the chapter are available from the author.

[9] See Laffan (2000) for a concise history of budgetary politics to 1999.

[10] Extended to seven under Delors II, 1992. Article 312 of TFEU requires the MFFs to be established for at least five years.

the annual budget negotiations but to limit them to the preset priorities and spending limits. This flexibility would allow the member states to redistribute funds within and across headings to improve efficiency as circumstances arose. The amounts under consideration were relatively small, and the financial perspective constrained what could be done with them. This was expected to make the annual negotiations more straightforward and lower the risk of failing to agree to a budget in any given year.

The reforms thus traded intense conflict every seven years for relative peace in between (Laffan and Lindner, 2014; Lindner, 2006).

The Primacy of the Council

The legal basis for the MFF is Article 312 of the Treaty on the Functioning of the European Union (TFEU), which requires that the MFF be established for at least five years, that the annual budgets must comply with the MFF, and that expenditures must be covered by EU's own resources. It sets up a special legislative procedure that gives primacy to the Council, which adopts the appropriate regulation after obtaining Parliament's consent. The Council must act unanimously unless authorized by the European Council to use qualified majority (Parliament always acts by a majority of its component members). The Commission, the Council, and Parliament are enjoined to "take any measure necessary" to ensure the adoption of a new MFF. If they fail, the provisions of the final year of the last MFF remain in force until they are supplanted by a new financial framework.

The practice of the MFF negotiations has been for the Commission to take the lead and draft a proposal, which it officially submits for consideration to both the Council and Parliament. This proposal outlines the Commission's vision for the EU, the priorities with relevant budget headings, the proposed annual commitments, and the estimated payments. Although this sets the agenda for the negotiations, the proposal usually follows months (sometimes years) of research and consultations with member states, and ends up incorporating their preferences for specific categories and for the overall structure of the budget. This bottom-up approach essentially aggregates the funding needs of individual member states to arrive at the commitment ceiling for each heading, and the Commission ensures that the payment appropriations do not exceed the own-resources ceiling.

The bargaining takes place in the Council, mostly in the General Affairs and External Relations and the Economic and Financial Affairs councils. The European Council, especially the heads of state of net contributors, can play an outsized role in this process by more or less setting the ceilings for appropriations and influencing the distribution of commitments across headings of special interest to them. Since member states are strongly motivated by the desire to limit their gross national income (GNI)-based payments, they tend to use a top-down approach, which fixes an overall size of the budget, and then redistributes the commitment ceilings. This practically ensures that the MFF they agree on will commit less money on almost every heading compared to the Commission's original proposal.

Once the Council produces its own version of the MFF, Parliament must act to consent to it. If it introduces any changes, the Council would have to approve them before the MFF can be adopted. Until 2009, the adoption was through an interinstitutional agreement between the Commission, the Council, and Parliament. Under the Lisbon Treaty, it is adopted once the Council reaches an agreement and the European Parliament ratifies it. Although in principle Parliament could make major modifications to the Council's proposed MFF, its *de facto* ability to do so is severely circumscribed. Because it moves so late in the game after the Commission, the Council, and the European Council have hashed out their differences and constructed a mutually acceptable financial framework, and because whatever Parliament does the Council still has to approve it, Parliament can only tinker with the MFF at the margins. For example, despite wanting higher spending and even after some creative accounting that "disappeared" more than €1.5 billion from the MFF while still keeping it available in a special instrument, it only managed to increase the Council's budget by a paltry 0.47 percent.[11]

Table 6.1 lists the five financial perspectives negotiated between 1987 and 2014, along with their negotiation and adoption dates. I took the start of the negotiations to be the month of the Commission's first proposal and the end to be the month of the Council's final agreement. The adoption date is when the interinstitutional agreement was concluded and, for the last MFF, when the Council's final regulation was ratified by Parliament.

[11] The Council committed €862.36 billion, but of these €1.547 billion under heading 4 were for the Emergency Aid Reserve. Parliament reclassified it as a special instrument, effectively reducing the commitment to €860.813 billion. It then tacked on €3.507 billion in new commitments yielding a new total of €864.32 billion. It further allocated another €0.5 billion to staff pensions, also off the headings. Overall, it increased the budget by over €4 billion but argued that only the difference of €1.96 billion in totals was relevant (European Commission, 2014, note to table 6.2). The calculation above considers the actual increase of €4.007 billion over the adjusted total of €860.813 billion. Schild (2008) takes the parliamentary position at face value and arrives at a 0.23 percent increase.

Table 6.1. *Negotiating the Financial Perspectives, 1987–2014.*

Period	Financial Perspective	Negotiations			Adopted
		Start	End	Months	
1988–1992	Delors I	Feb 1987	Feb 1988	12	Jun 29, 1988
1993–1999	Delors II	Feb 1992	Dec 1992	10	Oct 29, 1993
2000–2006	Agenda 2000	Jul 1997	Mar 1999	20	May 6, 1999
2007–2013	MFF 2007–2013	Feb 2004	Dec 2005	22	Jun 14, 2006
2014–2020	MFF 2014–2020	Jun 2011	Dec 2013	30	Dec 2, 2013

Negotiations begin with the first formal proposal by the Commission and end with the final agreement in the Council. The adoption date is when the Interinstitutional Agreement between the Commission, the Council, and Parliament is concluded (until 2009), or the ratification by Parliament.
Source: European Commission (2014) and author calculations.

If the Delors I reforms were overly optimistic about how easy agreement on annual budgets would be (as we have seen in Chapter 5), its pessimism about conflicts over the financial perspectives turned out to be spot on. The average time to negotiate a MFF exceeds a year and a half (nineteen months), with another four months to adopt it. It also appears that the conflicts have gotten worse over time.

Before we can ask why the MFF 2007–2013 took twenty-two months to negotiate, we need to understand what member states generally seek to achieve during these negotiations. For this, a brief account of the MFF structure and features is in order.

Balancing the Budget with Ceilings

The MFFs are commonly divided into at least five main headings, roughly corresponding to agricultural policies, structural operations, internal security and justice, external relations, and administration. Other headings, usually related to pre-accession aid or enlargement, are added as necessary. The names of these headings and precisely what gets included in them have changed over time, but the most important spending areas are readily identifiable. The agricultural category is mostly devoted to market-related expenses and direct payments under CAP, and the structural operations category is mostly concerned with developmental assistance and cohesion funds. These two take up the bulk of the budget: 68 percent in Agenda 2000 and 70 percent in MFF 2007–2013 (as seen later in Table 6.3).

6.1 The Multiannual Financial Perspectives

The EU practices fiscal discipline, expressed in two ceilings on resources – which limit how much revenue the EU can raise (own resources) and how much it can promise to pay (commitments) – and in the requirement that it must cover all actual payments with its own resources (balanced budget).[12]

The EU cannot expect to raise more money than its *own-resources ceiling*, which is calculated as a percentage of the total income of the EU. Introduced in 1988 at 1.15 percent of EU GNP, it was raised to 1.2 percent from 1992 to 1994, then increased gradually to 1.27 percent in 1999. In 2001, the Council decided that the relevant measure of income is GNI, and the ceiling was recalculated to be 1.24 percent of EU GNI. This stayed in place until 2010, when the Council changed the formula, which caused GNI to increase by 1 percent on average. To keep the ceiling commensurate with its previous value, the Council reduced it to 1.23 percent, where it currently remains.

The annual amounts for commitment appropriations in every budget heading limit how much the EU can promise to pay for that heading during a given year. The promises include both immediate disbursements and payments stretched over several years. The total annual commitment limits how much the EU can promise to pay overall during a given year. It is often expressed using the same measure as the EU's own resources because there is a separate limit that applies to them. Initially, the *commitments ceiling* was 1.335 percent of EU GNP, recalculated as 1.31 percent of EU GNI in 2001, and adjusted to 1.29 percent in 2010, where it has remained since.

The actual disbursements the EU expects to make every year are recorded as payment appropriations and obviously cannot exceed the commitments. The balanced budget requires that these payments be entirely covered by the EU's own resources; that is, they cannot exceed the own-resources ceiling, which is why they are often expressed using the same measure. The difference between expected payments and the own-resources ceiling is for unforeseen circumstances and usually ends up in some "special instrument" (a fund for specific goals). This allows some flexibility in the budgeting process because the amounts are not allocated to any heading.[13]

---

[12] For the following figures, see European Commission (2014, chapter 9).
[13] The fact that the MFFs tend to express both commitments and payments as percentages of GNI can also be confusing since the commitments ceiling is quite a bit higher than the own-resources ceiling. When some member states demanded that spending be limited to 1 percent of EU GNP, the Commission chose to interpret this as applying to payments, a readily achievable goal even for its ambitious plans. Apparently, this was not what the member states had meant, and the final budget reduced the commitments.

As with any budget, disagreements can be broadly classified into three areas: (1) contributions: how much should each member state pay to fund it, (2) ceilings: how much should the total spending be, and (3) distributions: how much should be allocated to each heading.

Almost all of EU's revenue comes from its "own resources": customs duties on imports from outside the EU, value-added taxes (VATs) in each EU country, and levies on members states based on their income (with reductions for particular member states). The GNI-based payments, introduced in 1988, have become the cornerstone of EU finance as they are used to cover expenditures in excess of the traditional customs duties and VAT-based payments.[14] This balances the EU budget when it is specified, but actual spending patterns vary depending on circumstances. The deficit between traditional resources and payments determines the total excess amount that must be financed with calls for GNI-based contributions from member states. Although a uniform call rate is applied, corrections reduce the payments from certain states, which opens up gaps between the amount called and the deficit that must be supplied. Except for the UK rebate, in whose financing the United Kingdom does not participate, these gaps are plugged by all member states in proportion to their GNI.[15]

The only limit to the GNI-based call rate, and therefore to what the EU can spend in any given year, is the own-resources ceiling, which is absolute. Trying to contain spending by lowering this hard budget constraint, however, is probably not the best thing to do. After all, member states have an interest in the EU continuing its operations, staying within its means, and being flexible enough to deal with unforeseen circumstances. Making the ceiling too low increases the risk that the EU might find itself starved of resources when it needs them most. Having a cumbersome procedure to change the ceiling makes it highly unlikely that the member states would be able to react quickly enough when the needs develop. It is more prudent to leave the ceiling high enough to absorb any special spending needs but control expenditures by reducing the commitments. Since this automatically depresses appropriations for payments, it would also ease pressure on the own-resources ceiling, while at the same time limiting the call rate for the GNI-based resources.

---

[14] In 2011, the Commission proposed eliminating the VAT-based resource as too cumbersome to administer and not worth much compared to the GNI-based resource, but the initiative did not get any traction (European Commission, 2014, pp. 107–113).

[15] Germany only paid two-thirds of its share of funding the UK rebate between 1985 and 2001. In 2002, this was reduced to one-quarter but extended to the Netherlands, Austria, and Sweden. This means that the UK rebate is uniquely disproportionately financed by the poorer countries.

Consequently, the conflicts during MFF negotiations tend to be over commitments, both their overall amount (which will determine how much each member state would have to contribute to keep the budget balanced) and their annual ceilings for various headers (which will determine how much each will receive in transfers). These conflicts set up the fault lines for the MFF 2007–2013 negotiations.

6.2 The Context: Four Fault Lines

There were four main conflicts during the MFF 2007–2013 negotiations, and none of them were new. Net contributors wanted to stabilize expenditures (i.e., keep the budget from expanding; shrink it if possible) while net beneficiaries wanted them to grow. The countries with large agricultural sectors wanted to keep CAP intact while everyone else wanted the subsidies eliminated. The richer countries with lagging regions wanted to preserve their access to the structural funds while the poor countries wanted them concentrated on themselves. And everyone that was not the United Kingdom wanted the UK rebate gone. These issues had been present with varying degrees of intensity for years, but now they came to a head like never before.

Restrain the Growth of the Budget

The struggle to contain the budget had been ongoing ever since the introduction of the GNI-based own resource removed the natural constraint of the small income generated by the traditional own resources. Indeed, this is why the Delors I reforms had capped the total of the own resources. As we have seen, after growing until 1999, the own-resources ceiling remained essentially constant; the only variations were due to changing the formula used to calculate GNI. The initial increase in the ceiling was necessary in order to accommodate more ambitious spending plans: the budget grew on average 3.9 percent per year during Delors I, and 3.3 percent per year during Delors II.[16] The member states – who had become increasingly concerned with this expansion – fixed the ceiling in 1999 and tried to control expenditures. The budget still grew, but at a substantially reduced rate: by 2.6 percent on average during Agenda 2000, and by 0.9 percent during MFF 2007–2013. Since these growth rates are in real terms, the decrease negotiated in

---

[16] The calculations of real growth rates are from Schild (2008, p. 536). See also Kölling and Leal (2014).

2004–2005 was quite dramatic.[17] In fact, the overall budget itself only grew by 9.7 percent from Agenda 2000 (in euros at 2004 prices, as seen later in Table 6.3). This showed remarkable restraint considering that the accession of the A10 was going to augment the population of the EU by almost a third. Somehow, the MFF 2007–2013 agreement kept commitments to merely 1.05 percent of EU GNI despite the own-resources ceiling remaining at 1.24 percent.

Reducing the total amount of resources available for any budget would greatly intensify the distributional conflicts over whatever remains, and it did so here. When the net contributors imposed their wishes for a smaller budget, all sorts of conflict cascades followed. The most obvious target was the UK rebate.

Reduce the UK Rebate

The UK rebate (or "correction") had been a permanent fixture almost from the moment the United Kingdom joined the Community. Two temporary corrections had been agreed to in 1975 and 1979, but in 1984 a more permanent one was put in place with the Fontainebleau Council. The problem was that when the United Kingdom acceded to the EU, the vast portion of the budget was going to pay for agricultural subsidies (and these, almost entirely to France). The United Kingdom had a relatively small and efficient agricultural sector, which meant that it would not receive back much of anything at all. Even worse, since the EU's main source of revenue was the VAT-based resource and the UK VAT base was relatively high compared to other members; applying even a uniform rate would extract a larger contribution from the United Kingdom than from another country with similar GNP. To add insult to injury, at the time, the United Kingdom was also among the poorest members, with its per capita income well below the EEC average. In other words, the United Kingdom did bear a disproportionately heavy burden, which is why the corrections had been introduced to prevent its contribution from being excessive.

The same circumstances prevailed in 1984, because despite attempts to reign in agricultural spending, about 70 percent of expenditures were still on CAP.[18] The Council agreed on a general exception:

---

[17] Although perhaps not as drastic as the −3.5 percent rate during MFF 2014–2020, this was the first time in its history that the financial perspective envisioned a real decline in the budget. This, of course, took place against the backdrop of the devastating financial crisis when many countries were undergoing painful adjustments, severely depressing both the ability to contribute to the EU budget and the political will to do so.

[18] European Commission. 2012. "CAP expenditure in total EU expenditure." http://ec.europa.eu/agriculture/cap-post-2013/graphs/graph1_en.pdf, accessed January 20, 2018.

6.2 The Context: Four Fault Lines

any Member State sustaining a budgetary burden which is excessive in relation to its relative prosperity may benefit from a correction at the appropriate time.[19]

Specifically, it would reimburse the United Kingdom 66 percent of the difference between its payments and receipts.

The circumstances that had rationalized the UK correction were, however, already changing. First, the accession of Spain and Portugal in 1986 immediately pulled down the average EU GNI, and the larger UK economy became "wealthier" purely by arithmetic. This discrepancy would widen even further with the accession of the A10, who were about to increase the EU-15 GNI by a mere 5 percent but the population by 30 percent (European Commission, 2004). Second, the United Kingdom had become quite a bit wealthier in real terms and was no longer a development laggard. Its per capita income had exceeded the EU average in 1997 and had consistently remained well above it since (Le Cacheux, 2005, chart 6). Third, the share of CAP expenditures in the budget had been in continuous decline, and was already at 38 percent under Agenda 2000 (as seen later in Table 6.3).

By 2003, then, the rationale behind the rebate had disappeared. It now even looked like other member states – in particular the newcomers – should have their contributions adjusted if the same logic applied. But the worst was probably the fact that the UK rebate was itself financed in what was beginning to look like a fundamentally unfair way. This is perhaps best explained with an example.

Because the GNI-based resource (and the VAT-based one as well) played a top-up role, the contributions from member states were calculated on as-needed basis, which meant that any reimbursement would create a deficit that had to be financed by the other member states. The individual shares of the UK rebate each had to pay were on top of their own contributions and were distributed in proportion to their income relative to the total EU GNP after the United Kingdom was excluded.

Consider the example in Table 6.2. If Germany's GNI was 21.99 percent of the EU-15 GNI in 2003 and the UK's was 18.26 percent, then Germany's share of the UK rebate financing would be $21.99/(100-18.26) = 26.90\%$. This was not what Germany would pay, however, since it had negotiated a 75 percent reduction of its share in 2002, along with Austria, the Netherlands, and Sweden. After this correction, Germany would only pay 6.73 percent of the UK rebate. Overall, the reductions for these four countries amounted to 29.74 percent of the

---

[19] Conclusions of the Sessions of the European Council (1975–1990): Fontainebleau, June 25–26, 1984.

Table 6.2. *Financing the UK Rebate.*

Country	Share of EU-15 GNI	Share of UK Rebate	75% Reduction	Share of UK Rebate	Excess for UK Rebate	Actual Share of UK Rebate
Austria	2.30	2.82	−2.11			0.70
Belgium	2.88	3.52		5.83	1.73	5.25
Denmark	1.92	2.35		3.89	1.16	3.51
Finland	1.51	1.84		3.05	0.91	2.75
France	16.57	20.27		33.59	9.99	30.26
Germany	21.99	26.90	−20.18			6.73
Greece	1.78	2.18		3.61	1.07	3.26
Ireland	1.24	1.51		2.51	0.75	2.26
Italy	13.83	16.92		28.03	8.34	25.25
Luxembourg	0.20	0.25		0.41	0.12	0.37
Netherlands	5.14	6.28	−4.71			1.57
Portugal	1.44	1.76		2.92	0.87	2.63
Spain	7.97	9.75		16.15	4.80	14.55
Sweden	2.98	3.65	−2.74			0.91
UK	18.26					
Total	100.00	100.00	−29.74	100.00	29.74	100.00

Author calculations based on UNSD GNI data.
Source: United Nations Statistics Division. National Account Estimates of Main Aggregates: GNI at current prices – US dollars.

rebate, and this had to be financed by the remaining ten member states. The distribution here was based on the individual shares in their total GNI. For France, this meant paying an additional 9.99 percent of the UK rebate, which brought its total to a whooping 30.26 percent. Between them, France, Italy, and Spain paid 70 percent of the UK rebate. Although this share would drop arithmetically once the A10 acceded, these three countries paid on average about 60 percent of the UK correction. Moreover, because the newcomers were much poorer than the rest of the EU, the fact that the four richest members had exempted themselves from financing the UK rebate meant that the burden would fall disproportionately on those least able to afford it.

The TFEU made no mention of any corrections whatsoever, which meant that the UK rebate rested squarely on the Fontainebleau Council agreement. Unfortunately, while it did set a general principle for corrections, this agreement clarified neither what it meant by a "burden which is excessive" nor how to measure "relative prosperity." This implied that newcomers, who were relatively underdeveloped, and the existing member states, who paid a disproportionate share of the UK rebate, had plausible reasons to complain that they were bearing excessive burdens. And if structural funds were to be mostly devoted to the development

6.2 The Context: Four Fault Lines

laggards, the United Kingdom could maintain the reasonable position that it still was benefiting disproportionately less from its contributions relative to other member states. But if the expenditures in new member states were to be included in the basis for calculating the UK rebate, the other pre-2004 members could complain that they were paying a disproportionately large share of the enlargement costs. This was especially galling since the United Kingdom had been the strongest promoter of this enlargement.

In the end, the rebate issue pitted the United Kingdom against everyone else although the four countries with their own special exemptions had weaker incentives to push very hard; after all, they had already shifted much of the burden onto others. A partial repeal of the UK rebate could, if accompanied by a revocation of their special status, actually increase their net contributions to the budget. Still, there was an obvious compromise, at least as a general outline: since the United Kingdom had championed the enlargement and stood to reap tremendous benefits from it, it would bear its proper share of its costs by having expenditures in new member states removed from the total, upon which the UK rebate was calculated. This would increase the UK contribution to the budget and reduce the extra burden on the other members.

Unfortunately, two interconnected factors militated against making this obvious compromise being an easy one to negotiate. The newcomers were going to double the disparity between rich and poor members, which would privilege their access to structural funds under the formulas that calculated eligibility based on EU averages. They were also going to bring in an additional four million farmers, which would enable them to lay claim to significant resources under CAP. This meant that as things stood, the United Kingdom would receive even fewer benefits after the enlargement. At the same time, if all resources going to newcomers were exempted from its rebate, the increase in the UK's contribution could be quite substantial. This would make it appear that suddenly the United Kingdom was getting much less from the EU while paying a lot more into it. This is never an easy sell, politically speaking, to the taxpayers who are funding the contribution, and would make nervous any government that contemplates it. Blair's Labour government was especially vulnerable to charges that it was giving away the gains that the (now opposing) Conservatives had worked so hard to achieve.

The UK government could seek to mitigate the negative impact of a rebate reform by aligning with net contributors in their demand to decrease the overall size of the budget. In particular, it could target both of the other traditional fissures in budgetary consensus: the CAP amount and the distribution of structural funds.

Table 6.3. *Context of the MFF 2007–2013 Negotiations, 2004.*

	Agenda 2000			Commission		Council	
	EUR (1999, bn)	EUR (2004, bn)	%	EUR (2004, bn)	%	EUR (2004, bn)	%
CAP	267.37	299.45	38	301.07	29	293.11	34
Structural Policies	213.01	238.57	30	344.91	34	307.62	36
Pre-Accession Aid	21.84	24.46	3	–	–	0.80[a]	<1
Enlargement	58.07	64.81	8	–	–	–	–
Total Commitments	704.26	786.03	100	1,025.04	100	862.36	100
% EU GNI[b]			1.22		1.26		1.05
Payment Appropriations % EU GNI			1.09		1.14		0.99
Own-Resources Ceiling % EU GNI			1.24		1.24		1.24

[a]Compensations for Bulgaria and Romania (2007–2009).
[b]Agenda 2000 used GNP, switched to GNI in 2002. Numbers adjusted for 2000 as 1.27 percent GNP ≈ 1.24 percent GNI.
The Agenda 2000 budget assumes that only six of the A10 would join.
Sources: Interinstitutional Agreement of 6 May 1999 (Annex II) for Agenda 2000, Cumulative inflation of 11.61 percent to 2004 (fxtop.com/en/inflation-calculator.php), Commission proposal (February 26, 2004), Council agreement (December 19, 2005), and author calculations.

Reform the CAP

Agricultural spending had been the prime mover of the initial rebate, and despite its decline, it still consumed a not insignificant chunk of the budget (Table 6.3). The costs of the CAP had also mushroomed. The market intervention to keep the prices of agricultural products high had been quite successful, and the farmers had begun to produce more than what the EU could consume. These expensive surpluses had been exported, partially offsetting the costs of the subsidy, but the new WTO rules prohibited that. The EU was in the process of reducing intervention prices but offsetting the decline in incomes of farmers with direct payments.

The Commission had proposed moving toward general rural development (including fisheries) during Agenda 2000, but that gambit had failed. CAP stayed essentially the same as under Delors II, so the pressure to reform it remained intense. With the Eastern enlargement around the corner, the French farmers were looking at massive cuts in their subsidies. President Chirac was about to face the polls amid much uncertainty and could not antagonize this influential bloc of voters. With Germany and the United Kingdom pressing for enlargement, Chirac demanded protections for CAP. Since France could veto the accession of new members, this was going to be the price of admission. The others relented, and in October 2002 France and Germany orchestrated a Council agreement that would preserve CAP spending until 2013, when the possibility of reform could be revisited. CAP spending would be €43 billion per year, with €9 billion going to French farmers.[20] This froze the commitment ceiling for that heading and took a large portion of the budget off the bargaining table. Reopening this debate a mere year after this agreement would be exceedingly difficult. Thus, while reforming CAP would result in substantial savings and lower UK's contribution, the timing for any such initiative was singularly inopportune.[21]

Redistribute the Structural Funds

The likelihood that the United Kingdom would manage to budge the other member states on the other big-ticket item – the structural funds – was just as remote. Here, the United Kingdom needed to preserve access to funds for its own relatively underdeveloped regions even though they could be disqualified when the A10 joined the EU. In this, it had a common interest with France, Germany, and Spain (among others), all of whom had regions that had gotten accustomed to EU receipts.[22] Of course, everyone recognized that the new member states would need significant aid to bring up their economies closer to the EU average. The Agenda 2000 architects had been aware that if the 2004 enlargement were to occur, the budget would be stretched to the breaking point. As Table 6.3 shows, for that eventuality they had appropriated total commitments of 1.27 percent of the EU GNP – right at the own-resources ceiling, and this under the assumption that only six of the A10 would join. They had kicked the can down the road in the

---

[20] "Trying to make the CAP fit." *The Scotsman*, June 15, 2005.
[21] As we shall see, CAP commitments in the new financial perspective decreased the Agenda 2000 allocation by a paltry 2 percent (Table 6.3). Since CAP commitments were already set to decrease slightly over the years of Agenda 2000, even this cannot be attributed to hard bargaining: the final year of Agenda 2000 envisioned spending €41.62 billion (in 2004 prices) on CAP, and the MFF 2007–2013 set the average annual commitment to €41.87 billion. In other words, the new perspective was a continuation of the existing CAP trajectory, per the Council agreement of 2002.
[22] Germany, for example, was a major beneficiary for its Eastern states (Länder). Not only did the federal government face huge domestic pressure to keep these funds, it was constitutionally required to account for the preferences of the Länder. This gave the poor among them, such as Saarland and especially the politically important Nordrhein-Westfalen, a direct say in policy, although they were opposed by the rich net contributors to the federal budget such as Bayern and Baden-Württemberg (Bachtler, Mendez, and Wishlade, 2016, pp. 164–167).

full knowledge that the negotiators of MFF 2007–2013. would have to revisit the issue and allocate many more funds to the newcomers. In other words, the structural funds were bound to increase, probably dramatically, and much of that increase would have to be directed to the new member states.

This is where the commonality of interest between the United Kingdom and the rest of the EU came to grief. If the UK rebate was to be reduced, especially through a mechanism that excluded spending in the new member states, then the United Kingdom would be paying more for the enlargement. Correspondingly, it had a very strong incentive to marry rebate reform to restrictions on spending on the newcomers. Whereas the other states also wanted to preserve access to structural funds, their need to do so at the expense of the new members was weaker. In fact, in the context of a UK rebate reform, they had a positive incentive to shift more of these funds toward the newcomers: the United Kingdom would be paying its full share of these expenditures, which would free up their extra contributions that had been used to finance its rebate. They could either contribute less overall, which would play well domestically, or increase their spending on the funds they qualified for, thereby reducing their net contribution, also a good political move. Thus, if the UK correction was going to happen, the United Kingdom wanted to decrease spending on new members as much as possible, while everyone else wanted to increase it, at least up to the point where the budget constraint would bind, forcing further increases to be matched by reductions in their own receipts.

Needless to say, the optics of the UK position were terrible: it could be accused of forcing the poorest member states to pay for the privilege accorded to one of the wealthiest. And indeed it was, when President Barroso of the Commission infamously labeled the United Kingdom's position a "Robin Hood in reverse."[23] In this atmosphere, where the other pre-2004 member states could pose as protectors of the weak and the new member states would be able to defend their interests with actual votes, it was exceedingly unlikely that the United Kingdom would make much headway toward its preferred position on the structural funds either.[24]

---

[23] "EU warns Blair against 'reverse Robin Hood.'" *Dawn*, December 1, 2005. www.dawn.com/news/167888/eu-warns-blair-against, accessed January 20, 2018.

[24] As we shall see, the new financial perspective increased the commitments for structural policies by 29 percent over the Agenda 2000 level, a raise all the more impressive for that it occurred in the context of a fairly strict dedication to keeping overall commitments down (Table 6.3).

In sum, as the EU was about to admit ten new members, the outline for the new financial perspective was apparent from the very beginning: the growth of the budget would be arrested, the UK rebate would have to be reduced, the CAP would remain mostly unchanged, and structural funds would increase. So why did it take almost two years to get to an agreement that had been essentially predetermined?

6.3 Negotiations under Predestination

The process of constructing the financial perspectives for 2007–2013 began long before the formal start of deliberations with the February 2004 proposal from the Commission. As part of the 2002 accession package for the 10(+2) CEE countries, the Council had negotiated an agreement to keep the agricultural subsidies more or less unchanged until 2013, with a gradual phase-in of the newcomers.[25] This severely limited the room for maneuvering on CAP, so when the Commission established, in April 2003, its working groups to canvass member states and identify the goals and needs of the EU, it was already handicapped in what had been the largest commitment in the budget (Table 6.3).

The budgetary impact of the substantial number of farmers that the enlargement would bring was already incorporated in the CAP deal. The rather woeful underdevelopment of the newcomers, on the other hand, had to be addressed now. This meant more structural funds.

Because the new members would not be able to contribute a whole lot, expenditures would grow faster than revenues for the foreseeable future. This meant that either the total commitments would have to increase, or the distribution of structural assistance would have to be shifted toward the newcomers, or both. This set up conflicts between net contributors and net recipients, as well as between existing beneficiaries of structural assistance and the newcomers. Because an expanded budget entailed larger contributions from all, and a redistribution of structural funds decreased receipts of the most important contributors, one thing was certain: the enlargement had painted a target on the UK rebate.

Little wonder, then, that member states had started to produce memoranda and to circulate position papers as early as 2002. What were the preference alignments along the four fault lines?[26]

---

[25] The "10(+2)" referred to the A10 that were to join in 2004 plus Bulgaria and Romania who were to join in 2007.
[26] The next section is based on Bachtler, Mendez, and Wishlade (2016), who summarize the policy positions of all member states.

The Order of Battle

When it came to the size of the overall budget, the alignments were very clear and would not change during the negotiations. The largest group was the net contributors who favored a reduction of the budget commitments. Its six members comprised 64 percent of the EU-25 GNI and 66 percent of the combined GNI of member states who took more or less explicit positions on the matter (Table 6.4). The second-largest group comprised member states interested in increasing the commitments, but at 18 percent of the EU-25 GNI, it was a very distant second. Since support for maintaining the budget "as is" was even weaker (15 percent), it was a foregone conclusion that the EU was facing some draconian cuts. It did not help that the most ardent wielder of the budget axe was Germany, who insisted on lowering the ceiling to 0.34 percent of EU GDP (as opposed to 0.45 percent favored by the more moderate ones) and on referencing absolute numbers rather than percentages whenever possible.

As it was, the budget hawks struck first. On December 15, 2003, they preempted the Commission's initial proposal by sending a joint letter to its then president, Romano Prodi. Citing their own "painful consolidation efforts" and citizens who would "not understand if the EU budget were exempt from this consolidation," they bluntly informed the Commission that average expenditure for the new financial perspective should be "stabilized around current expenditure levels, and should not exceed 1.0 percent of GNI" (to which they blithely added that this limit was to include the preset CAP spending).[27] This pretty much shut down any potential talk about larger budgets. The question now was whether the six would adhere strictly to the ceiling they were trying to impose.

On CAP, matters were slightly less lopsided. Even though the 2002 agreement had the support of its main beneficiary (France) and its closest ally (Germany), other member states with significant agricultural sectors wished to preserve the subsidies. Of the newcomers, Poland was especially vocal about that, and was, in fact, interested in getting access to the subsidies at the earliest possible date. In the opposite corner were the strong advocates of drastic reductions in these payments: the net contributors to the budget who did not benefit from receipts under

---

[27] The text of the *Joint Letter from Mr Blair, the Prime Minister, and the President of France, the Chancellors of Germany and Austria, and the Prime Ministers of the Netherlands and Sweden* could be found at www.bmdf.co.uk/blairlettereubudget.pdf, but is no longer available there. It can still be retrieved through the Wayback Machine for 2005, http://web.archive.org/web/20050701000000*/www.bmdf.co.uk/blairlettereubudget.pdf, accessed January 21, 2018.

Table 6.4. *Preference Alignments in the MFF 2004–2013 Negotiations.*

	Budget			CAP		Structural Funds			Rebate		
	Keep	Increase	Reduce	Keep	Reform	Keep	Reform	Shift	Keep	Reform	Eliminate
	Finland	Belgium	Austria	Belgium	Austria	France	Netherlands	Austria	UK	Austria	Belgium
	Italy	Greece	France	Cyprus	Netherlands	Germany	Sweden	A10		Germany	Denmark
		Portugal	Germany	France	Sweden	Greece	UK			Netherlands	Finland
		Spain	Netherlands	Germany	UK	Italy				Sweden	France
		A10	Sweden	Ireland		Luxembourg					Greece
			UK	Luxembourg		Portugal					Ireland
				Poland		Spain					Italy
											Luxembourg
											Portugal
											Spain
											A10
						Share of Group in EU-25 GNI					
15%	15%	18%	64%	43%	27%	61%	25%	7%	17%	31%	52%
						Share of Group among Position Takers					
15%	15%	18%	66%	61%	39%	66%	27%	7%	17%	31%	52%

Not all member states took explicit public positions on every policy issue.
Source for GNI: see note for Table 6.3.

CAP and who were especially concerned that the distortion in the price mechanism was hurting trade and commerce.

This CAP status quo group had merely 43 percent of the EU-25 GNI, but the rather more impressive 61 percent among those that took recognizable positions on the matter. The CAP reform group had only 27 percent of the EU-25 GNI, but 39 percent among position takers. The large differences were because most other member states (30 percent) declined to participate in these debates. Even though this effectively aligned them with the dominant status quo camp, most of them silently supported the reformers but recognized that altering the CAP would be impossible before the current agreement expired in 2013. Thus, while preserving the status quo commanded an effective 73 percent supermajority, reforms had the explicit or implicit approval of a majority as well (57 percent).

This made maintenance of CAP a foregone conclusion provided the status quo group held. If, however, that group wobbled, then its massive lead could collapse instantaneously. The key member of the group was Germany, which had almost reflexively supported France but which did not benefit nearly as much from CAP. If the Germans signaled that they wished to see some change in the firm 2002 commitments, then it would be quite difficult for the rest of the group not to go along with that on the pain of risking the radical changes sought by the reformers.

The situation with structural funds was even more complex (Maruhn and Emmanouilidis, 2005). There were, roughly speaking, three positions around which member states orbited. The existing beneficiaries wished to keep the system as is, meaning they sought to preserve access to assistance for their less developed regions. This *concentration model* envisioned spending the bulk of the resources on "convergence" (that is, on any region whose GDP was below 75 percent of EU average) and only a modest amount (up to 10%) on "cohesion" (that is, specifically on countries with GNP below 90 percent of the EU average).

With France, Germany, Italy, and Spain among its members, this was a formidable group. It accounted for 61 percent of the EU-25 GNI (66 percent among position takers). Still, even here, as with CAP, Germany was the odd one out. The problem was that the strategy of maintaining sizable structural commitments conflicted with Germany's status as a net contributor. The Länder that benefited from the "concentration" of these funds were very much in favor of the strategy, but the Länder that shouldered most of Germany's payments to the EU (the net contributors to the federal budget) were very much in favor of reducing them. Since the government had a legal obligation to take all these preferences into account, this put it between a rock and hard place.

6.3 Negotiations under Predestination

This made its negotiating position somewhat mercurial, dependent as it was on both domestic developments and on the evolution of intra-EU positions on the overall budget and distributions between headings.

The accession states had been worried that if the net contributors managed to hold the overall commitments down, the existing member states would crowd out their access to the structural funds. Why? Because the French president had told them this is how business was done. When, in early 2003, thirteen CEE countries backed the US position on Iraq, Chirac blasted them for their "infantile" letters and told them they had "missed a great opportunity to shut up." When asked why he did not direct some of that vitriol to the United Kingdom, Spain, Italy, Denmark, and Portugal – all of whom had already signed a similar letter in support of the United States – he was refreshingly honest:

> When you are in the family [...] you have more rights than when you are asking to join and knocking on the door.[28]

The newcomers clearly had failed to show the "minimum of understanding" of what entering the EU entailed. Commission President Prodi, whose native Italy was among the signatories, also declared himself saddened by this disappointing failure to understand what membership in the EU meant, adding cryptically that once these newcomers grew up, they would perhaps learn that "sharing the future means sharing the future."[29]

If not being in the family meant having fewer rights, then the A10's only real hope was for there to be more resources to go around. This was partially why the A10 clamored for an increase in the budget: with money plentiful, compromises are always much easier. In this they made common cause with Spain, Portugal, and Greece, but this alignment was not to last. With the easy solution quickly receding out of reach, the A10 pressed for eligibility rules that would give priority to the "poorer poor regions" rather than the currently favored "richer poor regions" (Bachtler, Mendez, and Wishlade, 2016, p. 191). This pitted them against their erstwhile budget expansionist allies and the dominant "concentration" group. This was not a fight the A10 group, which (together with Austria) accounted for a paltry 7 percent of EU-25 GNI, had any hope of winning unless it recruited some friendly heavy hitters.

---

[28] Quoted in "Chirac lashes out at 'new Europe'." CNN, February 18, 2003. http://edition.cnn.com/2003/WORLD/europe/02/18/sprj.irq.chirac/, accessed January 22, 2018.

[29] Staunton, Denis. 2003. "Chirac's testy outburst exposes fault lines at core of EU." *The Irish Times*, February 19, 2003. www.irishtimes.com/news/chirac-s-testy-outburst-exposes-fault-lines-at-core-of-eu-1.349403, accessed January 22, 2018.

And here they had every reason to expect a helping hand from the Dutch and especially from the advocate of enlargement, the British.

The radical – the Netherlands and the United Kingdom most prominent among them – had been critical of the system of structural allocations for a long time and wanted to overhaul it in order to minimize spending and improve efficiency. This *cohesion model* envisioned deep cuts in commitments and an exclusive focus on assistance for the poorest regions in the EU, with eligibility determined by national disparities of per capita GDP. It further aimed at decentralization and re-nationalization of cohesion policies to yank control of allocations from Brussels. The A10 states were on board with cohesion, but they opposed the efficiency measures because they feared that they would weaken EU's commitment to development (which is indeed part of the reason the United Kingdom was pushing for them), and they certainly were not enamored with any overall cuts. Even if they threw in their support behind the "cohesion" states, their combined share of EU-25 GNI would be 32 percent, only a little over half that of the "concentration" group. And the trouble did not end there, for the "cohesion" group was not cohesive itself.

The Netherlands, which was too developed to benefit from any aid, was unwavering in its commitment to reform: it had sought some version of reform since 1988 and had renewed the debate back in 2000. The positions of both the United Kingdom and Sweden, on the other hand, were more ambiguous. Both had important regions that had gotten used to structural funds, so there were domestic obstacles to pursuing serious cuts and to shifting entirely to cohesion. The Swedish government dealt with this by assiduously avoiding public statements and being circumspect even in closed meetings with like-minded member states.

The UK government also tried to mute the domestic discussion – the Labour party was running regional governments as well – but was less successful in doing so. The problem was that Blair was dealing not only with recalcitrant locals and a vigorous opposition by the Conservatives but also with internal discord in his own party due to personal animosities with Chancellor of the Exchequer (finance minister) Gordon Brown. Although the Treasury took the lead in formulating the UK position, there was little danger of things getting out of hand as long as the government did not hand the Tories something to harp about that would resonate widely with the electorate. The UK rebate, wrestled from the EU as it was by Margaret Thatcher, was just perfect in that regard. One could hardly devise a better flail for thrashing Labour with than an agreement to reduce it.

6.3 Negotiations under Predestination

On the UK correction, the United Kingdom stood alone. The various deals that largely exempted first Germany and more recently Austria, the Netherlands, and Sweden had kept it afloat. But as the net contributors dealt themselves out of financing the rebate, France, Italy, and Spain assumed an even heftier load. Even worse, the arcane method for calculating the basis for the correction was about to *increase* the UK rebate after the enlargement from €4.3 billion per year on average between 1997 and 2006 to about €7.1 billion per year starting in 2007. Not only would the unfortunate troika have to pay even more of the United Kingdom's share for a policy that counted the United Kingdom among the major beneficiaries, but the newcomers would be paying as well. The new member states were so much poorer than the existing ones that enlargement was going to cause the average per capita GDP of the EU to drop by 10 percent. And yet they had to contribute €294 million to the UK rebate (5.6 percent of its cost) immediately in the first year of their accession.[30] This oddity was not peculiar to the CEE countries: only 12 percent of the UK rebate was paid for by member states wealthier than the United Kingdom (Ackrill and Kay, 2006). This was not the sort of arrangement that anyone apart from the United Kingdom could be expected to tolerate.

Despite the consensus that the UK rebate had outlived its usefulness, no coherent anti-rebate coalition materialized. The problem here was the divergent preferences of the net contributors, who commanded 31 percent of the EU GNI, and everyone else, who held 52 percent. The net contributors had been concerned with reducing the discrepancy between what they paid into the budget and what they got out of it. They were sympathetic to arguments about "fair returns" and sensitive to any changes that would worsen their net balances.[31] This made them reluctant to push for the total abolition of the UK rebate, preferring some general "correction" mechanism that would apply to anyone who met certain transparent criteria. While they fully expected that any such arrangement would duly slash the UK rebate, they also wanted some protection from the unspecified "excessive" budgetary burdens that the Fontainebleau agreement had cited as its rationale for the original grant.

No such equivocation was to be found among the rebate eliminationists, who wanted all corrections gone, pure and simple. If it proved impossible to pry the rebate from the United Kingdom, they wanted the

---

[30] "Q&A: The UK budget rebate." BBC, December 23, 2005. http://news.bbc.co.uk/2/hi/europe/4721307.stm, accessed January 22, 2018.

[31] Whether net contributions are an appropriate way to think about what constitutes a "fair return" on investing in a collective entity like the EU is far from obvious (Le Cacheux, 2005).

exceptions for the net contributors removed so that financing it would be more equitable. But if neither was in the cards, then they would much rather throw in their lot with the moderates and attempt to maximize the reduction of the UK rebate. If these groups were to coalesce around a common position, their combined weight of 83 percent of the EU GNI would be irresistible except by a veto. Whether the UK government was prepared to exercise it under such circumstances was an open question.

Given the cross-cutting cleavages that were only consistent in that they ranged a Franco–German condominium against the distinctly smaller Anglo–Dutch coalition on everything save the UK rebate, and in light of the fact that the current arrangements largely favored the continental group, it is perhaps not surprising that the only position that commanded widespread, if unenthusiastic, support was for tinkering with existing policy. Any proposals for efficiency gains through simplification of regulations and streamlining of implementation would be welcome, of course, but very little else.[32]

It was in this delicate atmosphere that the Commission boldly marched to propose a 30 percent increase in the budget, total commitments in excess of its own-resources ceiling, and an elimination of the UK rebate in favor of an entirely new correction mechanism.

A Billion Here, A Billion There...

... and pretty soon we are talking real money, as the well-known saying goes.[33]

Yet, the proposal the Commission sent to the Council and Parliament on February 26, 2004, betrayed no awareness of financial constraints. The Commission proposed to raise average annual commitments from €112 billion in Agenda 2000 to €146 billion, a 30 percent increase, while claiming that it was adhering to strict budgetary discipline because it was leaving the own-resources ceiling untouched at 1.24 percent of EU GNI.[34] This accounting wizardry was but a sleight of hand: the new commitments would average 1.26 percent of EU GNI, so only the payments (at 1.14 percent) could be construed as not violating the ceiling. But even this deliberate misinterpretation of the budget hawks'

---

[32] See Bachtler, Mendez, and Wishlade (2016, pp. 150–151) on this point.
[33] Author unknown, often misattributed to Everett Dirksen, US senator from 1951 to 1969.
[34] See Table 6.3 for the Agenda 2000 figures at 2004 prices and Table 6.5 for the Commission's February 2004 proposal. The Commission did not express the commitments as percentages of EU GNI, only the payment appropriations. This ruse, defeatable by 30 seconds in Excel, fooled no one: the Council agreement and the final Interinstitutional Agreement listed both commitments and payments as percentages.

Table 6.5. *Commission Proposal and Council Agreement, MFF 2007–2013.*

Heading	Commission (Feb 2004) EUR, bn	Council (Dec 2005) EUR, bn	Change Amount	Change % Total	Change % Heading
Sustainable Growth	477.67	379.74	−97.93	−10	−21
Competitiveness	132.76	72.12	−60.64	−6	−46
Structural	344.91	307.62	−37.29	−4	−11
Natural Resources	404.66	371.24	−33.41	−3	−8
CAP	301.07	293.11	−7.97	−1	−3
Citizenship	18.51	10.27	−8.24	−1	−45
EU as Global Partner	95.59	50.01	−45.58	−4	−48
Administration	28.62	50.30	+21.68	+2	+76
Compensations		0.80	+0.80	0	
Commitments	1,025.04	862.36	−130.34		−13
% EU GNI	1.26	1.05	−0.21		−17
Payments	928.70	819.38	−109.32		−12
% EU GNI	1.14	0.99	−0.15		−13
Own-Resources Ceiling	1.24	1.24	0.00		0

The Council figure for heading 4 includes €1.547 billion for the Emergency Aid Reserve, which was excluded in the IIA (see fn. 11).
Sources: European Commission (2004), Council of the European Union (2005), and author calculations.

letter could not really work because the payments were nowhere near the 1.0 percent target they had set.

The Commission pleaded *force majeure* on agriculture, cleaved to the wishes of the CAP status quo group, and allocated an average of €43 billion to CAP per year, an imperceptible increase of less than 1 percent over Agenda 2000.[35]

On structural funds, it pursued a combination of the concentration policy that so many existing member states liked, and the cohesion variant preferred by the A10. This was the Commission's attempt to reconcile its own vision for balanced territorial development with the imperative of satisfying the wishes of a group that represented two-thirds of the EU's income. Naturally, it blew up the budget: the average annual commitment for this heading soared to €49 billion, an increase of 45 percent over Agenda 2000.

---

[35] As the Commission put it, "With the **CAP reforms of 2003 and 2004** so fresh and with agricultural spending fixed to 2013, the framework for the period covered by the Financial Perspectives is set" (European Commission, 2004, p. 16, emphasis in original).

Having thus summarily denied the United Kingdom on the budget, on CAP, and on structural funds, the Commission then invented a whole new way to dismay the British. It devised a "generalized correction mechanism" to replace the UK rebate, the first-ever concrete proposal to alter the Fontainebleau arrangement. After noting the "dramatic shift in the UK's position compared to the other net contributors" and explaining that the mechanism would apply to all net contributors without exception, the Commission blandly noted that the resulting adjustments to payments would be modest for everyone except for the United Kingdom, for whom they would more than double.[36]

Thus, while the proposal had also completely ignored the preferences of the Netherlands and Sweden, it was at least trying to propitiate them with some palliative concessions on their contributions. No such treatment awaited the United Kingdom, which was expected to swallow its bitter pill *and* pay a pretty penny for it. Even the most levelheaded government would be unnerved by something like this. And Blair's Labour was anything but levelheaded.

Chèque britannique, "non-negotiable"

The British public was apoplectic about Blair's handling of the Iraq crisis, as polls revealed in early 2003. Fully 77 percent opposed Britain joining an American-led military action against Iraq if this did not have UN approval. And the number of people who did not like how Blair was handling the crisis personally was also on the rise: 62 percent in January, a 32 percent increase over the 47 percent who thought so in October 2002.[37] By itself, this was no reason for the prime minister

---

[36] The mechanism would be activated as soon as the net contribution of a member state exceeded 0.35 percent of their national GDP. It would increase the United Kingdom's net contributions from 0.25 percent of its GDP to 0.51 percent. This was actually in line with what others had been paying under the old system: 0.56 percent for the Netherlands, 0.54 percent for Germany, 0.41 percent for Italy, and 0.37 percent for France (Maruhn and Emmanouilidis, 2005, p. 5). See also "Thatcher's rebate haunts EU's 2007–2013 budget plans." *EurActiv*, July 15, 2004. www.euractiv.com/section/eu-priorities-2020/news/thatcher-s-rebate-haunts-eu-s-2007-2013-budget-plans/, accessed January 31, 2018.

[37] If the invasion were sanctioned by the UN, then 61 percent supported Britain joining the United States. See "Blair losing public support on Iraq." *Ipsos MORI*, January 20, 2003. www.ipsos.com/ipsos-mori/en-uk/blair-losing-public-support-iraq, accessed January 22, 2018. When it appeared that a UN resolution might actually happen, the public became less anti-war, although even then most people opposed the use of force prior to the invasion (Strong, 2017). Of course, the public did not know that Blair had already approved the invasion plans and that he had given up on the UN inspections. See the declassified "Briefing to Prime Minister" on January 15, 2003. www.iraqinquiry.org.uk/media/236679/2003-01-15-minute-ma-dcjo-ops-to-ma-cjo-briefing-to-prime-minister.pdf, accessed with the Wayback Machine on

6.3 Negotiations under Predestination

to worry. Since the Conservatives were even more warlike than the government, public opposition to the war was unlikely to result in voters replacing Labour with the Tories.[38] Although the Conservatives could not capitalize on the unpopularity of the war, they were looking for an opportunity to pounce on a weakened opponent. Blair's approval levels had declined from over 70 percent in 1997 to about 30 percent in 2004, and the government's had sunk from 55 percent to 27 percent.[39] Crime and the economy were perennial favorites in that regard, but there was also another promising development that could be weaponized: the rise of Euroscepticism.

In 1991, the majority of the British public (57 percent) had supported the United Kingdom's membership in the EU. By 2004, this number had taken a nosedive: only 28 percent did so.[40] The Tories latched onto this discontent and became increasingly hostile to Blair's pro-EU policies (Baker and Sherrington, 2005, p. 308).

There was a certain irony in this reversal: it was Conservative governments that had pursued entry to the European Communities since the 1950s until finally managing to obtain it in 1973, and it was the Labour opposition that had consistently come out against it, most famously in its 2-1 vote to leave the Communities in 1975.[41] In the early 1980s, Labour began to support European integration but only allowed itself to be outmaneuvered on its previous stance when Margaret Thatcher negotiated the wildly popular (in the United Kingdom) rebate in 1984. Although the Iron Lady became the face of Euroscepticism, even she had to tread lightly in the end. When she returned from the failed Rome Summit in October 1990, she gave a speech in the House of Commons lambasting then Commission President Jacques Delors for suggesting that he wished the European Parliament to be the democratic body of the Community, and infamously roaring "No! No! No!" Foreign Secretary Geoffrey Howe, the last remaining member of her original

---

[38] January 22, 2018. Once the war began, the public quickly soured on it and by 2004 it was deeply antagonistic to the government over it.
Of the net average views expressed in parliamentary speeches between January 2002 and March 2003, 33 percent of Conservatives were pro-war, 28 percent of Labour were anti-war, and 61 percent of the Liberal Democrats were anti-war (Strong, 2017). Blair brought to heel the dissenting backbenchers of his party by threatening to resign if they failed to vote with him.

[39] Public opinion data from Ipsos MORI (www.ipsos-mori.com/researchpublications/researcharchive/88/Political-Monitor-Satisfaction-Ratings-1997Present.aspx, accessed December 2016).

[40] Data from the Interactive Eurobarometer (http://ec.europa.eu/COMMFrontOffice/PublicOpinion/index.cfm/Chart/index, accessed September 2016).

[41] "On this Day, 1950–2005, April 6. 1975: Labour votes to leave the EEC." BBC, April 6, 1975. http://news.bbc.co.uk/onthisday/hi/dates/stories/april/26/newsid_2503000/2503155.stm, accessed January 22, 2018.

1979 cabinet, characterized her attitude as a "tragedy" that was "running increasingly serious risks for the future of our nation."[42] He resigned two days later, widening the split in the Conservative party, and contributing to Thatcher's loss of the party leadership – and thus the premiership – two weeks later. The time was not yet ripe for extreme Euroscepticism, not even in the United Kingdom.

As the 1990s progressed, Labour became more staunchly pro-European, and the Conservatives remained split despite their historic electoral loss in 1997. When the dismal performance at the polls was repeated in 2001, however, the new party leader Ian Duncan Smith, whose Euroscepticism had been partially responsible for the victory in the leadership struggle with William Hague, marked a decisive shift of the party toward being consistently lukewarm on Europe.[43] They could not match the vehemence of the explicitly anti-European United Kingdom Independence Party (UKIP) – which was founded in 1993 to advocate a total withdrawal from the EU and which received 16 percent of the votes and twelve seats in the European Parliament election of 2004 – but for now it did not seem like they had to. They merely had to ride the wave of popular Euroscepticism while being resolutely amnesiac about the party's role in getting Britain integrated into the EU as much as it had. For this, the original Eurosceptic's greatest anti-EU achievement – the UK rebate – was absolutely perfect. Perfect, that is, if someone gave them the opportunity to bring it up.

That someone proved to be none other than Commission President Prodi. Undeterred by ominous admonitions about the unrealistic size of the intended budget, he unveiled the official Commission proposal on July 14, 2004, and it was nearly identical to the first.[44] It reduced slightly the total commitments by 3 percent, to €993 billion. Neither CAP, which remained unchanged, nor the structural funds, which were reduced by only 2 percent, were materially affected. The sole minor concession was to the budget hawks: the total commitments were now reported as a percentage of EU GNI, and, at 1.20 percent,

---

[42] "Democracy Live. 30 October 1990: 'No! No! No!'" BBC, October 30, 1990. http://news.bbc.co.uk/democracylive/hi/historic_moments/newsid_8189000/8189350.stm, accessed January 22, 2018.

[43] Lee (2011) emphasizes the evolving ideologies of the British parties and their changing approaches toward European integration and the UK rebate.

[44] The finance ministers of Germany and the United Kingdom had already clarified that expenditures had to be limited to 1 percent GNI (Osborn, Andrew. "Brown takes on Prodi in EU budget row." *The Guardian*, January 20, 2004. www.theguardian.com/politics/2004/jan/21/uk.eu, accessed January 22, 2018).

they were below the own-resources ceiling.[45] Whatever fleeting positive effect this concession might have had was immediately negated by Prodi serenely telling the budget hawks that their calls to reduce spending were "deeply flawed."[46] Although the French, as usual, were fully on board with anything that would cancel the hated "cheque Britannique," the German ambassador to the EU rejected the proposal as "very lopsided," asserted that it could not even be the "basis for negotiation," and said that Germany had already asked for "alternative proposals so we can negotiate."[47] But in terms of headline-grabbing, controversy-generating potential, all this paled in comparison to the Commission sticking to its original idea to eliminate the UK rebate.

The British press exploded. Instead of quoting the endless stream of outrage that poured out of the British press about the EU trying to lay its grubby hands on the cherished talisman, it is perhaps best to let Blair (2011, pp. 527–530) speak about his impression on the matter:

I had two problems over the rebate... The first was the near-hysterical—sorry, correct that—truly hysterical behaviour of the Eurosceptic media. Papers with a combined daily circulation of around eight million—a situation unique in Europe in terms of pervasion—were totally, wildly and irredeemably hostile to Europe, misrepresented what Europe was doing and generally regarded it as a zero-sum game: anything that pleased Brussels was bad for Britain. [...] Also, by this time the British rebate had assumed a mythical, almost cult status in the 2005 budget negotiation. To challenge it was like introducing Darwin to an ardent creationist. [...] To question it was to betray the nation.

Whatever Blair's opinion on the matter – and it was not pretty (he derided it as an "absurdly out of date delusion") – the government's defense mechanism went into high gear. The European Commissioners from the United Kingdom, who had valiantly fought and lost the battle with Prodi, called the proposal "manifestly unfair." British diplomats disparaged the plans as "ludicrous" and declared the rebate

---

[45] The cuts were mostly in Citizenship (heading 3) and EU as a Global Partner (heading 4), although spending on Administration (heading 5) doubled. Figures for this proposal from European Commission (2014, table 6.2, p. 84). The Commission must have updated its GNI estimates from the February report because if one were to use those numbers, the total commitments would be at 1.22 percent. Even the number reported in the table was rounded down from 1.205 percent.

[46] Black, Ian. 2004. "Battle erupts as Prodi tries to axe Britain's rebate." *The Guardian*, July 14, 2004. www.theguardian.com/politics/2004/jul/15/uk.eu, accessed January 22, 2018.

[47] Carter, Richard. "EU budget talks 'to be more difficult' than Constitution negotiations." *EUobserver*, June 21, 2004. https://euobserver.com/economic/16688, accessed on January 22, 2018.

"non-negotiable."⁴⁸ The government insisted that the rebate was "fully justified," "not on the table," and that it would be "fully protected."⁴⁹ The prime minister's rearguard action was, however, undermined by the fifth column headed by his own chancellor of the exchequer. Stories about Gordon Brown manning the barricades for a last stand while Blair was being bamboozled by Brussels proliferated, not the least because the Treasury encouraged them to.⁵⁰ In fact, Brown was the second of the "two problems over the rebate" that Blair (2011, p. 529) was having.

With the Treasury implying that Downing Street was lying, the opposition dismissed the government's statements as ritual denunciations and charged Blair with scheming to give away the farm. The Conservatives painted gloomy pictures of huge tax hikes under Labour to pay for lazy bureaucrats in Brussels, and of waves of EU regulations sweeping away all British freedoms. And of course, they brandished the talisman with vigor:

Why on earth should we contemplate for a single second allowing the commission to get rid of a rebate for which we fought so hard?⁵¹

Lashed from without and undermined from within, Blair vowed to veto the proposal over its reduction of the UK rebate (Laffan and Lindner, 2014). The problem was ... he did not really want to.

"When it comes to money, you have no friends"

The firestorm that the Commission had let loose in Britain made the already tense negotiations nearly impossible. The budget would now be harder to negotiate than the EU constitution, whose fate was also in peril.⁵² The government's stance appeared to echo Blair's performance in the 1999 row during the Berlin summit, when he had similarly

---

⁴⁸ Carter, Richard. "UK rebate 'non-negotiable' insists ambassador." *EUobserver*, October 13, 2004. https://euobserver.com/economic/17514, accessed January 22, 2018.
⁴⁹ Black, Ian. "Blair faces threat to £2bn EU rebate." *The Guardian*, July 8, 2004. www.theguardian.com/politics/2004/jul/08/uk.eu1, accessed January 22, 2018. Castle, Stephen. "Prodi threatens to cut Britain's EU rebate." *The Independent*, July 1, 2004. www.independent.co.uk/news/world/europe/prodi-threatens-to-cut-britains-eu-rebate-45499.html, accessed January 22, 2018.
⁵⁰ Gow, David. "Brown fights to save Britain's EU rebate." *The Guardian*, November 15, 2004. www.theguardian.com/business/2004/nov/16/politics.eu, accessed January 22, 2018. Brown (2005, p. 14) insisted that it was purely for unselfish reasons and that he was trying to avoid further decline in the party's popularity.
⁵¹ Oliver Letwin, the shadow chancellor, quoted in "Battle erupts as Prodi tries to axe Britain's rebate."
⁵² "EU budget talks 'to be more difficult' than Constitution negotiations." The "well-placed" German diplomat, the source for the title of this section, was quoted in this article.

6.3 Negotiations under Predestination

declared the UK rebate "utterly non-negotiable" and had pledged to accept "not a euro less."[53] He had prevailed, but back then the United Kingdom had been on the sidelines of EU policymaking, its strategy mostly reactive to initiatives from Brussels. Under Blair's leadership, however, the United Kingdom had assumed a more proactive position, especially on the Eastern enlargement. The prime minister himself had gained years of experience in European affairs and had evolved a much more pro-EU vision. Blair (2011, p. 527) summarized it rather succinctly:

In a world of new emerging powers, Britain needed Europe in order to exert influence and advance its interests. It wasn't complicated.

He believed that outside the EU, Britain was no longer an important world player, and that for all the talk of its "special relationship" with the United States, it was merely a junior partner, whose value to Washington was directly proportional to the degree of influence it had in Brussels. Instead of freeing Britain to boldly go a separate Anglo-Saxon way with the Americans, getting itself marginalized in the EU would diminish its influence everywhere. Being intransigent on the UK rebate was not the best strategy to make friends and influence people on the continent. Narrow nationalist concerns had to give way to a modern version of *realpolitik* (Chadwick and Heffernan, 2003).

An unbending commitment to the rebate also threatened vital economic and geopolitical interests of the United Kingdom. Given the dominance of the "concentration" countries, if the UK correction were to stay, "cohesion" policies would inevitably suffer, impeding the development of the new member states. This undermined the entire rationale for supporting the Eastern enlargement in the first place. The British government had hoped that the entry of the CEE countries would increase the economic benefits of its own membership in the EU, improve EU competitiveness, and help it recover some of its international influence (Bulmer, 2008; Gowland, Turner, and Wright, 2010). This was why it had been one of the few consistent strong promoters of admitting these states to the EU (Nugent and Mather, 2006; Schimmelfennig, 2001, 2003; Schneider, 2009). It simply would not do to stab the newcomers in the back and then twist the knife by making them contribute to the rebate. It was not fair.

---

[53] Walker, Martin and Ian Traynor. "Blair fights for 'not a euro less' in rebate." *The Guardian*, March 26, 1999. www.theguardian.com/world/1999/mar/26/tonyblair, accessed January 22, 2018.

Fair play, or at least the appearance of it, was, in fact, of some importance. The United Kingdom was about to assume the Council presidency in June 2005, making Blair the president of the Council. Whomever holds the presidency is supposed to help overcome deadlocks, foster compromise among the member states, and generally work on behalf of the EU (Tallberg, 2006). This could sometimes put presidents – who headed their own national governments – in an awkward position: They would sometimes have to prioritize the interests of the EU over their own national concerns and, in what could be an even more delicate position, have to recuse themselves when EU interests aligned uncomfortably close with national benefits (Laffan, 2000).[54] Blair seems to have expected to use the UK presidency to get France and Germany to agree to some reform on CAP in exchange for concessions on the rebate, but he also had to work under the immense weight of expectations to generate a compromise.

When all was said and done, the opposition was right to suspect that Blair was going to pursue a deal that neither they nor the majority of the British public would approve of. If anything, they might not have been suspicious enough: only recently did it come to light that he had apparently seriously considered quitting as prime minister in 2004 in order to run for EU's top job, the president of the European Commission.[55] But with the government doubling down on "we shall never surrender" on the rebate, there was not much the Conservatives could do but denounce the Labour government non-specifically for intending to genuflect to the next *diktat* from Brussels:

These are all words. The Commission's proposals are still on the table; nothing seems to have been achieved. Recently, there have been worrying reports that the Government has secured a deal with European leaders to postpone negotiations on the rebate until after the general election. What has the Government got to hide? It seems to me that the only possible reason for putting it off until after the election is that the Government is preparing for yet another possible surrender of British interests in Europe. In the unhappy event of Labour winning the election,

---

[54] This had already landed Jan Peter Balkenende, the prime minister of the Netherlands, in hot water during the Dutch presidency (July–December 2004): under the Commission's generalized correction mechanism, on whose behalf he was supposed to engineer an agreement, the Netherlands was going to make out like a bandit. Balkenende worked very hard to let the Dutch presidency expire without much action on that front, so that he could go back to full-throated support of the idea unencumbered by the ethical restrictions imposed by the presidency.

[55] Hope, Christopher. "Tony Blair 'considered quitting as Prime Minister in 2004 to stand for European president.'" *The Telegraph*, September 29, 2016. www.telegraph.co.uk/news/2016/09/29/tony-blair-considered-quitting-as-prime-minister-to-join-the-eur/, accessed January 23, 2018.

Britain will be landed with a Bill, not only for the black hole in the public finances but also potentially, and I certainly hope not, for the loss of the rebate.[56]

Any hint of a compromise on the rebate would quickly transform these unfounded accusations into an electoral indictment. Brown was also frantic that anything that smacked of surrender on the rebate would cost Labour the coming general elections (and thwart his plans for the premiership).

There was just no way that Blair would negotiate in good faith before May 2005. The only viable option here was blame avoidance through a strategic delay until after the British public had gone to the polls. Spending the rest of the year reassuring this public that there would be no deal on the EU budget that did not protect the rebate was the easy part. Getting the other EU member states to cooperate with this delay, on the other hand, looked more challenging. After all, they had to agree to play along for nearly half a year. And yet, in December 2004 this is exactly what they did. Why?

The (Almost) Hidden, (Mostly) Cooperative Delay

Officially, the EU was postponing negotiations until May 2005 in order "to concentrate on reforming the euro's growth and stability pact and on labour market reforms." Unofficially, as an anonymous Commission official helpfully explained, "we cannot touch the budget negotiations for the moment because of a sensitivity in one well known country."[57]

That country was not Luxembourg. In fact, its prime minister, Jean-Claude Juncker, was about to become president of the Council in January 2005. He was a shrewd operator. Pragmatic and deeply steeped in European politics, he had developed a reputation that gave him clout belied by the small size of his home country. And he favored reform. Blair could not have had much cause for optimism when the honest broker in the negotiations was going to be someone who liked to refer

---

[56] Tory spokesman Richard Spring, quoted in Joe Churcher and Jane Kirby. "Government 'set to surrender' on EU rebate." *Press Association*, March 7, 2005. This commentary came while Chancellor Brown was telling the Commons that the rebate was "fully justified" and financial secretary to the Treasury, Stephen Timms, was vowing that the rebate was "not up for negotiations" and asserting that no proposals had been made to change the method for calculating it. This was all true, of course. At this point, the deafening silence from all other member states had been going on for three months.

[57] Watt, Nicholas. "Blair wins deal to hold EU rebate talks after election." *The Guardian*, January 20, 2005. www.theguardian.com/politics/2005/jan/21/uk.eu, accessed January 23, 2018.

to the 1984 Fontainebleau summit, where the foundational myth of the UK rebate was forged, as "Fontainebluff."[58]

Nor could Blair expect cooperation from France or Germany. Both Chirac and Schröder were livid about the United Kingdom's participation in the Iraq invasion; the German for principled reasons and the French for anti-American ones. France had a huge stake in preserving the CAP – the prime target for any deal Blair would want to make on the rebate – and Germany was adamant about keeping expenditures down while backing the French on CAP, making rebate reform an absolute necessity. Both were also personally offended when Blair vetoed their choice for president of the Commission, the Belgian prime minister Guy Verhofstadt, in the summer of 2004 on the grounds that he was an arch federalist.[59] The problem here was not merely that Verhofstadt had solid Franco–German support, but that his appointment as president of the Commission had apparently been the quid pro quo so that those two countries would agree to meet Blair's demands on the EU constitution, shelving the UK rebate question until the following year.[60] Although this was not, as Blair (2011, p. 531) claimed, "the first time that the twin-engine motor of Europe had been stalled in respect of such a big issue" (the United Kingdom had torpedoed another Belgian bid for the presidency in 1994, and on the same grounds), he was probably right that his relationship with Schröder "never recovered."[61] And while one might wonder about his assessment that Chirac had taken this "more philosophically," if there was a straw that would break the camel's back, Blair had piled on a few lead pipes.[62]

---

[58] See, for instance, "Le Premier ministre Jean-Claude Juncker au CEPS (Center for European Policy Studies) à Bruxelles." February 22, 2005. https://gouvernement.lu/fr/actualites/toutes_actualites/discours/2005/02-fevrier/23-juncker-ceps.html, accessed January 23, 2018. That was not the only occasion.

[59] Blair had not been alone in this worry; there had been skepticism about Verhofstadt from the start. Michael White. "Blair in a quandary over Prodi's successor." *The Guardian*, May 31, 2004. www.theguardian.com/uk/2004/jun/01/eu.politics, accessed January 23, 2018.

[60] Evans-Pritchard, Ambros. "Europe fails to breach Blair's red lines." *The Telegraph*, June 17, 2004. www.telegraph.co.uk/news/worldnews/europe/1464774/Europe-fails-to-breach-Blairs-red-lines.html, accessed January 23, 2018.

[61] Brown, Colin and Andrew Marshall. "Major veto wrecks the summit: Britain blocks Dehaene as successor to Delors – Prime Minister 'unperturbed about the arithmetic of eleven to one.'" *The Independent*, June 25, 1994. www.independent.co.uk/news/major-veto-wrecks-the-summit-britain-blocks-dehaene-as-successor-to-delors-prime-minister-1425191.html, accessed January 23, 2018.

[62] This story, too, has an interesting postscript. Blair (2011, p. 531) accords a lot of credit to himself for organizing the resistance against Verhofstadt and getting José Manuel Barroso, who he opined was clearly the better choice if one "wanted Europe to reform in a non-federalist direction," appointed instead. In 2012, Barroso called for the EU to evolve into a "federation of nation-states" because the member states could

6.3 Negotiations under Predestination 183

Still, aside from outbursts by the understandably peeved Verhofstadt and irritating indiscretions by Blair's personal choice for the man who was chosen instead (José Manuel Barroso), everyone remained mum about the rebate.[63] All experienced policymakers and diplomats knew that the Conservatives were holding Blair's feet to the fire, and that the pressure to posture on the rebate would only ease after the general election. They also understood that Blair was prepared to strike a deal especially if it could be linked to some sort of promise to reform the CAP.[64] If they pushed too hard, too fast, or too openly, they might derail Labour's chances of success (as Brown feared they would) and actually contribute to the election of a government that would be implacable on the rebate, having, in effect, campaigned on the promise to keep it (Maruhn and Emmanouilidis, 2005, p. 6). The rational response was to play along with Blair's dilatory tactics. This was no indicator that they intended to fold. It was hidden cooperation to help out the government of a fellow member state signal responsiveness to its voters by avoiding blame before elections.

Of course, informal and voluntary cooperation also meant that occasionally someone might break ranks and embarrass the UK government prematurely. Commissioner Barroso had done that by suggesting that Britain was perhaps wealthy enough to be flexible although he was quick to offer praise for its "political realism."[65] Much more problematic was Chirac's (perhaps not entirely unpremeditated) outburst at a press conference on March 24 after Blair had already left following the conclusion of the EU summit in Brussels. The French president flatly asserted that the "British cheque" could "no longer be justified" and that it was only possible to "achieve a reasonable budgetary balance" if the debate were to reopen.[66]

This was no temper tantrum. Chirac had recently received very bad news: the "No" campaign on the upcoming French referendum on the

---

no longer "effectively steer the course of events." ("EU Commission chief Barroso calls for 'federation'." BBC, September 12, 2012. www.bbc.com/news/world-europe-19568781, accessed January 23, 2018).

[63] "Belgium says Britain's EU rebate 'no longer justifiable.'" *BBC Monitoring Europe*. October 13, 2004; Watt, Nicholas. "EU president supports cut in UK rebate." *The Guardian*, March 20, 2005. www.theguardian.com/politics/2005/mar/21/uk.eu, accessed January 31, 2018.

[64] "UK under pressure to share part of the EU rebate." *Financial Times*, March 11, 2005; "Blair wins deal to hold EU rebate talks after election."; "Financial Perspective 2007-2013." *EurActiv*, October 5, 2004.

[65] "EU president supports cut in UK rebate."

[66] "Blair battles French over bid to cut £3bn EU rebate." *The Scotsman*, March 24, 2005. www.scotsman.com/news/politics/blair-battles-french-over-bid-to-cut-163-3bn-eu-rebate-1-740830, accessed January 23, 2018.

EU constitution had taken the lead in the polls for the first time. The government was pushing back with tales of British-style "ultraliberalism" threatening Europe as much as communism had and was trying to appease its discontented citizens by signaling that it was responsive to their national concerns.[67] Since no deal on the budget was to be expected before the July summit – so after the May 29 referendum – bullying the British about the rebate and digging in on protecting the CAP were the next best thing. It was position taking *par excellence*, and it was deliberately public and blunt.

This broke the agreement that Blair had with Juncker to keep the lid on the rebate issue until after the election. But it was also an immediate and personal betrayal: Blair had just made concessions on economic liberalization to help Chirac win the referendum, and the French officials had "dropped heavy hints" that his help would be repaid with support on the rebate negotiations. After all, "This [was] the way Europe [had] worked for the last 50 years," as a French diplomat put it.[68] The confidence in this reciprocal assistance was probably what had led UK Foreign Secretary Jack Straw to say that he would support the exercise of Britain's "absolute veto" if that was necessary to protect the rebate.[69] Hidden cooperation could only hold together while no major government discovered an overriding domestic incentive to defect.

The UK reaction was swift and fierce. Blair retracted his help by telling the Commons that France should imitate the British model for labor markets and reform its creaking economy and out-of-date "social model."[70] British officials produced a four-page document outlining why the rebate had to be protected at all costs. The government indignantly insisted that it was still fully justified, adding for good measure that even when it was factored in, Britain was paying two and a half times as much as France.[71] And the Tories duly trotted out the sacred myth:

---

[67] Randall, Colin. "A nation of 'les miserables' threatens the EU vision." *The Telegraph*, March 24, 2005. www.telegraph.co.uk/news/worldnews/europe/1486368/A-nation-of-les-miserables-threatens-the-EU-vision.html, accessed January 23, 2018.

[68] Rennie, David and Toby Helm. "Blair under pressure to help Chirac win constitution vote." *The Telegraph*, March 23, 2005. www.telegraph.co.uk/news/worldnews/europe/1486274/Blair-under-pressure-to-help-Chirac-win-constitution-vote.html, accessed January 31, 2018.

[69] Rennie, David and Toby Helm. "Chirac betrays Blair on Britain's rebate." *The Telegraph*, March 24, 2005. www.telegraph.co.uk/news/worldnews/europe/1486370/Chirac-betrays-Blair-on-Britains-rebate.html, accessed January 31, 2018.

[70] Rennie, David and Toby Helm. "Blair attack on 'out-of-date' Chirac." *The Telegraph*, March 25, 2005. www.telegraph.co.uk/news/worldnews/europe/france/1486443/Blair-attack-on-out-of-date-Chirac.html, accessed January 23, 2018.

[71] "Chirac betrays Blair on Britain's rebate."

6.3 Negotiations under Predestination 185

The rebate was won by a Conservative government and is absolutely crucial to the UK. Given Labour's record of surrender in EU negotiations, we simply do not trust this Government to keep it.[72]

Amid this furor, the Germans remained conspicuously calm, not so much because of stoicism but because Schröder was paralyzed by the contradictions in the national position. The main thrust of the German policy was unambiguous: as the largest net contributor it sought to keep spending down as much as possible.[73] Beyond that generality, the specifics were rather murky. The 2002 deal with France meant that for the foreseeable future, no reductions in CAP would be forthcoming to alleviate the pressure on the budget. This meant cutting the structural funds, and here the Länder that benefitted from them were quite opposed. Among these was Nordrhein-Westfalen (NRW), Germany's most populous state, and a major recipient of transfers of European Structural and Investment Funds (ESIFs).[74] It was having serious economic problems and unemployment was high. These were not good things to have anytime, but 2005 was an election year, and the voters were going to express their feelings about the government on May 22.

The SPD, which was the senior partner in the ruling coalition with the Greens, was in electoral distress and the polls did not look good.[75] Its early lead had evaporated, and now it was trailing both the CDU and the liberal-conservative Freie Demokratische Partei (FDP). The NRW elections were something of a bellwether for the general disposition of German voters, but Schröder had more immediate reasons to worry. If the CDU prevailed in the state election, the SPD would lose its majority in the Bundestag. The only way for the chancellor to prevent the CDU from exercising its effective majority there would be to engineer a vote of no confidence and trigger federal elections in the hope of restoring SPD's dominance. These were not appetizing options, so Schröder muted the talk of ESIF cuts and mostly gestured to the wealthier Länder, where the opposition was polling well, that Germany's net contributions would

---

[72] Graham Brady, the shadow Europe minister of the conservative opposition, quoted in "Chirac betrays Blair on Britain's rebate."
[73] Afhueppe, Sven, Frank Dohmen, and Konstantin von Hammerstein. "Germany is tired of footing the European bill." *Spiegel Online*, March 26, 2005. www.spiegel.de/international/spiegel/eu-budget-conflict-germany-is-tired-of-footing-the-european-bill-a-348546.html, accessed January 26, 2018.
[74] "Germany's EU aid plan risks rift with France." *Financial Times*, March 4, 2005.
[75] The SPD–Green coalition had already lost the state elections in Schleswig-Holstein on February 20. Their majority in the regional parliament (Landtag) collapsed and their attempt to form a government failed on March 17. This forced them to enter negotiations with the CDU, and they worked out a compromise that saw CDU's Peter Harry Carstensen become prime minister of the state.

not go up. Beyond that, any deal that would keep the budget within reasonable bounds would depend on a compromise over the rebate. Germany had no interest in poking the British before their elections.[76]

With everyone else staying silent, Blair could (and did) dismiss Chirac's inflammatory remarks as the ravings of someone who just "had to come away from the European Council assuring the French people he is still the big man of Europe."[77] On May 5, the British electorate went to the polls and delivered the third consecutive victory for Labour. The Tories' stance on Iraq had neutralized them on what potentially could have been the decisive issue, and Blair's tactics on the EU had kept the rebate from becoming a slogan for the opposition. The Tories had to contend themselves with running on health, crime, and immigration. Even then, Labour was frazzled: it had lost 58 seats in the Commons compared to the previous election, and although this still afforded it a comfortable margin in parliament, its popular vote of 35.2 percent was the lowest of any majority government in UK electoral history. The Conservatives had won the popular vote in England and were nipping at Labour's heels nationally.

Blair was now free to bargain with the UK rebate, but the electoral message was also clear: whatever it was that he got, it could not play into the hands of the Eurosceptics. Brown seemed to think that any concession would be interpreted as abject surrender and dug in his heels on protecting the rebate at any cost. Blair, on the other hand, had some reason to hope for a decent deal: In late May and early June, the ground shifted under the pro-EU forces, particularly for France and Germany.

The first to stumble was Chancellor Schröder. On May 22, his SPD suffered its largest electoral defeat in more than half a century.[78] The victorious CDU formed a coalition with the FDP and could now block

---

[76] Neither did the other major governments. Spain's Socialist government, which had won the elections in March 2004, was very supportive of the EU generally and the structural transfers specifically. As the largest net beneficiary of the budget, it did not have much clout in the negotiations. Barroso's departure as prime minister of Portugal to become Commission president in July 2004 had caused some political instability, but in February 2005 the Socialists won in a landslide and all members of the assembly were renewed. From March that year, Portugal had a Socialist prime minister, and the country's EU preferences closely aligned with Spain's. Italy's Berlusconi, on the other hand, was confronted with a major crisis in April 2005, when Prodi's coalition won the regional elections in all but two regions. Although Berlusconi made some noises about threatening to veto any EU budget deal that did not include funds for Italy's southern regions, his priority was to survive domestically. He did not: Prodi defeated him (barely) in the general elections in April 2006.
[77] Quoted in "Blair attack on 'out-of-date' Chirac."
[78] "NRW-Wahl: SPD Abgewählt, CDU Triumphiert." *Spiegel Online*, May 22, 2005. www.spiegel.de/politik/deutschland/nrw-wahl-spd-abgewaehlt-cdu-triumphiert-a-357071.html, accessed January 31, 2018.

6.3 Negotiations under Predestination

any policy initiative of the government in the Bundestag. Predictably, Schröder called for a vote of confidence and then worked strenuously on losing it in order to force dissolution of the Bundestag and an early election. He managed to get the "No" vote on July 1, and although it took several weeks for the president to dissolve the Bundestag and for the Constitutional Court to reject challenges that the dissolution was invalid (because the Chancellor had lost the vote on purpose), the early general elections were set, as originally intended, for September 18. For their part, CDU/CSU nominated Angela Merkel for chancellor and entered the campaign with a massive lead in the opinion polls.

With a tough reelection campaign now looming in the fall, Schröder could not afford to antagonize the wealthier Länder, where the CDU/CSU was strong. The German line hardened perceptibly: the 1 percent ceiling for total commitments became "non-negotiable," throwing everything from a budget deal to the fate of the +2 accession countries into doubt. Juncker reflected gloomily that his presidency would "end badly."[79]

The next to get blindsided was President Chirac. On May 29, the French electorate delivered the first, and fatal, blow to the European constitution by rejecting it at the referendum. It did not matter that ten states had already approved it: Spain, in a referendum on February 20, and the others, Germany included, through the safer legislative action. With one of the founding member states refusing to ratify it, there was little chance of the constitutional project moving forward. When the Dutch voted "No" in their own referendum on June 1, it was all over.

With his approval ratings in the gutter, Chirac could scarcely afford any deal that would look to the voters like France giving away its benefits for the sake of the newcomers. It was 2002 all over again, and this time it was no longer the prospect of defeat at the polls; it was the reality. Even if he wished to compromise somehow on the CAP (and he did not), Chirac could not do so under the circumstances.[80] In fact, since many French citizens viewed the EU Constitution as a Trojan horse for economic liberalism, its rejection could be interpreted as a repudiation of the very policies that Britain was advocating. This in itself was enough to take a hard line with Blair, even at the cost of derailing the summit.[81]

---

[79] "E.U. budget deal unlikely as Germany refuses to pay more: Juncker." *Deutsche Press Agentur*, May 25, 2005; Mangasarian, Leon. "German vote hinders E.U. – May slow enlargement." *Deutsche Presse-Agentur*, May 26, 2005.

[80] Parker, George. "Blair and Chirac arm themselves for battle of Brussels." *Financial Times*, June 1, 2005. www.ft.com/content/ffdf2c12-d2c0-11d9-bead-00000e2511c8, accessed January 24, 2018.

[81] "Battling Blair takes fight to Chirac." *Sunday Times*. June 19, 2005.

Into the Maelstrom: The Luxembourg Presidency

It was amid these uncertain and troubled times that the Luxembourg presidency had to find a compromise. Juncker had tried really hard. The proposal from June 2 had hacked at the Commission's trillion euro budget until it had pared it down to €875 billion in commitments, or 1.056 percent of the EU GNI. This was no mean achievement: while it was not the 1 percent (€815 billion) demanded by the budget hawks, it was certainly within striking distance, and events would soon make it the focal point for all member states. The cuts had come from the cohesion funds, leaving CAP untouched. The UK rebate would be frozen at €4.7 billion, and the difference would give the Netherlands €1 billion in relief, while also reducing the contributions of Germany and Sweden. If the Germans would agree to raise the ceiling a bit and if the British would agree to revise the rebate, then the Dutch could get their billion and perhaps relent in their opposition to the CAP and the allocation of structural funds. The Netherlands was a net contributor, and its citizens had just delivered an unambiguous verdict about the current state of affairs. The Dutch government's demand for relief was persuasive (and supported by Britain). It was not clear what the French were being asked to give up.

The constitutional calamity suddenly made it imperative to achieve a resolution to the budget impasse, but the Franco–German motor was sputtering. Chirac's approval ratings plummeted and Schröder was already in a fight for his political life. The two met – *The Times of London* sneered that the meeting was between a lame duck and a dead duck – and tried to pretend there was still hope.[82] They insisted that the remaining countries should proceed with their national votes even though this was highly unlikely.[83] What they really needed was to signal that the "No" votes had not derailed the EU altogether; that the Eurosceptics were wrong about the unwieldy bureaucracy that was all talk and little to show for it; that action for the common good was still possible. What they needed was to show that the EU was working. The agreement on its budget at the coming Council summit suddenly acquired fresh urgency.[84]

The German position moderated again, with Schröder indicating that he was ready to consider increasing contributions if there was a way

---

[82] "Lame Duck meets Dead Duck." The Times (London), June 4, 2005.
[83] Julien, Cyril. "German and French leaders meet to revive faltering ties." *Agence France-Presse*, June 4, 2005.
[84] "Crucial week for EU's long-term budget plans." *Euractiv*, June 6, 2005. www.euractiv.com/section/future-eu/news/crucial-week-for-eu-s-long-term-budget-plans/, accessed January 23, 2018.

6.3 Negotiations under Predestination

to also increase Germany's receipts. There was a limit to how far he could go – the fiscal conservatives were leading in the polls and watching him very closely – but for the first time Germany parted ways with the budget hawks and moved closer to the Luxembourg position. Although Chirac denied that any changes to agricultural policy were on the table, he agreed that they had to offer answers to the rattled publics. The implication was that there might be a solution to the budgetary deadlock if Blair dropped the demand for reforming the CAP.[85] The pressure on Blair to agree to the necessary reductions in the UK rebate escalated.[86] Chirac demanded a "gesture of solidarity" while simultaneously ruling out any alteration of the 2002 CAP agreement. Blair retorted testily that paying two and a half times the French contribution over the past decade instead of the fifteen times it would have been without the rebate was gesture enough.[87]

This exchange reflected the British perception that the momentum had shifted to their advantage. Blair could argue that the "No" votes in France and the Netherlands meant that the public no longer agreed with the direction the EU was taking under its traditional Franco–German leadership. Perhaps it was time to nudge it into a more Anglo–Dutch direction instead?[88] Reforms were necessary, and these had to dismantle the archaic agricultural subsidy that consumed 40 percent of the budget and went to 5 percent of the EU population. The French president had dug in, but he would not be able to defend the CAP without German support, and Schröder was wobbling. His prospective replacement, Angela Merkel, did not have a close personal relationship with Chirac and was at any rate a fiscal conservative who had more in common with New Labour than the SPD had ever had (Blair, 2011, pp. 533–534). Why give in to help an outgoing chancellor without getting anything in return when Blair could delay again – with a veto if necessary – until

---

[85] "Schroeder, Chirac say rest of E.U. must vote on constitution." *Deutsche Presse-Agentur*, June 4, 2005.
[86] "Germany demands end to British E.U. rebate." *Deutsche Presse-Agentur*, June 3, 2005.
[87] Watt, Nicholas and Michael White. "Blair rebuffs Chirac call to give ground on EU rebate." *The Guardian*, June 9, 2005. www.theguardian.com/politics/2005/jun/10/uk.eu, accessed January 23, 2018.
[88] Blair did end up using this argument (Islam, Shada and Leon Mangasarian. "Failed E.U. budget deal spotlights deepening divisions." *Deutsche Presse-Agentur*, June 17, 2006). But this was a dangerous line of reasoning. The voters had rejected the EU constitution because they were afraid that globalization and economic liberalism were threatening their livelihoods, worried that immigration was altering the social fabric, and concerned that the enlargement was going to produce an influx of cheap labor. The open Anglo–Dutch model stood precisely for the policies that were being rejected wholesale (Tomforde, Anna. "Blair to lead the EU – from deal-wrecker to deal-maker?" *Deutsche Presse-Agentur*, June 29, 2005).

he assumed the Council presidency, and Germany got its new, possibly more sympathetic, chancellor? There was, of course, an element of risk in this: Schröder could pull off an electoral upset, but the polls suggested the odds of this were not likely. (This would turn out to have been too optimistic.)

This is how it came to pass that Blair repaid his German counterpart's tacit cooperation with the blame-avoidance strategy by delaying yet again, except now it was in order to deny Schröder a much-needed international win that would have allowed him to claim credit in the September elections. As one should recall from the theoretical argument, hidden cooperation is not likely to emerge if the government in distress is about to be replaced with someone else that a key actor prefers. In the fall of 2004, the Europeans wanted to cooperate with Blair because the Tory alternative was even worse from their perspective. In the summer of 2005, the British had no incentive to help Schröder because the Merkel alternative was much more promising. And so they did not.

Blair had already told the Commons on June 8, "The UK rebate will remain. We will not negotiate it away. Period."[89] A day later he clarified that by "not negotiate it away" he meant that he would negotiate it away but only in exchange for a "wider review" of the EU budget. The subtext was that the CAP had to go. Chirac immediately responded that he would neither compromise on the 2002 agreement nor deign to discuss the possibility.[90] The British gambit was plain for all to see: cast the blame for the now almost inevitable failure of the Luxembourg presidency on the French while simultaneously signaling that a deal was possible under the UK presidency.

Schröder was not going to remain passive. He needed an agreement on financing the budget by the end of the Luxembourg presidency.[91] His incentive to claim credit for success in the negotiations was so great that the German opposition got worried that he might be tempted to just buy a victory with taxpayer money. On June 11, the weekly *Welt am Sonntag* reported that "government sources" had said that Germany could offer to increase its annual contributions by up to €500 million to help get a deal on the budget. The CSU leader Edmund Stoiber immediately cautioned the chancellor not to "pull out the chequebook

---

[89] "Chirac meets presidency of EU, rocked by twin-pronged crisis." *Agence France-Presse*, June 9, 2005.
[90] Wintour, Patrick and Jon Henley. "Blair offers rebate deal as bait for EU reforms." *The Guardian*, June 10, 2005. www.theguardian.com/politics/2005/jun/11/uk.eu, accessed January 23, 2018.
[91] "Chirac, Schroeder draw battle lines against Blair." *Deutsche Presse-Agentur*, June 10, 2005.

6.3 Negotiations under Predestination

to get [himself] in the history books."[92] Whatever his desires to figure in the history books, there was one thing Schröder was certainly keeping an eye on: His "sudden flexibility" was all about his reelection bid.[93]

Schröder was, at any rate, busily laying the groundwork for ambushing Blair. On June 12, his spokesperson stated that while all countries would have to compromise on the budget, Germany "completely agreed" with the French position on CAP. Blair and Foreign Secretary Jack Straw shot back that it would be impossible to discuss the rebate without discussing the 40 percent that went to agriculture, with Straw saying that anyone who suggested that the rebate was the culprit behind the stalemate was "deluded." The Tories dutifully complained that the quarrelsome exchange had been a "victory for president Chirac" because the talisman was even mentioned.[94]

On the same day, Blair flew to Berlin and, in a stunning breach of protocol, met first with Merkel at the British embassy before trudging over to the chancellery for a meeting with Schröder. This was an obvious move – if Schröder was desperate for an international achievement to boost his electoral chances, his opponent would be strongly motivated to deny it to him – and it immediately paid off. On the following day, Merkel expressed sympathy for the UK position and said that if the others wanted to abolish the rebate, they should have negotiated with Britain back in 2002 when they had agreed on the CAP.[95] Schröder instead hectored Blair on the need for transcending "national egoism."[96]

On the eve of Schröder's departure for the Brussels summit, he and Merkel had their first parliamentary debate since his announcement of the early elections. The chancellor was vulnerable on many issues – high unemployment and his backing of the Turkish bid for full membership among them – but Merkel also zeroed in on his inability to confront the budgetary and constitutional crises enveloping the EU. The chancellor tried to deflect the charge by blaming the UK rebate, for which he said that there was "absolutely no justification any longer," and insisting

---

[92] "Germans reportedly offers [sic] 500 million euros in EU row." *Deutsche Presse-Agentur*, June 11, 2005.
[93] Mangasarian, Leon. "E.U. Big Three face off over money at summit." *Deutsche Presse-Agentur*, June 14, 2005.
[94] Tempest, Matthew. "Blair ties rebate talks to CAP reform." *The Guardian*, June 13, 2005. www.theguardian.com/world/2005/jun/13/eu.politics, accessed January 23, 2018.
[95] Harding, Luke and Nicholas Watt. "Britain finds an ally in row over budget rebate." June 13, 2005. www.theguardian.com/world/2005/jun/14/eu.germany, accessed January 23, 2018.
[96] "Blair's back against the wall over EU rebate." *Western Morning News*, June 16, 2005.

that his priority was to get the United Kingdom to align with other contributors. Merkel said that while she agreed that the British had to "demonstrate a willingness to budge on this issue" and that a conservative post-Schröder government would seek concessions from the United Kingdom, the chancellor's total support for the agricultural subsidies that overwhelmingly benefited the French was unacceptable.[97] Germany could not expect Britain to make concessions on the rebate while simultaneously agreeing that the French would not make any concessions on CAP. This laid the blame squarely on Schröder and without his reflexive support for Chirac, perhaps a deal was possible. Was this fair? Perhaps not. Politically astute? Absolutely.

The contrast between Merkel's studied neutrality and the chancellor's unequivocal embrace of the French position could not have been more unambiguous. It was designed to create the impression in Blair that he could expect more favorable treatment if Merkel were at the bargaining table instead of Schröder. This fits rather well with the prime minister's notion that the only way the inevitable rebate cut could play less than disastrously at home was to justify it with significant CAP reforms. Perhaps Merkel could be an impartial mediator between him and Chirac in a way Schröder never was? If so, it was better to wait for her to actually win the election she was so heavily favored to win (the polls gave the CDU a 19.5- to 22-point lead over the SPD). This meant that there would be no agreement during the Luxembourg presidency.

On the following day, Blair rejected Juncker's proposal.[98] Of course, this was precisely what Merkel had intended all along, and Schröder knew it. With the British press reporting about officials "heartened" by her comments and Blair being "hopeful" after talking to her, the chancellor accused Merkel of undermining the negotiations by giving the British reasons to be unreasonable. Her having had "energetically defended [UK's] rebate" would be a "disservice to Germany."[99] Schröder was fuming because he was right, and Blair's spokesman confirmed it:

> We don't need a deal at this summit. Things can continue. It is up to everybody to assess the advantages and disadvantages of doing a deal now.[100]

---

[97] Cole, Deborah. "Schroeder, challenger face off for first time ahead of early elections." *Agence France-Presse*, June 16, 2005; "Germany says Britain has no right to continued EU rebate." *Deutsche Presse-Agentur*, June 16, 2005.
[98] Watt, Nicholas and Patrick Wintour. "Rebate row wrecks EU summit." *The Guardian*, June 17, 2005. www.theguardian.com/politics/2005/jun/18/uk.eu3, accessed January 24, 2018.
[99] "Schröder adds to EU rebate pressure on Blair." *Financial Times*, June 17, 2005.
[100] "UK rejects EU budget compromise and threatens to use its veto." *Financial Times*, June 17, 2005.

6.3 Negotiations under Predestination

Table 6.6. *Proposals for the UK Rebate and Total Commitments, 2005.*

	Agenda 2000	Projected	Juncker	Blair	Chirac	Council
		UK Rebate (EUR, bn)				
Annual Average	4.6	7.1	5.5	6.0	5.1	5.6
Total Cut		0.0	11.2	8.0	14.0	10.5
Remaining Total	32.2	49.7	38.5	41.7	35.7	39.2
		Budget Commitments				
Total (EUR, bn)	786		875	849	865	862
% EU GNI	1.22		1.056	1.024	1.046	1.045

All figures in billions of euros at 2004 prices. Numbers for Juncker reflect the final proposal from June 17. Numbers for Blair reflect the United Kingdom's final proposal of December 14. Numbers for Chirac reflect his demand for the United Kingdom to reduce the rebate by €14 billion and restore that amount to the structural funds (the actual number was demanded by Poland).

It is saying something about Juncker's devotion to the cause that even now he plowed ahead. The indefatigable Luxembourger proposed another compromise (Table 6.6). Instead of freezing and then phasing out the UK rebate, the new deal kept it as is with respect to the EU-15, but expenditures on the new member states (except for CAP payments) were exempted from the rebate. This reduced the rebate to €5.5 billion per annum, still a rather drastic cut for the United Kingdom, and one that made it impossible to satisfy the Dutch demands for a correction of their excessive contribution. To make the deal more palatable to them, the presidency proposed to task the Commission with producing a plan to restructure the budget by the end of 2008. This would be reviewed by the Council, and the revisions could modify the financial perspective from 2009 on Puia (2010, p. 118).[101]

Under the circumstances, this was an exceptionally reasonable compromise. And it was certain to fail. Not because it was a bad deal, but because Blair (2011, p. 530) believed he "could do better." The Netherlands, Sweden, Finland, and Spain thought so too, at least when it came to scrapping the CAP – what their version of "better" meant beyond that was probably different from Blair's.[102] It was certain to fail because Chirac would not capitulate to the British vision for Europe

---

[101] Juncker gave the details of his final proposal during his farewell speech to the European Parliament on June 22, 2005. Government of the Grand Duchy of Luxembourg. "Luxembourg Presidency of the Council of the European Union." July 1, 2005. www.eu2005.lu/en/actualites/discours/2005/06/22jclj-pe/index.html, accessed January 24, 2018.

[102] "Failed E.U. budget deal spotlights deepening divisions."

(as expressed in trimming the CAP), and because Schröder supported him in that.

Juncker was ashen, having realized that bargaining had failed not because no mutually acceptable terms could be found, but because "some countries were seeking failure."[103] He clearly meant the British (and maybe the Dutch), but the reality was that as long as Blair hoped for a deal that included CAP reform, he was unlikely to budge on the rebate. This was the only "battering ram" the United Kingdom had to get the EU to align its policies with the British, and he would not give it up while it was still possible that Germany might come around. Chirac, who was probably far more finely attuned to continental moods, saw that Merkel was as unlikely to open the German purse as she was to antagonize the French. Not for the sake of policies that would be quite unpopular in Germany as well. In the end, both dug in their heels because both expected different things from Merkel, and so the two hostile blocs solidified. Juncker caustically remarked that now they could all go to Washington "to explain to the president of the United States in detail the vigor and strength of Europe."[104]

The summit collapse on June 17 was followed by an orgy of mudslinging and trash-talking. Blair tried to deflect blame for the outcome. The British refusal to a compromise was actually an act of "solidarity" with the common people of Europe, who had just rejected the out-of-touch EU leadership in the constitutional referenda. The bloc was overdue for a fresh direction. Chirac jeered at this "pathetic performance" but then outdid Blair by declaring that the farm subsidies were "modern."[105] Schröder blamed Britain and the Netherlands for being "stubborn." He thundered:

Those who want to destroy [the cherished continental welfare state model] due to national egotism or populist motives do a terrible disservice to the desires and rights of the next generation.

The French called the *chèque britannique,* apparently unironically, a relic of the "Ancien Régime" and an "antiquated legacy," and alleged that everyone except the British was willing to pay for the EU enlargement.[106] The CEE beneficiaries of the enlargement found themselves under fire

---

[103] Harding, Gareth. "Doom and gloom after EU summit." *United Press International,* June 20, 2015.
[104] Cooke, Lorne. "Crisis-hit EU seeks to keep lid on divisions." *Agence France-Presse,* June 20, 2005.
[105] Duval Smith, Alex. Nick Watt, and Ned Temko. "Inside the battle of Brussels." *The Guardian,* June 18, 2005. www.theguardian.com/politics/2005/jun/19/uk.eu, accessed January 24, 2018.
[106] "Strains deepen in hamstrung EU." *Agence France-Presse,* June 21, 2005.

too for nonconstructive behavior during the negotiations. Schröder, who was being battered by demonstrations against his domestic policies, threatened both Poland and, for good measure, Spain for their insistence on structural transfers (Dür and Gonzalez, 2007, p. 25; Heisenberg 2007, p. 115).[107]

The cacophony was so deafening that one could have easily missed a major change in the tone of the British government. On June 21, Blair went from insisting that the rebate was non-negotiable to flatly affirming that it had to go:

> We have made it clear all the way through that we are prepared not just to discuss and negotiate upon, but to recognise that the rebate is an anomaly that has to go, but it has to go in the context of the other anomaly being changed away.[108]

The government later explained that it would trade the rebate for cuts in the CAP and asserted that the British people would agree that this was "a price worth paying."[109]

Some of the participants in the Brussels summit were still reeling from its collapse and dismissed this position taking as nonsense. But it was, in fact, the first time that Blair aired in public what he had known all along: the rebate would not survive in its current form. This is why he had more or less put a lid on discussions about it until May. Now he merely added the cause of the second delay: the changing political landscape in Germany (and, to some extent, France and the Netherlands) had potentially given him a way to trade the inevitable rebate cut for something that he just might be able to sell domestically as a fair deal. What had transpired at the summit was part strategy, part opportunism. As a German government report dryly observed, despite repeated calls for reform, the United Kingdom had not put forward any reform proposals over the past 15 months. And you know you are in trouble when a bureaucratic paper says that you came up with arguments

---

[107] The treatment of Poland was unjustified and unfair. The Polish prime minister, Marek Belka, had offered to give up some of the development aid to facilitate a deal. Juncker was "ashamed" to hear new member countries, "each poorer than the other" offering to give up money for the common good. The British thought he had conspired in a setup engineered by the French. Quoted in "Inside the battle of Brussels." See also Jürgen-Schlamp, Hans and Frank Dohmen. "EU summit collapse is 'historic failure'." *Spiegel Online*, June 20, 2005. www.spiegel.de/international/spiegel/brussels-in-crisis-eu-summit-collapse-is-historic-failure-a-361374.html, accessed January 24, 2018.
[108] Tempest, Matthew. "Blair says UK rebate 'has to go.'" *The Guardian*, June 21, 2005. www.theguardian.com/world/2005/jun/21/eu.politics, accessed January 23, 2018.
[109] Grice, Andrew and Stephen Castle. "Blair's concession to European critics is rebuffed as Ahern joins attack on rebate." *The Independent*, June 21, 2005. www.independent.co.uk/news/world/europe/blairs-concession-to-european-critics-is-rebuffed-as-ahern-joins-attack-on-rebate-496106.html, accessed January 24, 2005.

for CAP reform "as if by magic" only at the last minute. People who act that way "do not want an agreement but are seeking an excuse for failure."[110] Indeed, they do.

Unlike the European statesmen, the domestic opposition immediately picked up on the core message. This begot another round of denunciations. After all, not even a fortnight had passed since the prime minister promised that the rebate would not be negotiated away. George Osborne, the shadow chancellor and a great source for anti-Blair quotes, was picturesquely disgusted:

> One minute Mr Blair says he will fight to the end for Britain's interests. The next he says Britain's rebate is an anomaly that has to go. He is more slippery than an eel in a tub of grease. There is no anomaly in trying to save billions of pounds of taxpayers' money. Britain should be paying less.[111]

Maybe so, but there was no upcoming election to get the government to pay attention. All eyes now turned to the UK presidency: Would Blair pull it off? Was he right to bet on Merkel altering the political landscape enough to get him the CAP reforms he hoped for?

From "fully justified" to "obviously wrong"

The Luxembourg presidency had ended with a 20-5 split on the budget. The EU now had to look forward to getting a deal on the financial perspectives under a UK presidency amid a constitutional crisis. It had to be done by the end of 2005, and Blair promised that he would "work hard" to solve the budget crisis. The hard working was, however, to start only with an informal summit outside London on October 27, supposedly because of the EU summer vacation. In private, the government was just waiting for the September elections to bring Merkel to power.[112]

As the summer wore on, this prospect became dimmer: the SPD was surging back in the polls, all but wiping the CDU/CSU lead by early August. On September 4, Schröder bested Merkel in a head-to-head debate, and the parties remained neck and neck on the eve of the election. The CDU had a 9 percent lead over the SPD, but with 25 percent of the electorate undecided, it was impossible to predict who

---

[110] "German official paper criticizes UK premier's views on EU farming." *BBC*, June 23, 2005. The text of the report had appeared on *Spiegel Online* the same day.
[111] Quoted in "Blair's concession to European critics is rebuffed."
[112] Grice, Andrew and Stephen Castle. "Blair delays reforms to repair rift with Brussels." *The Independent*, June 30, 2018. www.independent.co.uk/news/world/europe/blair-delays-reforms-to-repair-rift-with-brussels-295979.html, accessed January 24, 2018.

6.3 Negotiations under Predestination   197

would win. The only outcome that appeared certain was that neither party would be able to get enough seats to form a government.

On the September 18, CDU/CSU came ahead with 35.17 percent of the vote and 36.81 percent of the seats in the Bundestag. The SPD got 34.25 percent of the vote and 36.16 percent of the seats. The FDP, CDU/CSU's likely coalition partner, was third, with 9.83 percent of the vote and 9.93 percent of the seats, while the Greens, SPD's likely coalition partner, was fifth, with 8.12 percent of the vote and 8.31 percent of the seats. These numbers meant that even with their preferred coalition partners, the two big parties would be unable to get a majority and elect a chancellor. Naturally, both Schröder and Merkel claimed to have won the chancellorship. Downing Street declined to comment.[113]

The Germans now went through a dizzying set of multicolor combinations to somehow get to a coalition that would command a majority in the Bundestag. None looked good for Blair. One possibility was for the Greens to join with CDU/CSU-FDP, but this would bring back in power the party that had set Schröder's foreign policy. The other was for FDP to join with SPD-Greens, which would merely reinstate (likely, a very disgruntled) Schröder. The third possibility was for CDU/CSU and SPD to form a grand coalition, in which case it was not clear who would become chancellor. Even if it were Merkel, the extent to which she would be free to pursue policies in opposition to SPD preferences was also unclear.[114] Without a clear mandate for Merkel – now an impossibility – the UK's CAP reform dreams, never very realistic, started to look more like a hallucination. This did not bode well for the rebate.

Despite the center-left holding onto a majority, it was the CDU/CSU and SPD that negotiated a grand coalition on October 10 (Proksch and Slapin, 2006). Merkel was going to be chancellor, and Schröder would retire from politics. It took another six weeks before she was actually elected by the newly formed Bundestag, but on November 22, Blair finally got his negotiation partner ... sort of. The SPD was to control the finance and foreign affairs ministries.[115] With this tenuous hold on power and many unresolved questions about what it meant for her domestic policies, Merkel was not expected to indulge in any drastic

---

[113] MacPherson, Robert. "German election muddle seen as 'disappointment' for Blair." *Agence France-Presse*, September 19, 2005.
[114] "German election result leaves Blair in difficult position." *BBC*, September 20, 2005. Reporting on an editorial in the Portuguese daily *Diario de Noticias* on the same day.
[115] Fickling, David. "Merkel sworn in as German chancellor." *The Guardian*, November 22, 2005. www.theguardian.com/world/2005/nov/22/germany.davidfickling, accessed January 25, 2018.

departures from Schröder's approach to the EU (Heisenberg, 2007, pp. 115–116).

For Blair, this meant one thing: whether she had ever intended to pressure Chirac or not, Merkel was now highly unlikely to do it. The chances of getting any serious CAP reform were practically nil. With the British strategy in tatters, the only remaining play was to attempt to salvage as much of the rebate as possible. The final Luxembourg proposal had already introduced the principle that the rebate could be applied selectively – covering payments on policies that the United Kingdom objected to (CAP) but excluding policies for which it would have to pay its fair share (cohesion).[116] This had been eminently pragmatic back in June, and there was no reason it would not be acceptable to the others now. Under this arrangement, the United Kingdom would not get back anything for expenditures on the new member states. Since this was the rebate cut, the logical way to minimize it was to reduce these expenditures. In a complete reversal of its original (and, given its interests, rational) position on structural funds for the CEE countries, the United Kingdom was going to propose to rob the poor so it could pay the rich.

Indeed, when the plans leaked out at the end of November, this is what it amounted to: a 3 percent reduction in the Luxembourg overall budget, which was to come from a 10 percent cut to the structural funds aimed for cohesion.[117] Unimpressed by the fact that the feeler made no mention of any reductions in CAP, Chirac contemptuously dismissed the whole idea, while at home Blair was having trouble reining in Brown, who was still beating the CAP reform drums. In Europe, the prime minister was isolated.[118] Commissioner Barroso told Blair to stop acting like the Sheriff of Nottingham.[119] To add insult to injury,

---

[116] Correspondingly, in a speech to a domestic audience Blair revised his firm pledge to protect the rebate to an equally firm vow to defend it "from CAP spending." Rennie, David and Toby Helm. "Blair ready to surrender EU rebate with no payback." *The Telegraph*, November 30, 2005. www.telegraph.co.uk/news/uknews/1504332/Blair-ready-to-surrender-EU-rebate-with-no-payback.html, accessed January 31, 2018.

[117] Rennie, David and Anton La Guardia. "Blair targets new EU states with £118bn budget cut." *The Telegraph*, November 28, 2005. www.telegraph.co.uk/news/worldnews/europe/1504223/Blair-targets-new-EU-states-with-118bn-budget-cut.html, accessed January 31, 2018.

[118] Rennie, David and Anton La Guardia. "Blair too weak to win deal, says Chirac." *The Telegraph*, November 29, 2005. www.telegraph.co.uk/news/worldnews/europe/france/1504310/Blair-too-weak-to-win-deal-says-Chirac.html, accessed January 24, 2018.

[119] Watt, Nicholas and Michael White. "PM accused of taking from EU poor." *The Guardian*, November 30, 2005. www.theguardian.com/uk/2005/dec/01/eu.world, accessed January 24, 2018.

6.3 Negotiations under Predestination

Blair now embarked on a trip to Eastern Europe to explain to seven disbelieving governments how this was in their "true interest." There was some logic to this. After all, in the final round in June they had agreed to cuts in the cohesion funds, but the proposal had poisoned public opinion, leaving Britain's erstwhile allies little choice but to close ranks and condemn it.[120]

While on the continent Blair was pilloried for clawing the UK rebate back from the weakest of member states, at home the Tories were excoriating him for giving it up. Graham Brady, the Europe spokesman for the Conservatives, accurately summarized what had transpired thus far:

Before the general election there was an absolutely solid pledge the rebate would be maintained, then there was an offer it would be given away but only in return for solid fundamental reform of CAP, and now finally we see part of the rebate with nothing concrete in return at all.[121]

Amid howls of protest at home and abroad, the UK presidency formally tendered its proposal on December 5 (Table 6.6). The total budget was set at €847 billion to Juncker's €875 billion, a 3.2 percent reduction that brought it down to 1.022 percent of EU GNI on average (the spending was to drop below 1 percent by 2013). Under current rules, the projected UK rebate over the period was €7.1 billion per year, for an estimated total of €49.7 billion. The proposal was to cut it by €8 billion, whereas Juncker had offered €11.2 billion. The lion's share of the cut was to be financed by an €14 billion (about 8 percent) reduction in structural aid to the new member states and a much smaller share by reductions in rural development payments to the older members. The proposal also envisioned a midterm review of CAP spending in 2008, with possible changes from 2009, which, one should recall, was what Juncker had offered as well.[122]

Thus, all the "hard work" and frantic flurry of activity had culminated in an edit of the Luxembourg proposal, which was small in numbers but politically explosive enough to ensure that the deal was not viable. It also

---

[120] Mcooughln, Patrick. "Blair seeks smaller EU budget." *Times of Malta*, December 2, 2005. www.timesofmalta.com/articles/view/20051202/local/blair-seeks-smaller-eu-budget.70309, accessed January 24, 2018; Rennie, David. "Blair loses EU allies in budget rebate row." *The Telegraph*, December 2, 2005. www.telegraph.co.uk/news/1504558/Blair-loses-EU-allies-in-budget-rebate-row.html, accessed January 24, 2018.

[121] "UK prepared to reduce EU rebate." *BBC*, December 1, 2005. http://news.bbc.co.uk/2/hi/uk_news/politics/4489682.stm, accessed January 24, 2018.

[122] "Blair pushes EU budget proposals." *BBC*, December 8, 2005. http://news.bbc.co.uk/2/hi/europe/4509030.stm, accessed January 25, 2018.

enabled France to cast itself as the protector of the CEE countries that it had so recently disparaged over their support for the United States.[123] Merkel, who was already assuming her role as mediator between Chirac and Blair, observed that "this draft still [had] many rough patches throughout" but that it was "essential to continue to negotiate."[124] Although she later added that she did not want to prejudice these negotiations by making demands on specific countries, even she thought that the budget was "not sufficient."[125] The proposal was unceremoniously and unanimously rejected although several member states requested a revision, indicating that at least they thought that something along these lines could be acceptable. Sir Michael Butler, who had negotiated the original rebate, agreed:

Whatever the outcome of the negotiation it will continue to be worth several billion pounds a year to the UK up to 2013 because France has succeeded in defending her gains from the CAP up to that date and that is what makes our net contribution so large.

But nothing prevents, for example, an arrangement whereby some or all of the UK's contribution to economic development in the new member countries does not count when calculating the refund.[126]

Blair had to work fast because the deadline was just around the corner: the Brussels Council summit that would take place on December 15 and 16. Chirac had demanded that the €14 billion that Britain was proposing to yank from the CEE countries be financed by the equivalent reduction in the rebate. Poland had threatened to veto the budget over this, and soon the unthinkable happened: in a joint letter, France and Poland demanded a larger cut to the rebate and "privileged treatment" for the poorest member states.[127] The British tactics had produced an official Franco–Polish alignment, whose demands had to be taken seriously.[128] If Blair was going to offer something between the original

---

[123] Bennhold, Katrin. "Paris demands Blair accept cuts in EU rebate." December 11, 2005. www.nytimes.com/2005/12/11/world/europe/paris-demands-blair-accept-cuts-in-eu-rebate.html, accessed January 25, 2018.

[124] Kubosova, Lucia. "Merkel and Chirac call for new EU budget proposals." *EUobserver*, December 7, 2005. https://euobserver.com/economic/20494, accessed January 25, 2018.

[125] "Merkel, Chirac reject Blair's EU budget plans." *Deutsche Presse-Agentur*, December 9, 2005.

[126] Butler, Michael. "The great rebate debate." *The Guardian*, December 9, 2015. www.theguardian.com/world/2005/dec/09/eu.comment, accessed January 23, 2018.

[127] Rennie, David and Toby Helm. "Blair threatens Chirac with veto on Europe budget." *The Telegraph*, December 16, 2005. www.telegraph.co.uk/news/1505630/Blair-threatens-Chirac-with-veto-on-Europe-budget.html, accessed January 25, 2018.

[128] Rennie, David. "A high price to pay in lost friendships." *The Telegraph*, December 17, 2005. www.telegraph.co.uk/news/worldnews/europe/1505711/A-high-price-to-pay-in-lost-friendships.html, accessed January 25, 2018.

6.3 Negotiations under Predestination

€8 billion and the €14 billion France and Poland wanted, he would have to find money to plug the resulting hole in the structural funds. This could be accomplished if the budget were revised slightly upwards, perhaps to 1.04 percent of EU GNI.[129] But where would that money come from?

This question still had no answer when Britain submitted its revised proposal on December 14. The budget total had crept up by €2.5 billion, to €849 billion, still below the self-imposed 1.03 percent ceiling (Table 6.6).[130] This "tough but realistic budget" remained the "best basis for agreement," according to the UK presidency, which also warned that there was "very narrow room for negotiations."[131] The modifications from the rejected last offer were so small that the numbers looked the same due to rounding. There was no revision to the rebate or the demand for a midterm review of CAP spending. The government also insinuated that this was the best deal the others could hope for because the next two Presidencies – during whose terms the budget had to be adopted – were Austria, a net contributor, and Finland, not a known lover of CAP. It was not very likely that they would produce anything more generous. Barroso, who had already derided the last offer as a budget for "mini-Europe," told the European Parliament that the United Kingdom wanted the enlargement without having to pay for it.[132] The Franco–Polish axis rejected the proposal, with the French saying it was no basis for an acceptable agreement, and the Polish prime minister Kazimierz Marcinkiewicz threatening to veto it despite the €1 billion bribe it earmarked specifically for Poland.[133] Blair was seemingly heading into the summit with no apparent prospect for success.

---

[129] Watt, Nicholas. "Blair plans compromise on EU rebate." *The Guardian*, December 12, 2005. www.theguardian.com/politics/2005/dec/13/uk.eu, accessed January 25, 2018.

[130] Kubosova, Lucia. "France, Germany, Poland join forces against UK budget offer." *EUobserver*, December 15, 2005. https://euobserver.com/economic/20552, accessed January 25, 2018.

[131] "Blair stands firm on EU rebate." *The Independent*, December 14, 2005. www.independent.co.uk/news/world/europe/blair-stands-firm-on-eu-rebate-519470.html, accessed January 25, 2018.

[132] "Blair stands firm on EU rebate."; "When the CAP doesn't fit." *The Economist*, December 8, 2005. www.economist.com/node/5278954, accessed January 25, 2018.

[133] Rennie, David. "Blair isolated as Poland and France reject EU deal." *The Telegraph*, December 15, 2005. www.telegraph.co.uk/news/worldnews/europe/1505550/Blair-isolated-as-Poland-and-France-reject-EU-deal.html, accessed January 25, 2018. Poland then demanded that the budget be increased to €865 billion ("Another splendid compromise forged in Brussels." *The Economist*, December 17, 2005. www.economist.com/node/5323822, accessed January 25, 2018).

And then, after two days of frenetic activity and the occasional veto threat flare-up, predestination asserted itself.[134] On December 17, Blair, who had told Parliament back on June 20 that "Europe's credibility demands the right deal – not the usual cobbled-together compromise in the early hours of the morning," emerged in the early hours of the morning to announce that the European Council, as usual, had cobbled together a compromise.[135]

The deal essentially adopted the UK presidency's (edit of the Luxembourg) proposal but restored most of the structural aid to the CEE countries.[136] Under the now-official new dual-track method for calculating the UK rebate, these cohesion funds would be excluded. However, instead of paying the entire resulting difference, the United Kingdom would pay €10.5 billion, roughly midway between Blair's initial offer of €8 billion and Chirac's demand for €14 billion (Table 6.6).[137] Britain was back to being Robin Hood, which was much more in line with its interests in Eastern Europe anyway.[138] The spending on CAP stayed at €293 billion, which was where the previous proposals had it. In exchange for the rebate cut, Blair had only managed to get Chirac to agree for the Commission to draft a report reviewing all spending, including CAP, in 2008. Although in principle this could lead to the Council adjusting the budget for the remainder of the period, agreement would have to be unanimous. In practical terms, this meant that CAP would survive untouched at least until 2014.[139] In other words, the UK rebate was cut, and nothing came of the attempt to link that to meaningful reforms (or even promises of reforms) to the agricultural subsidies.

But with CAP holding steady and the structural funds increasing (Spain was to remain eligible for development aid longer than under existing rules), the total commitments had gone up as well, to €862.36

---

[134] See Mark Mardell's log of events for December 12–17, available at "Europe diary: Summit watch." BBC, December 17, 2005. http://news.bbc.co.uk/2/hi/europe/4529656.stm, accessed January 25, 2018.

[135] For his statement to Parliament on June 20, see "Nothing left to fight over." *The Economist*, June 23, 2005. www.economist.com/node/4104218, accessed January 25, 2018.

[136] See Council of the European Union (2005) for details.

[137] "Key points of the EU budget deal." *BBC*, December 17, 2005. http://news.bbc.co.uk/2/hi/europe/4537912.stm, accessed January 25, 2018.

[138] White, Michael and Nicholas Watt. "Blair clinches deal with offer of big rebate cut." *The Guardian*, December 16, 2005. www.theguardian.com/uk/2005/dec/17/eu.world, accessed January 25, 2018.

[139] Meade, Geoff and James Lyons. "Blair gives away £2.7bn to clinch EU budget deal." *The Independent*, December 17, 2005. www.independent.co.uk/news/world/europe/blair-gives-away-pound27bn-to-clinch-eu-budget-deal-519863.html, accessed January 25, 2018.

6.3 Negotiations under Predestination

billion, or 1.045 percent of GNI. Although this was not quite as high as Juncker's proposal of 1.056 percent, it fell short of the repeatedly referenced ceiling of 1 percent, and it exceeded Britain's limit of 1.03 percent as well. This had not pleased the net contributors, but the four member states that had mostly exempted themselves from paying for the UK rebate (see Table 6.2) retained that privilege and now obtained further corrections.[140]

The magic that allowed for the total commitments to increase concurrent with a decrease in contributions from key members was more money. And as usual, it was the Germans who had loosened the purse strings. Merkel had bowed to the obvious and agreed to let contributions climb to 1.045 percent of GNI, and she had even foregone certain benefits earmarked for Germany (e.g., she had reallocated €100 million from East German states to Poland).[141] This was one area where she had more flexibility than Schröder and so was able to offer more than he had in June. Back then, it was the CDU/CSU that was hammering home the idea that the government had been wasteful with its resources. Schröder might have found support for a larger EU budget in the Eastern states, but not among the wealthy southerners, like Bayern, the CSU stronghold. With the impeccable credentials of a fiscal conservative and as the leader of the party dominant in the south, Merkel could do something Schröder had not been able to: spend more. As the head of a grand coalition that included both supporters and opponents of a larger budget, and with her leadership of the opponents, it was necessary for Merkel to please the former and possible to do so with less resistance by the latter. She satisfied the suspicious Eastern states by relaxing the rules for accessing the structural funds so that their poor regions would benefit from these funds as well. And, in a bow to the interests of the CDU/CSU foundation, she got some aid specifically earmarked for Bayern as well. Her statement about the agreement was careful to note both, as clear an instance of credit claiming as one can find.[142]

---

[140] Austria, Germany, the Netherlands, and Sweden got reductions in the call rate for the VAT-based resource. The Netherlands and Sweden further got gross reductions in their annual GNI contributions of €605 million and €150 million, respectively [Council of the European Union, 2005, 78(b-d)].

[141] Dempsey, Judy. "In foreign policy, Merkel has a good first month as chancellor." *The New York Times*, December 20, 2005. www.nytimes.com/2005/12/20/world/europe/in-foreign-policy-merkel-has-a-good-first-month-as-chancellor.html, accessed January 25, 2018.

[142] The Federal Chancellor. "EU agrees on budget framework for 2007–2013." December 17, 2005. www.bundeskanzlerin.de/ContentArchiv/EN/Archiv17/Reiseberichte/eu-Eu-einigt-sich-auf-finanzielle-Vorausschau-2007-2013.html, accessed January 25, 2018.

Merkel was also able to do something Schröder seemed constitutionally incapable of doing because of his personal relationship with Chirac and the history of hostility to Blair over Iraq and Verhofstadt: she could play honest broker between Chirac and Blair. Her main role here was to provide shuttle diplomacy between the Brit – to explain to him that this was the end of the line – and the Frenchman – to get him to sign to a meaningless paragraph in the agreement.[143] Succeeding in that was no mean feat, although one would not know it from Merkel's description:

> I think that we clearly played an important role but that is always the case as we are a big country. We had a very good agreement with France, we prepared the groundwork, and then were able to reach a good consensus with the British.[144]

Merkel received universal acclaim for her mediation and for agreeing to an additional €13 billion to clinch a deal (Szemlér, 2006).[145] Blair, on the other hand, was torn to shreds by Brown (for not getting a firm commitment to CAP reform); by the Conservatives (for conceding 20 percent of the rebate); and by the Europhiles (for failing to lead the EU in a new direction).[146] The harsh domestic reaction explains why Blair had been so dedicated to not even hinting about a possible change to the rebate before the elections.

To get an idea of what might have happened if an analogous budget had been negotiated before May 5, just consider the treatment he received now.[147] Blair (2011, p. 537) had "the most frightful time" with Brown, especially near the end when the chancellor was refusing to agree to the compromise. And though he relented in the end, which meant that the Treasury would not veto the UK budget, his officials started to

---

[143] Mardell, Mark. "Blair deal avoids an EU crisis." *BBC*, December 17, 2005. http://news.bbc.co.uk/2/hi/europe/4537150.stm, accessed January 25, 2018. Helm, Toby and David Rennie. "A day is a very, very long time in EU budget negotiations." *The Telegraph*, December 17, 2005. www.telegraph.co.uk/news/worldnews/europe/1505708/A-day-is-a-very-very-long-time-in-EU-budget-negotiations.html, accessed January 25, 2018.

[144] "EU pulls itself back from the abyss." *EurActiv*, December 18, 2005. www.euractiv.com/section/uk-europe/news/eu-pulls-itself-back-from-the-abyss/, accessed January 25, 2018.

[145] "Merkel makes her mark as mediator in EU budget deal." *Deutsche Welle*, December 17, 2005. www.dw.com/en/merkel-makes-her-mark-as-mediator-in-eu-budget-deal/a-1823724, accessed January 25, 2018.

[146] Castle, Stephen and Francis Elliott. "Blair faces uproar at home after failing to consult with Gordon Brown over his rebate concessions." *The Independent on Sunday*, December 18, 2005.

[147] It is by no means certain that Blair could have gotten anywhere near the terms he obtained in December before the disastrous May referenda made it imperative for France and Germany to get an agreement. And while Schröder had been willing to make concessions similar to the ones Merkel made, his own electoral vulnerability and dedication to Chirac had encouraged Blair to reject the deal.

6.3 Negotiations under Predestination

leak that Labour would have to pay for the rebate difference from its own coffers and that there would be less to spend on the public sector, health, education, law and order, and transport, all because of a bad deal made at the European level.[148] Shadow foreign secretary William Hague alleged that the government had

> spectacularly failed to achieve any [CAP] guarantees–merely vague promises of a process of reform in the future. [...] Seldom in the course of European negotiations has so much been surrendered for so little.[149]

The Eurosceptic UKIP member of the European Parliament Nigel Farage described the budget deal as "game, set and match to President Chirac," who had stood up for French interests and had "outclassed, and outplayed [Blair] at every turn."[150] But it was David Cameron, the recently elected leader of the Conservative Party, who summarized just how this deal would play nationally. It is worth quoting at length from his response to Blair's statement on the EU budget in the House of Commons because it explicitly notes what appears to be an incoherent overall strategy:

> On the budget, does the Prime Minister remember having three clear objectives? First, to limit its size, when almost every country in Europe is taxing and borrowing too much. Second, to ensure fundamental reform of the CAP. And third, to keep the British rebate unless such reform occurs. Isn't it now clear that he failed in every single one? [...] the Prime Minister's position was clear. He used to say the rebate was non-negotiable. [...] Then the Prime Minister changed his mind. The rebate could be negotiated, he said, provided there was fundamental reform of the CAP. [...] But what happened? The farm subsidies remain. And £7 billion of the rebate has been negotiated away. If this was always the Government's plan, why wasn't any reduction in the rebate in the Chancellor's Pre-Budget Report? [...] Why did he give up £7 billion for next to nothing? And—vitally—how is the Chancellor going to pay for it? More taxes? More borrowing? Or cuts in spending? Which is it? [...] Europe needed to be led in a new direction. Aren't we simply heading in the same direction, but paying a bigger bill?[151]

---

[148] "British finance minister 'not consulted' over EU budget deal." *Agence France-Presse*, December 18, 2005.
[149] "Blair criticized over EU deal." *The Guardian*, December 17, 2005. www.theguardian.com/politics/2005/dec/17/uk.eu, accessed January 25, 2018.
[150] White, Michael. "Faced with Nigel Farage, what would Tony Blair do?" *The Guardian*, May 23, 2014. www.theguardian.com/politics/blog/2014/may/23/faced-nigel-farage-tony-blair, accessed January 25, 2018. Video of the exchange between Farage and Blair at the European Parliament can be found at www.independent.co.uk/video/News/tony-blair-nigel-farage-video-eu-parliament-ukip-brexit-prime-minister-immigration-a8151036.html, accessed January 25, 2018.
[151] The transcript of the full speech of December 19, 2005, "Cameron: Europe needs to be led in a new direction" can be found at http://conservative-speeches.sayit.mysociety.org/speech/600168, accessed January 25, 2018.

Barring unforeseen circumstances, the next general election was at this point five years in the future. One can imagine what would have happened if it were only five months after Labour negotiated a rebate cut.

The government defended itself, of course, but much of its reasoning fell on deaf ears. In part because of the mythological status of the rebate – after all, this was precisely why the government had delayed the announcement of a cut – and in part because the government's strategy looked duplicitous and incoherent when decontextualized, as it invariably was. Blair argued that another veto would have damaged relations with the new member states. Increasing funds for their development was good for the United Kingdom, he asserted, because it could stimulate British exports to the region (Ackrill and Kay, 2006).[152] All of this was true, of course, although one might have been confused by Blair trying to plunder these very development funds. It was also unclear how adding Germany to the Franco–Polish axis was going to help redirect Europe.[153] One might also have wondered why the "fully justified" rebate went from "non-negotiable" to negotiable in exchange for CAP reforms, to an "anomaly that had to go," and then finally to "obviously wrong."[154]

All of this would be puzzling without the story of the changing electoral landscape and the ebb and flow of incentives to signal responsiveness it furnished to the key policymakers.

6.4 Summing Up

Two years of wrangling had reduced the budget from €1,025 billion to €862 billion; spread over seven years, this meant from €146 billion to €123 billion per year (Table 6.5). To put this in perspective, in 2005 the US federal government spent about €3,187 billion, so the extravagant Commission proposal for the EU was to spend 4.6 percent of what the Americans did, and the Council set this to 3.9 percent. One could understand the bemusement of the American diplomat quoted in the epigraph to this chapter. Even if we took a EU member as the baseline, the magnitude of the stakes was not that great. The UK government antagonized the friendly CEE governments, risked a break

---

[152] "Blair criticised over EU deal."
[153] Poland's relationship with Germany was strained because of Schröder's penny-pinching ways. Merkel had managed to woo Marcinkiewicz during her December 2 visit to Warsaw (Scally, Derek. "Merkel offers reassurance to Poland." *The Irish Times*, December 3, 2005. www.irishtimes.com/news/merkel-offers-reassurance-to-poland-1.1172263, accessed January 25, 2018). After the successful summit, one of Poland's leading newspapers headlined with "Merkel – Miss Europe." See, for example, "In foreign policy, Merkel has a good first month as chancellor."
[154] "Blair criticised over EU deal."

6.4 Summing Up

with the Germans, and worsened its relationship with France over €10.5 billion over the entire period, or €1.5 billion annually. In 2005, the UK government budget was £519 billion, or about €756 billion. Thus, the entire rebate cut was merely 1.4 percent of that year's budget, and if one considered only the annual outlay, it would be a tiny 0.2 percent of the budget. The behavior of all governments during these negotiations would defy explanation if one focused on economic and international considerations only. In fact, doing so makes some of the interactions positively flabbergasting. How could one explain Blair's attempt to play "Sheriff of Nottingham" in the fall of 2005 when economic incentives pointed to increasing development funds to Eastern Europe and international incentives pointed to preventing France (and possibly Germany) from pulling these countries into their orbit? Without accounting for the domestic political factors, our explanations would be quite distorted indeed.

Domestic politics are like a magnifying glass, which can make the trivial look like the apocalypse. The United Kingdom (along with five other large contributors) had openly told the Commission that the budget needed to be restrained. Their reasoning in that letter was explicitly based on domestic political considerations: their citizens would not tolerate profligacy in the EU (especially if it were to go mostly to the new member states) when they had been subjected to rather harsh reforms themselves. The Commission chose to ignore the warning, and several months of discussions barely budged it from the original proposal to the one officially submitted in July 2004. Prodi had good reasons for wanting this budget, which in turn necessitated the reduction of the UK correction, but these were precisely the economic and financial reasons that are easily lost in a political stampede.

With the proposal for a cut in the UK rebate now official, the British audiences went into a state of agitation stirred by Eurosceptics and Tories alike. The Commission's logic was sound, however: A rebate cut was inevitable, and Blair knew it. But there was no way he could say any of this with elections just around the corner. Signaling responsiveness meant holding the line on the rebate at least until May 2005. This required the hidden cooperation of the other member states, and they obliged: after all, given the shift in the Conservative Party's position on the EU, Blair was almost infinitely better than a Tory alternative. As a result, the negotiations went into abeyance, and the UK government's grandstanding on the inviolability of its rebate went unchallenged. The only significant hiccup was President Chirac's March 24 outburst, which itself was precipitated by a domestic political event (the "No" campaign taking the lead in the polls), but the UK government managed to deflect it. Blair's blame-avoidance strategy paid off on May 2, and Labour won. However, the loss of the popular vote in England also indicated that it would be difficult to defy public opinion, which was almost uniformly hostile on the rebate cut issue. The fact that the government had spent nearly a year telling everyone that no such cut was in the cards only magnified the potential costs of defecting from this promise.

The election strengthened Blair's incentive to find some way to package the cut for domestic consumption. Since CAP had always been the cause of British financial grievances, it was a good target. It had been an untouchable target, however, because the French government defended it as if its life depended on it – which, for domestic political reasons, it did – and because the Germans had always played along, most recently in 2002 to get France to cooperate with the Eastern enlargement. But in May, some of the calculations changed. Schröder's loss in NRW put him on the defensive and made him keen to secure a major international victory before the September elections. And the rejection of the EU constitution in France tanked Chirac's standing and made it imperative for him to prove the critics wrong. This also meant willingness to secure an agreement on the EU budget. Whether he would want to do this by making concessions to Britain, on the other hand, was less clear. Blair thought that the referendum had rejected the Franco–German model of EU integration and (implicitly) approved the Anglo–Dutch model of liberalization. The perception was strengthened when the Dutch also rejected the constitution. Chirac thought exactly the opposite, and he was French (so in a better position to judge the domestic consequences of giving in to Blair).

From the British perspective, then, France and Germany should have become more willing to make compromises in June, and Blair thought that perhaps this made CAP fair game. Much to the consternation of his critics, he altered the government's position on the rebate, which went from non-negotiable to negotiable in exchange for CAP reform. Sustained by the notion that failure in June would not be terribly costly (and might even prove beneficial) because the favorite to win the German federal elections, Merkel, had signaled that she was more supportive of the British view, Blair took a hard line at the European Council meeting, and it predictably failed. Again, for domestic reasons. Even though he wanted to loosen the budget ceiling (and so reduce the magnitude of the rebate cut), Schröder was limited in how much he could offer: the opposition that had just won the state elections was preaching fiscal austerity. Chirac might have needed an EU agreement, but he needed the support of the farmers more. And he certainly could

6.4 Summing Up

not be seen giving in to the liberal Trojan horse that Britain had become in popular lore.

Since having Merkel on his side (or at least in the middle) was the essence of Blair's strategy, nothing whatsoever could happen with the budget before she got elected. The September elections, however, did not quite turn out as expected. They resulted in a hung Bundestag and nearly two months of negotiations before Merkel finally became chancellor. The coalitional government she headed, however, included Schröder's SPD, with the key posts of finance and foreign affairs in their hands. Blair might have gained a more sympathetic German leader, but she was far more constrained than he had hoped for.

This derailed the United Kingdom's rebate-for-CAP strategy, and forced Blair to look for alternative ways to sell the inevitable cut domestically. In practice there was only one thing to do: minimize it as much as feasible and hope for the best. This is how the reverse Robin Hood fiasco came to be. It might be possible to convince anyone other than the most rabid Eurosceptic that it was fair for the United Kingdom to pay its share of the funds aimed at developing the Eastern European countries, and thus exclude them from the calculations of the rebate.[155] This gave the United Kingdom the incentive to insist now that these funds be reduced. This shortsighted strategy backfired quite spectacularly, creating a new Franco–Polish alignment, to which Germany gravitated as well.

This is when Blair's strategy of waiting to see Merkel elected paid off. She managed to get Chirac to agree to a midterm review of the budget (including CAP), and even though this meant nothing about CAP spending, it could be used by the UK government to justify the rebate cut in the context of a promise of CAP reforms. More importantly, she was able to relax the budget constraint enough to restore most of the development aid to the CEE countries and meet the British halfway on the rebate cut. Beyond her doubtless formidable personal skills and expertise, the recently elected Merkel was less handicapped by domestic politics than Schröder had been in the midst of an electoral campaign. She was the head of the party that had opposed his attempt to increase the EU budget and could count on a muted disagreement when she did it. And as the chancellor of a grand coalition with the former ruling

---

[155] This did not mean that the CEE countries would not pay for the UK rebate. They were in the same pool as everyone else when it came to financing the budget hole it left. The concession was that the size of this hole would be reduced by the amount spent in CEE countries. Given that, however, everybody paid *modulo* whatever special exemptions they had negotiated for themselves.

party, she was careful to ensure that its constituents got their due as well. This was credit claiming at its best.

If nothing else, this analysis shows that domestic politics generally – and elections more specifically – matter for the dynamics of European cooperation. The analysis complements the statistical results, which demonstrate the relevant correlations by providing direct evidence that the correlations matter in the ways anticipated by my theoretical mechanism. The positions the governments took, the signaling strategies they adopted, the shifts in their negotiating stances, and the timing of these shifts were all driven by domestic concerns. The detailed study was also able to document something that no statistical analysis can: an instance of hidden cooperation with the blame-avoidance strategy of a fellow member government, the limits of that cooperation, and the absence of cooperation when the alternative is preferable to a key member. In other words, the electoral threat to a particular government might increase the chances of hidden cooperation or decrease them, depending on whether the party that is threatening it is preferable to those on whose participation that cooperation depends.

The analysis also shows just how important a country's bargaining leverage is in the Council. When a group of countries representing 64 percent of EU GNI says that the total commitments must be 1 percent, it does not matter what the Commission and the others want. When a group of only 27 percent of GNI wants to reform CAP, this reform will not happen. When a group with a combined total of 67 percent of GNI wants to preserve the fundamental allocations of development funds, there will be no cohesion policies strictly reserved for the poor states. And most clearly, when a group with 83 percent of GNI wants the UK rebate cut, the UK rebate will get cut. The pivotal importance of Germany, which would not surprise anyone who studies the EU, was also at full display in these negotiations. As long as it stuck with France, not even a hint of a reform could enter the agreement. And only when it relented on the budget ceiling did it become possible to limit the cut to about 20 percent of the rebate without pauperizing the Eastern Europeans in the process. In this instance, it also showed that while the formal rules could have given veto power to a smaller member state such as Poland, the structurally advantaged one (Germany) could compensate it at least partially and then rely on the strong informal norm of consensus to get it to accept less than what it wanted.

Of course, the case also reveals the extraordinary importance of idiosyncratic and contextual factors that are nearly impossible to capture in a statistical analysis. For instance, Blair and Chirac interpreted differently the meaning of the constitutional referenda in France and

6.4 Summing Up

the Netherlands, and shifted their bargaining strategies into incompatible directions, making agreement less likely. Blair, like everyone else, overestimated CDU/CSU's chances of success and expected Merkel to emerge as a chancellor with solid party support behind her, and not as the (not very popular) leader of a grand coalition with her rivals. Finally, the importance of Merkel's intervention cannot be denied. Although her success can in part be accounted for by systematic domestic factors (the composition of the grand coalition), some of it was due to her personal qualities and the lack of "baggage" that her predecessor had accumulated with both Chirac and Blair. One should not underestimate Merkel's extraordinary savvy in this: she managed to get the German press to hail her for masterminding an international agreement even though she had, in fact, committed Germany to larger contributions than Schröder had intended.

At this point one might be persuaded – by the statistical evidence in Chapter 5 for the annual budgets and the pathway analysis in this chapter for the multiannual financial framework – that domestic politics matter for EU budget negotiations. But one might still wonder: Could that be it? Or do they matter for non-budgetary policies as well? After all, bargaining over the budget is clearly redistributive. This makes it easy to identify winners and losers, and so allows unambiguous signals of responsiveness that voters can readily interpret. The MFFs are also highly politicized (which is why they were established in the first place), and in a sense are the most likely case for these signaling strategies to appear. Although it is nice to know that the EU governance structures make it responsive to national audiences when it comes to the budget, it would be even better to know whether this holds for its vast legislative activities as well. The rest of the book is dedicated to convincing the reader that yes, it does.

7   The Legislative Leviathan Marionette

The EU is a prodigious legislator. It adopts on average about 40 acts each month, and the number easily tops 100 for many months.[1] Most of this legislative output is regulatory – which means that it impinges on the lives of Europeans whether they know it or not, and highly technical – which means that they probably do not. Thus, while citizens ought to be concerned with legislative politics, they might be quite unable to exercise the requisite oversight to do so effectively. Is it the case that the hope for responsive governance in the legislative arena is merely the hope for a benevolent dictatorship?

In this and the following chapters, I will show that national elections shape government strategies even in legislative negotiations. Although the nature of the policies makes it tough to claim credit for any particular outcome, the governments engage in position taking and position defending to shift the bargains closer to outcomes they believe will enhance their electoral standing. When this proves impossible, they are apt to delay unavoidably disadvantageous outcomes until after elections. The vaunted legislative leviathan is still dangling on the strings of national interests as governments negotiate the policies in the Council. The question is why.

Legislative negotiations differ from bargaining over the budget in several respects. First, despite the multiannual financial perspectives, the budgets tend to focus on the near term and the strategies of the member states to prioritize immediate and readily forecast losses and gains. There is not much planning beyond the multiannual financial framework (MFF) horizon: if something is not in the period covered by the financial perspective, it might well not exist. This "short-termism" could be detrimental to cooperation because it reduces the value of future gains one might promise in exchange for better terms today,

---

[1] The data are from "European Union Legislative Output Dataset (EULO)," assembled by Hertz and Leuffen (2011) using PreLex and EUR-Lex, the main databases for monitoring EU legislative processes.

while making others less worried about the future costs of adopting unyielding positions in the present. But it could also be quite conducive to cooperation because statutory deadlines can force governments to compromise, and because any truly divisive unpleasantness can be kicked down the road leaving subsequent, and potentially different, governments to deal with it.

The pros and cons are exactly reversed when it comes to general legislation. Once adopted into the regulatory framework, policies become difficult to reverse and, because they might affect a myriad of other rules and regulations, not that easy to modify. They represent long-term commitments and so worries about future costs loom large in present calculations. Moreover, potentially negative effects today cannot be brushed aside with the argument that one could expect better terms in just a year or five. Without the pressure of deadlines, negotiations can be stretched indefinitely as long as there are some particularly recalcitrant holdouts. On the other hand, the absence of a predictable schedule means that governments might be less susceptible to the need to play to domestic audiences, and so perhaps might be more likely to cooperate. It could also be much easier to induce strategic delays in adoption to tide distressed governments over the next election.

There are, however, several aspects of legislative bargaining that make it much harder for governments to signal responsiveness compared to budget negotiations. While nearly every policy has its winners and losers, the budgets have unambiguous indicators of success: larger shares. Not so with most other EU policies, where the "national" interest gets interpreted through the lens of various pressure groups. For instance, when it comes to CO_2 emission allowances for the aviation industry, is the national interest to set them at 95 percent of the 2005–2007 annual average or at the 2004–2006 annual average? Environmentalists, the airlines, and related business groups would provide conflicting answers, and it is not clear *a priori* that a government that wishes to maximize general welfare would know which of these answers is consistent with its own goals. Nor can it reliably predict what the voters would want: if the battles over the alternatives spill into newspaper editorials and become talking points on popular shows, it is quite possible that the voters themselves will become conflicted on the issue.

When technical matters get politicized – as they are increasingly wont to – even narrow policies can get tied into more generic questions about the responsiveness of the government. Thus, while it is true that the majority of legislative proposals are so arcane that even the specialized news sources do not cover them, policies with clear redistributive domestic implications and policies that defy the preferences of influential interest groups always have the potential of getting politicized, which in turn compels governments to worry about the electoral consequences.

But herein lies the other problem: the secretive negotiations in the Council and the largely cooperative decision-making norms are not very conducive to straightforward evaluations of the contributions of any individual government. As convenient as it might be for one of them to cast aspersions on the twenty-eight others when a policy outcome blows up domestically, it is proportionately challenging to pat oneself on the back when a policy outcome is well liked. The easier it is to avoid blame, the harder it is to claim credit.[2]

Coupling this difficulty with the fluid structure of negotiations makes it nearly impossible to time a favorable outcome in order to claim credit before elections. This means that the strategies for signaling responsiveness must be front-loaded, focusing on position taking and position defending (studied in this chapter), and when these fail, on blame avoidance (studied in Chapters 8 and 9).

Since a government cannot usefully parlay a positive outcome into electoral advantage, it would have to rely on its bargaining behavior to do the signaling. This implies that it would have to adopt and defend positions it believes are in the interests of the politically relevant constituencies. This has a very important implication for its negotiation strategy: *it cannot adopt an extreme position as an opening bid in the hopes of selling concessions for a compromise closer to its ideal policy.* The reason for this is that the reward for this strategy comes in the form of the outcome achieved (potentially too late for the government) and its costs are incurred immediately (the government appears unreasonable and not in sync with the wishes of its own constituents). Moreover, since other governments often have access to the same information on the basis of which the position is formulated, they will discount any extreme position taking as cheap talk, and the bargaining ploy will most likely not work anyway.

The upshot of all of this is that in order to signal responsiveness, *governments must adopt a position in line with the preferences of their constituents and defend it consistently throughout the negotiations.* Since defying the collective is costly, governments can credibly show that they are fighting the good fight. Since it does not take a group for one government to dig in its heels, these strategies can be implemented unilaterally, which makes them more accessible. Even if they do compromise in the end, governments can still use their behavior up to that point for

---

[2] See Cruz and Schneider (2017) on claiming undeserved credit in low-information environments. This is not common in the oversaturated European context.

electoral gain, especially if they also delay that compromise until after the elections.

In this chapter, I present evidence supporting this hypothesis. I begin by showing that governments engage in position defending that is especially pronounced during election periods (Section 7.1). I then describe the "Decision-Making in the European Union" (DEU) data set of legislative negotiations used for the analyses in Section 7.2. Whereas they often do compromise in the end, governments are much more likely to refuse to do so when facing elections. Since these strategies are accessible (and do not necessarily prejudice the outcomes), governments do not need to be strongly motivated to resort to them. Consistent with this, I find that the traditional measures of electoral distress, which proved useful in predicting behavior in budget negotiations, are not relevant here. Of course, if position defending were unrelated to policy outcomes, governments could not use it as a signal; the voters would ignore it. This means that governments that defend their positions should be more likely to attain outcomes more in line with their preferences (even though the timing of these outcomes keeps them unsuitable for credit claiming). I show that this is indeed the case (Section 7.5).

The evidence that position taking is related to policy success combined with the evidence that position taking tends to occur during electoral periods provides strong support for the notion that governments can signal responsiveness even in legislative negotiations.

7.1 Why Focus on Position Defending?

The principal hypothesis is that governments signal responsiveness in legislative negotiations by defending their initial policy positions during electoral periods. This assumes that the initial position reflects the government's estimate of what might be electorally advantageous, which is why holding the line can persuade the relevant political constituents that the government is trying to deliver on their preferred policy. Note that this position need not be the government's own ideal point on the policy and that the government might adopt it for strategic reasons.

Ideally, one might want to estimate with what the initial position is correlated. Unfortunately, data limitations preclude an assessment of the correspondence between the initial position and the government's perception (or, rather, definition) of "national interest." Since there are no objective measures of national interests, governments tend to formulate specific definitions of these interests depending on the information provided to them by partisan and nonpartisan interest groups, as interpreted through the lens of the governing ideology and accounting for governance and electoral concerns. It is nearly impossible to unpack these types of considerations systematically for many governments and many policies over time. Some rough-and-ready methods could be used to calculate the congruence between public opinion and government position taking, but they require some fairly restrictive assumptions (e.g., that positions could be placed on a left–right or pro–anti EU dimension) that are inappropriate for many policies. It is also by no means certain (or even probable) that the governments or their constituents view the desired congruence in this manner.

At the end of the day, the governments are the ones who are highly motivated to get their positioning right. Instead of forcing policies to comply with an arbitrary ideological dimension to gauge whether they have done so, I assume that governments are aware of the preferences of politically relevant constituents that would be affected by the policy – these constituents have strong incentives to make their preferences known – and that the governments have their own reasons to decide how to incorporate conflicting preferences into their policy positions. Since much of this information is inaccessible to outsiders and because insiders are loath to share anything that might be potentially awkward if made public, we must rely on the publicly adopted positions to make our inferences.

There are three potential threats to these conclusions, and fortunately none are particularly troublesome in our context. First, if the outcome of negotiations is to be realized before the elections, then the government would either hold the line to the end or compromise for the sake of agreement. If it holds out, then the government's behavior and its effect on the policy outcome are identical, regardless of its "true" motivations. From the perspective of the citizens, the government would have been responsive, and there is no reason to penalize it at the polls. If it compromises, on the other hand, one could infer with more confidence that the government was insincere in its original positioning.[3] The appropriate remedy for this type of dishonesty is punishment at the polls. Putting these two possibilities together tells us that holding the line should be a signal of responsiveness whether or not the government was defending a policy it genuinely prefers or one that it merely believes its constituents prefer. Conversely, folding at the last minute should not be electorally rewarded.

---

[3] With more confidence, but not with certainty. It is also possible that the government compromised because of side payments it received during the negotiations or because of the strong norms of consensus in the Council. It could have been genuinely committed to the policy its constituents want, but gave way for pragmatic reasons.

7.1 Why Focus on Position Defending? 217

Second, if the outcome is not realized before the elections, then the government could hold the line until the citizens vote and compromise afterwards. For this strategy to work at all, one must assume that domestic politics matter for EU negotiations (which is what I am trying to demonstrate). Moreover, the tactic will fail if the citizens do not assign a relatively high probability to the initial position that truly reflects the government's ideal point. The reason is simply that if citizens thought their government was engaged in blame avoidance by delaying unpleasant outcomes, they would not reelect it. But if the citizens are not entirely deluded, then it cannot be the case that the government adopts insincere positions very often. In other words, for this argument to go through, it has to be the case that the initial position the government adopts is more likely than not to be its preferred policy. If this went against the wishes of its constituents, then holding the line would merely result in losing office. Position defending would have the positive effect the government hopes for only if its position also pleases its constituents, that is, if the government is responsive. Thus, the only relevant possibility is that the government adopted the initial position to signal responsiveness but once the threat receded, it moved toward its ideal point. This lack of position defending should be concentrated in non-electoral periods.

It follows then that if domestic politics affect the adoption of the initial position, this position would very likely reflect the government's best guess about what its constituents want.

The third, and final, potential threat is that the government adopts an initial position for reasons unrelated to domestic politics. One possibility could be that the government strategically chooses a more extreme position in order to shift the bargaining outcome closer to its ideal point by offering "concessions" from its initial demand. For this to work, however, the other governments must not be able to see through the strategy: there is no reason to offer real concessions in exchange for fake ones. Since governments have to motivate their positions whenever they try to persuade others to change theirs, and because they have to rely on data that are observable by all, it is highly unlikely that bazaar-haggling tactics would be successful. Even in the unlikely event that they were, the government would have to retreat from its initial position toward the "compromise." This movement would indicate the absence of position defending and would therefore be associated with domestic costs. Indeed, the precommitment tactic is premised on the assumption that the government faces political costs for compromising – this is why the others are making concessions in order to reach an agreement (Leventoğlu and Tarar, 2005). But this essentially takes the domestic threat mechanism for granted and merely argues that the government might be willing to incur the costs in exchange for a better international deal. If we were to find that on average governments defend their positions during electoral periods, then it would not be possible to rationalize their initial positions in these strategic terms.

For these reasons, I will not attempt to discern just how the initial position is meant to reflect the preferences of relevant constituents, I will simply assume that it does.[4] The analysis is meant to test the implications of that assumption in the context of my theory: governments should be more likely to defend their initial position when facing elections. The next step is to measure the main variables.

7.2 Data and Variables

It has proven exceedingly difficult to analyze position taking and position defending more systematically outside of case studies. The innovative data set "Decision-Making in the European Union" (DEU), however, has gone a long way to rectifying that deficiency.[5] This massive effort has collected detailed information about EU legislative proposals across policy areas and over time. Among its many variables several are pertinent to my analysis: the positions of member states' representatives in the Council (as well as in the European Commission and in the European Parliament), and the outcomes of negotiations. These allow me to construct measures of position taking (whether governments stick to their initial positions throughout) and of success (whether the outcomes correspond to the positions governments defended).

The most recent update, DEU II, includes 125 legislative proposals introduced between January 1999 and August 2008.[6] There are three criteria for selecting a proposal for inclusion: (1) it must have been

---

[4] There is, in fact, empirical support for this assumption. I provide very clear instances of initial positioning meant to reflect public attitudes in the case studies in Chapters 6 and 9. More generally, several studies find robust correlations between public opinion and government positions during European negotiations (Thomassen and Schmitt, 1997; Schmitt and Thomassen, 1999, 2000). When it comes to initial position taking, Thomson (2007, 2011) demonstrates that policy positions that are announced at the beginning of the negotiations generally provide a good representation of the national or ideological interest of the government. Wratil (2017) further demonstrates that governments' initial positions on proposals that can be placed on a left–right (pro–anti EU) dimension are affected by voters' self-placement on a left–right (pro–anti EU) dimension.

[5] Stokman and Thomson (2004); Thomson et al. (2006); Thomson (2011); Thomson et al. (2012).

[6] A complete list of these proposals can be found at www.robertthomson.info/wp-content/uploads/2011/01/Issues_list_new_26March2012.pdf, accessed October 15, 2016.

7.2 Data and Variables

discussed in the Council at various levels between the end dates, (2) it must have been subject to either the consultation or the co-decision procedure, and (3) it must have generated at least some controversy. Since the first two are strictly objective criteria, the third one requires some clarification. A proposal is said to have satisfied the controversy criterion if (a) it was mentioned in a report that was longer than four lines and that was published by either *Agence Europe* or *European Voice*, the news services devoted to European affairs (Thomson et al., 2012, p. 608) and (b) experts identified at least one substantive disagreement among the actors.[7] The non-random selection of proposals for the data set is appropriate for my analysis because I do not expect that domestic electoral politics would have any influence on technical legislation that does not even rate a mention in the specialized news sources. Selecting minimally controversial proposals avoids inflating the data set with cases where the theoretical mechanism should not be operational. I would have had to drop such cases anyway, and the DEU authors have done so in a systematic and replicable way.

To assess the positions that the various governments and their agents adopted with respect to these proposals, the researchers conducted 349 extensive semi-structured face-to-face interviews (with average duration of 100 minutes) with more than 125 experts. The respondents were recruited from the permanent representations of the member states, the European Commission, and the European Parliament. They were mostly civil servants responsible for representing their countries during Council discussions, and they tended to be well informed about the legislative negotiations.[8] Each policy was divided into anywhere between one and five individual issues, and the experts were asked to indicate the positions their governments, the Commission, and Parliament adopted on these issues both immediately after the proposal was introduced (initial position) and before the Council formulated its common position (final position).[9] For instance, Thomson et al. (2012, p. 610) describes the coding process for initial positions as follows:

---

[7] The pre-enlargement data set only used *Agence Europe* as the source, but it is more specialized and read mostly by EU bureaucrats. The post-enlargement data set excludes directives because they are meant for specific states or legal entities, and because they tend to be uncontroversial.

[8] The face-to-face interviews were also used to assess the expertise of the respondents (Thomson and Stokman, 2006).

[9] The individual issues are meant to represent the main points of the controversy. They must contain positions that define the substance of the alternative outcomes and be unidimensional so that preferences over the policy alternatives are single-peaked (Thomson and Stokman, 2006, p. 36). The European Commission and the European Parliament were treated as unitary actors.

The experts were first asked to identify the main disagreements or controversies raised by the legislative proposal in question. [...] For each issue, the expert was first asked to identify the actors that favoured the most extreme policy alternatives. These policy alternatives then defined the endpoints of the issue continuum used to represent this controversy, which for convenience we gave a range of 0–100.[10]

The experts had to justify their opinions, and most referred to positions their governments took when the proposal was introduced or as soon as the governments formulated a stance. The same method was used to code the final positions and the actual outcome.

Figure 7.1 shows an example of the coding of initial positions on a proposal to amend Directive 2003/87/EC (Thomson et al., 2012, p. 605). The proposal sought to include the aviation sector into the EU emissions trading scheme designed to combat climate change. Experts identified two controversial issues: (1) actors were divided over the total amount of CO_2 allowances that should be allocated to the airline industry [Figure 7.1(a)] and (2) they disagreed over the auctioning limits [Figure 7.1(b)]. On the first issue, the new member states preferred generous allowances, and in this they were ranged against the old EU-15 member states and the Commission (where the eventual outcome lay), with Parliament being most aggressive on limitations. On the second issue, preferences were more evenly dispersed, with most new member states preferring no auctioning at all at one extreme and Parliament, Sweden, and Ireland preferring maximum flexibility on the other. Most member states distributed themselves between these positions. The outcome (favored by Belgium and the Netherlands) was a compromise between the positions favored by the Commission, Germany, and France (along with several other member states) and the position favored by the United Kingdom.

When it came to final positions, many (but not all) governments moved toward the common Council position (marked as "outcome"). For example, Sweden did not compromise on its initial rather extreme stance of maximum flexibility in auctions, and its final position diverged considerably from the outcome. This is a clear instance of position defending. Now I turn to its more systematic analysis.

---

[10] The positions recorded in the data set are not averages of the estimates provided by different experts. The researchers made judgments about which estimates to include based on the information provided by the respondents and their reliability. See Thomson et al. (2012, p. 609ff.) for an explanation.

7.2 Data and Variables

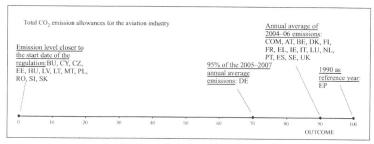

(a) Total Emission Allowances

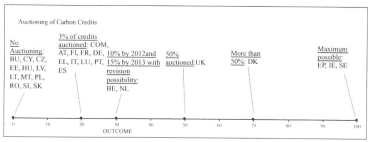

(b) Auctioning of Carbon Credits

Figure 7.1 Issues in CO_2 Emission Allowances for the Aviation Industry (COD/2006/304). The panels show the initial positions taken by EU actors on the proposed directive for emission allowances in the aviation sector. The experts identified two controversial issues: size of allowances (a) and auctioning of carbon credits (b). The member states are identified with the standard EU codes, which use the two-letter abbreviations of ISO 3166 alpha-2 except for Greece (EL) and the United Kingdom (UK). See http://ec.europa.eu/eurostat/statistics-explained/index.php/Tutorial:Country_codes_and_protocol_order. The two additional actors are the Commission (COM) and the European Parliament (EP).
Source: Thomson et al. (2012, p. 606).

The Dependent Variable: Position Defending

The studies of responsiveness often focus on the willingness of actors to move away from their initial legislative positions.[11] I adopt an analogous approach here to measure whether the governments of member states defend the positions they announce near the beginning of negotiations. The initial statements represent the official positions of the governments

---

[11] Arregui, Stokman, and Thomson (2004, 2006); Arregui (2008); Thomson (2011); Aksoy (2012).

and are shared with their domestic audiences and the media. They can be thought of as precommitment devices that are supposed to bind the governments to some aspects of the policy in the hopes that the final outcome reflects their preferences. They provide the anchor from which subsequent behavior during the negotiations can be evaluated. Of particular interest to me is the difference between the initial statement and the government's final position before a vote is taken or a consensus policy announced. If the positions are more or less identical, then the government has held the line throughout and can be said to have defended its original stance. If, on the other hand, the positions diverge, then the government has compromised and can be said to have failed to defend its original stance. My principal dependent variable is thus defined as:

> *Position Defense*: an indicator variable that takes the value of 1 if the final position of the government on an issue is substantially the same as its initial position, and the value of 0 otherwise.

It is perhaps worth repeating that unlike studies that interpret these positions as indicators of the government's policy preferences, I impose no such assumption here. For all we know, these positions could be strategic and so diverge quite a bit from a government's ideal points. However, since such a divergence can only be caused by domestic considerations, and it can achieve its electoral effects only if the constituents believe the government wishes to see the adopted position implemented, and because, on average, these expectations would have to be correct, it follows that a government's willingness to hold onto its initial position is a signal of responsiveness.

Figure 7.2 provides an overview of the frequency of position-defending strategies for the issues in the DEU II data set. On average, governments held the line in about 40 percent of cases (the vertical short-dashed line). Another way of saying this is that compromise is more likely than not, an observation consistent with the collegial decision-making style of the Council. There is considerable variation among countries even if we account for different lengths of memberships. For example, we should probably discount the very high rates of position defense for Romania and Bulgaria (nearly 60 percent) because the data set ends in 2008. This is barely a year after these countries acceded to the EU; as a result, their averages are based on very few instances of participation in policymaking (so they might not be representative).

The high rate for Poland (about 50 percent), on the other hand, is not so easily dismissed: it is very similar to France's (among the oldest

7.2 Data and Variables

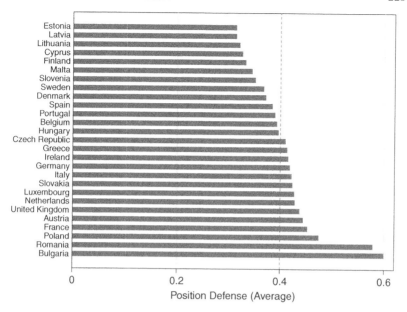

Figure 7.2 Position Defense across Member States, 1998–2008. Average rates of position defense for each EU member for DEU II policies between 1998 and 2008. Countries ranked by their median value of *Position Defense*. The average *Position Defense* across all member states and all issues is indicated by the short-dashed vertical line.
Source: DEU II data set and author calculations.

members) and substantially different from the three Baltic states (which joined at the same time as Poland). In fact, of the A10 that acceded in 2004, six are among the ten member states least likely to defend their positions, and four are at the very bottom (with rates around 30 percent). Among the established members, France, Austria, and the United Kingdom all exceed the sample average and are close to 50-50 on defense and compromise, whereas the Netherlands, Italy, and Germany are closer to the overall mean. There are no obvious differences between net contributors and net beneficiaries, or between older and newer members.

Principal Explanatory Variable

As I expect that electoral concerns should motivate governments to signal responsiveness with position defending, the main explanatory variable is whether elections occurred at any time during the negotiations over the issue:

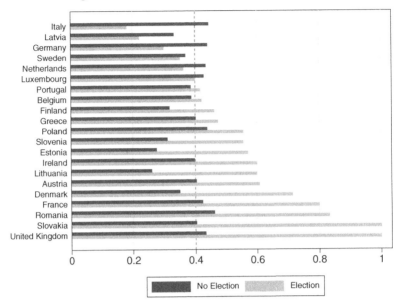

Figure 7.3 Position Defense in and out of Election Periods, 1998–2008. The average rates of position defense for each EU member for DEU II policies between 1998 and 2008 when governments faced elections (light gray) and when they did not (dark gray). Countries are ranked by their median value of *Position Defense* during election periods. The average *Position Defense* across all member states and all issues is indicated by the short-dashed vertical line.
Source: DEU II data set, Döring and Manow (2015), and author calculations.

Election Period: an indicator variable that takes the value of 1 if the government held an election while the issue was being negotiated, and the value of 0 otherwise.

During the decade covered by the DEU II data set (1998–2008), twenty-two member states held at least one national election. Although governments have incentives to signal throughout the entire legislative process, the effect should be strongest when the elections are close to the first Council reading (where most positions get solidified). I do not examine this hypothesis in my main analyses presented here, but the results are robust to considering only elections that occur prior to the first reading in the Council (see below).

Figure 7.3 provides an overview of the frequency of position-defending strategies for the issues in the DEU II data set, separated by periods in which the governments experienced an election while the issue was being negotiated (light-gray bars) and periods in which they did not (dark-gray bars).[12] The average rate of position defense when no elections are held during ongoing negotiations is 39 percent. It climbs to 47 percent on average when elections occur during the negotiations. In other words, the rate of compromise increases by 20 percent when governments do not have to face the polls. Almost two-thirds (14 of 22) of the governments that negotiated both in and out of electoral periods exhibit higher propensities to defend their positions when elections occur during the legislative bargaining process.[13]

There is also significant variation in these propensities, with the United Kingdom experiencing the largest swing: from slightly more prone to position defending than the group average during non-electoral periods, to almost certain position defending during electoral ones. Slovak governments seem just as concerned with appearing to compromise during election periods. The interesting thing here is that neither seems to be particularly recalcitrant outside elections (Slovakia is right at the mean rate.) On the other hand, Portugal and Belgium are only very slightly more likely to hold the line when elections happen during the negotiations.

Of course, it could be that some omitted variable explains both the timing of elections and the reason for position defending, so in my analysis I control for several factors that might be relevant.

Control Variables

My choice of controls is largely derived from the studies of position shifts and legislative outcomes in EU legislative bargaining.[14] The first set of controls accounts for the placement of the government's position in relation to the positions adopted by other important actors:

> *Distance from Commision*: the absolute distance between the government's initial position on the issue and the position adopted by the Commission.

---

[12] Bulgaria, Cyprus, the Czech Republic, Hungary, Malta, and Spain held no national elections during the negotiations covered by the data set. (This does not mean that they held no elections during that decade. Spain, for example, held general elections in 2000, 2004, and 2008.) These member states do not appear in Figure 7.3, but they are included in the statistical estimations.
[13] The exceptions are Italy, Latvia, Germany, Sweden, the Netherlands, and Luxembourg.
[14] Arregui, Stokman, and Thomson (2004); Arregui (2008). Appendix F, available online at https://quote.ucsd.edu/cjschneider/books/, has further details on the codings and the data sources.

> *Distance from Parliament*: the absolute distance between the government's initial position on the issue and the position adopted by the European Parliament.
>
> *Distance from Council Mean*: the absolute distance between the government's initial position on the issue and the average of the initial positions of all other members of the Council.

The second set of control variables pertains to characteristics of the issue itself:

> *Salience*: measures the importance of the issue to the government, as rated by experts. Values range from 0 (not important at all) to 100 (of highest importance).
>
> *Multiple Issues*: an indicator variable that takes the value of 1 if the proposal has more than one issue over which member states have conflicting preferences, and the value of 0 otherwise.

The final set of control variables captures aspects of the formal decision-making rules and some of the structural power of individual member states:

> *Qualified Majority*: an indicator variable that takes the value of 1 if the issue is decided by qualified majority vote, and the value of 0 if it has to be unanimous.
>
> *Voting Power*: the Shapley–Shubik index (SSI) of formal bargaining power, which measures the frequency with which a state's membership in a coalition is pivotal when all voting coalitions are equally likely. Index defined by Shapley and Shubik (1954), data from Bräuninger and König (2005).

Summary statistics can be found in Appendix F.

7.3 During Election Periods, Hold the Line

The dependent variable is dichotomous and policy issues are nested in their proposals. The appropriate estimator is a multilevel mixed-effects probit with robust standard errors. The results are robust to the inclusion of country fixed effects, controlling for different types of Council configurations, controlling for the economic importance of the member state, and using relative salience. (Details in Appendix F.)

7.3 During Election Periods, Hold the Line

Table 7.1. *Position Defending in Legislative Negotiations, 1998–2008.*

	Position Defense			
	Main	Proposal-Restricted	Election-Restricted	Placebo
Election Period	0.224*	0.232*	0.216*	0.087
	(0.118)	(0.130)	(0.115)	(0.072)
	Relative Positioning			
Distance from Commision	0.002	0.000	0.002	0.002
	(0.003)	(0.004)	(0.003)	(0.004)
Distance from Parliament	−0.011**	−0.011**	−0.011**	−0.011**
	(0.004)	(0.004)	(0.004)	(0.004)
Distance from Council Mean	−0.018**	−0.010	−0.018**	−0.017**
	(0.007)	(0.007)	(0.007)	(0.007)
	Proposal Characteristics			
Salience	0.007*	0.006	0.007*	0.007*
	(0.004)	(0.005)	(0.004)	(0.004)
Multiple Issues	−1.431**	−1.440**	−1.431**	−1.435**
	(0.265)	(0.312)	(0.265)	(0.266)
	Formal Decision-Making Power			
Qualified Majority	0.299	0.287	0.297	0.287
	(0.446)	(0.482)	(0.446)	(0.441)
Voting Power	0.018	0.017	0.018	0.017
	(0.016)	(0.017)	(0.016)	(0.016)
constant	0.205	0.130	0.206	0.212
	(0.480)	(0.522)	(0.480)	(0.477)
Observations	2073	1797	2073	2073
Wald χ^2	65.19**	55.46**	65.22**	75.23**

Note: $^*p < 0.10$, $^{**}p < 0.05$.
Multilevel mixed-effects probit with robust standard errors in parantheses. The *main* model uses elections that occur throughout the negotiations; the *proposal-restricted* model uses only proposals that conclude within 36 months; the *election-restricted* model uses only elections that occur prior to the Council vote; and the *placebo* model uses only elections that occur within six months after the Council decision.

Table 7.1 presents the estimation results for four specifications: the *main* model, which considers elections that occur throughout the negotiations, and which is used for interpreting the findings; a *proposal-restricted* model limited to proposals that were concluded within 36 months; an *election-restricted* model limited to elections held prior to the Council vote; and a *placebo* model that changes the *Election Period* coding to 1 if the election occurs within six months after the final adoption of the proposal, and 0 otherwise. The idea behind the placebo test is to check whether holding the line really is about signaling responsiveness through position defending or simply the government digging its heels on a policy it wants quite apart from electoral considerations. A significant coefficient for *Election Period* in the placebo model would be inconsistent with the electoral motivation, and would constitute evidence that the argument about strategic position taking – which I advanced at the beginning of this section – is flawed.

The models fit the data well. The highly significant Wald tests indicate that we can reject the null hypothesis that the coefficients are jointly equal to zero. If the hypothesis that governments are particularly prone to position defending during election periods is valid, the *Election Period* variable should have a positive and statistically significant estimated coefficient in the presence of the relevant control variables in all model specifications except the placebo test. This is precisely what we find: the predicted probability that a government would refuse to compromise in the negotiations is 31 percent absent elections and 36 percent when it has to face the polls. The effect is stronger when only shorter negotiations are considered (proposal-restricted model), and robust when considering only elections that took place prior to the final Council vote (election-restricted model). As expected, the *Election Period* variable is not even close to being statistically significant in the placebo model. This is a strong indicator that the effect uncovered by the other specifications is due to electoral concerns: when a government refuses to compromise because of its own preference for the policy, it is no more likely to do so during electoral periods than outside them.

The electoral effect, while statistically significant, is not substantively very large (although a 16 percent increase in the probability of position defense is not small either). This is analogous to what we observed for negotiations over shares of the annual budget in Chapter 5, and the explanation is very similar. Holding the line against the wishes of other member states is costly because it affects their willingness to reciprocate on other issues and because it goes against the consensual decision-making norm in the Council. As a result, governments would not be willing to do this unless they must.

The analysis supplies evidence for this: the coefficients on the distance from Parliament and the Council mean are both significant and negative. The more discrepant a government's initial position is from the position taken by Parliament and the average (excluding itself) in the Council, the less likely is it to refuse to compromise. In other words, the initial "extremism" does not persist throughout the negotiations. This is consistent with the notion that sometimes countries could stake out a relatively extreme claim for bargaining purposes, but the fact that *Election Period* is significant even after accounting for this possibility tells us the electoral motivation remains key.[15]

It is also interesting to note that distance from the position taken by the Commission does not play a role in the likelihood of position defending. This makes sense: the Commission might set the agenda (often by incorporating what it knows about the preferences of member states that indicate preferences) but it does not play a significant formal role in determining the final outcome. In this it is very different from the other members of the Council and, under the co-decision procedure, from Parliament as well.

The strength of the consensus norm is also evident in the finding that the decision to defend one's position is unrelated to either the voting rule (qualified majority or unanimity) or to one's centrality to winning coalitions (voting power). One might have expected that having a veto (under unanimity) would increase the value of resistance because it would cause the other member states to offer concessions and side payments (although then one would have to compromise in the end) or because it could force them to move to one's preferred position. One might also have thought that the more structurally powerful member states would have better chances of getting the others to make such a move, so they would be more prone to digging in their heels. Neither expectation is borne out by the data, most likely because of the collegial decision-making procedures in the Council.

The fact that *Voting Power* is insignificant also provides some nuance to the interpretation of *Election Period*. Recall that *Position Defense* is coded without reference to the final outcome of negotiations: it takes the value of 1 for governments whose recalcitrance resulted in their remaining an outlier on the adopted policy (as clear an instance of position defending as one could hope for) but also for governments whose initial position was adopted. It could be the case that some member states are more pivotal: their positions tend to become final outcomes and so there is no reason for them to alter their initial stance. If this were true, we would expect *Voting Power* to pick it up. It does not, which suggests that we are looking at position defending instead. Another possibility is that governments simply pick positions they expect to emerge as compromises. Unless it just so happens that for some reason

---

[15] The inverse relationship between initial extremism and the tendency to compromise is consistent with other findings in the literature (Thomson et al., 2006; Arregui, 2008).

governments that face elections are more likely to have preferences that coincide with those of the majority in the Council, the only reason to adopt such a stance is electoral: the government is backing what it believes would be the "winning horse" so it can signal responsiveness both through position defending and credit claiming.

Proposal characteristics matter as well. When the issue is part of a proposal that has other aspects over which members have conflicting preferences, it is less likely that governments would become recalcitrant on that issue. This makes sense: multiple dimensions allow for trade-offs that make compromises more likely (McKibben and Western, 2014). Moreover, sticking to one's guns on one of the issues might make others quite unwilling to give in on other issues, which increases the costs of position defending. Hence, *Multiple Issues* is both negative and highly significant.

Finally, governments are more likely to defend their positions if the issues are salient. The effect, however, is tiny and barely significant. On the one hand, the DEU II set already selects on controversial policies, which means that for many governments the baseline level of salience is already high. The additional marginal effect of *Salience* might be too small to get picked up by the estimations. On the other hand, salience is almost the *sine qua non* for signaling responsiveness, so it is worth taking a closer look.

7.4 The Unconditional Absence of Public Compromise

Does salience matter? It should. Highly salient issues are more likely to be debated domestically, which implies more awareness and, potentially, more interest in what the government is doing about them. The incentive to signal responsiveness should be stronger, which seems to imply that the government should be more likely to defend its initial position. Indeed, this is what the coefficient on *Salience* indicates, except that the indication is really more like a suggestion.

Figure 7.4(a) gives a sense of the distribution of the DEU II issues by their salience. Unlike the vast majority of mundane and highly technical legislative activity of the EU, these issues have an average salience of 49 (recall that the scale is between 0 and 100). This does not mean, of course, that everyone in the Council finds the issues especially relevant; about 20 percent of cases involve salience that does not exceed 20. It also does not mean that the issues are exceptionally important to many; about 22 percent of cases involve salience that exceeds 80. It is, however, clear from the histogram that the majority of cases exceed the midpoint of 50 (the average is smaller only because of the roughly 16 percent of

7.4 The Unconditional Absence of Public Compromise 231

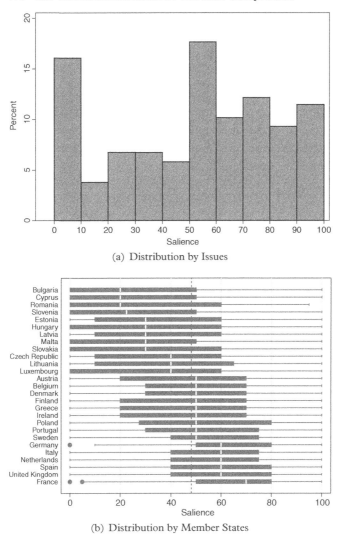

Figure 7.4 Salience of Legislative Issues in DEU II, 1998–2008. Panel (a) shows a histogram of issues, and panel (b) shows box plots for *Salience* by country. Countries are by their median value of *Salience*. The average *Salience* across all member states and all issues is indicated by the short-dashed vertical line.
Source: DEU II.

issues where it was exceptionally low). In other words, as one would have expected, among the issues selected for their potential to generate controversy, most are quite salient.

Sometimes a proposal would involve issues highly salient to almost everyone and issues that only a few member states seem to care about. For example, consider the 1998 Commission proposal on cigarette taxation (Directives 92/79/EEC, 92/80/EC, and CNS/1998/189). The negotiations involved two issues: the frequency with which the tax should be reviewed (with an average salience score of 68, many member states cared about this) and the extension of a derogation for the German tobacco industry (nobody but Germany cared about this).

This example raises another aspect of salience that is worth exploring: its variation by country. Figure 7.4(b) shows box plots for the salience across all member states, ranked by their median salience.[16] All governments have participated in negotiations over issues that were not salient for them, and all of them have been involved in at least some negotiations where they found the stakes high. There is considerable variation in the propensity to get involved in high salience negotiations, however. The issues seem to have been of moderate concern for all the A10(+2) countries that joined in 2004 and 2007, except for Poland. The average median salience of these member states (about 30) is well below the sample average, and most of the issues do not exceed it by much (recall that the boxes include the first and third sample quartiles). This group is clearly distinguishable from the group of old net contributors (Germany, the Netherlands, the United Kingdom) and large important states such as France, Italy, and Spain. The average median salience for this group is above 60; few of their issues drop below 40. It is not immediately obvious what could be driving this pattern.[17]

The mild clustering of issues in the higher salience categories [Figure 7.4(a)] and the clustering of higher salience among the established member states and especially net contributors [Figure 7.4(b)] suggests that it might be beneficial to unpack the effect of salience on the electoral incentives to hold the line during negotiations. To this end, I estimated the *main* model, and this time interacted *Election Period* with *Salience*.

---

[16] See fn. 11 in Chapter 2 for a description of this type of plot.
[17] It could be that the experts overrepresented these countries because of their longer histories, and because of the abundance of information about them. It could be that legislation is more transparent there and so more likely for potential controversies to become salient problems. It could also simply mean that the A10 (and especially the +2) have had very little opportunity to engage in EU-level negotiations over the time span of the data set – four years for the former group and just one year for the latter – and so have either inherited agendas with issues they do not care much about or have not had the opportunity (or capacity) to bring forward legislative proposals on issues they do care about. It also could simply be that there are too few observations for them to make any meaningful inferences.

7.4 The Unconditional Absence of Public Compromise

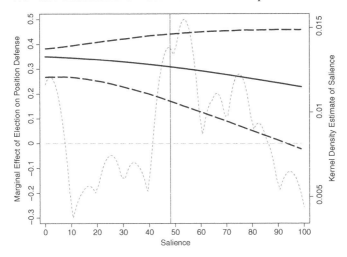

Figure 7.5 The Electoral Incentive, Position Defense, and Issue Salience. Probit estimation as described in Table 7.1 for the *main* model but with *Election Period* interacted with *Salience*. Estimated coefficient (solid line) and 90 percent confidence intervals (dashed lines) plotted over all levels of *Salience* in the sample. Kernel density estimate of *Salience* (short-dashed line) and its mean (vertical light solid line) also shown.

The regression coefficients are reported in Appendix F. Here I present them in a more easily digestible form.[18]

Since the coefficients of the probit model are not easily interpretable, Figure 7.5 shows the marginal effect of elections on position defense across all levels of salience (the solid line) and its 90 percent confidence interval (the two dashed lines). The plot also displays the kernel density estimate of the conditioning variable (indicated by the short-dashed line), which gives us an idea where most observations for *Salience* are in the sample, and its mean (the vertical solid line).

The plot shows that governments are more likely to engage in position defending when they face elections *regardless of the salience* of the issue. The estimated effect of elections is everywhere positive and the confidence intervals do not include zero except at the highest level of salience.[19] Additional tests reveal that the exclusion of the early years from the sample strengthens the significance of the effect across the

---

[18] I adapted the Stata program for interaction effects provided by Matt Golder. http://mattgolder.com/interactions, accessed October 2016. See also Brambor, Clark, and Golder (2006); Berry, Golder, and Milton (2012).
[19] The mean of the estimate is decreasing in salience but the decrease is not statistically significant.

entire range. The results do not change if we control for old and new members, for the average salience of the proposal or the issue, and for the enlargement period.[20]

We can conclude that the effect of salience on position defending is unconditional, and fairly robustly so. One possible explanation is that the incentive to resort to this strategy is so strong during electoral periods that extra salience does not have any additional effect. For this to work, however, it must be that the costs of using this strategy must remain relatively low. If the other member states were to sanction this behavior consistently, then the resulting political costs should serve as a deterrent, and a government would resort to the strategy only if the issue is particularly salient.

One reason to think that this is what might be going on comes from the way I measure position defense. Recall that this variable indicates whether there is a difference between the initial position adopted by a government on an issue and the final known position before the vote in the Council. That is, it is independent of the actual outcome and, more to the point, of how the government voted. In some cases, it might simply reflect the government not announcing publicly a modification of its original position while signaling something quite different behind the closed doors of Council meetings. If this position defending is decoupled from what the government does – which is mostly what other member states care about – then it is truly a costless strategy to implement. Of course, this means that its effectiveness as a signal will be severely undermined. However, remaining committed (from the public's perspective) to the position still keeps alive the possibility of a favorable outcome, and the negative electoral effect can be avoided with a higher probability.

This argument directly yields an empirical implication that we can verify. If the incentive to defend an initial position is strong enough that a government will not deviate from it before a final decision is announced, then this incentive should be overwhelming in other situations as well. That is, other variables that we might expect to influence governments in their position defending should not have an independent effect.

As we found in Chapter 5, when it comes to budget receipts, *Unemployment*, *Number of Elections*, and *Voting Power* strongly condition the signaling behavior of governments.[21] If the effect of position defending would persist no matter how far apart the position is from the average

---

[20] Results available upon request. At one point I threw in everything but the kitchen sink to see if the result would go away, but it appears to be quite robust (at least to my imagination).

[21] I do not have approval data for much of the period covered by DEU II.

7.4 The Unconditional Absence of Public Compromise

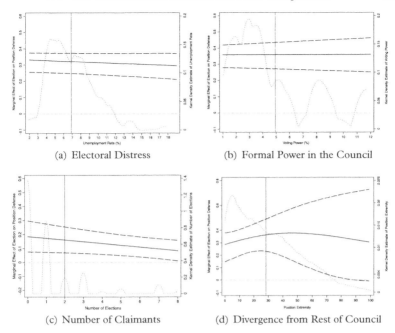

Figure 7.6 Electorally Motivated Unconditional Position Defending. Probit estimation as described in Appendix F for the *main* model but with *Election Period* interacted with each of *Unemployment*, *Voting Power*, *Number of Elections*, and *Distance from Council Mean*. The estimated coefficient (solid line) and 90 percent confidence intervals (dashed lines) are plotted over all values of the corresponding variable. Its kernel density estimate (short-dashed line) and mean (vertical light solid line) are also shown.

in the Council, then this would imply that position defending is relatively easy to pursue (i.e. cheap), *Distance from Council Mean*. For each of these four variables, I estimated the *main* model again but included both the variable and an interaction term with *Election Period*.

Figure 7.6 shows the (absence of) conditional effects across the board (Appendix F presents the results in tabular form). *Election Period* is everywhere significant, and nowhere is any change of its mean estimate significant itself. Electorally motivated position defending occurs irrespective of the level of unemployment, the formal voting power in the Council, the number of other governments facing elections while negotiations are ongoing, and the extent of divergence from the mean position in the Council. It appears, then, that even though EU governments frequently move from their initial policy position, they instantly become far less likely to do so when negotiations coincide with an electoral period.

The incentive to avoid any public hint of a compromise appears especially overwhelming to the point that the mere presence of an election is sufficient to trigger position defending. This is in stark contrast to bargaining over budget shares where the effect was very much conditional on the strength of the electoral incentive, the formal power in the Council, and the number of potential claimants with the need to defend their own positions. In the budget case, however, we analyzed the relationship between the electoral motivation and actual policy outcomes (receipts). It was the redistributive nature of the negotiations that made position defending costly and informative as a signal of responsiveness.

This suggests another way to test whether the unconditional adoption of position defense here is because it is not costly: if the strategy were to somehow incur costs, then salience and the other conditioning variables should come to matter. Let us see whether this implication is consistent with the empirical record.

7.5 Potential Costs Discourage Frivolous Defense

One way position defending could become costly is suggested by the budget case – it must materially affect the other member states. This will happen whenever a government does not merely refuse to abandon its initial position publicly but actually votes consistently with it. We cannot observe the votes, but we do know that they should affect the content of the policy – strongly so under unanimity rules but possibly also under qualified majority rules. This means that we could use the divergence between the initial position and the policy outcome to gauge whether a government is likely to have maintained its position when it mattered. Only governments willing to bear the cost of antagonizing other member states would be willing to go through with this, and this would deter frivolous grandstanding, i.e., the effect should become conditional and only show up when there are additional incentives to engage in position defense. This further implies that a government's ability to achieve an outcome closer to what it had committed can itself be a credible signal of responsiveness. In other words, it can be used for credit claiming.

Variables and Model

Studies of legislative bargaining often define how successful a government is in achieving its goals by looking at the distance between its initial

7.5 Potential Costs Discourage Frivolous Defense

position (which is taken to reflect its ideal point on the issue) and the policy adopted in the end.[22] I use the analogous measure here:

> *Bargaining Success*: measures the inverse of the absolute difference between the member state's initial policy position and the final outcome on the issue. It varies from 0 (the outcome is on the other end of the policy spectrum relative to the position adopted by the government) to 100 (the outcome coincides exactly with the position adopted by the government), with a mean of 65.[23]

This measure is appropriate for my analysis as well, insofar as greater success on a controversial policy implies that someone else must have compromised. Since the proposals in the DEU II data set are deliberately chosen to ensure that there is at least some conflict among the member states on at least one issue, *Bargaining Success* is a decent proxy for the costs of position defending. Moreover, since the policy range on each issue is defined by the actual policy positions taken by the member states, movement toward one's preferred point necessarily implies that someone else is moving away from theirs. The greater the bargaining success, the more concessions someone else must have made, and the higher the costs of achieving the preferred outcome.

Figure 7.7 shows the distribution of *Bargaining Success* by member state. One pattern that becomes immediately evident is that there is no pattern: all EU members are very similar in their ability to achieve legislative outcomes that are relatively close to their initial positions. The median scores are well above the sample mean with the exception of France (right at the mean) and Bulgaria and Romania (which joined in 2007 and thus are not party to many negotiations included in the data set).[24] In other words, almost all countries tend to be successful most of the time.

The absence of any clear patterns of success among the member states is quite encouraging, because I am interested in the willingness to incur political costs and therefore in the difference between defending a position when elections are "around the corner" and when they are not. What "around the corner" means is rather arbitrary, so I provide two operationalizations of my main explanatory variable:

---

[22] Bailer (2004, 2006); Arregui and Thomson (2009).
[23] Cross (2012) defines success by weighing the distance by the salience. These are separable effects, however, and I can estimate them more precisely by keeping them that way and analyzing their interaction.
[24] New members also tend to be less successful during the first years after their accession (Schneider, 2011, 2013).

238   The Legislative Leviathan Marionette

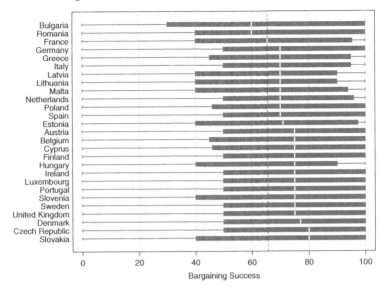

Figure 7.7 Bargaining Success by Member State, 1998–2008. Countries ranked by their median value of *Bargaining Success*. The average *Bargaining Success* across all member states and all issues is indicated by the short-dashed vertical line.
Source: DEU II.

> *Pending Elections (6 Months)*: an indicator that takes the value of 1 if the government expects a national election within six months after the adoption of the proposal, and 0 otherwise.
>
> *Pending Elections (Year)*: an indicator that takes the value of 1 if the government expects a national election within twelve months after the adoption of the proposal, and 0 otherwise.

Since the costs of the position-defending strategy are only incurred if the government pursues it to its completion, elections that occur prior to the final policy outcome should not affect the government's incentive to pursue the strategy. In fact, with the election safely in the past, the government should be more likely to compromise. I define an electoral variable that should have a negative effect on the prospects of bargaining success:

> *Past Elections*: an indicator variable that takes the value of 1 if the government experienced a national election during the negotiations but *before* the outcome was realized, and 0 otherwise.

The other variables are standard for models of bargaining success, and most of them can be found in the estimations reported in Table 7.1.

7.5 Potential Costs Discourage Frivolous Defense

Table 7.2. *Bargaining Success in Legislative Negotiations, 1998–2008.*

	Bargaining Success		
	(6 Months)	(12 Months)	(Placebo)
Pending Elections (6 Months)	1.893*		
	(1.014)		
Pending Elections (Year)		2.597**	
		(1.166)	
Past Elections			−4.523**
			(2.027)
Position Defense	20.879**	20.900**	21.099**
	(4.713)	(4.722)	(4.715)
	Relative Positioning		
Distance from Commision	−0.110	−0.109	−0.107
	(0.090)	(0.090)	(0.090)
Distance from Parliament	−0.102	−0.102	−0.101
	(0.094)	(0.093)	(0.094)
Distance from Council Mean	−0.449**	−0.449**	−0.447**
	(0.133)	(0.133)	(0.133)
Distance from Status Quo	0.180*	0.181*	0.179*
	(0.093)	(0.093)	(0.093)
	Proposal Characteristics		
Salience	0.050	0.049	0.051
	(0.053)	(0.052)	(0.052)
	Formal Decision-Making Power		
Voting Power	−0.115	−0.121	−0.114
	(0.232)	(0.231)	(0.232)
Constant	69.290**	68.547**	69.845**
	(10.351)	(10.320)	(10.367)
Observations	1506	1506	1506
Wald χ^2	138.49**	144.89**	158.29**

*$p < 0.10$, **$p < 0.05$.
Multilevel mixed-effects linear regression model with Huber–White robust standard errors in parantheses.

The two exceptions are *Position Defense*, which should be positively correlated with the outcomes, and *Distance from Status Quo*, which is the absolute distance of the initial position from existing policy.[25]

---

[25] Aksoy (2012) makes a convincing case for including *Distance from Status Quo* into models of bargaining success. The theory makes no predictions about the expected sign.

Because *Bargaining Success* is a continuous variable, and the issues are nested within different proposals, I estimate a multilevel mixed-effects linear regression model with Huber–White robust standard errors.[26]

Table 7.2 shows the estimation results with the three principal explanatory variables. The models fit the data very well. The significant Wald tests in all specifications indicate that we can reject the null hypothesis that the coefficients are jointly equal to zero.

As my argument suggested, when elections are pending, governments are more likely to obtain outcomes closer to their initial positions. Conversely, with elections concluded, governments are far more likely to make concessions. We must be careful how we interpret this, however. At first glance, it would appear that this sort of result should give voters no warrant to expect their government to hold the line, and so they should not reward it at the polls even if they are uncertain. The model, however, does not differentiate between concessions made by the same government and those made by a new one after the elections. It could very well be the case that the constituents the previous government was trying to please were not electorally strong enough to keep it in power, and that the new government has an entirely different set of interests to satisfy. This would have to be answered in future work.

Turning back to pending elections: How big are their effects? Governments increase the convergence between their initial position and the final outcome by about 2 percent during electoral periods. As with budget receipts, the effect is not very large (although one must be wary about making statements like that since the metric is issue specific and not easily comparable across issues). It is also worth noting the strong positive effect of *Position Defense* on *Bargaining Success*. This is as should be: one could hardly interpret clinging to one's initial position throughout the negotiations as position defending if this were not making it more likely that the outcome would be closer to that position as well.

These results provide some evidence for the notion that position defending is associated with outcomes that are less favorable to other member states, which in turn can substantiate the notion that it can become costly for the government when it carries it through the voting stage. This implies that the willingness to pay this cost should rise and fall with the salience of the issue, the extent of electoral distress, the number of claimants, the formal voting power, and the ease of forming supporting coalitions.

---

[26] Details about the model specification and a number of robustness checks can be found in Appendix F.

7.5 Potential Costs Discourage Frivolous Defense

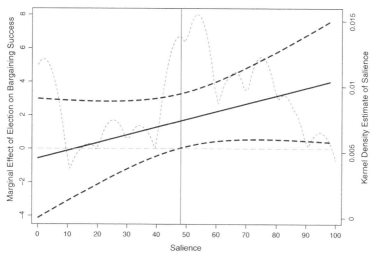

Figure 7.8 The Electoral Incentive, Bargaining Success, and Issue Salience. Estimation as described in Table 7.2 for *Pending Elections (6 Months)*, which is also interacted with *Salience*. The estimated coefficient (solid line) and 90 percent confidence intervals (dashed lines) are plotted over all levels of *Salience* in the sample. Kernel density estimate of *Salience* (short-dashed line) and its mean (vertical light solid line) are also shown.

Since the puzzling effect of salience is what triggered this inquiry, let us start with it. Figure 7.8 shows the marginal effect of elections on *Bargaining Success* across all levels of salience (the solid line) and its 90 percent confidence interval (the two dashed lines).[27] As before, the plot also displays the kernel density estimate of the conditioning variable (indicated by the short-dashed line), which gives us an idea where most observations for *Salience* are in the sample, and its mean (the vertical solid line).

The result strongly supports the hypothesis that governments are only willing to pay the position-defending costs when the issue is relatively salient to them. The electoral incentive is not strong enough until *Salience* exceeds the sample mean; the effect is not statistically significant for values below that mean. Elections do become motivating when salience is high. Governments are more likely to obtain policy outcomes closer to their initial positions, which is what allows them to claim credit

---

[27] Appendix F presents the results in tabular form.

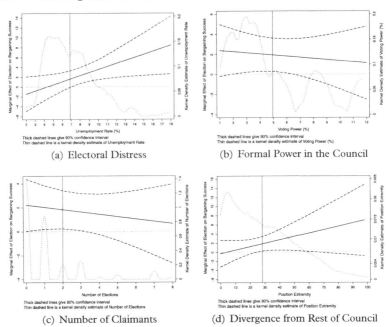

Figure 7.9 Electorally Motivated Unconditional Position Defending. Estimation as described in Appendix F for the *main* model but with *Pending Elections (6 Months)* interacted with each of *Unemployment, Voting Power, Number of Elections*, and *Distance from Council Mean*. The estimated coefficient (solid line) and 90 percent confidence intervals (dashed lines) are plotted over all values of the corresponding variable. Its kernel density estimate (short-dashed line) and mean (vertical light solid line) are also shown.

after the fact. At the high end of salience, elections increase congruence by 4 percent, double the unconditional effect we detected in Table 7.2.

Figure 7.9 exhibits similar patterns for the other four conditioning variables: when position defense is costly, the strength of the electoral incentive varies with the conditions. Take, for instance, electoral distress operationalized through the level of unemployment. The electoral effect is nonexistent until unemployment exceeds the sample mean. Once this happens, however, the government becomes very highly motivated indeed: at very high levels, governments manage to increase the convergence of the policy outcome and their initial position by 8 percent [Figure 7.9(a)]. This is reminiscent of the findings for the budget, where the electoral incentive also did not kick in until *Unemployment* hit 7 percent.

7.5 Potential Costs Discourage Frivolous Defense

Another result that echoes conclusions for budget negotiations is that while elections might motivate a government to achieve more favorable outcomes, the presence of other similarly motivated governments lowers the likelihood of success. As Figure 7.9(c) shows, the pending elections are only positively and significantly associated with favorable bargaining outcomes when there are fewer than four other governments facing elections.

As one might expect, increasing the number of member states that might work at cross-purposes with a government has contradictory effects on the signaling strategy. On the one hand, the costs of plowing through and defending the initial position to its end are higher, which makes the signal more credible, and the credit claiming more effective. On the other hand, it makes it much harder to achieve a positive outcome, which drastically lowers the probability that a government would be in a position to claim credit at all. This result suggests that when there are more than three other member states eyeing the polls, the latter effect dominates the former. No matter how effective the costly signal would be, the government is simply unable to send it.

This logic is also in evidence in Figure 7.9(d), which correlates the effect of the electoral motivator to the degree of divergence from the policy preferences of the others in the Council. When the position is too close to the Council average, there are no costs associated with defending it (because the others will not have to make concessions), and so the signal of responsiveness is ineffective. As a result, the government has no incentive to send it – the electoral effect is statistically insignificant. As a government's position diverges from the group, however, getting the final outcome closer to its position must involve concessions from others; thus the costs of pushing through increase. This makes the signal more informative, and the incentive to send it becomes stronger; the electoral effect is statistically significant at moderate levels of position divergence. However, when the government departs too far from the Council mean, adopting anything close to an extreme position would require very serious concessions from other member states, which are unlikely to be forthcoming. As with the number of claimants, achieving success under these conditions would be incredibly useful for credit claiming, but the very thing that endows it with such signaling potential also makes it nearly impossible to achieve in practice. Since the government will be unable to attain such an outlier of an outcome, the incentive to hold the line weakens, and the government compromises; the electoral effect is statistically insignificant yet again.

If there is one aspect in which legislative negotiations do not track bargaining over budget shares, it is in the inability of structurally powerful member states to throw their weight around. As was already evident from the box plots in Figure 7.7, the countries one normally associates with having tremendous pull in Council negotiations – France, Germany, Italy, the United Kingdom – are not notably more successful than others in their ability to attain legislative outcomes closer to their initial positions. In fact, except for Bulgaria and Romania, France, Germany, and Italy are among the most likely to compromise. The United Kingdom seems generally better at pulling outcomes toward its position, but its median success is on par with Portugal, Luxembourg, and Ireland, none of which is generally known as a legislative heavyweight. The United Kingdom is, in fact, outperformed by Denmark and the Czech Republic (and Slovakia, although it has a higher variance).

Figure 7.9(b) corroborates this impression: having more formal power (at least the one measured by the Shapley–Shubik voting power index) does not enable a government to extract more favorable deals during electoral periods. In fact, the electoral effect quickly disappears (becomes statistically insignificant) for countries whose power exceeds the sample mean. The effect also does not exist for those among the least powerful. It only shows up for intermediate values of the index, where the kernel density indicates most of the countries cluster anyway. In other words, pending elections can enable governments to wrest better deals but not if these governments are too powerful.

One possible explanation is that much of the budget gets allocated under access rules that are designed to benefit specific member states, and in many cases these are precisely the ones with significant formal powers. When it comes to non-budget legislation, there is no such built-in privilege. Although it would be an exaggeration to say that in these policy matters everything is up for grabs, it would not be going too far to suggest that the outcomes here depend much more directly on bargaining specifics rather than on any formal rules. This would be especially true when the policy must be adopted unanimously, but it would also hold under qualified majority, where the interested member state would have to prevent the formation of blocking coalitions.

All of this suggests that the bargaining over these policies could be subject to an even stronger norm of consensus decision-making. When this is coupled with the idea that in legislative negotiations small states tend to have narrower interests and more clearly defined priorities than larger states, one could easily see how the formally powerful states could fail to exercise a lot of influence (Arregui and Thomson, 2009, p. 670). This, of course, is speculative. Disentangling the reasons why *Voting Power* affects the electoral incentive differently for budget bargaining and legislative negotiations must await future study.

7.6 Conclusion

The preponderance of evidence presented in this chapter establishes that domestic electoral politics affect the conduct of legislative negotiations much in the way they do those over the budget. With elections pending, governments tend to obtain policy outcomes that are closer to their initial positions (and the positions they defend throughout the negotiations) compared to outcomes they agree to during non-electoral periods. The correlations are maintained even when we account for a variety of procedural and structural factors.

We can, in fact, go beyond this general conclusion. Table 7.3 summarizes the findings for total budgetary receipts from Table 5.3 and summarizes the new results from the analyses in this chapter.

Table 7.3. *Revised Summary of the Empirical Findings.*

	Signals of Responsiveness		
	Budget	Legislative Acts	
	Total Receipts	Position Defense	Bargaining Success
The Fundamental Result			
Impending Elections	✓	✓	✓
Politicization over Time	Yes		
Salience		No	Yes
Electoral Distress			
Bad Economic Times	Yes	No	Yes
Disapproval of the Government	Yes		
Volatile Swing Voters	Yes		
Structural and Informal Powers			
Voting Power in the Council	Yes	No	Weak
Ideological Divergence	Weak		
Divergence in EU Support	Yes		
Divergence from Council		No	Yes
Constraining Factors			
Number of Claimants	Yes	No	Yes

For all conditioning variables, "yes" means that the size of the electoral effect depends on the variable and is significant; "weak" means that the relationship is tenuous; "no" means that there is no evidence that the effect depends on the variable. Empty cells mean that the relationship was not tested.

It turns out that posturing during negotiations – defending the position initially adopted and refusing to compromise through a public revision – is a relatively cheap strategy to pursue. Since the final vote and any accompanying concessions are made in private, if the elections were to occur before the outcome is realized, then the fact that a government stands firm on its position imposes little cost on its fellow member states. There is no reason for them not to cooperate with its position defending. Consequently, governments seem to resort to that strategy whenever elections are pending irrespective of any other additional motivating factors. None of the conditioning variables (salience, unemployment, voting power, divergence from the Council, and even the number of potential claimants) has an effect on the strength of the incentive to cling to the initial position throughout the negotiations.

Things are different, however, when a government's position defending materially affects other member states. Since securing a preferable outcome on an issue over which there is disagreement immediately implies that someone else must have made a concession, it follows that holding the line behind closed doors in the Council is costly to the government in a way that mere refusal to compromise in public is not. The more the outcome reflects a government's position, the larger the concessions others must make to reach an agreement on those terms, and thus the higher the costs of forcing them to do so.

This generates contradictory incentives for a government to pursue its position on an issue to its completion. The higher costs of attaining a favorable outcome discourage frivolous position defending of the type that is available prior to the final vote. Only highly motivated governments would be willing to pay them, and when they do succeed, they can credibly claim credit for that success. But the larger the required concessions, the less cooperative other member states become, and so the less likely the government is to obtain a favorable outcome. Moreover, without the clarity of a larger budget share, the policy minutia of legislative deals often makes for a rather weak mark of success. This inclines the government toward compromise and dilutes the credit-claiming potential. When a deal is preferable to no agreement at all, the government will retreat from its initial position, and the outcomes will not be clear-cut achievements.

In these situations, the additional motivating factors regain their influence. Governments are only willing to insist, and able to obtain, more favorable deals when the issue is particularly salient to them, and when they are in electoral distress because of high unemployment rates. Conversely, they become increasingly unlikely to do any of these things when there are other member states who might need to signal

7.6 Conclusion

their own responsiveness because of pending elections. The trade-off between the credibility of the signal and the probability of obtaining a favorable outcome is most evident in the conditioning effect of the distance between the government's preferred position and the average in the rest of the Council.

The electoral incentive has a Goldilocks property: it does not work if the government is too close to the rest of the Council or if it is too far from them; it has to be "just right." This is because a position that is likely to prevail without others having to make concessions is not costly to insist upon, which weakens the impact of the signal. If anyone could get this, there is no reason for domestic audiences to infer that the government is particularly responsive. This in turn means that there is no reason to be especially motivated by electoral considerations either. If the position is too far from the Council average, insisting upon it requires serious sacrifices from others, which seriously lowers a government's chances of success. In these cases, position defending would be extremely beneficial for the information a favorable outcome would convey; however the probability of getting this outcome is practically nil. As a result, the government would not be especially motivated by electoral considerations either. Only when the divergence is moderate can signaling work: it is costly enough to deter frivolous position defending, and yet not too costly to make the outcome an impossibility; it is "just right."

Accounting properly for the costs of the signaling strategy made it possible to explain the otherwise surprising absence of conditioning in position defending during negotiations but without reference to the final outcome. Still, one result remains puzzling even after the extended analysis: we found formal voting power in the Council does not influence the effect of the electoral incentive. On one hand, one might have expected this for member states with little heft in the Council, and indeed this is the case. On the other hand, the inability of those who do command greater power to do better for themselves in electoral periods is not easy to explain. In a sense, this is quite encouraging because it implies that might does not make right in the EU, at least when it comes to legislative acts – it does when it comes to the budget – but then it would be nice to know why this is so. I have offered some speculative possibilities, but more work is needed to understand this.

An important implication of this analysis is that governments can use legislative negotiations to signal responsiveness by claiming credit for success. Although not as straightforward to interpret as budgetary receipts, it appears that achieving more favorable outcomes is important enough to constituents who care that governments are trying their best to procure them on their citizens' behalf when governments have to face the polls. The fact that they are more successful in this during electoral periods than on average is testament enough for their efforts. The vaunted legislative leviathan of the EU is still very much a marionette where the national governments pull the strings in their deliberations in the Council.

But with so many masters, there is a limit to the coordination that can benefit any one of them. What happens when a government knows that it is not likely to prevail? What happens if it knows that the majority is arrayed against it or that there are powerful states that are unlikely to make concessions and could organize a blocking coalition? What happens when there are other member states trying to move the outcome closer to their positions for the exact same reason that the government is trying to move it closer to its own?

The findings here suggest that the prospects for success look rather dim. But this means that if an agreement is reached before the elections, an unfavorable outcome is going to undermine whatever position defending the government had done prior to the final vote. It would have to defend itself against charges of incompetence, bad faith, or both. Having to deal with this is bad no matter the timing, but having to do it in the midst of an electoral campaign is the worst. The only sensible thing for the government to do in this situation seems to be stalling the negotiations until the elections have passed. I now turn to the systematic analysis of this possibility.

8   The Waiting Game: *Après les élections, le déluge*

The most persuasive signal of responsiveness for a government is to deliver a policy outcome that its constituents favor in time for the election (credit claiming).[1] When it anticipates that the collective outcome is unlikely to reflect that position, the government can signal by adopting the stance the constituents prefer (position taking) and sticking to it throughout the negotiations despite the costs incurred (position defending). When the outcome is realized prior to the elections, the government can at least claim it did its best on the behalf of its constituents and try to explain away any disparity between what they wanted and the outcome by attributing it to the political process, to the strongly held preferences of other member states, or, in a pinch, to the EU itself.

This is not likely to be especially persuasive: After all, any government that fails to deliver has strong incentives to pin the blame somewhere else and virtually no incentive to admit to its own disability, incompetence, or, perhaps worst, divergent preferences. And neither it is likely that the government would be able to keep the lid on the information: the opposition is very motivated to publicize its deficiencies, magnify the expected losses, and harp on the inadequacy of its feeble attempts at rationalizing the outcome (Novak, 2013). The press, of course, loves nothing more than stories of botched performances, government-induced fiascos, and policy flops.

To get a sense of what might happen, consider the consequences of the Commission announcing in October 2014 that the United Kingdom would have to pay an extra €2.1 billion into the EU budget. Aside from the fact that the sum was unusually large, this was a technical matter: contributions are calibrated to the state of the economy, and

---

[1] It is not a perfect signal because everyone wants to claim credit for success. In fact, governments often interpret outcomes to their advantage even though their claims might be difficult to substantiate when details are examined: Witness the aftermath of any EU summit when all governments without exception tell their domestic audiences how they managed to defend national interests while simultaneously working for the bright future of the EU.

the UK's had grown faster than anticipated by Eurostat, which automatically increased the call rate on the GNI-based resource relative to the forecasts. The recalibration is standard procedure and had been neither controversial nor (until now) politicized domestically. The United Kingdom was not even the only member state whose call rate had gone up: eight others were in the same boat, among them the Netherlands and Italy, which got bills with additional €640 million and €340 million, respectively.[2] The Commission had not anticipated that the corrections would become politicized. As the EU budget commissioner explained:

Because in previous years they were relatively small, they stayed under the radar screen of politicians and I admit, for us in the European Commission as well.[3]

But politicized the corrections got, and fast. The opposition Labour Party denounced the Commission for springing "a backdated bill"; the tabloids screamed that Brussels was "back for MORE of your cash"; and the UK Independence Party (UKIP) leader Nigel Farage melodramatically likened the EU to "a thirsty vampire feasting on UK taxpayers' blood."[4] Prime minister David Cameron was already under pressure from his own Conservative party to revisit the United Kingdom's relationship with the EU, and he had promised a referendum on whether Britain should leave the EU if he were to win the elections scheduled for May 2015. UKIP had also just gotten its first MP elected to the House of Commons, and was fielding another Conservative defector in a November by-election in Rochester and Strood in Kent. Facing an insurgent UKIP and a general election, Cameron angrily vowed that Britain would not pay this bill by the December 1 deadline. Farage ridiculed the idea that the United Kingdom could avoid meeting the EU's "outrageous" demands.[5] As Cameron's carefully worded denial – that he would not pay by the deadline rather than at all – implied, the UKIP leader was right: there was not much the United Kingdom could

---

[2] Fox, Benjamin. "Cameron slapped with new €2bn EU bill." *EUobserver*, October 24, 2014. https://euobserver.com/political/126238, accessed February 3, 2018; Fox, Benjamin. "Cameron vows to reject €2 billion EU bill." *EUobserver*, October 24, 2014. https://euobserver.com/news/126239, accessed February 3, 2018.

[3] EU budget commissioner Kristalina Georgieva, quoted by Valentina Pop, "UK, Netherlands get nine extra months to pay EU bill." *EUobserver*, November 7, 2014. https://euobserver.com/economic/126437, accessed February 3, 2018.

[4] "Anger in Britain over EU's 'thirsty vampire' payout demand." *Agence France-Presse*, October 24, 2014. www.yahoo.com/news/anger-britain-over-eus-thirsty-vampire-payout-demand-103003354.html, accessed February 3, 2018.

[5] "Cameron: UK won't pay £1.7bn EU bill." *BBC*, October 24, 2014. www.bbc.com/news/uk-politics-29754168, accessed February 3, 2018.

do except reschedule the payments so that they would not have to come all at once.⁶

In the aftermath of this imbroglio, public support for UKIP surged to 19 percent (about a 4 percent increase) while support for EU membership dropped by 10 percent.⁷ Mark Reckless (the UKIP candidate) won the Rochester and Strood seat, and other Tory MPs were said to have gotten ready to defect as well.⁸ A Conservative MP could only ruefully observe:

> The timing and content of the EU budget demand shows how inept Brussels is. Brussels needs to work with the UK Government, not work against it.⁹

In cases like this, the problem (from the government's perspective) is that the outcome is there for all to see; it cannot be denied, only interpreted. It would be far better if the outcome remained a possibility – something that had yet to occur, something that could potentially be unfavorable for the constituents but that could potentially be favorable as well. There would be no need to explain anything away, only to convey the impression that the government was working hard on their behalf and that it expected to prevail. Position taking and position defending are much more effective when they are not undermined by their factual failure to achieve the stated goals. Thus, if the government can delay the realization of an unfavorable outcome until after the elections, it would much rather do that than having to fend off charges of ineptitude or unresponsiveness.

---

⁶ The compromise was already evident by early November with both Britain's new EU commissioner and the Dutch finance minister indicating that the main problem was the short time to meet such large demands ("David Cameron says he will reject installment plan for £1.7bn EU bill." *The Guardian*, November 6, 2014. www.theguardian.com/politics/2014/nov/07/david-cameron-no-compromise-over-eu-demand, accessed February 3, 2018). The Commission initially threatened that unless there are compelling reasons for the delays, non-payment would result in penalties but in the end acquiesced to interest-free rescheduling (Pop, Valentina. "EU commission warns UK about its rebate." *EUobserver*, October 27, 2014. https://euobserver.com/political/126262, accessed February 3, 2018).

⁷ Chroley, Matt. "Ukip surges to record poll high after the 'gift' of Brussels demanding Britain pay an extra £1.7billion." *Daily Mail*, October 28, 2014. www.dailymail.co.uk/news/article-2810938/Ukip-surges-record-poll-high-gift-Brussels-demanding-Britain-pay-extra-1-7billion.html, accessed February 3, 2018.

⁸ Lyons, James. "Ukip popularity surge because people are still struggling financially, says Tory grandee John Major." *Daily Mirror*, November 16, 2014. www.mirror.co.uk/news/uk-news/ukip-popularity-surge-because-people-4639198, accessed February 3, 2018.

⁹ Morris, Nigel. "Nigel Farage says David Cameron will have no choice but to meet EU's 'outrageous' demand for an extra £1.7bn from Britain." *The Independent*, October 24, 2014. www.independent.co.uk/news/uk/politics/nigel-farage-says-david-cameron-will-have-no-choice-but-to-meet-eus-outrageous-demand-for-an-extra-9816287.html, accessed February 3, 2018.

The downside is that when the outcome is finally revealed, the government would have to confront the inevitable fallout that would also pile accusations of bad faith and deliberate stalling. But with the citizens having to cast their votes again years in the future, the government would have reasonable expectation that these ill effects might dissipate or be supplanted by its subsequent successes and so play little role in future elections. And this is provided the government wins the present ones. If it loses, the former ruling party can always lay any bad outcome that follows at the door of the new government.

Tactical delays are not really an option when it comes to annual budgets: they have a fairly strict schedule and can be adopted by qualified majority vote. As we saw in Chapter 5, credit claiming is the only viable strategy here. Tactical delays become possible during bargaining over the multiannual frameworks, as evidenced by the UK behavior I studied in Chapter 6. But even then there is a deadline: the new financial perspective has to be adopted in time for it to come into effect. Unless the elections happen to be conveniently scheduled before that deadline, there is little chance of any government being able to resist the collective pressure to come to an agreement to keep the EU funded.

Legislative negotiations, on the other hand, are not critical the way the budget is: the EU machinery would happily keep chugging along while the issues are being deliberated. Negotiations have no time schedules and could potentially be delayed as long as necessary to obtain the votes to adopt the legislation. It is far more likely that any government that wishes to delay for electoral reasons would be accommodated by the other member states, especially if its acquiescence to the final policy is deemed important. EU bureaucrats are also not generally as politically insensitive as the Commission was in 2014 and are likely to steer clear of controversy if it means getting legislative outcomes closer to where they want them.

The theoretical argument suggests that negotiations over legislative proposals that involve issues that member governments might find objectionable (as almost every proposal that involves negotiations does almost by definition) would tend to last longer when governments face national elections. Using data for all legislative activities of the EU between 1976 and 2009 (14,396 proposals), I find that this is indeed the case and that the delay is especially noticeable when the elections are highly competitive and when there are many of them.

8.1   Data and Variables

The information about EU legislative negotiations I use for the analyses in this chapter comes from the *European Union Legislative Output*

8.1 Data and Variables

(EULO) data set (Hertz and Leuffen, 2011).[10] Unlike the selective DEU II data set, EULO includes all 14,396 legislative proposals negotiated between January 1976 and July 2009. It encompasses regulations (binding in their entirety and directly applicable to all EU member states), directives (binding in their entirety but leaving form and transposition method to national authorities), and decisions (binding only for a subset of member states). I use all three legislative instruments, as argued by König (2008, p. 149).[11]

The Dependent Variable: Length of Negotiations

The hypothesis relates electoral considerations to incentives to delay the adoption of legislative proposals, so the natural unit of analysis is the individual proposal and the dependent variable is the time it took to negotiate its adoption:

> *Length of Negotiations*: the number of days between the introduction of a legislative proposal by the Commission and its final adoption by the Council.

Figure 8.1(a) shows the distribution of *Length of Negotiations*. More than three-quarters of proposed legislation is adopted within the first 346 days of its introduction, and 90 percent is finalized within 882 days. There are a few outliers – most notably COM(1975)490-2, "Proposal for a Council Directive on the Establishment of Common Rules for Certain Types of Carriage of Goods by Road Between Member States," which was initiated in October 1981 but not adopted until March 2005, a delay of 10,767 days – but they are uncommon. The results are robust to excluding unusually lengthy negotiations.

Figure 8.1(b) displays the variation in adoption times over the years. It shows that with the exception of a brief period in the 1980s (when it spiked and then dropped precipitously for a few years, most likely because of the Single European Act of 1986), the median duration of legislative negotiations has not varied by more than a couple of months.

---

[10] EULO codes information from the PreLex and EUR-Lex databases of EU legislative processes. It is very similar to the data set used by Häge (2011).

[11] Research has shown that directives are most prone to conflict (Schulz and König, 2000; Golub, 2007; Hertz and Leuffen, 2011). My results are robust to limiting the sample to directives only. In fact, the results are even stronger because elections reduce the probability of adoption by 51 percent in the inclusive data set, but by 65 percent in the restricted one. See Appendix G, available online at https://quote.ucsd.edu/cjschneider/books/, for details.

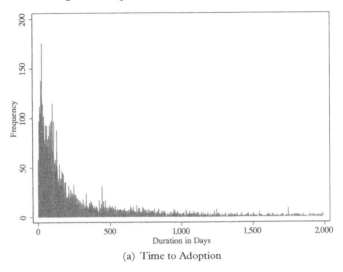

(a) Time to Adoption

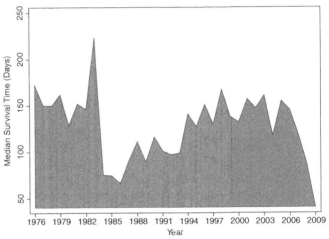

(b) Median Time to Adoption by Year

Figure 8.1 Duration of Legislative Negotiations, 1976–2009.
Source: EULO.

Principal Explanatory Variables

My hypothesis is that legislative acts are unlikely to be adopted close to national elections. The delay should be caused by governments that are facing elections and anticipate unfavorable outcomes. Unfortunately, it was not feasible to measure these expectations for more than

8.1 Data and Variables

14,000 proposals, and thus we must remain agnostic about the identity of the footdraggers. Correspondingly, I shall use a generic measure that indicates whether any government is close to elections at the time of adoption. Since the theory is not (and cannot be) very specific about what "close" means, I use two alternative operationalizations:

Elections in 30 Days: an indicator variable that takes the value of 1 if the proposal was adopted within 30 days prior to a national election in any member state. Overall, 34 percent of proposals are adopted within 30 days.

Elections in 60 Days: an indicator variable that takes the value of 1 if the proposal was adopted within 60 days prior to a national election in any member state. Overall, 53 percent of proposals are adopted within 60 days.

Although these measures do not distinguish among member states, I provide some country-specific estimates in the analysis that follows. This is not entirely satisfactory, so I try to approximate the likelihood of *someone* becoming obstructionist during the negotiations by measuring the number of governments standing for reelection around the time the proposal is adopted:

Number of Elections: measures the number of national elections that take place within 60 days after the adoption of the proposal. It ranges from 0 to 5, with a mean of 1.5.

We know from the findings in Chapters 5 and 7 that member states become less cooperative when several of their governments face elections, and I expect that this will increase the probability that someone would have to resort to delaying tactics to avoid a bad outcome.

Control Variables

The extant studies of EU legislative decision-making have identified several important variables that could influence the duration of negotiations apart from electoral concerns.[12] The first set of variables accounts for procedural reasons for delays:

Qualified Majority: an indicator variable that takes the value of 1 if the act is to be adopted by qualified majority, and 0 if it requires unanimity.

---

[12] See, for example, Schulz and König (2000); König and Pöter (2001); König and Bräuninger (2002); Golub (2007, 2008); Golub and Steunenberg (2007); König (2007, 2008); König and Junge (2009); Leuffen and Hertz (2010); Hertz and Leuffen (2011); Kleine and Minaudier (2018).

Cooperative Procedure: an indicator variable that takes the value of 1 if the legislation is to be decided by the cooperation procedure (where the Council is more influential), and 0 otherwise.

Co-decision Procedure: an indicator variable that takes the value of 1 if the legislation is to be decided by the co-decision procedure (where Parliament plays an important role), and 0 otherwise.

Proposal for a Directive: an indicator variable that takes the value of 1 if the legislative proposal is a directive, and 0 if it is either a regulation or a decision.

Number of Pending Acts: measures the number of proposals pending decisions. The more undecided acts there are, the higher the pressure to adopt some in order to relieve the workload of the Council.

Summer Vacation: an indicator variable that takes the value of 1 for the month of August, when most EU employees take their vacations, and 0 otherwise.

The second set of controls accounts for possible increases in the potential for conflict as a result of enlargements, which brings in more governments, and governments themselves that are far apart ideologically:

Preference Heterogeneity: measures the extent of preference divergence among member state governments as represented by the range of their placements on a left–right dimension.[13] Data from Hertz and Leuffen (2011).

EU-9: an indicator variable that takes the value of 1 from January 1976 through December 1980, when the EU had nine members, and 0 otherwise.

EU-10: an indicator variable that takes the value of 1 from January 1981, when Greece joined, through December 1985, and 0 otherwise.

EU-12: an indicator variable that takes the value of 1 from January 1986, when Spain and Portugal joined, through December 1994, and 0 otherwise.

EU-15: an indicator variable that takes the value of 1 from January 1995, when Austria, Finland, and Sweden joined, through April 2004, and 0 otherwise.

---

[13] The results are robust to using the standard deviation of partisan preferences instead of the range. Results available upon request.

8.2 With Elections Pending, Stall

The reference category for the successive expansion indicators is the Central and Eastern European (CEE) enlargement (the A10 in May 2004, and Bulgaria and Romania in January 2007).

8.2 With Elections Pending, Stall

The dependent variable is not distributed normally, which violates the central assumption of ordinary least squares (OLS). Consequently, I use survival analysis (nonparametric Cox duration models) with time-varying covariates and year fixed effects.[14] Table 8.1 reports the estimation results. Overall, the models fit the data well. The robustly significant Wald tests suggest that the variables are jointly significantly different from zero.

If the hypothesis that legislative proposals are less likely to be adopted when there are governments nearing elections is valid, the principal explanatory variables should have negative and statistically significant coefficients. And indeed, this is what we find: irrespective of the measure used, the hazard is decreasing, meaning that the likelihood that a proposal is adopted when elections are pending is smaller.

Apart from their sign, the interpretation of coefficients is not straightforward. To gauge the magnitude of the substantive effects, I calculate the hazard ratios instead. The probability that a proposal is adopted within 60 days prior to elections is about 51 percent lower than if there are no elections during the following 60 days.[15] The probability is reduced by about 48 percent if elections are to occur within 30 days following the adoption. Finally, for each election that is to occur within 60 days after the adoption, the probability of adoption goes down by 29 percent. In other words, with three or more elections happening within that time frame, the probability of adoption plunges by 90 percent. This corroborates the findings in Chapter 5 (for the EU budget) and Chapter 7 (for DEU II proposals): as the number of governments that face elections goes up, the prospects for timely policy decisions go down.

It is possible that the effects are not constant over time. To check this, I interacted the time-varying covariates with time (the estimations are reported in Appendix G. The results indicate that although the

---

[14] The results do not change if the fixed effects are omitted. Details about the variables, model specification, the interaction of time-varying covariates with time, and the results with time-varying coefficients can be found in Appendix G.
[15] Consistent with my arguments about politicization, the post-1990 effect is even stronger: proposals are 61 percent less likely to be adopted if elections are to occur within 60 days. See Appendix G for details.

Table 8.1. *Elections and Legislative Delays.*

	Length of Negotiations		
	(1)	(2)	(3)
Elections in 60 Days	−0.719**		
	(0.021)		
Elections in 30 Days		−0.655**	
		(0.025)	
Number of Elections			−0.344**
			(0.010)
Procedural Hurdles			
Qualified Majority	0.437**	0.441**	0.435**
	(0.020)	(0.020)	(0.020)
Cooperative Procedure	−1.065**	−1.068**	−1.071**
	(0.042)	(0.042)	(0.044)
Co-decision Procedure	−0.948**	−0.996**	−0.956**
	(0.040)	(0.043)	(0.040)
Proposal for a Directive	−0.864**	−0.868**	−0.840**
	(0.031)	(0.032)	(0.031)
Number of Pending Acts	0.003**	0.003**	0.003**
	(0.000)	(0.000)	(0.000)
Summer Vacation	−1.212**	−1.167**	−1.053**
	(0.121)	(0.119)	(0.116)
Potential for Conflict			
Preference Heterogeneity	0.025**	0.009**	0.034**
	(0.002)	(0.002)	(0.003)
EU-9	1.459**	1.195**	1.386**
	(0.169)	(0.170)	(0.169)
EU-10	1.263**	1.079**	0.682**
	(0.137)	(0.137)	(0.131)
EU-12	0.683**	0.539**	0.588**
	(0.108)	(0.110)	(0.107)
EU-15	0.261**	0.011	0.319**
	(0.079)	(0.083)	(0.076)
Time-Varying Covariates	Yes	Yes	Yes
Year Fixed Effects	Yes	Yes	Yes
Observations	32,784	32,784	32,784
Wald χ^2	6790.76**	5946.60**	6586.52**

*$p < 0.10$, **$p < 0.05$.
Nonproportional Cox hazard models.

probability of electoral delay goes down as the proposals mature, the change is rather small. For example, it would take more than 7,000 days for the effect of *Elections in 60 Days* to wear off. This is almost eight times longer than the 882 days in which 90 percent of proposals

8.2 With Elections Pending, Stall

are concluded. In other words, the prospect of impending elections decreases the probability of adoption regardless of how long the negotiations have been going on. This is despite the fact that the pressure for adoption increases substantially after about two years. Similar conclusions hold for the other two operationalizations of the explanatory variable.

Delays due to Elections in a EU4 Country

Although the argument is not specific to any particular government, one might wonder whether some member states have a particularly strong influence on the timing of the adoption of proposals. Many examples in this book leave the impression that the United Kingdom seems quite prone to delaying tactics and that other member states are often accommodating because it is such an important member. Could there be others? To answer this question, I estimated the model separately for each of the Big Four (EU4) member states – France, Germany, Italy, and the United Kingdom – with *Elections in 60 Days* now reflecting only elections that occurred in the relevant country within 60 days after the final adoption of a proposal. A negative and significant coefficient would indicate that elections in the country under consideration systematically reduce the likelihood of adoption even when the entire dataset is considered.

Limiting the elections to those occurring in one of the EU4 also allows me to be more precise about the strength of the incentive to delay because we have data on how competitive the elections were. To this end, we define the following:

> *Close Elections in 60 Days*: an indicator variable that takes the value of 1 if the country under consideration held competitive elections within 60 days following the adoption of a legislative proposal, and 0 otherwise. Elections are defined as competitive if public support for the incumbent government falls below the average support for governments in that country.[16]

Table 8.2 reports the estimation results for the two principal explanatory variables for each of the EU4 (full results can be found in Appendix G. All coefficients are significant and, with one exception, in the expected direction. They all have large substantive effects as well. Elections in Germany reduce the probability of adoption by 34 percent while

---

[16] See Chapter 5 for a discussion of different measures of competitiveness.

Table 8.2. *EU4 Elections and Legislative Delays.*

	All Elections		Close Elections	
	Coefficient	Hazard Change (%)	Coefficient	Hazard Change (%)
France	0.134**	+14	−0.232**	−21
Germany	−0.417**	−34	−1.105**	−67
Italy	−0.380**	−32	−0.160**	−69
United Kingdom	−0.210**	−19	−0.932**	−61

**$p < 0.05$.
Nonproportional Cox hazard models, with estimated coefficients and the change in probabilities computed from the hazard ratios for each of the Big Four member states. Only the principal explanatory variables, *Elections in 60 Days* (All Elections) and *Close Elections in 60 Days* (Close Elections), are reported; full results in Appendix G.

elections in France increase that probability by 14 percent. When only close elections are considered, all coefficients are significant and in the expected direction. The substantive effects are much larger too: the probability of adoption falls by 69 percent when there are competitive elections in Italy, and now even elections in France cause delays (21 percent).

Aside from the fact that close elections in any of these member states consistently tend to prolong negotiations, two further observations are in order. First, despite the fact that the United Kingdom ends up in so many narratives as the arch-obstructionist, it is actually Germany and Italy that appear to be more strongly associated with delaying tactics. We already saw a glimpse of that in Chapter 6 when Angela Merkel seemed to have encouraged Tony Blair to derail the Luxembourg compromise in June 2005 so that her competitor Gerhard Schröder would not be able to turn an international triumph into an electoral advantage. We shall see in Chapter 9 how Merkel directly engaged in dilatory tactics herself. This is not to say that the United Kingdom is unlikely to do it (elections for the House of Commons reduce the likelihood of adoption by 19 percent on average, and by 61 percent when competitive).

The strong impact of close elections is consistent with results reported by Kleine and Minaudier (2018, p. 19), although they attribute the effect to a desire for ambiguity. As they explain, competitive elections increase the uncertainty about retaining office and encourage

"incumbents to remain ambiguous on a wide range of issues out of fear that their decision at the international level might contradict their electoral stance at the domestic level. This ambiguity, under certain circumstances, inhibits progress in international negotiations."

8.2 With Elections Pending, Stall

This mechanism is partially consistent with my arguments about strategic delay in the sense that governments that expect unfavorable outcomes would seek to convey a contrary impression to the electorate. The most effective strategy in that case, however, is not to be ambiguous but to adopt the position favored by the electorate and defend it throughout. The evidence from Chapter 7 supports this idea but not the notion of remaining ambiguous.

The other interesting result is the unexpected positive effect for France when elections are not necessarily competitive. That France is anomalous is also evident from the relatively modest substantive effect of its competitive elections: they reduce the likelihood of adoption but only by about a third of the magnitude of the reduction among the other three member states of the EU4. At this point, I can offer an educated guess why this might be the case.

Recall that France has a relatively high positive variability when it comes to achieving successful legislative outcomes (Figure 7.7 in Chapter 7). That is, although it is not necessarily more successful than others on average, it is often more successful – especially so – compared to Germany and Italy. When a government expects a favorable outcome, it has incentives to push for a speedy adoption of the legislation so that it can claim credit for it. If France does tend to obtain favorable outcomes more often than Germany or Italy, then the presence of elections in France might be associated with a higher probability of adoption.

Reality Check: Procedural Hurdles

As numerous studies have found, there are various nonpolitical reasons for legislative negotiations to take a long time. The results here replicate these findings so I will only summarize them briefly. When decisions do not require unanimity but can be imposed by a qualified majority vote, legislation is more likely to be adopted in a timely manner: the probability of adoption increases by 54 percent. Getting the Parliament involved slows everything down, by 64 percent in the cooperative procedure and 61 percent in the co-decision procedure (the reference category is the consultative procedure where the Council gets to make the decisions). Backlog matters but very marginally so; it increases the likelihood of adoption by about 0.2 percent. And, to nobody's surprise, when many EU bureaucrats and politicians go on vacation, not much gets done; the probability of a proposal being adopted drops by 60 percent in August.

Table 8.3. *Time Constraint or Electoral Delay?*

	Coefficient	Hazard Change (%)
All Proposals	−0.719**	−51
Directives Only	−1.054**	−65
Post-1990 Proposals	−1.022**	−64

**$p < 0.05$.
Nonproportional Cox hazard models for proposals that involve only regulations and decisions, proposals that involve only directives, and proposals introduced after 1990. Only the principal explanatory variable, *Elections in 60 Days*, are reported; full results in Appendix G.

8.3 Time-Constrained or Electorally Motivated?

Directives – legislative acts that are directly binding for all member states – are both more likely to generate controversy and be more relevant to a government's electoral prospects (Schulz and König, 2000). Consistent with this, I find that directives are about 58 percent less likely to be adopted than regulations and decisions.

This result bears on an important alternative explanation for the association between longer duration of negotiations and pending elections. The correlation I found could simply reflect the fact that the government is laboring under a time constraint: there are only so many hours in the day, and if it has to spend many of them campaigning for reelection, it has that many fewer to spend on crafting compromises and passing legislation. In other words, governments do not delay because they wish to avoid an unfavorable outcome right before the elections, but because they just do not have the time to put *any* proposal through the process. This is not implausible, but it is also not inconsistent with lacking the motivation to find the time for the proposal, especially when the outcome might be unfavorable.[17] In fact, absent the electoral motive, there should be no difference in adoption times for proposals that are more controversial and those that are less so, and it should not make any difference whether the EU is politicized or not.

To examine this alternative, I estimated the model with *Elections in 60 Days* again but restricted the proposals to directives only, and to those that were introduced since 1990. Table 8.3 summarizes the substantive effects (the full analysis is in Appendix G. Consistent with the alternative

---

[17] In plain English, a government might be time constrained, but it also has no incentive to find the time to push for a proposal that will make it look bad.

hypothesis, elections are associated with delays regardless of the proposal type. However, as suggested by the delays specifically associated with directives we found previously, the prospect of elections is less likely to delay the adoption of regulations and decisions than it is to delay the controversial directives (51 percent versus 65 percent reduction, respectively). This is not consistent with the alternative explanation. The effect of elections in the politicized environment after 1990 is also very strong: the prospect of a government having to face the polls decreases the chances of adoption by 64 percent. Thus, while it is still possible that the time constraint plays a role in lengthening negotiations, it seems that quite a bit of that variation is due to the electoral incentive.

8.4 The Potential for Conflict

The positive and statistically significant coefficient on *Preference Heterogeneity* indicates that legislative delays are less likely when governments are more heterogeneous in their preferences. This is consistent with results reported by Hertz and Leuffen (2011), who also find that ideological divergence speeds up decision-making in the Council. At first glance, the result appears counterintuitive; after all, one would expect that diverse interests should make it harder to find a mutually acceptable deal. But if that were the only effect, then one would also expect that some of that conflict would manifest itself in procedural tactics as well: for example, one way to minimize the potential for disruption is to use regulations and decisions rather than directives. Another result could be that many proposals would remain on the legislative docket without resolutions.

All of these potential effects are already accounted for by the procedural variables, so we need to consider more carefully what *Preference Heterogeneity* tracks over and above them. One natural explanation consistent with my theory is that a government is only able to successfully stall legislation if it can threaten to veto it or if it can assemble a sufficiently large coalition to block it under qualified majority rules. The political costs of unilateral action are not trivial, which means that even under unanimity, governments would look for allies to make their position defending more credible and principled. The upshot is that delays often require at least the tacit cooperation of other member states, and preference heterogeneity makes that cooperation harder to obtain. In fact, as Blair's cooperation with Schröder's domestic political opponent in 2005 shows (Chapter 6), governments might have an incentive to work against incumbents with whom they disagree.

This implies that wider ideological divergence has contradictory effects on the duration of legislative negotiations. On one hand, it makes bargaining more difficult and compromises more scarce, which should delay the adoption of proposals. But if governments use procedural tactics to shield themselves from deals they do not like, this effect would be mediated through the procedural variables. On the other hand, because it makes cooperation less forthcoming, it undermines governments' ability to stall negotiations for electoral purposes. In extreme cases, it might even tempt them to bring decisions forward precisely because they expect these decisions to hurt electorally a government they disagree with.

This might account for *Preference Heterogeneity*'s positive contribution to the likelihood of adoption. This effect, while statistically significant, is substantively rather small – an increase of about 2 percent – which itself is consistent with the notion that most of the direct consequences of a larger conflict potential are channeled through the procedural variables.[18]

The potential for conflict should also increase mechanically with enlargements, especially when the new member states are substantially different (usually lagging) in economic development relative to the existing members. The coefficients of the enlargement variables indicate that this is indeed so. Recall that the reference category is the largest expansion in 2004–2007 to the CEE countries, and so the four indicators show the effect of having fewer members. We should expect that as the number of existing member states goes down, legislative delays should become less likely as well. All four indicators have positive and statistically significant coefficients, which means that indeed the probability of adoption is higher compared to the baseline after the CEE enlargement. Moreover, the coefficients get larger as the number of existing member states declines (it is smallest for *EU-15*, larger for *EU-12*, larger still for *EU-10*, and largest for *EU-9*), which provides further evidence for this effect: timely adoptions of proposals are most likely when there are fewest members, and negotiations get increasingly protracted as the number of governments involved goes up. As a robustness check, I replaced the indicators with a variable that measures the number of member states, and find the exact same pattern: more governments mean slower decision-making.

---

[18] In addition, different aspects of heterogeneity might be more relevant than others depending on context (Schneider, 2014).

8.5 Conclusion

The findings in this chapter lend consistent support for the hypothesis that legislative negotiations get systematically delayed when governments of member states – especially important ones – face impending elections. The effect persists even after taking into account the procedural reasons why some types of legislation might take longer to process, as well as for slower decision-making because more (and more diverse) preferences are represented in the Council.

In fact, the entire legislative output of the EU slows down come national elections time.[19] On average, the EU adopts about 39 proposals in any given month, and only 3 percent of these are close to national elections (i.e., elections that occur within 60 days after the adoption). When there are no such elections, the EU adopts 46 proposals per month, an 18 percent increase. Conversely, if the adoption of even 20 percent of current proposals were to occur close to elections, legislative output plunges to four adoptions, a 90 percent drop.[20] And if an election is so close that the adoption of all current proposals would fall in the 60-day period, then none of them would be adopted. This is an extreme counterfactual, though, and an out-of-sample prediction. In general, between 0 percent and 9 percent of the proposals in any given month would, if adopted, become realized within 60 days of an impending election. The expected contraction in output would involve anything between six and eighteen proposals. That is, an upcoming election in a member state reduces EU's legislative activity by 15 percent to 46 percent. The further out that election, the weaker its delaying effect, and the more active the EU is. Domestic politics induce a *legislative tide* rhythm in EU policymaking.

---

[19] See Appendix G for the analyses whose results are described here.
[20] The effect is so drastic because the 60-day limit is somewhat artificial, and in fact the pending election is likely to affect proposals whose adoption would occur within 65, 70, or even 90 days of its scheduled date, albeit more weakly. Since the data are aggregated to the month, the 60-day window codes some proposals as unaffected by the coming election. For instance, if the election is scheduled for July 20 and we consider proposals that could be adopted in May, any adoption before May 21 would fall outside the 60-day window. Only adoptions that occur on or after May 21 would be within 60 days of that election. The sample average is that 3 percent of adoptions fall in that category. Of course, this does not mean that if a proposal were to be adopted on May 20 it would be totally unaffected by the election. In fact, it is probably just as likely to be affected as a proposal adopted on May 21. There is no theoretical reason to limit the window to any particular number of days, and my choices of 60 and 30 days are rather conservative in that regard, as indicated by the fact that elections do influence the adoption of proposals that occur further out as well.

One might be surprised (I know I was) that the magnitude of the effect is so large. When close elections in three of the Big Four member states reduce the likelihood of adoption by two-thirds, and when the average election does so by half, then we know that stalling is a prevalent strategy, and that it works (at least in terms of extending the duration of negotiations). The large substantive effect of the electoral incentive on delay is in stark contrast to the marginal size it had on actual policy outcomes (which we found in Chapters 5 and 7). It is not difficult to see this should be so: claiming credit for a favorable policy is great, but getting that outcome is quite challenging (indeed, this is what makes claims more persuasive). Delaying, on the other hand, is far more accessible as a tactic, and it can be very appealing when the government realizes that it is unlikely to meet the challenge of producing a favorable outcome. And so it is that a substantial fraction of the signals of responsiveness seem to involve blame avoidance through strategic delays.

This prevalence of blame avoidance and the strong temptation to resort to deliberate delays should make voters highly suspicious and reduce the effectiveness of the tactic. The opening example in this chapter suggests that this is precisely what can happen: Cameron's defiant refusal to pay the Commission's updated assessment of the UK contribution was dismissed by the opposition (on both the right and the left) as empty posturing, and the subsequent surge of support for the opposition in the polls indicates that the voters agreed with that assessment. The Tories could not make their position defending stick, and the citizens knew that, so they punished the Conservatives even before Cameron worked out the deal that confirmed their suspicions.

Sometimes, however, a government can be quite credible when it takes a position voters agree with and then defends it throughout negotiations. It is especially interesting when it does so even though its own preferences are, in fact, divergent from that position but it needs to postpone the outcome until after crucial elections. We already examined a case where the delaying tactic worked – the United Kingdom during the MFF 2007–2012 negotiations. Now we turn to one where it failed – Germany during the 2010 Greek bailout negotiations. This case is particularly intriguing because the government did manage to convince the voters that it would hold the line, but then external developments forced it to change its strategy before elections took place. As we shall see, the government was far less successful in persuading the electorate that it had done so out of necessity, and so it got clobbered at the polls.

9 When the Music Stops: The German Politics of the Greek Bailout

When all else fails or is in doubt, stall until the polls are out. This seems to be the lesson taught by the analyses of legislative delays in Chapters 7 and 8. Prolonging negotiations could be a Fabian tactic when the mounting costs of delay end up compelling others to offer better terms. This requires that the lack of decision itself be costly, making the delay a war of attrition. But the vast majority of legislative proposals do not have this property and thus are not very suitable for the competitive imposition of the costs of disagreement. Even when it comes to the annual budgets or the multiannual frameworks, all of which have more or less explicit deadlines by which decisions must be made, delays are not costly in and of themselves, and the failure to reach an agreement before the deadline merely causes expenditures to revert to an established default. In EU negotiations, the principal cause of legislative delay is politics – domestic politics to be exact.

For the footdragging strategy to work – success here being defined as avoiding the electoral costs of an unfavorable policy outcome – a government must be able to persuade the relevant constituents that a favorable outcome is likely. Persuasion can only be effective if the signals of responsiveness a government sends – its position taking and position defending – are credible in the sense that they either increase the probability of a favorable outcome or at the very least strengthen the perception among the voters that the government is genuinely committed to their preferred policy. These perceptions cannot be wrong on average – governments cannot lie to everyone and get away with it all the time – so it follows that when a delay occurs there is a good chance that the government does in fact prefer its existing policy position. In other words, for the tactical delay strategy to work, it must be the case where voters assign a strictly positive probability that the delay is nonstrategic. If they were sure that the government was bluffing, they would call that bluff instantly.

The upshot of this line of reasoning is that when a government delays negotiations right before an election, the opposition will always accuse it of acting in bad faith, the government will always profess its genuine commitment, and the voters will always remain uncertain about its true motivations. The strategy succeeds if, despite their uncertainty, voters are more favorably disposed toward the incumbent than they would have been had the government agreed to the unpleasant outcome before the election. The relevant comparison – what the government should have expected to happen had it not delayed – is absolutely crucial and, in all cases of successful delay, an unobservable counterfactual. This is great for plausible deniability. When the unfavorable outcome finally gets revealed, the government can always claim that it tried its best; at any rate, the voters can express their displeasure only in hypothetical fantasy voting surveys. It is not so good for a researcher trying to figure out whether the delay was no more than an electoral tactic.

In some special cases, we can be reasonably sure that the government was not genuinely committed to the position it had been defending (see the study in Chapter 6 of the United Kingdom's strategy), but in most cases things will not be that straightforward even after the fact. Since we do not see what would have happened had the government chosen to agree to the policy before the elections, the conclusions must necessarily remain more speculative.

The great thing about the situation we will explore in this chapter is that it is a rare instance of something that would have stayed a counterfactual under usual circumstances but instead became an actual fact. It is a case of a failed strategic delay, where the government was forced by exogenous and exigent events to adopt the policy of which its constituents did not approve, and one that the government had been advocating against since the beginning. The case is unusual because the ground was shifting even under the government that had been impeding the negotiations, which made the time horizon endogenous to the delay. The overall effect was for the implicit deadline to move forward in time, which in turn denied the government the luxury of delay right before its critical election. The price of inaction, which normally does not constrain governments (and few voters are even aware of it), became the main cause of this dramatic turnabout. This gives us the opportunity to see what happens if a government misjudges where the horizon is; when it tries to stall the legislative process but the deadline arrives sooner than expected and, to its great discomfiture, right before the elections – a premature arrival that forces the outcome the government had been trying to avoid, thereby releasing its negative electoral potential.

This bountiful case study involves the negotiations over the first financial rescue package for Greece in the wake of the European debt crisis of 2010. Of particular interest here is the behavior of the German government, which started, sensibly enough, by demanding that the Greeks implement certain austerity measures in exchange for an infusion of cash – but then proceeded to adamantly deny that it would agree to a comprehensive bailout despite the deteriorating financial situation in the eurozone and against all advice from fellow member states, the Commission, and the International Monetary Fund (IMF). The Germans finally reversed their position rather abruptly, but by this time the crisis had engulfed other states, and Germany's own contribution to the rescue package had become nearly as large as the total that had originally been estimated.

Why did the German government behave so erratically: dithering despite the pleas of everyone involved and despite objective evidence that the situation was getting worse, but then suddenly doing a *volte-face* and agreeing to pay a lot more than what it had initially refused to pay? Why did it choose a strategy that European Green Party leader Daniel Cohn-Bendit characterized as "incomprehensible and politically very stupid"?[1]

Because of elections, that's why.[2]

I present evidence from in-depth personal interviews, archival research, and secondary sources that supports the primacy of domestic politics as an explanation for this behavior.[3] Before delving into specifics, I should like to point out two things. First, I use the term "Greek bailout" because it has become the convention in the literature and the media. This term is neither neutral – it shoves all the blame for the crisis on the Greek government – nor correct, because it implies that the Greeks were the primary beneficiaries of the aid. "Greek bailout" was deliberately chosen as the label precisely because of these

---

[1] "Germany policy toward Greece 'very stupid': Cohn-Bendit." *Agence France-Presse*, April 26, 2010, www.expatica.com/de/news/country-news/Germany-policy-toward-Greece-very-stupid-Cohn-Bendit_173298.html, accessed February 4, 2018.

[2] In Schneider and Slantchev (2017), we develop a game-theoretic model of international cooperation in the shadow of domestic elections and explore (among other things) the conditions under which governments might delay the implementation of necessary policies due to electoral concerns. We provide a stripped-down version of the Greek bailout case as an analytical narrative to illustrate how the model can be applied.

[3] In addition to the personal interviews, the analysis relies on a number of archival resources, including technical reports, academic books and articles, speeches, official government announcements, and newspaper articles. I searched for newspaper sources in two steps. First, I retrieved newspapers using systematic keyword searches on the relevant topics. Second, I searched for further articles on specific questions that became relevant for the line of argumentation. For the newspaper articles, I added the author names and website address (URL) whenever available. Since many newspaper articles were retrieved from newspaper databases and archives in the United States and Germany, they often do not contain information on either author names or URLs (I use accessible online versions whenever possible). All newspaper articles, speeches, letters, and reports cited in the chapter are available from the author.

implications. In fact, German and French banks had been complicit in the unsustainable profligacy of the Greek government with their reckless spending there. These investments were so massive that a default by the Greek government would have bankrupted many of these banks, triggering another financial collapse across Europe. The bailout was as much a rescue package for the European banks as it was for the Greeks, but the German government could not admit to it. Not after the very unpopular taxpayer-funded bailout of local banks it had engineered just two years prior. So "Greek" the bailout was going to be.

Second, for my analysis, I draw upon a wide range of sources, many of them critical of the German government. Many attribute motives to political actors that are plausible but that are imputed rather than corroborated. Indeed, most of the time it is impossible to find direct evidence for these motives especially if the strategy relies on them remaining obscure. I have tried to correct for this throughout the personal interviews, and the experience has been especially rewarding. I talked to administrative and political elites who work in the German Chancellery, the Ministry of Finance, the Ministry of Commerce, and the Bundestag. All of the interviewees were directly involved in some capacity in decisions throughout this episode. They represent a rich variety of viewpoints both in terms of their ideology and in terms of the position they occupied during the deliberations (e.g., within the German government or at the EU level). They paint a remarkably consistent picture of the crisis, and with the events safely in the past there is no reason to doubt their sincerity.

9.1 The Genesis of the Greek Crisis

The origins of the Greek financial crisis go back to years of excessive government spending and corruption, aided and abetted by reckless foreign investors and banks. But the problems did not begin in earnest until the snap elections in the fall of 2009 brought the Socialists to power. George Papandreou, the new prime minister, disclosed that the pervasive mismanagement of the economy by previous governments had saddled the country with a crushing debt of 129.7 percent of gross domestic product (GDP) and an unsustainable deficit of 12.7 percent of GDP (Figure 9.1).

This was a startling revelation for two reasons. First, the mountain of debt and the ongoing levels of borrowing not only far exceeded the limits that all eurozone members had agreed to observe, but it outstripped even the commonly tolerated noncompliance by some of them. Under the Stability and Growth Pact (SGP), all EU member states had committed

9.1 The Genesis of the Greek Crisis

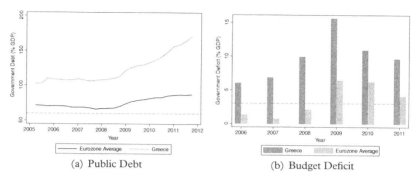

(a) Public Debt (b) Budget Deficit

Figure 9.1 Public Debt and Budget Deficits for Greece and the Eurozone, 2005–2012. Debt and deficit as a percentage of GDP. The gray dashed lines indicate the ceilings under the Stability and Growth Pact (60 percent for debt and 3 percent for deficit).
Source: Eurostat, Quarterly Data.

to ceilings of 60 percent of GDP for public debt and 3 percent of GDP for budget deficits.[4] While it was true that many governments were in violation of these ceilings – the average public debt in the eurozone at the time was 80 percent and the average budget deficit was 6.4 percent – the Greeks really stood out. Their public debt was more than twice the ceiling (and 62 percent higher than the EU average), and their budget deficit was more than four times the ceiling (and twice the EU average).

The magnitude of the violations was shocking, but that was not the worst of it. The truly potentially calamitous impact of the revelation was in the realization that violations of these magnitudes had somehow gone undetected by Eurostat. There was, of course, a simple explanation: the Greek governments had supplied the agency with doctored numbers. The EU inquiry into Greek accounting practices revealed serious irregularities in their procedures, and the Papandreou government admitted that its predecessors had failed to report the correct statistics. On January 11, 2010, Eurostat published its report that made these lies official, and even the recently reported budget deficit was soon adjusted

---

[4] The SGP is a framework of rules that was established by the EU in order to ensure sound fiscal policies in the EU. It is composed of a preventive arm – cooperation to achieve sustainable fiscal policies – and a corrective arm – procedures to correct excessive deficits. The corrective arm is used when the public deficit exceeds 3 percent of GDP, or when the public debt exceeds 60 percent of GDP. The European Commission can impose sanctions on noncompliant members. The SGP's legal basis is in Articles 121 and 126 of the Treaty on the Functioning of the EU (TFEU). The Pact came into existence in 1997 and was revised in 2005 (to relax the rules under which a country would be declared noncompliant) and 2011 (to automate the imposition of penalties).

to 13.6 percent, and then to the eyepopping 15.6 percent, more than five times the ceiling. This was not the first time the Greek governments were caught peddling fake statistics: In 2004 Eurostat had discovered that the actual deficit for 1997–2004 was 6.1 percent rather than the reported 1.4 percent, which would have disqualified Greece from entrance in the eurozone. The difference now was breathtaking.[5]

The financial markets had reacted immediately after the initial announcement, and the Eurostat report only made things worse. The rating agency Fitch downgraded Greek sovereign debt from A− (upper medium grade) to BBB+ (lower medium grade).[6] Starting in October 2009, Greek debt was downgraded six times by Standard and Poor's (S&P), six times by Moody's, and seven times by Fitch before July 2011. With each downgrade, Greek bonds became riskier for investors, and their yields increased, diverging ever further from the German standard.

Figure 9.2(a) tracks the deterioration of Greek bonds relative to both Germany and the eurozone average. It shows how the introduction of the euro in 1999 had caused bond yields for eurozone countries to converge to positions very close to the exceptionally safe German bonds. (In 1995, the Greek bond yield had been 18 percent, and the German bond yield had varied between 2 percent and 4 percent.) Since there was never a formal mechanism to guarantee the financial rescue of a troubled economy in the eurozone, the decision made by foreign investors and banks to treat Greek and German bonds as equivalent was, shall we say, questionable. After the 2004–2005 Eurostat revisions of the Greek deficit figures, that decision seems to have been singularly unwarranted.

And yet it persisted – the Greek bond yield was around 5 percent at the time of the 2008 bankruptcy of Lehman Brothers. It went into the dangerous territory of about 6 percent, but then dropped below the precrisis levels. Over that fluctuation, much of the difference with Germany was due to investors rushing to park their money in safe German bonds. But after this period of deceptive calm, suspicions about the creditworthiness of the Greek government began to accumulate.

It was the Papandreou announcement that started the inexorable climb of the Greek bonds yield: by the time of the Eurostat intervention, it was nearing 7 percent, effectively shutting Greece out of international

---

[5] Flanders, Stephanie. "The bitter taste of a Greek bail-out." *BBC*, April 27, 2010. www.bbc.co.uk/blogs/thereporters/stephanieflanders/2010/04/the_bitter_taste_of_a_greek_ba.html, accessed February 4, 2018.

[6] The credit rating is an indicator to potential investors in debt securities. Supposedly independent credit rating agencies use letter designations that represent the quality of bond. The designations vary somewhat across agencies, but AAA is generally assigned to the safest bonds, and C/D for the riskiest ones.

9.1 The Genesis of the Greek Crisis

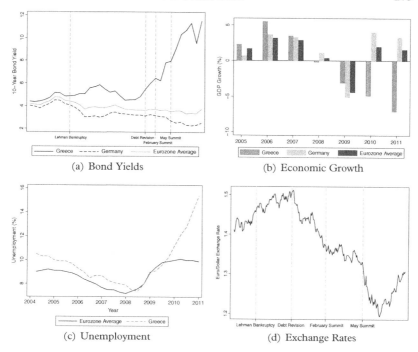

Figure 9.2 Economic Indicators during the Eurozone Crisis.
Source: Eurostat.

financial markets. By the time of the bailout it was at 8 percent, and in February 2012, it hit the incredible yield of 29.2 percent. One thing was certain by early spring 2010: the Greek government could not borrow its way out of its predicament because nobody was willing to lend to it.

The economic and social consequences for Greece were devastating. GDP growth had already dipped below zero in 2008, and having dropped to −3 percent in 2009, it further declined to −5 percent in 2010 when the other eurozone countries were already on their way to recovery. In 2011, it plumbed to new depths with −7.1 percent [Figure 9.2(b)]. Unemployment skyrocketed from being on par with the eurozone average of 7.5 percent in 2007 to 14.1 percent in 2010 [Figure 9.2(c)]. When Papandreou, incredibly, insisted that Greece would not need a bailout but would get its house in order with a series of draconian austerity measures (which the government implemented in early 2010), the streets exploded with violent demonstrations to protest "turning the screws on" the very people who were also being hurt by the economic downturn. In 2013, unemployment reached an astounding 27.6 percent.

While it matters whether Papandreou believed a bailout was necessary, it was far more important whether the creditor countries thought it was. The euro had gained on the US dollar as the financial crisis enveloped America in the wake of the Lehman Brothers bankruptcy [Figure 9.2(d)]. The revision of the Greek debt figures reversed that trend, and the exchange rate declined from 1 euro = 1.51 USD in December 2009 to 1 euro = 1.36 USD in February 2010. The Greek crisis began to threaten the eurozone and rumors about a potential bailout started to circulate after the special summit of the European Council on February 11, 2010.

The bailout issue was tricky because Article 125 of TFEU explicitly prohibited EU institutions (such as the European Central Bank) and member states from assuming liability for the debts of local, regional, and central governments within the eurozone. Creative proposals ranged from using EU structural funds to support Greece to supplying loans from government-owned savings institutions.[7] Experts warned that policymakers should not get tangled up in legal matters, and that time was of the essence:

It's a crisis that develops at the pace of the markets, not at the pace of official meetings. There is a risk of being behind the curve. [...] Policymakers need to be clear about the endgame and make sure the markets grasp what is the endgame. If you get behind the curve, you lose credibility. To avoid this you have at some point to take the initiative and risks.[8]

Back in 2009, the German finance minister, Peer Steinbrück, had struck an upbeat note by indicating that a bailout of overly indebted eurozone members was likely in spite of the treaties that made no provisions for such financial rescues.[9] With Germany counted among the main

---

[7] "EU can't afford to let Greece fail." *The Guardian*, April 9, 2010. www.theguardian.com/commentisfree/2010/apr/09/greece-cant-afford-fail, accessed February 5, 2018.

[8] Jean Pisani-Ferry, director of Bruegel, the Brussels economic think tank, quoted in Traynor, Ian. "The euro's darkest hour. European leaders gather in Brussels amid rumors that struggling Greece will be bailed out." *The Guardian*, February 10, 2010. www.theguardian.com/business/2010/feb/09/eu-economic-summit-greece-bailout, accessed February 5, 2018.

[9] Charlemagne. "A Greek bailout, and soon?" *The Economist*, January 28, 2010. www.economist.com/blogs/charlemagne/2010/01/greek_bailout_within_months, accessed February 5, 2018. Steinbrück was a member of the Social Democratic Party (SPD), and had become finance minister as part of the grand coalition formed after the 2005 federal election (see Chapter 6). The coalition cabinet was headed by Angela Merkel, but before the 2009 elections Steinbrück had joined her opponent (and foreign minister) Frank-Walter Steinmeier in a campaign to unseat her. The maneuver failed, and he was replaced by CDU's Wolfgang Schäuble as finance minister. Steinmeier was also ousted as both foreign minister and vice chancellor in favor of Guido Westerwelle of the Free Democratic Party (FDP) in both positions.

9.1 The Genesis of the Greek Crisis

beneficiaries of the eurozone, and with German banks on the hook over their investments in Greece, it might have seem a foregone conclusion that Chancellor Angela Merkel would not permit the destabilization of the area or expose the national banks to the risk of bankruptcy. It was thus doubly ironic that the international impetus for a concerted action to stem the Greek crisis foundered on Germany's stiff opposition.

Despite mounting evidence that the crisis was being exacerbated by the unbounded nature of Greek commitments and that it was threatening to spill over to the weaker members of the eurozone, Merkel remained uncompromising in her insistence that the Greeks had to solve their own problems:

[T]here is no looming insolvency. [...] I don't believe that Greece has acute financial needs from the European Community and that's what the Greek prime minister keeps telling me.[10]

When an increasingly larger chorus of governments and financial institutions started to clamor even more vociferously for immediate action, Merkel even implied that countries in persistent violation of the SGP (read: Greece) could be expelled from the eurozone.[11] In fact, Merkel would refuse to act until post-downgrades panic seized the markets at the end of April.

Merkel's actions are particularly puzzling because she had been, and continued to be, strongly supportive of the eurozone. From such a perspective it must have been clear by March that the crisis was likely to be very serious and that Germany would be the linchpin for any collective action to resolve it. My interviewees indicated that Greece had already become a subject of concern back in 2008. Government officials from several eurozone countries had participated in low-key meetings throughout 2008 and 2009 to discuss how to avert a financial crisis, how to handle one should it come to pass, and how to work around the "no-bailout" clause if a rescue became necessary. The European Commission had also sent delegates to several German ministries to increase awareness of the looming crisis among members of the German political and administrative apparatus.

---

[10] Wray, Richard. "Angela Merkel: EU summit should not discuss bailout for Greece." *The Guardian*, March 21, 2010. www.theguardian.com/business/2010/mar/21/eu-greece-angela-merkel, accessed February 5, 2018.

[11] Buckley, Chris. "Greece bailout will prevent spillover: EU's Barroso." Reuters, April 30, 2010. http://in.reuters.com/article/2010/04/30/us-eu-greece-china-idUSTRE63T0P920100430, accessed February 5, 2018; Peel, Quentin. "Merkel damps bailout expectations." *The Financial Times*, March 21, 2010. www.ft.com/cms/s/7315d8a8-34db-11df-9cfb-00144feabdc0.html.

By January 2010 (when Greece published the new statistics) it was clear to the major actors involved that a concerted action was inevitable, and that the German government "would not be able to get out of this anymore." The delay not only made the crisis appreciably worse (Matthijs, 2016), but drastically increased the funds that had to be committed to its resolution. As late as April 11, the Eurogroup's rescue package had envisioned a total of €30 billion, with about €10 billion additional funding provided by the IMF. Germany's contribution had been set by the European Central Bank (ECB) at €8.4 billion.[12] A month later, the price tag would be up nearly threefold.

Why would Merkel mortgage the financial stability of the entire eurozone and the solvency of Germany's largest banks on delaying a policy that her own government officials thought inevitable?

9.2 The *Schwäbische Hausfrau* Policy

There was no shortage of speculation, both at home and abroad, that Merkel was attempting to postpone what she knew would be a highly unpopular decision.[13] The culprit was an election in – where else? – the crucial state of Nordrhein-Westfalen (NRW).[14] The voters there were going to the polls on May 9 to choose its next state parliament (Landtag), and the election could potentially disrupt the entire domestic policy agenda of the government. The Christlich Demokratische Union/Christlich-Soziale Union (CDU/CSU) had managed to edge the SPD out of the governing grand coalition after the October 2009 elections. This was not because of Merkel's campaign skills (by all accounts she had run a campaign notable only for being excruciatingly boring), but in part because the SPD could not attack the performance of the incumbent government (since it had been in it), and mostly because of the unexpectedly strong showing of CDU's preferred partner, the Free Democratic Party (FDP) (which promptly replaced SPD in the governing coalition). Now in opposition, the SPD was beaten but not defeated; it was within striking distance of the CDU in the Bundesrat

---

[12] In the eurozone crisis, the contributions to the bailout, as most other financial matters, were tied to the size of the economy of individual members. It is therefore also unlikely that Merkel used the delay to negotiate deviations from existing ECB formulas.

[13] Schneider and Slantchev (2017) examine two alternative explanations and dismiss them as inconsistent with the evidence. I provide a brief overview of that argument in Appendix H, available online at https://quote.ucsd.edu/cjschneider/books/.

[14] Recall from Chapter 6 that NRW was the Golgotha for the previous chancellor, Gerhard Schröder. The defeat in that populous state had caused his governing party, the SPD, to lose its majority in the Bundestag, prompting him to engineer the no-confidence vote that brought about the general elections that led to his ouster in favor of Merkel.

(the upper house of the federal parliament), and was running neck-and-neck with the CDU in the NRW polls.

The NRW election was critical because it was seen as a referendum on the policies of the seven-month-old government, but more directly because a CDU defeat there would cost it the working majority in the Bundesrat. This would put paid to Merkel's plans for a radical overhaul of the taxation and health systems, and for an extension of the nuclear power program. The SPD had thwarted all these initiatives when it was in the grand coalition, and if it were to gain enough seats in the Bundesrat, it was sure to obstruct them again.[15] The election had acquired such a significance that some analysts argued that all federal politics had come to a standstill. Not only that, but NRW was "historically speaking, a seismograph for national politics."[16]

In this situation, the chancellor would not willingly do anything that would jeopardize the CDU's chances in NRW. Why this meant holding the line on a bailout for Greece requires some explanation.

Most German voters believed that bailing out the Greeks was both unfair and unnecessary, and in addition, they did not believe that the Greek crisis was serious enough to affect their own well-being. Consequently, they were opposed to a bailout. While their chancellor was telling them that Greece would solve its own problems, the media was regaling them with stories of astounding Greek government largesse and endemic corruption (Mylonas, 2012; Tzogopoulos, 2013). The examples of this are too numerous to cite, but one egregious example provides a useful encapsulation of the issues and a glimpse at the tenor. On the day of Papandreou's March 5 visit to Berlin, *Bild* published an inflammatory "Dear Prime Minister" open letter full of assorted accusations:

> If you're reading this, you've entered a country different from yours. You're in Germany. Here, people work until they are 67 and there is no 14th-month salary for civil servants. Here, nobody needs to pay a €1,000 bribe to get a hospital bed in time. Our petrol stations have cash registers, taxi drivers give receipts and farmers don't swindle EU subsidies with millions of non-existent olive trees.

---

[15] Boyes, Roger. "Greece is like a rat's tail. It will come round to hit us." *The Times*, May 8, 2010. www.thetimes.co.uk/article/greece-is-like-a-rats-tail-it-will-come-round-to-hit-us-lpz2zk6lk8w, accessed February 5, 2018.

[16] Peters, Katharina. "Wahlkamp in Letzter Minute: Rüttgers kämpft gegen Griechenland-Effekt." *Der Spiegel*, March 18, 2010. www.spiegel.de/politik/deutschland/wahlkampf-in-letzter-minuteruettgers-kaempft-gegengriechenland-effekt-a-693779.html, accessed February 5, 2018; "German voters poised to punish Merkel party over Greece." *Agence France-Presse*, May 8, 2010. www.expatica.com/de/news/German-voters-poised-to-punish-Merkel-party-over-Greece_176477.html, accessed February 5, 2018.

Germany also has high debts but we can settle them. That's because we get up early and work all day. We want to be friends with the Greeks. That's why since joining the euro, Germany has given your country €50 billion.[17]

This came only a day after its interview with two German MPs, who had suggested that before asking for loans, the Greek government should consider selling off its stakes in companies, some government-owned buildings, and land such as uninhabited islands. These remarks were widely reported as the Germans telling the Greeks to sell the Acropolis, the Parthenon, ancient works of art, and their islands.[18] One might be tempted to dismiss these as typical tabloid hyperbole, but *Bild* is one of the few national newspapers and it far outstrips the rest in circulation (with more than 2.5 million daily readers it has the highest circulation of any publication in Europe).[19] Its editorials are also often in line with the less-shocking weeklies (Oltermann, 2012).

Given these sentiments, most Germans instinctively approved of the *schwäbische Hausfrau* strategy that Merkel had debuted in 2008 when she warned that doling out credit to rescue the American finance sector would exacerbate the meltdown caused by the bursting of the real estate bubble. For wide swaths of the population, fear of inflation and aversion to debt had become part of a culture that emphasized frugality and solvency (Lynn, 2011).[20] Many Germans believed that a bailout would endanger the stability of the euro rather than support it.[21]

---

[17] Translated in "Get up earlier, Germans tell Greeks." *The Guardian*, May 3, 2010. www.theguardian.com/business/2010/mar/05/bild-open-letter-greece-papandreou.

[18] "Verkauft doch eure Inseln, ihr Pleite-Griechen ... und die Akropolis gleich mit!" *Bild*, March 4, 2010. www.bild.de/politik/wirtschaft/griechenland-krise/regierung-athen-sparen-verkauft-inseln-pleite-akropolis-11692338.bild.html, accessed February 5, 2018; "Greece should sell islands to keep bankruptcy at bay, say German MPs." *The Guardian*, March 4, 2010. www.theguardian.com/business/2010/mar/04/greece-sell-islands-german-mps, accessed February 5, 2018.

[19] Several interviewees explicitly referred to the *Bild*, and its massive campaign against the bailout, when they discussed the fears of German politicians to go forward with the bailout in light of negative public opinion.

[20] "In Greek debt crisis, a window to the German psyche." *New York Times*, May 4, 2010. www.nytimes.com/2010/05/04/business/global/04iht-euro.html, accessed February 5, 2018.

[21] In light of the enormous exposure of German banks in Greece, it is possible to argue that the bailout was about saving these banks rather than helping the Greeks. However, the German voters were even less disposed to bail out their banks because of the billions already spent since 2008 on doing just that and because of the widespread perception of corruption in the banking sector. This might also help explain why Merkel never mentioned the German banks when discussing the bailout and instead focused entirely on Greece (Ewing, Jack. "In Germany, little appetite to change troubled banks." *New York Times*, August 9, 2013. www.nytimes.com/2013/08/10/business/global/in-germany-little-appetite-to-change-troubled-banking-system.html, accessed February 5, 2018).

9.2 The *Schwäbische Hausfrau* Policy

It should, therefore, come as no surprise that the Germans were dead set against a bailout, in part because of austerity measures that had been necessary to meet fiscal consolidation targets in Germany (Bechtel, Hainmueller, and Margalit, 2014, 2017). Polls consistently showed that only 20–25 percent supported helping Greece, and Germans tended to be distant outliers compared to other Europeans on the causes and consequences of the crisis.[22] In March, an Institut Francais D'Opinion Publique (IFOP) survey reported that 78 percent of Germans believed that the Greek government was responsible for the crisis as opposed to it being part of a global crisis or a result of financial speculation. The average of those who shared that sentiment among those surveyed in Spain, France, Italy, and the United Kingdom was only 54 percent.

The majority of Germans (55 percent) did not think that the crisis was significant either personally or to those around them (compared to an average of 36 percent among the other Europeans). Germans were also far more confident that their country could not suffer the same fate as Greece: 66 percent compared to an average of only 41 percent for the others. Since they blamed the Greeks for the crisis and did not believe it would affect them, 76 percent did not want to help Greece. Majorities in Italy (67 percent), Spain (55 percent), and France (53 percent) thought that their governments should help Greece in the interests of European solidarity. The only citizens the Germans resembled in their hawkishness on the bailout were the British (78 percent opposed a bailout), but the United Kingdom was not a member of the eurozone (IFOP, 2010). In fact, about a third of the Germans preferred to see Greece expelled from the eurozone than pay to bail out its government, and in this sentiment they again exceeded everyone else.[23]

In addition, the costs of continuing a serious crisis were not initially seen as excessive by political elites and publics alike. By March, the other eurozone members and the IMF had reached a consensus that the crisis was serious, but in their initial bailout agreement from April 11, they estimated that only about €45 billion in loans would be necessary to rescue Greece. The €15 billion IMF share was comparable to its loans

---

[22] "Mehrheit der Deutschen lehnt Griechen-Hilfe ab." *Die Welt*, April 27, 2010. www.welt.de/politik/deutschland/article7354187/Mehrheit-der-Deutschen-lehnt-Griechenland-Hilfe-ab.html, accessed February 5, 2018; "Poll finds 57% of Germans oppose Greek aid." *Agence France-Presse*, April 27, 2010. www.expatica.com/de/news/Poll-finds-57-percent-of-Germans-oppose-Greek-aid_173437.html, accessed February 5, 2018.

[23] Atkins, Ralph. "Athens crisis highlights pressure on Merkel." *Financial Times*, March 21, 2010. www.ft.com/cms/s/0/57f5217c-350e-11df-9cfb-00144feabdc0.html, accessed February 5, 2018.

to Brazil in 1999 and Mexico in 1994, and the overall package was akin to the bailout for Argentina in 2001.[24] In other words, while the crisis was clearly serious from a eurozone perspective, it was perceived as manageable. The economic costs were also not expected to be grievous. The Greeks did not even request the activation of the emergency loans under this agreement until April 23, and the credit ratings on government bonds in Greece itself but also in Portugal, Ireland, Italy, and Spain (the PIIGS countries where the crisis was most likely to spill over) remained at investment-grade levels until April 27–28.

In this political climate, it was not surprising that Merkel wanted to delay the bailout decision until after the elections. She might have wanted to act earlier because of the economic indicators in Greece and other Southern European countries, but it would have almost certainly cost the CDU the election in NRW.[25] So instead, she talked tough on Greek debt in an attempt to reassure German voters that their own beliefs about the crisis were correct and that she agreed with them. According to the public officials that I interviewed, Merkel took a calculated risk, hoping that she still had enough time before markets turned ugly on Greece. She intended to spend it holding the hard line until May 9 and then act.[26]

The SPD opposition openly charged Merkel with employing electoral tactics that had caused her "to be celebrated as the 'Iron Lady'" and even insinuated that she and Finance Minister Schäuble were "already hatching the plan for Germany to contribute its billions" in

---

[24] In comparison, during the banking crisis in Germany, which started in 2008, the German government committed more than €600 billion between 2008 and 2011; about €259 billion were actually called upon during that time period, and it was estimated that taxpayers would end up paying €50 billion (Frühauf, Markus. "Teuer für den Steuerzahler. Milliardengrab Bankenrettung." *Frankfurter Allgemeine Zeitung*, August 16, 2013. www.faz.net/aktuell/wirtschaft/wirtschaftspolitik/teuer-fuer-den-steuerzahler-milliardengrab-bankenrettung-12535343.html, accessed February 5, 2018).

[25] "Die Bundeskanzlerin versucht, Zeit zu gewinnen." *Badische Zeitung*, April 26, 2010. www.badische-zeitung.de/wirtschaft-3/die-bundeskanzlerin-versucht-zeit-zu-gewinnen--30135537.html, accessed February 5, 2018; Kulish, Nicholas. "Merkel tested as escalating Greek crisis hurts Europe." *The New York Times*. April 28, 2010. www.nytimes.com/2010/04/29/world/europe/29germany.html, accessed Feburary 5, 2018.

[26] The interviewees noted two reasons for the delay. The first reason was legal: the bailout had to be reconciled with the EU treaties and the German Basic Law. In light of the speed with which this was accomplished in early May, it is unlikely that this could explain months of dithering. The second was electoral and was emphasized by respondents who had participated in internal political discussions. They all noted the negative public opinion (especially fueled by the vicious attacks in *Bild*), and the regional elections in NRW.

a coming bailout.[27] The Parliamentary leader of the SPD, Frank-Walter Steinmeier, who had served as foreign minister until 2009 (and would again do so starting in 2013), flat out accused the chancellor of covering up the unpopular aid package and called on her to bring it up for discussion in Parliament immediately (ahead of the elections), because "the financial markets and the German public need clarity."[28]

Many foreigners also thought that Merkel's refusal to act was a transparent political ploy and that she was merely "hoping to stave off a bailout decision that many believe is inevitable until after voters in NRW go to the polls."[29] As an EU official put it, the "statements of German officials on Greece are aimed mainly at their electorate. I think that eventually Berlin will agree to hand over the aid."[30] The leader of the Eurogroup, Jean-Claude Juncker, rued that

> [The German government is] excessively hesitant when it comes to Europe [...] Taking a domestic political look at European issues first, instead of looking at domestic issues with a European eye, definitely worries me.[31]

But with her entire domestic policy agenda on the line there was precious little a European eye could do to budge Merkel from her position defending. Not unless the eye looked upon an apocalypse.

9.3 Fiddling While Rome Burns

Germany would not pay. There was no need for a bailout. Greece had to help itself by imposing austerity measures that had worked for the Germans. Rescuing the Greeks would set a bad precedent and endanger the eurozone. This is what German voters wanted to hear, and this is what their chancellor preached.

---

[27] Joachim Poss, deputy head of SPD, quoted in Chambers, Madeline. "Merkel tries to sell Greek bailout to Germans." *Reuters*, May 3, 2010. www.reuters.com/article/us-eurozone-greece-germany-idUSTRE6424KI20100503, accessed February 5, 2018; Sigmar Gabriel, the head of the SPD, quoted in Connolly, Kate. "Greek debt crisis: IMF chief to woo Germany over bailout deal." *The Guardian*, April 28, 2010. www.theguardian.com/business/2010/apr/28/greek-debt-crisis-imf-chief-imf-chief-to-woo-germany, accessed February 5, 2018.
[28] "Verzögerungs-Vorwürfe. Steinmeier kritisiert Merkels Griechenland-Politik." *Frankfurter Allgemeine*, April 22, 2010. www.faz.net/aktuell/wirtschaft/eurokrise/verzoegerungs-vorwuerfe-steinmeier-kritisiert-merkels-griechenland-politik-1969913.html, accessed February 5, 2018.
[29] "Merkel tested as escalating Greek crisis hurts Euro."
[30] "Euro leaders to debate Greek aid on May 10." *EU Business*, April 27, 2010. www.eubusiness.com/news-eu/greece-finance-aid.4b, accessed February 5, 2018.
[31] "Euro chief Juncker hits out at 'hesitant' Germany." *Agence France-Presse*, April 15, 2010. www.eubusiness.com/news-eu/finance-economy.44x/?searchterm=eurozone, accessed February 5, 2018.

This *laissez-faire* policy had three other things going for it: (1) it was similar to what Germany had done to get out of its own painful recession, (2) it would not appear to reward the Greeks for having lived beyond their means (and having lied about it), and (3) it would not encourage other profligate governments to emulate Greece in the expectation of a bailout. "Moral hazard fundamentalists" argued that the stability of the eurozone required fiscal discipline and that governments mired in unsustainable debt should either be allowed to default or asked to leave the eurozone altogether. Providing a bailout would undermine the credibility of the sanction for profligacy and provide incentives to others to spend irresponsibly. According to this view, whereas the Greek crisis itself would not threaten the eurozone, an international rescue of the Greeks would. Members of the government, the coalition parties, and leading newspapers all insisted that Greece should cope alone (Meiers, 2015, p. 18).[32]

This position was not difficult to sustain in the early months while the crisis seemed localized and within Athens's ability to stem. The European Council meeting on February 11 limited itself to assurances of political support for Greek reforms while emphasizing the need to abide by the rules. As Merkel put it, "The rules must be obeyed – but Greece is one of us."[33] The message was calibrated to reassure Germany's partners in the eurozone while simultaneously denying that a bailout would come. Unsurprisingly, the signal was decidedly mixed; some interpreted it as an implicit assurance to help refinance the debt as long as Athens reined in its deficit, whereas others thought Germany had committed to inaction.[34] The immediate aftermath seemed to justify this response: when the Greek government announced additional austerity measures on March 3 (in compliance with a February 16 demand of the Economic and Financial Affairs Council), the markets reacted favorably to its ten-year bonds for €5 billion that it floated on the following day.

---

[32] One of the officials whom I interviewed, explicitly noted the massive lobbying efforts of CDU/CSU and FDP politicians who all demanded a tough line on Greece. The rise of the nationalist Alternative für Deutschland (AfD) party was also worrisome because it tended to paint anyone who supported a Greek bailout as a "traitor to the fatherland." The lobbying was not limited to the bailout but affected the austerity measures (stricter) and the haircut (smaller).

[33] *Deutsches Bundeskanzleramt.* February 11, 2010. "EU special summit meeting emphasizes shared responsibility." www.bundesregierung.de/ContentArchiv/EN/Archiv17/Artikel/2010/02/2010-02-11-eu-sondergipfel_en.html, accessed November 1, 2017.

[34] Traynor, Ian. "Angela Merkel dashes Greek hopes of rescue bid." *The Guardian*, February 11, 2010. www.theguardian.com/theguardian/2010/feb/11/germany-greece-merkel-bailout-euro, accessed February 5, 2018.

9.3 Fiddling While Rome Burns 283

This did not last. When the Greek parliament passed the austerity program on March 5, its increases in taxes, freezes of pensions, and cuts in salaries provoked nationwide protests. Even as the situation in Greece deteriorated, the Eurogroup refused to commit to any financial help and instead pressed for further austerity measures. In exasperation, Papandreou warned that Greece might have no choice but turn to the IMF for help if the Eurogroup did not put together a rescue package at the EU summit scheduled for March 25. His particular concern was that the waffling EU response had fanned the flames of speculation, causing Greek bond yields to top 6 percent. At such an exorbitant rate, Athens had no hope of financing itself out of the crisis via the markets. The only way to stop the betting against Greek debt was through a firm commitment to a bailout by the Eurogroup or, failing that, assurances of loans from the IMF.[35] Everyone – markets, Eurogroup finance ministers, the head of the Organisation for Economic Co-operation and Development (OECD), and the president of the European Commission – agreed with him. Everyone, that is, except the Germans.[36]

Reflecting both the moral hazard perspective and the widespread popular opposition to a bailout, Merkel told the Bundestag on March 17 that rushing aid to Greece in "a quick act of solidarity" was wrong and that a fundamental solution had to be devised, a solution that would allow for the expulsion from the eurozone of countries that persistently break its financial rules.[37] When the inevitable hue and cry arose over broaching the expulsion taboo, Merkel reminded everyone that Greece had yet to ask for financial aid, insisted that she did not believe the country was facing imminent insolvency, and flatly stated that any discussion of a bailout was off the table for the upcoming EU summit.[38]

Consequently, the statement released at the March 25 summit harped, much like its February 11 predecessor, on the need to follow the rules, but went further by promising "a package involving substantial IMF

---

[35] Traynor, Ian. "Greek PM gives European leaders a week to produce rescue plan." *The Guardian*, March 18, 2010. www.theguardian.com/business/2010/mar/18/greek-pm-gives-eu-leaders-rescue-deadline, accessed February 5, 2018.

[36] "Barroso demands solidarity: Europe increases pressure on chancellor Merkel." *Der Spiegel*, March 22, 2010. www.spiegel.de/international/europe/barroso-demands-solidarity-europe-increases-pressure-on-chancellor-merkel-a-684997.html, accessed February 5, 2018.

[37] "Merkel wants scope to expel eurozone troublemakers." *Euractiv*, March 18, 2010. www.euractiv.com/section/eu-priorities-2020/news/merkel-wants-scope-to-expel-eurozone-troublemakers/, accessed February 5, 2018.

[38] "Angela Merkel: EU summit should not discuss bailout for Greece."; "Merkel damps bail-out expectations."

financing and a majority of European financing." This seemed to have committed the Eurogroup to a bailout and satisfied Germany's demand to get the IMF involved. On the other hand, the statement also insisted that since Greece had not requested any financial help, the rescue mechanism was not being activated. It also emphasized that the loans would be at non-concessionary rates, that they would only be provided as an absolutely last resort, and that their provision would require the unanimous consent of the euro area members after assessments by the European Commission and the ECB (European Union, 2010).

Unsurprisingly, interpretations of what, exactly, the Eurogroup had committed to immediately diverged. Most officials signaled satisfaction with the outcome and either explicitly or implicitly indicated that a bailout was coming.[39] The official statement from the chancellor's office, however, chose to emphasize just how hedged that promise was. In only thirteen sentences of text, it managed to say that the package was a "last resort," "very last resort," and "absolutely last resort." After professing a commitment to the common currency, it clarified that any disbursements would involve "strict criteria" and had to be "authorized unanimously," and that the loans would be priced "in line with the *de facto* risks" (Bundeskanzlerin, 2010).

Merkel's tough talk on Greece brought her political gains domestically. Figure 9.3 shows that initial rumors of a bailout at the end of 2009 led to declining support for Merkel. However, after her staunch opposition to the Greek bailout, support increased and stabilized in March and April 2010. We can see the same, even slightly stronger, pattern in support for the CDU. This period also saw a stabilization in the share of voters that believed that the CDU government had competently handled the economy. Merkel's actions were largely supported by the German media. *Bild* gloated, "By taking on our chancellor, Europe has bit off more than it can chew," and "Our Chancellor is forcing the rest of Europe to bite its teeth out!"[40]

---

[39] "Eurozone leaders hammer out Greece rescue plan." *EurActiv*, March 26, 2010. www.euractiv.com/section/euro-finance/news/eurozone-leaders-hammer-out-greece-rescue-plan/, accessed February 5, 2018; Traynor, Ian. "Angela Merkel agrees on Greece rescue package – but wants new euro rules." *The Guardian*, March 26, 2010. www.theguardian.com/business/2010/mar/25/angela-merkel-greece-package, accessed February 5, 2018.

[40] Translated in Carsten Volkery. "The Greek bailout plan: Merkel's risky hand of Brussels poker." *Der Spiegel*, April 26, 2010. www.spiegel.de/international/europe/the-greek-bailout-plan-merkel-s-risky-hand-of-brussels-poker-a-685771.html, accessed February 5, 2018; "The iron Frau: Angela Merkel." *The Independent*, April 12, 2010. www.independent.co.uk/news/world/europe/the-iron-frau-angela-merkel-1941814.html, accessed February 5, 2018.

9.4 On the Road to Damascus

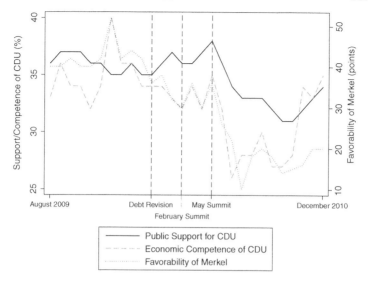

Figure 9.3 German Public Opinion during the Eurozone Crisis. The dashed line indicates the timing of the agreement on the Greek bailout.
Source: Forschungsgruppe Wahlen (Politbarometer).

9.4 On the Road to Damascus

The financial support mechanism that the eurozone heads of state had committed to on March 25 became fully operational on April 11 when the finance ministers provided the details, along with the requirement that Greece implement further austerity measures and report frequently on the status of their implementation. Athens immediately began negotiations on the extent and severity of these additional measures. On April 22, Eurostat revised Greece's estimated deficit to 13.6 percent of GDP (up from 12.7 percent).[41] This caused the rating agency Moody's to cut Greece's bond rating to A3, citing "significant risk" and warning that the rating would slide further "unless the government's actions can restore confidence in the markets and counteract the prevailing headwinds of high interest rates and low growth."[42] The ten-year bond yield surged to an astonishing 8.8 percent, and the spread from Germany's

---

[41] Forelle, Charles. "EU sees wider Greek deficit, roiling markets." *Wall Street Journal*, April 23, 2010. www.wsj.com/articles/SB10001424052748703876404575199520197362174, accessed February 5, 2018.

[42] Censky, Annalyn. "Another bad day for Greece." *CNN*, April 22, 2010. http://money.cnn.com/2010/04/22/news/economy/greece_debt/index.htm?postversion=2010042214, accessed February 5, 2018.

bond widened by 5.75 percent. Schäuble still clung to the established narrative, claiming in an interview in *Deutschlandfunk* the very same day, that the Greeks would not ask for help for weeks, perhaps until mid-May.[43] The Greek government formally requested financial assistance under the new mechanism on the following day.

Despite that, on April 25, German Foreign Minister Guido Westerwelle bluntly told the ZDF television channel that it was "not all agreed that Greece will actually receive aid from Europe." This sentiment was echoed by Schäuble, who also stated that Germany could still refuse to aid Greece. Both ministers and the chancellor insisted that Germany would only act if there was no other way to ensure the stability of the common currency and only if Athens produced a "credible austerity plan."[44] On the next day, the interest on Greek debt climbed to 9.1 percent, and the Italian foreign minister openly accused Germany of intransigence.[45] Merkel insisted that the ball was in the Greek court: Germany stood ready to help but only Athens could ensure that the preconditions were met, and "that will take a few days."[46] What she meant by this was not entirely clear since the Greeks had already signaled that they would make "drastic" cuts to their deficit.[47]

By the end of April, the economic and financial situation in Greece had worsened so much that experts no longer thought that the bailout package – even if it were to come – would suffice to stem the crisis. Greece's debt had reached almost €300 billion, and after the 4 percent interest rate hike, its borrowing costs were 67 percent higher than they

---

[43] Schulz, Sandra. "Griechenland muss zu soliden finanzpolitischen Verhältnissen zurückkehren." *Deutschlandfunk*, April 22, 2010. www.deutschlandfunk.de/griechenland-muss-zu-soliden-finanzpolitischen.694.de.html?dram:article_id=68442, accessed February 5, 2018.

[44] "Germany 'not ready to write blank cheque' for Greece: Minister." *Agence France-Presse*, April 25, 2010. www.expatica.com/de/news/Germany-not-ready-to-write-blank-cheque-for-Greece-minister_173176.html, accessed February 5, 2018; "New austerity a precondition for Greek aid: Germany." *Reuters*, April 25, 2010. www.reuters.com/article/us-greece-germany-idUSTRE63O1OP20100425, accessed February 5, 2018; "Germany could say no to Greece aid: Finance minister." *Agence France-Presse*, April 25, 2010. www.expatica.com/de/news/Germany-could-say-no-to-Greece-aid-finance-minister_173128.html, accessed February 5, 2018.

[45] "Greek crisis drives wedge in EU ranks." *Agence France-Presse*, April 26, 2010. www.expatica.com/de/news/Greek-crisis-drives-wedge-in-EU-ranks_173265.html, accessed February 5, 2018.

[46] "Merkel seeks to calm Greece crisis, but keeps tough line." *Agence France-Presse*, April 26, 2010. www.expatica.com/de/news/Merkel-seeks-to-calm-Greece-crisis-but-keeps-tough-line_173342.html, accessed February 5, 2018.

[47] "Finance minister says Athens ready to make 'drastic' cuts to deficit." *Agence France-Presse*, April 26, 2010. www.expatica.com/nl/news/Finance-minister-says-Athens-ready-to-make-drastic-cuts-to-deficit_173346.html, accessed February 5, 2018.

had been in February 2010.[48] It was unlikely that Greece would be able to service the €8.2 billion that were about to mature on May 19 at such prohibitive rates.[49] With the country headed toward almost certain default and financial markets in turmoil, experts predicted that a restructuring of Greek sovereign debt was unavoidable, although Schäuble denied it.[50] The yields on two-year Greek government bonds had increased to over 13 percent; it was now safer to lend money to Iraq or Venezuela than to Greece.[51]

In this heated atmosphere, S&P's April 27 downgrade of Greek government debt to junk (BB+ for long-term and B for short-term bonds) and Portugal's to low investment grade (A−, closing on the territory previously occupied by the Greek bonds) unleashed a veritable panic. As the downgrade was accompanied by a warning that the agency expected investors to lose between 50 and 75 percent if Greece defaulted, the fallout was immediate and severe.[52] European stock markets plummeted as investors voiced fears over the crisis and the risk of contagion.[53]

On April 28, S&P downgraded the Spanish long-term debt to AA, and an Italian bond issue failed to garner expected support. The borrowing costs for Ireland, Italy, and Portugal climbed as experts became increasingly convinced that a Greek default would unleash a series of defaults in the other PIIGS countries.[54] The crisis threatened to engulf the entire eurozone, not just its weakest members. Sales of the euro accelerated, leading the common currency to plunge to its lowest value against the dollar in more than a year and, since the yuan was

---

[48] Traynor, Ian. "Markets tremble while Merkel plays for time over Greek rescue deal." *The Guardian*, March 27, 2010. www.theguardian.com/business/2010/apr/26/markets-greece-rescue-imf-package, accessed February 5, 2018.
[49] Beatty, Andrew. "Pressure mounts for swift Greek bailout." *The Sydney Morning Herald*, April 25, 2010. www.smh.com.au/breaking-news-business/pressure-mounts-for-swift-greek-bailout-20100425-tkz9.html, accessed February 5, 2018.
[50] Pabst, Adrian. "EU can't afford to let Greece fail." *The Guardian*, April 9, 2010. www.theguardian.com/commentisfree/2010/apr/09/greece-cant-afford-fail, accessed February 5, 2018; "Greece warns speculators as it races for bailout." *Agence France-Presse*, April 26, 2010. www.expatica.com/es/news/country-news/Greece-warns-speculators-as-it-races-for-bailout_173195.html, accessed February 5, 2018.
[51] "The bitter taste of a Greek bail-out."
[52] Ewing, Jack and Jack Healy. "Cuts to debt rating stir anxiety in Europe." *The New York Times*, April 27, 2010. www.nytimes.com/2010/04/28/business/global/28drachma.html?mtrref=www.google.com, accessed February 5, 2018.
[53] "Desperate Greece presses EU for quick debt rescue." *Agence France-Presse*, April 27, 2010. www.smh.com.au/world/desperate-greece-presses-eu-for-quick-debt-rescue-20100427-tqgz.html, accessed February 5, 2018; Kiberd, Damien. "The fall of Greece may topple us all." *The Sunday Times*, May 2, 2010; "The bitter taste of a Greek bail-out."
[54] Graydon, Eric. "Germany finds bailing out is hard to do." *BBC*, April 28, 2010. www.bbc.com/news/10090578, accessed February 5, 2018.

tracking the dollar, against the Chinese currency as well.[55] The *New York Times* reported that a vice president of the ECB believed that the EU was "facing its biggest challenge since the adoption of the Maastricht Treaty in 1993."[56]

The eurozone was speeding toward a cliff. The managing director of the IMF, Dominique Strauss-Kahn, declared that "it is the confidence in the whole eurozone that is at stake."[57] The secretary-general of the OECD, Angel Gurria, went even further and compared the eurozone crisis to Ebola: "You have to cut your leg off in order to survive." And the former Greek finance minister, Yannos Papantoniou, warned that Greece was becoming "the Lehman Brothers of the sovereign debt crisis."[58] *The Sunday Herald* summarized it cogently[59]:

> Greece's economic problems are on the point of triggering an economic avalanche that will engulf other eurozone countries with high borrowing levels (Spain, Portugal, Italy and Ireland), roll relentlessly on through the eurozone and its trading partners (notably Britain) and push the struggling global economy into the second dip of the recession triggered by the collapse of Lehman Brothers in 2008.

The heads of the IMF and the ECB turned the screws on Germany to act, emphasizing the "absolute necessity to decide very rapidly" and "to act swiftly and strongly."[60] Astonishingly, even now Merkel insisted that Greece had to implement an "ambitious" austerity program, and while she believed that the negotiations had to be "accelerated," they would only after they had concluded that Germany would "make its decisions" on whether to grant aid.[61] A source close to the EU Spanish presidency indicated that the summit to discuss aid would be held on May 10, a day after the NRW vote.[62] The peculiar scheduling would not be surprising to anyone who was aware that the latest polls found 57 percent

---

[55] Buckley, Chris. "Greece bailout will block spillover – EU's Barroso." *Reuters*, April 30, 2010. https://in.reuters.com/article/idINIndia-48120320100430, accessed February 5, 2018.
[56] Thomas Jr., Landon. "Europeans fear Greek debt crisis will spread." *The New York Times*, April 27, 2010. www.nytimes.com/2010/04/28/business/global/28euro.html, accessed February 5, 2018.
[57] *Agence France-Presse*. April 28, 2010. "Pressure mounts on Germany to aid Greece."
[58] "Debt crisis in Greece is a warning to us all." *The Sunday Herald*, April 30, 2010.
[59] "Debt crisis in Greece is a warning to us all."
[60] "IMF, ECB pressure Germany to help Greece." *Agence France-Presse*, April 28, 2010. www.expatica.com/de/news/IMF-ECB-pressure-Germany-to-help-Greece_173762.html, accessed February 5, 2018.
[61] "Merkel says Greek rescue talks must be 'accelerated.'" *Agence France-Presse*, April 28, 2010. www.expatica.com/de/news/Merkel-says-Greek-rescue-talks-must-be-accelerated_173783.html, accessed February 5, 2018.
[62] "Euro leaders to debate Greek aid on May 10."; "Cuts to debt rating stir anxiety in Europe."

9.4 On the Road to Damascus

Figure 9.4 Stuck between a Rock and a Hard Place.
Source: Süddeutsche Zeitung, April 28, 2010 (by Pepsch Gottscheber).

of Germans adamantly opposed to a bailout (and only 33 percent in favor).[63]

The electoral motivation came to the fore again. An official from the EU predicted that "the election campaign can't justify anything ... [Germany's government leaders] will have to explain their position later to their citizens if the euro area as a whole is destabilized ... This is not and has never been only about Greece."[64] The incongruity between Merkel's position and what everyone else outside Germany seemed to be saying was not lost on the domestic press. Merkel's dilemma was well illustrated by the *Süddeutsche Zeitung* cartoon published at the end of April (Figure 9.4). She could act now and almost certainly tank the elections in NRW, or she could wait and let the eurozone collapse. It did not help that the months of delay had raised the costs of a bailout drastically.[65] It now was clear that €45 billion would not suffice to bail out the Greek economy. The IMF and the ECB stated on April 28 that the aid to Greece could be between €100 billion and €120 billion. Germany's contribution would rise from €8.4 billion to more than €25 billion. This was not something the chancellor was eager to tell the

---

[63] "Poll finds 57% of Germans oppose Greek aid."
[64] "Greece warns speculators as it races for bailout." *Agence France-Presse*, April 26, 2010.
[65] "Greece said to be close to deal on rescue plan." *New York Times*, April 30, 2010. https://dealbook.nytimes.com/2010/04/30/greece-said-to-be-close-to-deal-on-rescue-plan/, accessed February 5, 2018.

German voters, not when only as few as 16 percent of them favored a bailout.[66]

With the ship rapidly sinking, however, political action was unavoidable. On May 3, the German government introduced the "Act on Financial Stability within the Monetary Union" that would clear the way for Germany's contribution to the bailout. The act passed on May 7 after heated debate, and became effective on the following day. On May 9, the EU finance ministers assembled for an emergency meeting and approved the rescue package totaling €500 billion, of which Germany's guarantees were €123 billion (with a possible additional €24.6 billion). The IMF also approved Greece's request for a Stand-by-Arrangement of €30 billion, with an immediate release of its first tranche of €5.5 billion to refinance the Greek bonds maturing in ten days.

Having stood her ground for weeks in the face of immense economic and external political pressure, the chancellor finally caved in when it became almost certain that further dithering would be catastrophic for the eurozone. As one of the interviewees explained, the German government had not wanted a decision on the bailout before the NRW election, which is why it had persisted in its public denials that the problem even existed. It was only at the end of April that Merkel agreed that this was not a viable strategy anymore. This interpretation is corroborated by another interviewee, who noted that at the end of April it had become clear that the German government had a responsibility to act despite the potential public backlash. The economic and financial costs of waiting even a few more days far outweighed the political benefits. With the survival of the common currency at risk, the German government became intensely focused on expediting a financial rescue package. The flurry of activity resulted in a bailout agreement even before it was resolved what the bank participation was going to be. But the Eurogroup had to send a signal to the financial markets, and so it did.[67]

The attempt to signal responsiveness by position defending, or, more to the point, the strategy of blame avoidance through delay, had failed. What were the voters going to do?

9.5 The Wages of Defiance

Electoral concerns can rationalize Merkel's opposition to a bailout despite her knowledge that the crisis was serious. However, the strategy

---

[66] "Germany finds bailing out is hard to do."
[67] "Huge Greece bail-out deal agreed." *BBC News*, May 2, 2010. http://news.bbc.co.uk/2/hi/business/8656649.stm, accessed February 5, 2018; "Greece bailout will prevent spillover: EU's Barroso."

9.5 The Wages of Defiance

required her to delay all the way until after the elections and she did not. The German bailout agreement passed in the Bundestag two days before the election in NRW. What now?

With the delay strategy in shambles, and with everything that was at stake domestically, Merkel tried very hard to persuade the German voters that the bailout was crucial for the German economy.[68] The German government switched to damage-control mode almost immediately after the second downgrade. Schäuble now insisted that loans for Greece were good for Germany.[69] It was, he argued, about the eurozone: "It is our mission to defend the stability of the euro zone in its entirety. The better we do that, the better it is for all Europeans and for Germans."[70] He also met with directors of private German banks to get their voluntary commitment to buy Greek debt. Polls had indicated that 53 percent of Germans would support aiding Greece provided the banks participated.[71] Merkel doubled down, "It does not just mean we are helping Greece but also that we are stabilising the euro as a whole, thereby helping people in Germany, for whom a stable European currency is of extraordinary value."[72] She even managed to defend the delay in her policy statement, when she insisted that

It is about nothing more and nothing less than the future of Europe, and therefore the future of Germany in Europe. [...] A good European is not necessarily the one who helps quickly. A good European is the one who respects the European treaties and the relevant national law, and helps accordingly to ensure the stability of the Eurozone (Bundesregierung, 2010).

The chancellor also contrived to present the bailout as a potentially profitable enterprise because the loans would be provided through a state-owned bank, which would make money if the Greeks paid it back.[73] As one economist put it, in the long term, the bailout should have no

---

[68] Dempsey, Judy and Jack Ewing. "Germany approves assistance for Greece." *The New York Times*, May 4, 2010. www.nytimes.com/2010/05/04/business/global/04ecb.html, accessed February 5, 2018; "Merkel faces voter backlash over Greece." *Deutsche Presse-Agentur*, April 26, 2010.

[69] "Aid for Greece won't put squeeze on Germany, says Schaeuble." *Deutsche Welle*, April 29, 2010. www.dw.com/en/aid-for-greece-wont-put-squeeze-on-germany-says-schaeuble/a-5517080, accessed February 5, 2018.

[70] "110 Billion Euro package: EU agrees to prop up Greece." *Der Spiegel*, May 3, 2010. www.spiegel.de/international/europe/110-billion-euro-package-eu-agrees-to-prop-up-greece-a-692619.html, accessed February 5, 2018.

[71] "German finance minister to press banks on Greek rescue: report." *Agence France-Presse*, April 30, 2010. www.expatica.com/de/news/German-finance-minister-to-press-banks-on-Greek-rescue-report_174304.html, accessed February 5, 2018.

[72] "Germany warns Greece to deliver on cuts." *Agence France-Presse*, May 3, 2010.

[73] "Merkel tries to sell Greek bailout to Germans."

impact on the taxpayers because Germany would lend the money at 5 percent interest while only paying for it at 3 percent.[74]

Merkel went on a veritable media blitz with news conferences and interviews on the day the eurozone members approved the bailout package.[75] She made fifteen personal appearances in NRW alone and spent the week before the election giving numerous interviews on TV.[76] The head of the CDU-FDP government in NRW, Jürgen Rüttgers, also tried to sound confident that voters would realize that the Greek bailout was in their own best interest and would not punish the government for agreeing to it.[77]

The voters were not buying it. Since June 2009, the fraction of Germans who thought that the current economic situation was good or very good had been steadily increasing. The same trend obtained for the expectations about the future.[78] Compared to January 2010, when 64 percent of Germans thought that the worst of the crisis was still to come, by May only 56 percent thought so.[79] In mid-April, 78 percent of Germans believed that their own economic situation would either not be affected by the crisis or improve over the next few years; 59 percent believed that the German unemployment rate would either remain stable or decline; and 71 percent believed that the economy would either remain as is or improve.[80]

Even after the rating downgrade, the majority (59 percent) considered the Greeks responsible for the crisis, as opposed to the banks (13 percent), politicians (11 percent), or speculators (9 percent). Moreover, the vast majority (76 percent) were convinced that the Greeks would

[74] "Merkel stumps up for Greece, but demands change." *Agence France-Presse*, May 4, 2010. www.expatica.com/de/news/Merkel-stumps-up-for-Greece-but-demands-change_174913.html, accessed February 5, 2018.
[75] "Rüttgers kämpft gegen Griechenland-Effekt."; "Griechenland entscheidet die Wahl." *RP Online*, May 8, 2010. www.rp-online.de/nrw/landespolitik/griechenland-entscheidet-die-wahl-aid-1.877336, accessed February 5, 2018.
[76] "German voters poised to punish Merkel party over Greece."
[77] "Verhagelt Ihnen Griechenland die Wahl, Herr Rüttgers?" *Bild*, May 5, 2010. www.bild.de/politik/2010/juergen-ruettgers-interview-12425094.bild.html, accessed February 5, 2018. Unfortunately, Rüttgers' own credibility was already in tatters over the "Rent-a-Rüttgers" scandal and the allegations that his staff had been trafficking in private conversations with him for donations of €6,000. "Merkel party fears voter lashing over Greece aid." *Agence France-Presse*. May 8, 2010.
[78] See the figures "Gegenwärtige wirtschaftliche Lage: Zeitverlauf" and "Zukünftige wirtschaftliche Lage: Zeitverlauf" in Infratest Dimap (2010).
[79] See the figure "Aussagen zur Krise: Der schlimmste Teil der Krise steht uns noch bevor" in Infratest Dimap (2011).
[80] Presseportal, "N24-EMNID-UMFRAGE: Deutsche vorsichtig optimistisch – Wirtschaftliche Lage wird weitgehend stabil eingeschätzt." *Presseportal*, April 15, 2010. www.presseportal.de/pm/13399/1595863, accessed May 10, 2016.

9.5 The Wages of Defiance

not repay their debts.[81] With 61 percent now fearing that helping the Greeks would only be the first step in a never-ending series of bailouts for other heavily indebted Eurozone members, 65 percent opposed a bailout (only 16 percent were in favor). In fact, while 42 percent believed the government claim that the delay was necessary to extract more austerity measures, 23 percent suspected that it had always planned to provide the aid. More worryingly, only 20 percent thought that membership in the EU was economically beneficial to the country (28 percent thought it disadvantageous), which further undermined calls to stabilize the euro in the name of that membership.[82]

It is instructive that even after the bailout, 56 percent of Germans continued to believe that aid to Greece was wrong (only 39 percent were in favor), even though 67 percent thought that the euro would destabilize over the next year.[83] Moreover, only 4 percent believed that the government would come through with the promised tax cuts (51 percent expected a tax hike).[84] The government's initial strategy of telling voters that everything was fine and Greece did not need rescuing had worked all too well.

The anti-bailout flames were relentlessly fanned by *Bild*, which referred to the rescue as the "fattest cheque in history." A sampling of headlines in the run-up to the NRW election can give one a pretty good idea what the government had to contend with[85]:

The Greeks want even more billions from us! – 25,000,000,000 EURO! Suddenly our politicians have got billions of euros for Greece. It is a country that has been living beyond its means for decades. It cheated to get the euro and well and truly lied to the rest of Europe. Congratulations, Dear German Government.

---

[81] *Presseportal*, "N24-EMNID-UMFRAGE Deutsche bewerten Griechenlandkrise als hausgemacht – Mehrheit glaubt nicht an Kreditrückzahlung." *Presseportal*, April 29, 2010. www.presseportal.de/pm/13399/1604651, accessed May 10, 2016.

[82] Köcher, Renate. "Allensbach-Analyse Vertrauensverlust für den Euro." *Frankfurter Allgemeine Zeitung*, April 28, 2010. www.faz.net/aktuell/wirtschaft/eurokrise/allensbach-analyse-vertrauensverlust-fuer-den-euro-1970252.html, accessed May 10, 2016.

[83] "Der Schicksalstag des Euro." *Bild*, May 10, 2010. www.bild.de/politik/wirtschaft/milliarden-hilfe-griechenland-pleite-krise-12397612.bild.html, accessed February 5, 2018.

[84] "Der Schicksalstag des Euro."

[85] Translated in "Greek aid up to 120 billion euros." *Agence France-Presse*, April 28, 2010; "As size of Greek bailout soars, supply of German sympathy runs short." *The Independent*. April 30, 2010. www.independent.co.uk/news/world/europe/as-size-of-greek-bailout-soars-supply-of-german-sympathy-runs-short-1958681.html, accessed February 5, 2018; "Warum zahlen wir den Griechen ihre Luxus-Renten?" *Bild*, April 27, 2010. www.bild.de/politik/wirtschaft/wir-zahlen-luxus-rente-mit-milliarden-hilfe-12338430.bild.html, accessed February 5, 2018; 'Liebe Politiker, würden Sie mit Ihrem Privatvermögen für die Griechen-Milliarden bürgen?" *Bild*, May 5, 2010.

Dear politicians, would you agree to be liable for the Greek-billions with your personal wealth?

Why should we pay for Greeks' luxury pensions?

We are the idiots of Europe! [The Greek government] tricked, camouflaged and fooled for years in a way that would make the gods on Olympus blush... With all respect to the world's oldest democracy, if you lie once, no one will believe you. Particularly when it's about money.

The furor over Merkel's *volte-face* fatally weakened her party. A survey conducted on the day of the announcement revealed that 62 percent of Germans were unhappy with the government, and that the CDU-FDP coalition would lose the vote in NRW.[86] Figure 9.3 shows the abrupt decline in support for both the chancellor and CDU in the wake of the bailout decision. According to a Forsa Institute poll for *Stern*, only 48 percent of Germans would elect Merkel again (a drop of 6 percent from the previous week), and only 41 percent approved of her performance in the debt crisis in Greece.[87] The *Frankfurter Allgemeine* editorialized that "there is nothing of the Iron Lady left now."[88]

The opposition parties had been playing up the Greek issue and Merkel's perceived inability to deal with it for a while but could not point to anything specific aside from ominous conspiracy theories.[89] Now they had their proof. Recognizing the inherent weakness of the chancellor's newly revealed position, the opposition pounced, making it the most important topic in the electoral campaign in NRW.[90] As Klaus-Peter Schöpener, head of the polling institute Emnid, said, "The issue has electrified people as seldom before and is going to play a determining role" in the election.[91] The last poll published by *Bild* on the eve of the

---

[86] "Germany warns Greece to deliver on cuts." *Agence France-Presse*, May 3, 2010. www.expatica.com/de/news/Germany-warns-Greece-to-deliver-on-cuts_174471.html, accessed February 5, 2018.

[87] "Merkel popularity drops over Greek crisis: poll." *Agence France-Presse*, May 5, 2010. www.expatica.com/de/news/Merkel-popularity-drops-over-Greek-crisis-poll_175465.html, accessed February 5, 2018.

[88] Paterson, Tony. "Merkel gets Germany to sign the 'fattest cheque in history'." *The Independent*. May 8, 2010. www.independent.co.uk/news/world/europe/merkel-gets-germany-to-sign-the-fattest-cheque-in-history-1968230.html, accessed February 5, 2018.

[89] Connolly, Kate. "Merkel's dilemma: Germans rage at picking up bill for 'pampered' Greeks." *The Guardian*, April 29, 2010. www.theguardian.com/world/2010/apr/28/debt-crisis-germans-bill-greeks, accessed February 5, 2018.

[90] "Wahlkampf in letzter Minute: Rüttgers kampft gegen Griechenland-Effekt." *Der Spiegel*, May 8, 2010. www.spiegel.de/politik/deutschland/wahlkampf-in-letzter-minute-ruettgers-kaempft-gegen-griechenland-effekt-a-693779.html, accessed February 5, 2018; "SPD nutzt die Griechenland-Krise." *Handelsblatt*, May 6, 2010. www.handelsblatt.com/politik/deutschland/wahlkampf-spd-nutzt-die-griechenland-krise/3429284.html, accessed February 5, 2018; "Griechenland entscheidet die Wahl: Umfragen zeigen Kopf-an-Kopf-Rennen."

[91] "German voters poised to punish Merkel party over Greece."

9.5 The Wages of Defiance

elections showed that 20 percent of NRW voters said that the bailout would affect their decision.[92] Discontent was so deep that when Merkel appeared at a rally near Wuppertal, the police had to step in to contain protests that were about to turn into a riot.[93]

At the end of the day, German voters had no reason – in evidence or in logic – to believe Merkel's sudden conversion. And so they did not. Greece was not their concern, and the government had no business throwing taxpayer money down the black hole of Greek finances. All of Merkel's position taking and position defending had been a sham: the government had finally revealed what it had wanted to do all along, and it was not what the voters wanted. There was only one thing to do: deliver the electoral punishment this lack of responsiveness warranted.

The NRW election was an unmitigated disaster for the CDU, which lost by 10.2 percent relative to its 2005 performance, making this its worst electoral defeat in NRW ever. The SPD, which had abstained from the bailout vote, lost 2.6 percent, while the parties most critical of Merkel's government, the Greens and the Left Party, gained the most.[94] The NRW government was replaced with a coalition of SPD and Greens, and Merkel lost the majority in the Bundesrat.[95] The media erupted in outrage. *Bild* was hysterical, "Yet again, we are the idiots of Europe" for paying so much for "bankrupt neighbors" without money for tax cuts at home.[96] *Tagesspiegel* solemnly editorialized,

> Never before has a federal government's fear of a state election had such a disastrous impact on the EU and the stability of the euro. Merkel played tactical games for weeks before having to make promises after all, and what is the

---

[92] "Merkel's party braces for electoral backlash over Greece." *Agence France-Presse*, May 9, 2010. www.expatica.com/de/news/country-news/Merkels-party-braces-for-electoral-backlash-over-Greece_176567.html, accessed February 5, 2018.

[93] Pancevski, Bojan. "Angela Merkel faces voter revolt over generous Greece bailout." *The Sunday Times*, May 9, 2010. www.thetimes.co.uk/article/angela-merkel-faces-voter-revolt-over-generous-greece-bailout-x9v69x09n3n, accessed February 5, 2018.

[94] The Greens almost doubled their share from 6.2 percent to 12.1 percent, and the Left Part went from 3.1 percent to 5.6 percent (Medick, Veit, Philipp Wittrock, and Sebastian Fischer. "Elections in North Rhine-Westphalia: Key state vote handicaps Merkel." *Der Spiegel*, May 10, 2010. www.spiegel.de/international/germany/elections-in-north-rhine-westphalia-key-state-vote-handicaps-merkel-a-693917.html, accessed February 5, 2018).

[95] "Merkel loses state poll, upper house majority." *Agence France-Presse*, May 9, 2010. www.expatica.com/de/news/country-news/Merkel-coalition-loses-state-poll-upper-house-majority-exit-polls_176640.html, accessed February 5, 2018; "Merkel government sees 'double debacle' in pivotal poll." *Agence France-Presse*, May 10, 2010. www.expatica.com/de/news/Merkel-government-sees-double-debacle-in-pivotal-poll_176713.html, accessed February 5, 2018.

[96] "German cabinet approves euro crisis fund." *Agence France-Presse*, May 11, 2010. www.expatica.com/de/news/German-cabinet-approves-euro-crisis-fund_177192.html, accessed February 5, 2018.

end result? Black-yellow bankruptcy in North Rhine-Westphalia and a crisis for Europe.[97]

In the wake of the "double debacle," the chancellor faced an "unprecedented hail of criticism from within her own ranks," which only got worse when it became clear that the government would have to plug the €75 billion deficit hole with lower tax revenues and a new constitutional "debt brake."[98] The political ramifications of the NRW loss were not merely temporary setbacks; they proved as costly and persistent as the gloomy forecasts had predicted. As Figure 9.3 illustrates, public support for Merkel fell by more than 18 percent to an all-time low, and support for the CDU fell to a low of 31 percent. Support for Merkel would not recover to the (uncharacteristically low) levels of the immediate precrisis months for two years, and support for the CDU would take even longer.

All of this made it very difficult to pursue the domestic agenda Merkel and her CDU intended, and even though they still could push some legislation with compromises after long negotiations, by early 2013 the Greens and the Left had acquired 36 of the 69 votes, enough to block or renegotiate any government bill without exception.[99]

The political bill for the failed dilatory tactic was quite substantial.

9.6 Conclusion

Under normal circumstances, stalling on EU policies seems to be a favored strategy that allows governments to avoid blame for unfavorable outcomes right before elections (Chapter 8). Unless impelled by political rivalries, other governments appear to be willing to provide the electoral assist through hidden cooperation. This means that most of the time, legislation gets put on the back burner long enough for the elections to precede its adoption. Even in situations where the outcome appears more or less predestined, the government can take the position preferred by its constituents and defend it throughout the negotiations, fully expecting that as long as the outcome remains undecided, the uncertainty can work to its advantage. This is what Tony Blair had done in 2004–2005, and Labour survived a bruising election despite lingering doubts about the extent of his commitment to keep the UK rebate intact (Chapter 6).

---

[97] Translated in "Merkel under fire after 'double debacle' election defeat."
[98] Beste, Ralf, Christian Reiermann, and Merlind Theile. "Plans for sweeping cuts: Germany tries to plug gaping hole in its budget." *Der Spiegel*, May 26, 2010. www.spiegel.de/international/germany/plans-for-sweeping-cuts-germany-tries-to-plug-gaping-hole-in-its-budget-a-696760.html, accessed February 5, 2018.
[99] "Opposition to set up new hurdles for Merkel." *Deutsche Welle*, February 28, 2013. www.dw.com/en/opposition-to-set-up-new-hurdles-for-merkel/a-16634647, accessed February 5, 2018.

9.6 Conclusion

But the British government had the luxury of time, and so it obstructed agreements while there was hope of clinching something in return that it could use domestically to blunt the pain of the inevitable "betrayal."

The German government tried a similar strategy in 2010, but the circumstances were not normal. As was abundantly clear to experts, other governments, the Commission, the IMF, and even the German opposition, a financial rescue package for Greece was practically inevitable. And yet, the German government repeatedly denied that it was necessary and persisted in its opposition to a bailout even as the eurozone was slipping into financial chaos. Chancellor Merkel's predicament was strikingly similar to prime minister Blair's five years earlier: her ruling coalition was facing important elections where defeat would mean a collapse of the government's domestic agenda, and the voters were dead set against the obvious policy. Merkel's track record of fiscal conservatism made it possible for her to take the anti-bailout position preferred by the voters and to defend it credibly throughout the negotiations that were unfolding before that election.

Unlike the British, however, the German government ran out of time. The blame-avoidance strategy got derailed by the unexpected and extremely rapid deterioration of the economic situation in the eurozone triggered by the sudden steep downgrades of the sovereign debt of several governments. When this "bolt out of the blue" struck, the elections were less than two weeks away. The German government made a last-ditch effort to cling to its stance, but with chaos enveloping the eurozone, its position became untenable. With a week remaining to the elections, Merkel abruptly reversed course and pushed through the domestic legislation that made it possible for Germany to pay its portion of the massive bailout bill. The package was adopted on the day of the elections. The chancellor tried very hard to convince the voters that she had been committed to their preferred position all along but that exigent circumstances had compelled her to act. However, they did not believe her, and the CDU suffered a crushing defeat.

It is this drubbing at the polls that makes this case so interesting: it is one of the few instances where the government's putative electoral concerns that were supposed to motivate its strategy became very real when the strategy could not be implemented. It is not very often that exogenous events impinge so dramatically on the government's footdragging capacity, which is why most delays continue past elections without much trouble (as long as other member states are willing to allow them). Unlike these usual situations where we must be content with inferring government fears from opinion polls that ask hypothetical questions about vote intentions, the German case gives us the raw and unvarnished opinion of the voters: their actual choice.

10   The European Republic

> St. Simonianism is finished. It can't work when you have to face democratic opinion.   – Pascal Lamy, European Commission

Jean Monnet's grand vision was one of lasting peace and prosperity for Europe. As desperately needed this vision was for the war-ravaged continent, it was by no means obvious how it could be attained. Europe had known spells of peace before: The long nineteenth century had seen one that had lasted for fifty years and another that lasted for forty, but war had always come back, each time more vicious and destructive. The last one had left most of Europe a smoldering ruin, and it had come on the heels of another that itself had been so unprecedented in its intensity that people had simply called it the Great War. Now it had merely become the first.

Among the myriad explanations for how Europeans were plunged into madness not once but twice in a single generation, one stood out. Governments had not considered the status quo sufficiently attractive, either because they found the existing distribution of benefits unsatisfactory or because they believed it was changing to their ultimate ruin, and they had been willing to disrupt it with violence. They were motivated by domestic concerns and ambitions that the international system had repeatedly proven to be incapable of restraining. The remedy for this diagnosis was simple: governments had to have reasons to want the status quo preserved, and reasons to prefer that any necessary revisions be made peacefully. But, to paraphrase Carl von Clausewitz, everything in peace is simple, but the simplest thing is difficult.

Monnet's fundamental insight was that it would be futile to place one's faith in an international institution when governments could still pursue their nationalist designs unfettered by anything but the potential that others might fight back. A peace secured only by the threat of war cannot last; governments must have a stake in preserving it.

This meant, first and foremost, that Germany would have to be fully re-integrated into the postwar system. This was how the victorious allies had treated the vanquished French in 1815, and this was the lesson neglected by the writers of the Treaty of Versailles in 1919. The winners of this war would have to set aside their thirst for revenge and their desire to have the losers pay for their recovery. Instead, the victors would have to focus on building toward common prosperity that would give the defeated ones reasons to live in peace. This had proven beyond the political will of the victors of World War I, and there was no guarantee that governments would not set out to appease their domestic audiences again. If new arrangements were to be made – and World War II was the terrible reminder that it was imperative to try – then governments would have to be protected from the buffeting of national politics.

Attempting to do everything at once would certainly doom the project from the start: the more interests the new institutions affect, the stronger the pressure on the government to consider them. Monnet realized that the only way forward was incremental: starting small with something that could be implemented with minimal agreement and then using the success of each individual step to build a momentum toward the next one, all the while improving the conditions of living in peace. This process would not only aid in the economic development of the states, it could make the governments and their publics believe that a future of shared prosperity was possible while also teaching them how to attain it. Hopefully, these would be reasons enough to preserve the peace.

And thus it was that the architect of the European Union started small – with the integration of the coal and steel industries of France and Germany – and insisted on institutional arrangements that would insulate the governments against the vicissitudes of domestic politics. National sovereignty was diluted by design, as was the muting of the publics. The process of ever-deepening integration would be self-sustaining, propelled by the tangible benefits that it created for the participants.

The principle of delegating authority so that policies for the common good are not determined by short-term parochial interests is quite entrenched domestically. Indeed, this is one reason why all modern democracies are representative rather than direct, and why federalism is so prevalent among the larger ones.[1] When people elect representatives to make the laws that govern them and design the policies that affect

---

[1] See Caramani (2017) for a recent discussion of representative democracy and its two most prominent challenges.

their lives, they do so knowing that it is quite likely that there will be some divergence between what they want and what gets done. Indeed, if the representatives do their jobs properly, then it is almost inevitable that there would have to be some divergence. Hewing too closely to the wishes of one's constituents might make a representative responsive, but it would defeat a key reason for having that representative in the first place.[2]

Citizens do not need a mirror that just reflects their wishes – inchoate and ill-informed as they might be – they need agents who would faithfully account for their interests but settle on a policy that appropriately balances these interests against other considerations. For the representatives to have the freedom to act in this way, they must be somewhat protected against immediate public backlash. The danger is that providing them such protection makes them unaccountable for their actions, which deprives them of a powerful incentive to be faithful to the interests of the people they represent.

This is the fundamental tension between the benefits of delegation and the costs of losing control of the agent (Scharpf, 2003, p. 5). It is never fully satisfactorily resolved, as the countless variations in electoral systems, term limits, and extents of direct popular involvement can attest.

This is also the tension inherent in the delegation of authority to international organizations, part of whose design is to prevent national interests from undermining the possibility for cooperation. Conflicts between general welfare and short-term particularistic interests can arise in areas as diverse as trade, human rights, economic development, and peacekeeping operations. Issues of intergovernmental cooperation could be at least partially depoliticized if they are transferred to the domain of an organization that is staffed with experienced bureaucrats mostly concerned with the technical aspects of achieving common goals. When their apolitical approach does not founder at the hard realities of politics, there is a good chance that such an organization could produce policies that are close to optimal from the perspective of the collective. This, at least, is the promise that makes international organizations so attractive.

---

[2] This is the conflict between demands for responsiveness that emphasize the need for the government to act in accordance to the preferences of the citizens, and demands for responsibility that emphasize the need for the government to take into account long-term needs of the citizens and domestic (constitutional) as well as international commitments, if any (Dahl, 1956; Birch, 1964; Scharpf, 1999). What it means for a government to be "responsible" is also not entirely straightforward. Some identify it with accountability, others talk of predictability and consistency, while others focus on efficiency and effectiveness (Mair, 2009).

The desire to wall off the organizations from the hurly-burly of national politics is easily seen in their institutional design. Shifting trade policies and related dispute resolution to the World Trade Organization (WTO) or the North American Free Trade Agreement (NAFTA) insulates decision-makers from the pressure of various domestic economic groups whose clamoring for exceptions, tariffs, or subsidies would otherwise raise protectionist barriers to trade that would be economically inefficient. Delegating developmental policies to the World Bank or the African Development Fund makes it possible to implement projects that maximize goals other than strategic geopolitical interests, goals such as sustainable social and economic development, or environmental protection and conservation. Delegating peacekeeping to the United Nations (UN) enhances the legitimacy of the operations by signaling broad consensus among the great and minor powers, increases the costs of resisting them with force, and in the end improves the chances of their success.

The downside of all this insulation is that national interest groups, elites, and citizens might have precious little control over what these organizations do and even over what their own governments are up to behind the closed doors, where much of the interaction at the highest levels takes place. When the outcomes diverge from their preferences, these audiences could come to regard them as unrepresentative, undemocratic, and therefore illegitimate. This can undermine the organization because it would erode the goodwill that is supposed to keep it functioning, and because it might generate a push for the national government to operate outside the confines of an organization that repeatedly fails to deliver outcomes these audiences would like.

Organizations to whom authority is delegated must therefore tread carefully between two extremes. On the one hand, they cannot be too responsive to national demands or they risk losing all the advantages that motivated their establishment. On the other hand, they cannot be too nonresponsive to these demands or they risk losing the support that sustains them. This means that the responsiveness of international organizations, much like representation in democracies, is not a question of either/or, but rather a matter of balance (Sartori 2005; Mair 2009).[3] In this context, legitimation is neither purely procedural nor entirely instrumental, and it has elements of both.

When European integration started, it was guided by Monnet's perception that democratic responsiveness to domestic publics would

---

[3] Scharpf (1999) says that the challenge is to be both democratic and effective.

be a serious obstacle to progress, especially when the benefits might take several years to begin to materialize. Starting small with particular industries and only six members ensured that only few domestic interest groups would be affected, and so resistance to the approach would be minimal. Starting with the key industries related to war making ensured that the practical aim of reducing the chance of war could be furthered by making it, as Robert Schuman said, "materially impossible" to wage war (since coal and steel production would be governed by a supranational centralized authority).

The European Coal and Steel Community could be regarded as a proof of concept, and it worked. Governments found it beneficial to transfer a growing number of policies over which they had traditionally exercised sovereign rights to the set of institutions that morphed into what eventually became the EU. But as the range of delegated policies widened, as their scope deepened, and as the number of members expanded, more and more domestic interests became directly affected, more and more people started to pay attention to what the EU was doing, and more and more of them discovered that they did not approve of what their own governments were doing. That this should occur had been "part and parcel" of the vision for an ever-strengthening EU.

In this sense, the idea that European integration could proceed indefinitely in an insulated technocratic cocoon was always utopian. It was inevitable that this elitist and top-heavy version of the EU would become a victim of its own success. The hue and cry raised by those who allege that the EU suffers from a democratic deficit – a charge that has become especially potent since the ratification of the Maastricht Treaty – must be understood in its proper context. The EU does not face a crisis of legitimacy but a problem of balance: it must be more responsive (in publicly visible ways), but it must continue to function. It is just that its traditional trade-off that privileged superior policy outcomes over procedural legitimation at the domestic level – its "policies without politics" model – had become unsustainable precisely because it had worked so well.[4]

One of the main goals of this book is to convince the reader that a proper understanding of how the fundamental tension resolves itself in the EU shows that both its defenders and detractors have overstated their concerns. Simply put, it does not matter how much one tries to ward off the spirit of domestic politicking through institutional designs. Politics

---

[4] Schmidt (2006) notes how this model of governance in the EU has contributed to what people perceive to be its democratic deficit.

always finds a way. The institutions can only hope to channel it; often, shutting off one route merely causes politics to burrow another.

The EU has not been insulated against domestic politics nearly as much as its technocratic defenders would have liked it to be. The findings strongly support the idea that member state governments are quite sensitive to electoral concerns, and this causes them to signal that they are responsive to their relevant constituencies. The signals range from something as mild as adopting policy stances that are congruent with the wishes of their constituents, to stubbornly defending these positions throughout negotiations at the EU level, and to the most persuasive signal of all: delivering policy outcomes to their constituents' liking. Governments do these things because voters tend to reward them for such performance, as I found in both experimental (Chapter 4) and quasi-experimental (Chapter 5) settings. The pervasive worry about looking bad at the polls motivates legislative behavior so strongly that governments are exceptionally unlikely to publicize any concessions they make irrespective of how non-salient they might be to the constituents. There is also evidence that governments understand these incentives quite well and are willing to cooperate with fellow members experiencing electoral distress, even behind the closed doors of the Council (provided, of course, that they would not rather see the opposition replace the incumbent government). With the citizens in EU member states having become more aware of the EU's role in their lives – for good or bad – domestic opposition parties have found it expedient to politicize the incumbent government's actions at the EU level, further strengthening the linkage between what the publics want and what the governments do at the supposedly insulated intergovernmental level.

All of this should make the detractors of the EU less despondent. But the problem is, the way domestic pressure manifests itself and gets reflected in policymaking might often be quite unsatisfying. When it comes to negotiations over the annual budgets (Chapter 5) or the multiannual financial frameworks (MFFs) (Chapter 6), governments seem quite responsive in uncontroversial ways: they seek to secure larger shares of the total receipts and redirect expenditures toward headings where the access rules favor their own constituents. However, as the MFF case study shows, when governments expect that they will have to compromise in ways their publics will disapprove of, they will try to evade being held accountable for their actions by delaying the unfavorable outcome until the elections are safely in the past. This seems to be the prevalent *modus operandi* in legislative bargaining, where cheap public posturing on behalf of constituents (Chapter 7) often resolves itself in private concessions after the fact (Chapter 8). And all of this is enabled by the opaque decision-making in the Council, the organ that still retains primacy in much of the EU's policymaking. When these sorts of considerations are combined with policy proposals from the Commission that are sometimes extraordinarily apolitical, it is no wonder that detractors of the EU often see a supranational entity run amok, with national governments either permitting this through disability or inaction, or actively conniving with it out of public glare.

For one who considers the fundamental tension, however, it is not difficult to argue that a government that resorts to a strategic delay is doing exactly what a responsible representative of its constituents' interests should do: It makes the hard decision that goes against their wishes and protects itself against an unjustified backlash. This backlash might arise for no other reason than it is advantageous for the government's political opposition to make the decision an electoral issue. When the electoral threat is especially potent, a government might fail to discharge its policymaking responsibilities in a timely manner. In extreme cases, the government might wind up hurting the constituents it was aiming to protect with the unpopular policy, and, ironically, it might get punished by these same constituents for even trying to protect them (Chapter 9).

The findings that EU governments are responsive to domestic interests, at least around election time, have several implications that bear on different strands in the literature on the EU and democracy more generally. First, it is uncontroversial that the EU's widening and deepening reach has changed and constrained national and subnational governance in its member states. If this entailed only a surrender of sovereignty in the name of economic efficiency, then the process would truly be problematic from a representative perspective. But if governments actively influence EU-level policies for the same national (and, as we have seen in the German case during the MFF negotiations, subnational) interests, then the supposed loss of autonomy is not nearly as great as critics fear. National governments have become more sensitive to domestic political concerns and have used the institutional structure of the EU to negotiate deals that reflect them. As one might have supposed, when constituents start to worry about EU policies that will impact their lives without their knowledge nor subject to their control, their own government must seek to reassure them that it is working on their behalf.

Second, it is not really a problem that these governments are responsive to national audiences. Critics of the EU argue that the EU should be responsive to the "European" citizenry, which has led many of them to pin their hopes on an increasing role of the European Parliament. Setting aside the very basic (and in reality almost insurmountable) difficulty posed by the nonexistence of a European *demos* – exactly whose interests is the EU supposed to be representing? – the trouble with these criticisms is that they posit an artificial standard against which they propose to judge the EU. I do not mean that the standard is merely unrealistic, I mean that it is undesirable.

Why should "national" be a dirty word when it comes to interests represented at the European level? The justly vaunted consociational democracies in the EU have managed to protect their ethnic, cultural, linguistic, and religious minorities (McCrae, 1974; Lijphart, 1999). There is no reason to suppose that the EU would fail to protect its "national minorities." The patterns of electoral accountability and responsive governance in the EU are strikingly similar to those found in many advanced democracies, including majoritarian ones like the United States, where governments are responsive even when accountability is weak.[5]

In fact, if we were to apply the same standards of representation demanded of the EU toward national governments, we would find fault with every federal state. In a federal system, the central government signals responsiveness to citizens of its various subnational units by promulgating policies that are often determined in the give-and-take of negotiations designed to satisfy specific constituencies in these units (Wlezien and Soroka, 2011). This is not only so by design, it is considered as a fundamental aspect of the legitimation of these policies.

In the United States, the House of Representatives is expressly set up to give the elected politicians reasons to be responsive to their home state districts that elected them. And whereas the US Senate was constructed in part to balance the inevitable centrifugal tendencies of the House, its construction – wherein each state gets two votes – was intended to protect the interests of the smaller states so they would not be trampled by the larger ones (since the allocation of seats in the House depends on population size). Along these lines, the German upper house, the Bundesrat, represents the sixteen states (Länder) at the federal level. Unlike the US Senate, its members are not even elected – they are appointed by state governments – and the number of votes depends on the population, although not proportionally (again, to ensure that the smaller ones do not end up with too few votes to make a difference). One might quibble with the effectiveness of representation in the United States and Germany, but few would call these systems undemocratic.

The analogy with existing democratic federations should not be pushed too far: there is a lot more variation among the citizens of the

---

[5] Przeworski, Stokes, and Manin (1999); Ashworth and de Mesquita (2014); Achen and Bartels (2015).

EU than in any single federal state, even the most diverse one. This suggests that perhaps national interests *are* an appropriate aggregation of subnational preferences around which representation should be organized, much as it is in the Council, in conjunction with a more direct representation, as it is in the Parliament. And before a true "European" *demos* is formed, it is unrealistic to suppose that the member states whose governments must champion these national interests, would fail to consider both their contributions to and their benefits from the common policies.

This harkens back to the ancient principle of no representation without taxation: those who contribute the most toward the common good get a disproportionate voice in deciding the contours of the policies to achieve it and, in some limited instances, what constitutes that good. In this, the EU resembles the celebrated Dutch Republic of the seventeenth and eighteenth centuries, in which sovereignty lay with the provinces and their states. Contributions to the "federal" budget depended on the relative wealth of each province, and each province had one vote in the States-General, where unanimity was the rule. The most important decisions, however, were made in the Council of State, in which the wealthy provinces had more votes.[6] Even the EU's funding system is reminiscent of the Dutch one. The States-General had its "traditional" resource that mostly consisted of customs duties, but its largest source of revenue was the analogue to the gross national income (GNI)-based resource: the provincial contributions based on negotiated quotas. For someone accustomed to the EU's Big Four to be disproportionately influential in setting policies for the EU, it would not come as a surprise that with Holland contributing an average of 58 percent to the common budget of the Republic, and jointly with Zeeland and Utrecht, an average of 75 percent, the Republic's Big Three decided most of its policies.

One could continue with the astonishing parallels that could justify calling the EU the European Republic, but the point is that a system of representation that attempts to balance the reality of important contributors that must be motivated to pony up the cash for the common policies with the ideal that all constituents have equal voices should not be faulted for failing to implement that ideal to the hilt.

Most of the work on responsive governance in the EU has focused on its supranational aspect, which is why it privileges the Parliament as the directly elected representative of the European *demos* (of course, even there groupings linked to national parties play an important role).

---

[6] For a concise overview of the system of governance in the Dutch Republic, see Israel (1995, pp. 276–306).

Just as one would get a distorted picture of German politics by studying only the Bundestag, one cannot fully understand responsiveness in the EU by focusing only on its Parliament. Domestic democratic legitimacy depends on the functioning of the institutional complex, which must be considered in its entirety. Separate institutions are often designed to address certain shortcomings of the others, and the function of the collective depends on the interactions of its constituent parts. And so it must be with the EU. My book is intended to complement the extant studies by drawing attention to the fact that responsiveness is also the reality in that governing body that was supposedly immune to it, the Council.

The finding that even the secretive negotiations in the Council end up being an arena were national interests get played out in the electoral shadow has implications beyond the EU. Many international integration projects such as Mercosur, NAFTA, the WTO, and even to some extent the UN, are said to face legitimacy crises similar to the EU's. The breakneck speed with which some of these processes have unfolded has generated fears that governments are delegating so much authority to these organizations that they are becoming unaccountable to their publics, and so ordinary citizens are being left behind. Scholars have noted, of course, that interest group pressure would motivate governments to pursue certain benefits from these organizations, but as a rule not much attention is paid to public opinion or elections except when they throw a monkey wrench into the smooth operation of the international machinery.[7]

If the EU could serve as an example, however, then there is no reason to believe that the publics could not influence delegated policies constructively. One might raise the objection that the EU is *sui generis*, and so no such parallels could be drawn. But in this case, the atypical nature of the EU works to the argument's advantage: if it is the case that the governments of member states remain responsive to their publics even in the most integrated international political system in the world, then why should one fear what they do in institutions much less binding than the EU?[8]

---

[7] Caraway, Rickard, and Anner (2012); Chaudoin (2014); Pervez (2015). A notable exception is the formal model developed by Dai (2005).

[8] We do, in fact, have evidence that perhaps one should not, at least in two such organizations. Dreher and Vaubel (2004) find that new net credits from the IMF are significantly larger in preelection periods, and that borrowing from the International Bank for Reconstruction and Development significantly declines after elections. Likewise, Rickard and Caraway (2014) argue that elections give countries more leverage in their negotiations with the IMF, and they manage to obtain less stringent labor market conditions in IMF loan programs.

For the mechanism I identified to work, however, the constituents must be at least minimally aware of the policies that affect their wellbeing and that are being decided in these organizations. I do mean minimally, as in: there must at least be a potential that the issue could become politicized domestically. The process through which that happens is not that important. It could be that powerful interest groups press strenuously for benefits on behalf of their members, such as the agricultural lobbies in the United States and the EU that caused so much grief to proponents of trade liberalization during the Uruguay and Doha rounds of WTO negotiations (Hudec, 1993; Davis, 2004). It could be that opportunistic politicians deliberately inflame domestic passions in order to enhance their own electoral prospects (as we have seen repeatedly in the case studies in this book). It could be the government officials themselves when they seek to trumpet their international achievements (even when these achievements are illusory, as in the case of Filipino mayors who put up billboards announcing World Bank grants for their municipalities to claim credit for policies over which they had absolutely no influence whatsoever [Cruz and Schneider, 2017]). A government that cannot guarantee that something it does internationally would not have domestic repercussions will very much care about the electoral optics of its actions.

On this dimension, developments have mirrored the European experience. Many of these international organizations have come under increased public scrutiny, and the globalization of communications has spread information faster and wider than ever before. Governments have become acutely aware of the need to defend national interests that are defined more broadly and of the possibility that they might be called to account for the agreements they have struck. The danger now is not that the technocratic train would run over the national publics but that the politicians terrified by the polls would derail it.

And this danger brings us back to the EU. Whither the Union?

Critics allege that the EU is in a crisis of legitimacy but as I have argued above, if this is indeed a crisis, then it is one that engulfs all democracies. Research on the responsiveness of European institutions – supranational bureaucrats in the Commission, political elites in Parliament, national politicians in the Council – shows that many of the specific allegations are overstated. The Commission has not become unmoored from member state concerns (indeed, if it ever was), and the institutions with some sort of national representation exhibit clear patterns of responsive behavior. But much somber assessment is lost in the cacophony of assaults from both the left – charging that the EU does not do enough to promote the rights of various underrepresented groups – and the right – charging that the EU tramples on national interests. The dilemma created by the fundamental tension is real enough, but its ruthless politicization has been exploited by populists of all stripes. Euroscepticism is on the rise, and politicians who often seek to evade blame by pinning bad outcomes on the EU are getting trapped by their own rhetoric (Schmidt, 2006). The EU has singularly failed to raise awareness of the valuable role it has played in keeping the peace and in promoting European prosperity after World War II.

The book has both good news and bad news on this front. The findings that governments try to signal that they are responsive in EU negotiations and that this conduct tends to be associated with outcomes closer to their preferences are encouraging. Even more so is the evidence that this is not limited to the Council,[9] but also clear in Parliament and even the Commission.[10] The institutions are adjusting as policy without politics has become untenable. The politicization of the EU can also instruct citizens about responsible governance and the limits of purely democratic processes (Rose, 2014). Knowing more about the situation in other member states is also helpful. For instance, voters are now much more likely to judge the economic performance of their own government in reference to how other states are doing rather than in absolute terms. Presiding over a slumping economy is no longer a political death sentence if the economic troubles are widespread (Duch and Stevenson, 2010).

The bad news is that it is not clear that voters have updated their beliefs about the state of European democracy. The findings also show that governments try to evade taking responsibility for outcomes their publics would find objectionable. Legislative delays are pervasive, and the case studies revealed the lengths to which some governments would go to avoid being blamed for policies they either favor or at least acknowledge as necessary. These strategies work in the short term – as long as governments can maintain the facade of being resolute defenders of the positions their audiences prefer – but the weight of accumulated evidence must eventually catch up with them. The consequences of electorally induced deception could be catastrophic if citizens lose faith in the institutions, and one can be certain that domestic political opposition would never be far away to remind voters about past transgressions.

---

[9] Aside from my own work, see also Hagemann, Bailer, and Herzog (2016); Alexandrova, Rasmussen, and Toshkov (2016); Wratil (2017).

[10] Van der Eijk, Franklin, and Marsh (1996); Thomassen and Schmitt (1997); Rittberger (2007); Williams and Spoon (2015); de Bruycker (2017); Rauh (2016); Spoon and Williams (2017).

The generation that fought the last great war is gone, and the generation that remembers the desperate postwar years is receding from the stage as well. The instinctive support for policies that countered nationalist tendencies has weakened, and ideologies that would have been considered beyond the pale because of their associations with the dark past only two decades ago have resurfaced. It is another one of the sad ironies of European success that the prosperity and peace that had been the *raison d'être* of the EU have caused many of its citizens to underestimate the costs and risks of abandoning the common project to pursue narrow national goals. Although the EU is not blameless in allowing the rot to take place by not taking action when politicians pecked at it for domestic gains, it is inherently challenging to claim credit for avoiding the dreadful paths not taken (where one must argue a counterfactual) while confronting dissatisfaction with the path that was (where one must deal with facts).

The EU is attempting to reform itself to cope with the perceived crisis of legitimacy, and among its leading efforts is the push to increase the transparency of policymaking. It is not at all clear that this would solve the problem in light of the above considerations. People often have this notion that more information and more deliberation are more likely to produce consensus, but there is no evidence for this in either fact or logic. Quite often, all they produce is a realization that the goals are further apart than they had seemed initially, and that the gulf might be unbridgeable. And yet, democratic decisions still have to be made, preferably without resorting to means that endanger the peace.

Some transparency is, of course, necessary because delegation must remain a fact, not just a meaningless trope for a form of governance more often honored in the breach. It could help alleviate the problem of governments trying to camouflage their complicity in unpopular but necessary policies by pretending that they are diktats imposed by Brussels. It could prevent governments from usurping credit for success when they festoon their campaigns with accomplishments to which they contributed little or nothing while conveniently omitting any mention of the crucial role played by the EU.

Radical transparency, however, would certainly increase the politicization of the EU. Some believe this would be a good thing because it would enhance democratic accountability of political actors at the EU level.[11] But it is too much to expect that elected politicians would stop politicking for office. Few would have the courage of conviction

---

[11] Transparency is not the only proposed means of increasing politicization in this belief of its salutary effects. See Hix (2008) for a concise summary.

to swim against the popular tide, and if they did, their parties would probably make short work of their careers. There is precious little in these schemes that guards against swinging too far toward responsiveness and abandoning responsibility altogether. They also fail to consider the reality of European compromises that are often forged precisely because of hidden cooperation in the Council. In the context of divergent public preferences, transparency is likely to increase the levels of conflict in policymaking. This would drastically reduce the effectiveness of the EU, which in turn would undermine its legitimacy even further because it would aggravate the doubts about its necessity and desirability. It is not at all clear that the technocratic extreme is worse than its populist variant.

Responsiveness without responsibility would doom the European project, and, unfortunately, it is often well-nigh impossible to impress upon people what they have until it is gone. This book was written before the British public voted to take the United Kingdom out of the EU, and although the argument anticipated the possibility, I would not have predicted it. The silver lining is that the shock of this withdrawal has forced Europeans to think harder about the value of the EU and to realize that there is much more to it than faceless bureaucrats in Brussels twiddling their thumbs or spending their time penning long memoranda about the size and shape of bananas. According to the Bertelsmann Foundation, which conducts surveys in the six most populous member states, in the aftermath of the Brexit vote, public approval of the EU has risen in all of them except Spain (Hoffman and de Vries, 2016). And while before Brexit 41 percent of Danes and 49 percent of Austrians had favored holding referenda on continuing their membership, only 32 percent and 30 percent did afterwards.[12]

It is painful to contemplate that it might have taken the self-immolation of one of the most valuable members of the EU to awaken the nascent European *demos* from its complacent slumber. But perhaps there is no other way. No institutional wizardry or economic pyrotechnics can substitute for the bedrock of a steady popular support. At the end of the day, the key to the survival of the European Republic is the support of its citizens.

---

[12] Rick Noack. "After Brexit and Trump's victory, Europeans are beginning to like the E.U. again." *The Washington Post*. November 24, 2016. www.washingtonpost.com/news/worldviews/wp/2016/11/24/europeans-start-liking-the-e-u-again/?utm_term=.ae84462cd828, accessed: February 5, 2018.

References

Abrajano, Marisa A., Christopher S. Elmendorf, and Kevin M. Quinn. 2018. "Label vs. Pictures: Treatment-Mode Effects in Experiments About Discrimination." *Political Analysis* 26: 20–33.

Achen, Christopher H. 2006. Evaluating Political Decision-Making Models. In *The European Union Decides*, eds. Robert Thomson, Frans N. Stokman, Christopher H. Achen, and Thomas König. Cambridge: Cambridge University Press, pp. 264–298.

Achen, Christopher H. and Larry M. Bartels. 2015. *Democracy for Realists: Why Elections do not Produce Responsive Governments*. Princeton: Princeton University Press.

Ackrill, Robert and Adrian Kay. 2006. "The EU Financial Perspective 2007–13 and the Forces That Shaped the Final Agreement." Discussion Papers in Applied Economics and Policy No. 2006/1.

Aksoy, Deniz. 2010. "Who Gets What, When, and How Revisited: Voting and Proposal Powers in the Allocation of the EU Budget." *European Union Politics* 11(2):171–194.

2012. "Institutional Arrangements and Logrolling: Evidence from the European Union." *American Journal of Political Science* 56(3):538–552.

Alesina, Alberto and Howard Rosenthal. 1995. *Partisan Politics, Divided Government, and the Economy*. Cambridge: Cambridge University Press.

Alexandrova, Petya, Anne Rasmussen, and Dimiter Toshkov. 2016. "Agenda Responsiveness in the European Council." *West European Politics* 39(4): 605–627.

Alt, James E. and David Dreyer Lassen. 2006. "Transparency, Political Participation, and Political Budget Cycles in OECD Countries." *American Journal of Political Science* 50(3):530–550.

Anderson, Christopher J. 1995. "The Dynamics of Public Support for Coalition Governments." *Comparative Political Studies* 28:350–383.

Anderson, Jeffrey J., ed. 1999. *Regional Integration and Democracy. Expanding on the European Experience*. Lanham: Rowman & Littlefield Publishers.

Arnold, Christine, Eliyahu V. Sapir, and Catherine E. de Vries. 2012. "Parties' Positions on European Integration: Issue Congruence, Ideology or Context?" *West European Politics* 35(6):1341–1362.

Arregui, Javier. 2008. "Shifting Policy Positions in the European Union." *European Journal of Political Research* 47:852–875.

References

Arregui, Javier, Frans N. Stokman, and Robert Thomson. 2004. "Bargaining in the European Union and Shifts in Actors' Policy Positions." *European Union Politics* 5(1):47–72.
  2006. Compromise, Exchange and Challenge in the European Union. In *The European Union Decides*, eds. Robert Thomson, Frans N. Stokman, Christopher H. Achen, and Thomas König. Cambridge: Cambridge University Press, pp. 124–152.
Arregui, Javier and Robert Thomson. 2009. "States' Bargaining Success in the European Union." *Journal of European Public Policy* 16(5):655–676.
Arrow, Kenneth J. 1963. *Social Choice and Individual Values*. New York: John Wiley & Sons.
Ashworth, Scott and Ethan Bueno de Mesquita. 2014. "Is Voter Competence Good for Voters?: Information, Rationality, and Democratic Performance." *American Political Science Review* 108(3):565–587.
Aspinwall, Mark. 2002. "Preferring Europe: Ideology and National Preference on European Integration." *European Union Politics* 3(1):81–111.
  2007. "Government Preferences in European Integration: An Empirical Test of Five Theories." *British Journal of Political Science* 37(1): 89–114.
Atikcan, Ece Özlem. 2015. *Framing the European Union: The Power of Political Arguments in Shaping European Integration*. Cambridge: Cambridge University Press.
Axelrod, Robert and Robert O. Keohane. 1985. "Achieving Cooperation under Anarchy: Strategies and Institutions." *World Politics* 38(1):226–254.
Bachtler, John, Carlos Mendez, and Fiona Wishlade. 2016. *EU Cohesion Policy and European Integration: The Dynamics of EU Budget and Regional Policy Reform*. London: Routledge.
Bailer, Stefanie. 2004. "Bargaining Success in the European Union: The Impact of Exogenous and Endogenous Power Resources." *European Union Politics* 5(1):99–123.
  2006. *Nationale Interessen in der Europäischen Union. Macht und Verhandlungserfolg im Ministerrat*. Frankfurt: Campus.
Bailer, Stefanie, Mikko Mattila, and Gerald Schneider. 2015. "Money Makes the EU Go Round: The Objective Foundations of Conflict in the Council of Ministers." *Journal of Common Market Studies* 53(3):437–456.
Baker, David and Philippa Sherrington. 2005. "Britain and Europe: The Dog that Didn't Bark." *Parliamentary Affairs* 12(24):125–176.
Barnes, Samuel H. 1977. *Representation in Italy: Institutionalized Tradition and Electoral Choice*. Chicago: University of Chicago Press.
Bartels, Larry M. 1996. "Uninformed Votes: Information Effects in Presidential Elections." *American Journal of Political Science* 40(1):194–230.
  2008. The Study of Electoral Behavior. In *The Oxford Handbook of American Elections and Political Behavior*, ed. Jan E. Leighley. Oxford: Oxford University Press, chapter 14.
Bechtel, Michael, Jens Hainmueller, and Yotam M. Margalit. 2014. "Preferences for International Redistribution: The Divide Over the Eurozone Bailouts." *American Journal of Political Science* 58(4):835–856.
  2017. "Policy Design and Domestic Support for International Bailouts." *European Journal of Political Research* 56(4):864–886.

Benedetto, Giacomo and Bjørn Høyland. 2007. "The EU Annual Budgetary Procedure: The Existing Rules and Proposed Reforms of the Convention and Intergovernmental Conference 2002–04." *Journal of Common Market Studies* 45(3):565–587.

Berelson, Bernard, Paul Lazarsfeld, and William McPhee. 1954. *Voting: A Study of Opinion Formation in a Presidential Campaign*. Chicago: University of Chicago Press.

Berry, William, Matt Golder, and Daniel Milton. 2012. "Improving Tests of Theories Positing Interaction." *Journal of Politics* 74(3):653–671.

Birch, Anthony. 1964. *Representative and Responsible Government*. London: George Allen and Unwin.

Bischoff, Carina S. 2013. "Electorally Unstable by Supply or Demand? An Examination of the Causes of Electoral Volatility in Advanced Industrial Democracies." *Public Choice* 156(3):537–561.

Blair, Tony. 2011. *A Journey: My Political Life*. New York: Vintage.

Bølstadt, Jørgen. 2015. "Dynamics of European Integration: Public Opinion in the Core and Periphery." *European Union Politics* 16(1):23–44.

Börzel, Tanja. 2005. "Mind the Gap! European Integration Between Level and Scope." *Journal of European Public Policy* 12(2):217–236.

Börzel, Tanja and Thomas Risse. 2009. "Revisiting the Nature of the Beast - Politicization, European Identity, and Postfunctionalism: A Comment on Hooghe and Marks." *British Journal of Political Science* 39(1):217–220.

Bostock, David. 2002. "Coreper Revisited." *Journal of Common Market Studies* 40(2):215–234.

Brambor Thomas, William Roberts Clark, and Matt Golder. 2006. "Understanding Interaction Models: Improving Empirical Analyses." *Political Analysis* 14(1):63–82.

Bräuninger, Thomas and Thomas König. 2005. *Indices of Power IOP 2.0 [computer program]*. [www.tbraeuninger.de/IOP.html]. University of Konstanz.

Brender, Adi and Allan Drazen. 2005. "Political Budget Cycles in New versus Established Democracies." *Journal of Monetary Economics* 52:1271–1295.

Brown, Gordon. 2005. *Global Europe: Full-employment Europe*. London: HM Treasury.

Bueno de Mesquita, Bruce and Frans N. Stokman. 1994. *Twelve into One: Models of Decision-Making in the European Community*. New Haven: Yale University Press.

Bulmer, Simon. 2008. "New Labour, New European Policy? Blair, Brown, and Utilitarian Supranationalism." *Parliamentary Affairs* 61(4):597–620.

Bundeskanzlerin. 2010. "A Solution for Greece: 'An Important Day for the Euro.'" Statement of the Federal Chancellor.
URL: www.bundeskanzlerin.de/Content/EN/Artikel/2010/03/2010-03-26-eu-rat-hilfen-griechenland_en.html

Bundesregierung. 2010. "Regierungserklärung von Bundeskanzlerin Merkel zu den Hilfen für Griechenland." Statement of the Federal Chancellor.
URL: www.bundesregierung.de/ContentArchiv/DE/Archiv17/Regierungserklaerung/2010/2010-05-05-merkel-erklaerung-griechenland.html

Burley, Anne-Marie and Walter Mattli. 1993. "Europe Before the Court: A Political Theory of Legal Integration." *International Organization* 47(1): 41–76.

Butler, Daniel M. and Eleanor Neff Powell. 2014. "Understanding the Party Brand: Experimental Evidence on the Role of Valence." *The Journal of Politics* 76(2):492–505.

Caramani, Daniele. 2017. "Will vs. Reason: The Populist and Technocratic Forms of Political Representation and Their Critique to Party Government." *American Political Science Review* 111(1):54–67.

Caraway, Teri L., Stephanie J. Rickard, and Mark S. Anner. 2012. "International Negotiations and Domestic Politics: The Case of IMF Labor Market Conditionality." *International Organization* 66(1):27–61.

Carrubba, Clifford J. 1997. "Net Financial Transfers in the European Union: Who Gets What and Why?" *Journal of Politics* 59(2):469–496.

2001. "The Electoral Connection in European Union Politics." *Journal of Politics* 63(1):141–158.

Carrubba, Clifford J., Matthew J. Gabel, and Charles Hankla. 2008. "Judicial Behavior under Political Constraints: Evidence from the European Court of Justice." *American Political Science Review* 102(4):435–452.

Chadwick, Andrew and Richard Heffernan. 2003. Britain in the World, Labour in the European Union. In *The New Labour Reader*, eds. Andrew Chadwick and Richard Heffernan. Oxford: Blackwell Publishing Ltd, pp. 223–224.

Chaudoin, Stephen. 2014. "Audience Features and the Strategic Timing of Trade Disputes." *International Organization* 68(1):235–256.

Clark, Nick and Robert Rohrschneider. 2009. "Second-Order Elections versus First-Order Thinking: How Voters Perceive the Representation Process in a Multi-Layered System of Governance." *Journal of European Integration* 31(5):645–664.

Clark, William R. 2002. *Capitalism Not Globalism: Capital Mobility, and the Political Control of the Economy*. Ann Arbor: University of Michigan Press.

Clark, William R. and Mark Hallerberg. 2000. "Mobile Capital, Domestic Institutions, and Electorally Induced Monetary and Fiscal Policy." *American Political Science Review* 94(2):323–346.

Coen, David and Jeremy J. Richardson, eds. 2009. *Lobbying the European Union: Institutions, Actors, and Issues*. Oxford: Oxford University Press.

Colgan, Jeff D. and Robert O. Keohane. 2017. "The Liberal Order Is Rigged." *Foreign Affairs* 96: 36–44.

Council of the European Union. 2005. Note from the Presidency of Council of EU to European Council: Financial Perspective 2007–2013. Technical Report Council of the European Union. 15915/05 (CADREFIN 268), December 19.

Cox, Gary W. 1987. "Electoral Equilibrium under Alternative Voting Institutions." *American Journal of Political Science* 31(1):82–108.

Cramme, Olaf and Sara B. Hobolt, eds. 2015. *Democratic Politics in a European Union under Stress*. Oxford: Oxford University Press.

Crombez, Christophe. 1996. "Legislative Procedures in the European Community." *British Journal of Political Science* 26(2):199–228.

1997. "The Co-Decision Procedure in the European Union." *Legislative Studies Quarterly* 22(1):97–119.

2003. "The Democratic Deficit in the European Union: Much Ado about Nothing?" *European Union Politics* 4(1):101–120.

Crombez, Christophe and Bjørn Høyland. 2015. "The Budgetary Procedure in the European Union and the Implications of the Treaty of Lisbon." *European Union Politics* 16(1):67–89.

Crombez, Christophe, Bernard Steunenberg, and Richard Corbett. 2000. "Understanding the EU Legislative Process." *European Union Politics* 1(3):363–381.

Cross, James P. 2012. "Everyone's a Winner (Almost): Bargaining Success in the Council of Ministers of the European Union." *European Union Politics* 14(1):70–94.

Cruz, Cesi and Christina J. Schneider. 2017. "Foreign Aid and Undeserved Credit Claiming." *American Journal of Political Science* 61(2):396–408.

Dahl, Robert A. 1956. *A Preface to Democratic Theory*. Chicago: University of Chicago Press.

1973. *Polyarchy: Participation and Opposition*. Yale: Yale University Press.

1999. Can International Organizations be Democratic? A Sceptic's View. In *Democracy's Edges*, eds. Ian Shapiro and Casiano Hacker-Cordon. Cambridge: Cambridge University Press, 19-36.

Dai, Xinyuan. 2005. "Why Comply? The Domestic Constituency Mechanism." *International Organization* 59(2):363–398.

Dalton, Russell J. 1985. "Political Parties and Political Representation: Party Supporters and Party Elites in Nine Nations." *Comparative Political Studies* 18(3):267–299.

2000. The Decline of Party Identifications. In *Parties without Partisans: Political Change in Advanced Industrial Democracies*, eds. Russell J. Dalton and Martin P. Wattenberg. Oxford: Oxford University Press, pp. 19–36.

2004. *Democratic Challenges, Democratic Choices*. Oxford: Oxford University Press.

Dalton, Russell J., Ian McAllister and Martin P. Wattenberg. 2000. The Consequences of Partisan Dealignment. In *Parties without Partisans: Political Change in Advanced Industrial Democracies*, eds. Russell J. Dalton and Martin P. Wattenberg. Oxford: Oxford University Press, pp. 37–63.

Dalton, Russell J. and Martin P. Wattenberg, eds. 2000. *Parties without Partisans. Political Change in Advanced Industrial Democracies*. Oxford: Oxford University Press.

Dassonneville, Ruth and Marc Hooghe. 2017. "Economic Indicators and Electoral Volatility. Economic Effects on Electoral Volatility in Western Europe, 1950-2013." *Comparative European Politics* 15(6):919–943.

Davis, Christina L. 2004. "International Institutions and Issue Linkage: Building Support for Agricultural Trade Liberalization." *American Political Science Review* 98(1):153–169.

de Bruycker, Iskander. 2017. "Politicization and the Public Interest: When do the Elites in Brussels Address Public Interests in EU Policy Debates?" *European Union Politics* 18(4):603–619.

de Haan, Jakob and Jan-Egbert Sturm. 2000. "Do Financial Markets and the Maastricht Treaty Discipline Governments? New Evidence." *Applied Financial Economics* 10:221–226.

de Vries, Catherine E. 2007. "Sleeping Giant: Fact or Fairytale? How European Integration Affects Vote Choice in National Elections." *European Union Politics* 8(3):363–385.

2009. "The Impact of EU Referenda on National Electoral Politics: Evidence from the Dutch Case." *West European Politics* 32(1):142–171.

2010. "EU Issue Voting: Asset or Liability? How European Integration Affects Parties' Electoral Fortunes." *European Union Politics* 11(1):89–117.

de Vries, Catherine E. and Sara B. Hobolt. 2012. "When Dimensions Collide: the Electoral Success of Issue Entrepreneurs." *European Union Politics* 13(2):246–268.

de Vries, Catherine E. and Marco Steenbergen. 2013. "Variable Opinions: The Predictability of Support for Unification in European Mass Publics." *Journal of Political Marketing* 12(1):121–141.

de Vries, Catherine E., Wouter Van der Brug, Marcel van Egmond, and Cees Van der Eijk. 2011. "Individual and Contextual Variation in EU Issue Voting: The Role of Political Information." *Electoral Studies* 30(1):16–28.

de Wilde, Pieter. 2011. "No Polity for Old Politics A Framework for Analyzing the Politicization of European Integration." *Journal of European Integration* 33(5):559–575.

de Wilde, Pieter and Michael Zürn. 2012. "Can the Politicization of European Integration be Reversed?" *Journal of Common Market Studies* 50(1): 766–783.

Dellmuth, Lisa M. and Jonas Tallberg. 2015. "The Social Legitimacy of International Organisations: Interest Representation, Institutional Performance, and Confidence Extrapolation in the United Nations." *Review of International Studies* 41(3):451–475.

Dixit, Avinash and John Londregan. 1998. "Fiscal Federalism and Redistributive Politics." *Journal of Public Economics* 68:153–180.

Dolezal, Martin and Johan Hellström. 2016. The Radical Right as Driving Force in the Electoral Arena? In *Politicising Europe. Integration and Mass Politics*, eds. Swen Hutter, Edgar Grande, and Hanspeter Kriesi. Cambridge: Cambridge University Press, pp. 166–180.

Döring, Holger and Philip Manow. 2015. "Parliaments and Governments database (ParlGov): Information on Parties, Elections and Cabinets in Modern Democracies." Development Version.

Downs, Anthony. 1957. "An Economic Theory of Political Action in a Democracy." *Journal of Political Economy* 65(2): 135–150.

Drazen, Allan. 2000a. "The Political Business Cycle after 25 Years." *NBER Macroeconomics Annual* 15:75–117.

2000b. *Political Economy in Macroeconomics*. New Jersey: Princeton University Press.

Dreher, Axel and Roland Vaubel. 2004. "Do IMF and IBRD Cause Moral Hazard and Political Business Cycles? Evidence from Panel Data." *Open Economies Review* 15:5–22.

Druel, Elisabeth, Pierre Chrzanowski, Rufus Pollock, and Jonathan Gray. 2015. "Where Does Europe's Money Go?" Open Knowledge Report. URL: www.europarl.europa.eu/ftu/pdf/en/FTU_1.4.3.pdf

Duch, Raymond M. and Randolph T. Stevenson. 2008. *The Economic Vote: How Political and Economic Institutions Condition Election Results.* Cambridge: Cambridge University Press.

Duch, Raymond M. and Randolph T. Stevenson. 2010. "The Global Economy, Competency, and the Economic Vote." *Journal of Politics* 72(1):105–123.

Dullien, Sebastian and Daniela Schwarzer. 2009. "Bringing Macroeconomics into the EU Budget Debate: Why and How?" *Journal of Common Market Studies* 47(1):153–174.

Dür, Andreas and Gemma M. González. 2007. "Hard and Soft Bargaining in the EU: Negotiating the Financial Perspective, 2007–2013." Paper Presented at the European Union Studies Association, 17–19 May, Montreal.

Easton, David. 1965. *A Systems Analysis of Political Life.* New York: John Wiley and Sons.

Elgström, Ole and Christer Jönsson. 2000. "Negotiation in the European Union: Bargaining or Problem-solving?" *Journal of European Public Policy* 7(5): 684–704.

European Commission. 1999. "Interinstitutional Agreement of 6 May 1999 between the European Parliament, the Council, and the Commission of Budgetary Discipline and Improvment of the Budgetary Procedure." *Official Journal of the European Communities, 1999/C 172/01.*

2004. "Building our Common Future" – Policy Challenges and Budgetary Means of the Enlarged Union. Technical Report European Commission. COM(2004)101 final/2, February 26.

2008. *European Union Public Finance.* 4th ed. Luxembourg: Office for Official Publications of the European Communities.

2014. *European Union Public Finance.* 5th ed. Luxembourg: Publications Office of the European Union.

European Parliament. 2014. "Activity Report on Codecision and Conciliation, 2009–2014." No. 1031024.

European Parliament. 2016. "The Budgetary Procedure." Fact Sheets on the European Union.
URL: www.europarl.europa.eu/ftu/pdf/en/FTU_1.4.3.pdf

European Union. 2010. "Statement by the Heads of State and Government of the Euro Area." Consilium.
URL: www.consilium.europa.eu/uedocs/cms_Data/docs/pressdata/en/ec/113563.pdf

Evans, Geoffrey. 1998. "Euroscepticism and Conservative Electoral Support: How an Asset Became a Liability." *British Journal of Political Science* 28(4): 573–590.

2002. European Integration, Party Politics, and Voting in the 2001 Election. In *British Elections and Parties Review*, eds.. Lynn Bennie, Colin Rallings, Jonathan Tonge, and Paul Webb. London: Frank Cass Publishers, pp. 95–110.

Finke, Daniel, Thomas König, Sven-Oliver Proksch, and George Tsebelis. 2012. *Reforming the European Union. Realizing the Impossible.* Princeton: Princeton University Press.

Fiorina, Morris P. 1981. *Retrospective Voting in American National Elections.* Yale: Yale University Press.

Franklin, Mark and Christopher Wlezien. 1997. "The Responsive Public: Issue Salience, Policy Change, and Preferences for European Unification." *Journal of Theoretical Politics* 9(3):347–363.

Franklin, Mark N., Thomas T. Mackie, and Henry Valen. 1992. *Electoral Change*. Colchester: ECPR Press.

Franzese, Robert Jr. 2002. "Electoral and Partisan Cycles in Economic Policies and Outcomes." *Annual Review of Political Science* 5:369–421.

Follesdal, Andreas and Simon Hix. 2006. "Why There Is a Democratic Deficit in the EU: A Response to Majone and Moravcsik." *Journal of Common Market Studies* 44(3):533–562.

Gabel, Matthew J. 1998. "Public Support for European Integration: An Empirical Test of Five Theories." *The Journal of Politics* 60(2):333–354.

2000. "European Integration, Voters, and National Politics." *West European Politics* 23(4):52–72.

Gabel, Matthew J. and Kenneth Scheve. 2007. "Mixed Messages: Party Dissent and Mass Opinion on European Integration." *European Union Politics* 8(1):37–59.

Gallagher, Michael, Michael Laver, and Peter Mair. 2011. *Representative Government in Modern Europe*. New York: McGraw-Hill.

Gali, Jordi and Roberto Perotti. 2003. "Fiscal Policy and Monetary Integration in Europe." *Economic Policy* 18(37):533–572.

Garrett, Geoffrey, R. Daniel Keleman and Heiner Schulz. 1998. "The European Court of Justice, National Governments, and Legal Integration in the European Union." *International Organization* 52(1):149–176.

Garrett, Geoffrey and George Tsebelis. 1996. "An Institutional Critique of Intergovernmentalism." *International Organization* 50(2):269–299.

2001. "The Institutional Foundations of Intergovernmentalism and Supranationalism in the European Union." *International Organization* 55(2): 357–390.

Gelman, Andrew and Gary King. 1993. "Why Are American Presidential Election Campaign Polls so Variable When Votes are so Predictable?" *British Journal of Political Science* 23(4):409–451.

Gerring, John. 2008. Case Selection for Case Study Analysis: Qualitative and Quantitative Techniques. In *Oxford Handbook of Political Methodology*, eds. Janet M. Box-Steffensmeier, Henry E. Brady, and David Collier. Oxford: Oxford University Press, 645-684.

Giger, Nathalie and Heike Klüver. 2016. "Voting against Your Constituents? How Lobbying Affects Representation." *American Journal of Political Science* 60(1):190–205.

Golub, Jonathan. 2007. "Survival Analysis and European Union Decision-Making." *European Union Politics* 8(2):155–179.

2008. "The Study of Decision-Making Speed in the European Union: Methods, Data and Theory." *European Union Politics* 9(1):167–179.

Golub, Jonathan and Bernard Steunenberg. 2007. "How Time Affects EU Decision-Making." *European Union Politics* 8(4):555–566.

Gowland, David, Arthur Turner, and Alex Wright. 2010. *Britain and European Integration Since 1945: On the Sidelines*. London: Routledge.

Gray, Julia. 2009. "International Organization as a Seal of Approval: European Union Accession and Investor Risk." *American Journal of Political Science* 53 (4): 931–949.

Gray, Julia. 2013. *The Company States Keep: International Organizations and Investor Perceptions.* New York: Cambridge University Press.

Gray, Julia and Jeffrey Kucik. 2017. Leadership Turnover and the Durability of International Trade Commitments. Comparative Political Studies 50(14): 1941–1972.

Gray, Julia and Raymond Hicks. 2014. "Reputations, Perceptions, and International Economic Agreements." International Interactions 40 (3): 325–349.

Green-Pedersen, Christoffer. 2012. "A Giant Fast Asleep? Party Incentives and the Politicisation of European Integration." *Political Studies* 60:115–130.

Greenwood, Justin. 1997. *Representing Interests in the European Union.* Houndmills: Macmillan Press Ltd.

Grimmer, Justin, Solomon Messing, and Sean J. Westwood. 2012. "How Words and Money Cultivate a Personal Vote: The Effect of Legislator Credit Claiming on Constituent Credit Allocation." *American Political Science Review* 106(4):704–719.

Grimmer, Justin, Sean J. Westwood, and Solomon Messing. 2014. *The Impression of Influence: Legislator Communication, Representation, and Democratic Accountability.* Princeton: Princeton University Press.

Grossman, Gene M. and Elhanan Helpman. 2001. *Special Interest Politics.* Cambridge: MIT Press.

Haas, Ernst. 1958. *The Uniting of Europe.* Stanford: Stanford University Press.

Häge, Frank M. 2011. "The European Union Policy-Making Dataset." *European Union Politics* 12(3):455–477.

Hagemann, Sara, Stefanie Bailer, and Alexander Herzog. 2016. "Signals to Their Parliaments? Governments' Strategic Use of Votes and Policy Statements in the EU Council." Unpublished Working Paper.

Hagemann, Sara and Julia De Clerck-Sachsse. 2007. "Decision-Making in the Council of Ministers: Evaluating the Facts." CEPS Policy Brief No. 119.

Hagemann, Sara, Sara B. Hobolt, and Christopher Wratil. 2016. "Government Responsiveness in the European Union: Evidence from Council Voting." *Comparative Political Studies* 50(6):850–876.

Hainmueller, Jens, Daniel J. Hopkins, and Teppei Yamamoto. 2014. "Causal Inference in Conjoint Analysis: Understanding Multidimensional Choices Via Stated Preference Experiments." *Political Analysis* 22(1):1–30.

Hallerberg, Mark, Lucio Vinhas de Souza, and William R. Clark. 2002. "Political Business Cycles in EU Accession Countries." *European Union Politics* 3(2):231–250.

Hayes-Renshaw, Fiona. 2009. Least Accessible but Not Inaccessible: Lobbying the Council and the European Council. In *Lobbying the European Union*, eds. David Coen and Jeremy J. Richardson. Oxford: Oxford University Press, pp. 70–88.

Hayes-Renshaw, Fiona, Wim Van Aken, and Helen Wallace. 2006. "When and Why the EU Council of Ministers Votes Explicitly." *Journal of Common Market Studies* 44(1):161–94.

Hayes-Renshaw, Fiona and Helen Wallace. 2006. *The Council of Ministers.* Houndmills: Palgrave Macmillan Press Ltd.

Heisenberg, Dorothee. 2005. "The Institution of 'Consensus' in the European Union: Formal versus Informal Decision-Making in the Council." *European Journal of Political Research* 44(1):65–90.

2007. Merkel's EU Policy: "Kohl's Mädchen" or Interest-driven Politics? In *Launching the Grand Coalition: The 2005 Bundestag Election and the Future of German Politics,* ed. Eric Langenbacher. New York: Berghahn Books, pp. 110–121.

Hendriks, Gisela. 1991. *Germany and European Integration, the Common Agricultural Policy: An Area of Conflict.* New York: Berg.

Hertz, Robin and Dirk Leuffen. 2011. "Too Big to Run? Analyzing the Impact of Enlargement on the Speed of EU Decision-Making." *European Union Politics* 12(2):193–215.

Hix, Simon. 2008. *What's Wrong with the European Union & and How to Fix it.* Manchester: Polity Press.

Hix, Simon and Christopher Lord. 1997. *Political Parties in the European Union.* New York: St. Martin's Press.

Hix, Simon, Abdul Noury, and Gérard Roland. 2006. "Dimensions of Politics in the European Parliament." *American Journal of Political Science* 50(2): 494–511.

Hobolt, Sara B. 2015. "The 2014 European Parliament Elections: Divided in Unity?" *Journal of Common Market Studies* 53:6–23.

Hobolt, Sara B. and Catherine E. de Vries. 2016. "Public Support for European Integration." *Annual Review of Political Science* 19:413–432.

Hobolt, Sara B. and Robert Klemmensen. 2005. "Responsive Government? Public Opinion and Government Policy Preferences in Britain and Denmark." *Political Studies* 53(2):379–402.

Hobolt, Sara B. and Jae-Jae Spoon. 2012. "Motivating the European Voter: Parties, Issues and Campaigns in European Parliament Elections." *European Journal of Political Research* 51:701–727.

Hobolt, Sara B., Jae-Jae Spoon, and James Tilley. 2008. "A Vote against Europe? Explaining Defection at the 1999 and 2004 European Parliament Elections." *British Journal of Political Science* 39(1):93–115.

Hobolt, Sara B. and James Tilley. 2014. *Blaming Europe? Responsibility without Accountability in the European Union.* Cambridge: Cambridge University Press.

Hoffman, Isabell and Catherine de Vries. 2016. "Brexit Has Raised Support for the European Union." Flashlight Europe, Bertelsman Stiftung.

Hooghe, Liesbet and Gary Marks. 2009. "Postfunctionalist Theory of European Integration: From Permissive Consensus to Constraining Dissensus." *British Journal of Political Science* 39(1):1–23.

Houweling, Robert Van and Mike Tomz. 2016a. "Political Repositioning." Princeton University Press (forthcoming).

2016b. "Political Repositioning: A Conjoint Analysis." Unpublished Working Paper.

Hudec, Robert. 1993. *Enforcing International Trade Law: The Evolution of the Modern GATT Legal System.* Salem, NH: Butterworth.

Hug, Simon. 2003. "Endogenous Preferences and Delegation in the European Union." *Comparative Political Studies* 36(1):41–74.

Hug, Simon and Thomas König. 2002. "In View of Ratification: Governmental Preferences and Domestic Constraints at the Amsterdam Intergovernmental Conference." *International Organization* 56(2):447–476.

Hug, Simon and Tobias Schulz. 2007. "Referendums in the EU's Constitution Building Process." *The Review of International Organizations* 2(2):177–218.

Hutter, Swen, Edgar Grande, and Hanspeter Kriesi, eds. 2016. *Politicising Europe. Integration and Mass Politics*. Cambridge: Cambridge University Press.

IFOP. 2010. "Europeans and the Greek Crisis." IFOP Report.
URL: www.ifop.fr/media/poll/1118-2-study_file.pdf

Infratest Dimap. 2010. ARD DeutschlandTREND – November 2010. Technical Report Infratest Dimap.
URL: www.infratest-dimap.de/umfragen-analysen/bundesweit/ard-deutschlandtrend/2010/november

2011. ARD DeutschlandTREND – November 2011. Technical Report Infratest Dimap.
URL: www.infratest-dimap.de/umfragen-analysen/bundesweit/ard-deutschlandtrend/2011/november/

Irwin, Galen A. and Jacques J. A. Thomassen. 1975. "Issue-Consensus in a Multi-Party System: Voters and Leaders in the Netherlands." *Acta Politica* 10(4):389–420.

Israel, Jonathan I. 1995. *The Dutch Republic: Its Rise, Greatness, and Fall, 1477–1806*. Oxford: Clarendon Press.

Jacobson, Gary C. 1987. Running Scared: Elections and Congressional Politics in the 1980s. In *Congress. Structure and Policy*, eds. Mathew D. McCubbins and Terry Sullivan. Cambridge: Cambridge University Press, pp. 39–81.

Joseph, Sarah. 2011. *Blame It on the WTO?: A Human Rights Critique*. Oxford: Oxford University Press.

Karp, Jeffrey, Susan A. Banducci, and Shaun Bowler. 2003. "To Know It Is to Love It? Satisfaction with Democracy in the European Union." *Comparative Political Studies* 36(3):271–292.

Kayser, Mark A. and Christopher Wlezien. 2011. "Performance Pressure: Patterns of Partisanship and the Economic Vote." *European Journal of Political Research* 50(3):365–394.

Keohane, Robert O. 1986. "Reciprocity in International Relations." *International Organization* 40(1):1–27.

King, Anthony. 1997. *Running Scared. Why American Politicians Campaign Too Much and Govern So Little*. New York: Free Press.

Kleine, Mareike and Clement Minaudier. 2018. "Negotiating Under Political Uncertainty: National Elections and the Dynamics of International Cooperation." *British Journal of Political Science* (forthcoming), doi:10.1017/S000712341600051X.

Klüver, Heike. 2013. *Lobbying in the European Union. Interest Groups, Lobbying Coalitions, and Policy Change*. Oxford: Oxford University Press.

Klüver, Heike, Caelesta Braun, and Jan Beyers. 2015. "Legislative Lobbying in Context: Towards a Conceptual Framework of Interest Group Lobbying in the European Union." *Journal of European Public Policy* 22(4):447–461.

Koenig-Archibugi, Mathias. 2004. "Explaining Government Preferences for Institutional Change in EU Foreign and Security Policy." *International Organization* 58(4):137–174.

Kölling, Mario and Cristina Serrano Leal. 2014. "An Analysis of the Agreement on the Multiannual Financial Framework 2014–2020." Real Instituto Elcano Working Paper No. 2/2014.

König, Thomas. 2007. "Divergence or Convergence? From Ever-growing to Ever-slowing European Legislative Decision Making." *European Journal of Political Research* 46(3):417–444.

2008. "Analysing the Process of EU Legislative Decision-Making: To Make a Long Story Short ..." *European Union Politics* 9(1):145–165.

König, Thomas and Thomas Bräuninger. 2002. From an Ever-Growing towards an Ever-slower Union? In *Institutional Challenges in the European Union*, eds. Madeleine O. Hosli, Adrian van Deemen, and Mika Widgrén. London/New York: Routledge, pp. 155–172.

König, Thomas and Daniel Finke. 2007. "Reforming the Equilibrium? Veto Players and Policy Change in the European Constitution-building Process." *The Review of International Organizations* 2(2):153–176.

König, Thomas and Dirk Junge. 2009. "Why Don't Veto Players Use Their Power?" *European Union Politics* 10(4):507–534.

König, Thomas and Mirja Pöter. 2001. "Examining the EU Legislative Process: The Relative Importance of Agenda and Veto Power." *European Union Politics* 2(3):329–351.

König, Thomas and Jonathan B. Slapin. 2006. "From Unanimity to Consensus. An Analysis of the Negotiations at the EU's Constitutional Convention." *World Politics* 58:413–445.

Koopmans, Ruud and Paul Statham, eds. 2010. *The Making of a European Public Sphere: Media Discourse and Political Contention*. Cambridge: Cambridge University Press.

Kramer, Gerald H. 1971. "Short-Term Fluctuations in U.S. Voting Behavior, 1986–1964." *American Political Science Review* 65(1):131–143.

Kriesi, Hanspeter. 2007. "The Role of European Integration in National Election Campaigns." *European Union Politics* 8(1):83–108.

Kriesi, Hanspeter and Edgar Grande. 2016. The Euro Crisis: A Boost to the Politicisation of European Integration? In *Politicising Europe. Integration and Mass Politics*, ed. Swen Hutter, Edgar Grande, and Hanspeter Kriesi. Cambridge: Cambridge University Press, pp. 240–276.

Kriesi, Hanspeter, Edgar Grande, Martin Dolezal, Marc Helbling, Dominic Höglinger, Swen Hutter, and Bruno Wüest. 2012. *Political Conflict in Western Europe*. Cambridge: Cambridge University Press.

Kriesi, Hanspeter, Edgar Grande, Romain Lachat, Martin Dolezal, Simon Bornschier, and Timotheos Frey. 2008. *West European Politics in the Age of Globalization*. Cambridge: Cambridge University Press.

Kriesi, Hanspeter, Anke Tresch, and Margit Jochum. 2007. "Going Public in the European Union: Action Repertoires of Western European Collective Political Actors." *Comparative Political Studies* 40(1):48–73.

Laffan, Brigid. 1999. "The Berlin Summit: Process and Outcome of the Agenda 2000 Budgetary Proposals." *European Community Studies Association Review* 12(4):6–8.

2000. "The Big Budgetary Bargains: From Negotiation to Authority." *Journal of European Public Policy* 7(5):725–743.

Laffan, Brigid and Johannes Lindner. 2014. The Budget. Who Gets What, When and How? In *Policy-Making in the European Union*, eds. Helen Wallace, Mark A. Pollack, and Alasdair R. Young. New York: Oxford University Press, pp. 220–242.

Lasswell, Harold D. 1936. *Who Gets What, When, and How*. New York: Whittlesey House.

Le Cacheux, Jacques. 2005 European Budget: The Poisonous Budget Rebate Debate. Technical Report Notre Europe. Notre Europe Studies & Research No. 41.

2008. "European Budget: The Poisonous Budget Rebate Debate." Notre Europe Etudes & Recherches Working Paper No. 41.

Lee, Chung Hee. 2011. "The UK's Negotiation of Its EU Budget Rebate." Phd diss. University of Glasgow.

Leuffen, Dirk and Robin Hertz. 2010. "If Things Can Only Get Worse: Anticipation of Enlargement in European Union Legislative Politics." *European Journal of Political Research* 49(1):53–74.

Leuffen, Dirk, Berthold Rittberger, and Frank Schimmelfennig. 2013. *Differentiated Integration. Explaining Variation in the European Union*. Basingstoke: Palgrave MacMillan.

Leventoğlu, Bahar and Ahmer Tarar. 2005. "Pre-Negotiation Public Commitment in Domestic and International Bargaining." *American Political Science Review* 99(3):419–433.

Lewis, Jeffrey. 1998. "Is the 'Hard Bargaining' Image of the Council Misleading? The Committee of Permanent Representatives and the Local Election Directive." *Journal of Common Market Studies* 36(4):479–504.

2003. "Institutional Environment and Everyday Decision Making in the European Union." *Comparative Political Studies* 36(1–2):97–124.

2005. "The Janus Face of Brussels: Socialization and Everyday Decision Making in the European Union." *International Organization* 59(4):937–971.

Lewis-Beck, Michael S. and Thomas Rice. 1992. *Forecasting Elections*. Washington, DC: Congressional Quarterly Press.

Lewis-Beck, Michael S. and Mary Stegmaier. 2000. "Economic Determinants of Electoral Outcomes." *Annual Review of Political Science* 3:183–219.

Lijphart, Arend. 1999. *Patterns of Democracy. Government Forms and Performance in Thirty-Six Countries*. New Haven: Yale University Press.

Lindbeck, Assar and Jörgen W. Weibull. 1987. "Balanced-Budget Redistribution as the Outcome of Political Competition." *Public Choice* 52:273–297.

Lindberg, Leon and Stuart Scheingold. 1970. *Europe's Would-Be Polity*. Englewood Cliffs: Prentice-Hall.

Lindner, Johannes. 2006. *Conflict and Changes in Budgetary Politics*. New York: Routledge.

Lynn, Matthew. 2011. *Bust: Greece, the Euro, and the Sovereign Debt Crisis.* Hoboken: John Wiley & Sons.

Magee, Stephen P., William A. Brock, and Leslie Young. 1989. *Black Hole Tariffs and Endogenous Policy Theory: Political Economy in General Equilibrium.* New York: Cambridge University Press.

Mair, Peter. 2000. "The Limited Impact of Europe on National Party Systems." *West European Politics* 23(4):27–51.

2005. "Democracy Beyond Parties." UC Irvine: Center for the Study of Democracy.

2007. "Political Opposition and the European Union." *Government and Opposition* 42(1):1–17.

2008a. "The Challenge to Party Government." *West European Politics* 31(1):211–234.

2008b. "Electoral Volatility and the Dutch Party System: A Comparative Perspective." *Acta Politica* 43(2):235–253.

2009. "Representative versus Responsible Government." MPifG Working Paper 09/8.

Malamud, Andrés. 2008. The Internal Agenda of Mercosur. Independence, Leadership and Institutionalization. In *Los Nuevos enfoques de la integracion: mas alla del regionalismo*, ed. Grace Jaramillo. Quito: FLASCO, pp. 115–135.

Manin, Bernard, Adam Przeworski, and Susan C. Stokes. 1999. Elections and Representation. In *Democracy, Accountability and Representation*, eds. Adam Przeworski, Susan C. Stokes, and Bernard Manin. Cambridge: Cambridge University Press.

Maruhn, Roman and Janis A. Emmanouilidis. 2005. "Agenda 2007 – The Conflict over the Financial Framework 2007–2013." *Spotlight Europe* 01(05):1–11.

Matthijs, Matthias. 2016. "Powerful Rules Governing the Euro: The Perverse Logic of German Ideas." *Journal of European Public Policy* 23(3):375–391.

Mattila, Mikko. 2004. "Contested Decisions: Empirical Analysis of Voting in the European Council of Ministers." *European Journal of Political Research* 43:29–50.

2006. "Fiscal Transfers and Redistribution in the European Union: Do Smaller Member States Get More than their Share?" *Journal of European Public Policy* 13(1):34–51.

Mattila, Mikko and Jan-Erik Lane. 2001. "Why Unanimity in the Council? A Roll Call Analysis of Council Voting." *European Union Politics* 2(1):31–52.

Mattli, Walter and Anne-Marie Slaughter. 1998. "Revisiting the European Court of Justice." *International Organization* 52(1):177–209.

Mayhew, David. 1974. *Congress. The Electoral Connection.* New Haven: Yale University Press.

McIver, Iain. 2008. "The European Union Budget Review." SPICe Briefing Paper No. 08/50.

McKelvey, Richard D. and Peter C. Ordeshook. 1986. "Information, Electoral Equilibria, and the Democratic Ideal." *Journal of Politics* 48(4):909–937.

McKibben, Heather. 2013. "The Effects of Structures and Power on State Bargaining Strategies." *American Journal of Political Science* 57(2):411–427.

McKibben, Heather and Shaina Western. 2014. "Levels of Linkage: Across-Agreement versus Within-Agreement Explanations of Consensus Formation among States." *International Studies Quarterly* 58(1):44–54.

McCrae, Kenneth D., ed. 1974. *Consociational Democracy: Political Accommodation in Segmented Societies*. Toronto: McLelland & Steward.

Meiers, Franz-Josef. 2015. *Germany's Role in the Euro Crisis: Berlin's Quest for a More Perfect Monetary Union*. Cham: Springer.

Meirowitz, Adam. 2005. "Informational Party Primaries and Strategic Ambiguity." *Journal of Theoretical Politics* 17(1):107–136.

Meyer, Christoph. 1999. "Political Legitimacy and the Invisibility of Politics: Exploring the European Union's Communication Deficit." *Journal of Common Market Studies* 37(4):617–639.

Miller, Warren E. and Donald E. Stokes. 1963. "Constituency Influence in Congress." *American Political Science Review* 57(1):45–56.

Milner, Helen V. 1997. *Interests, Institutions, and Information: Domestic Politics and International Relations*. Princeton: Princeton University Press.

Milner, Helen V. and Benjamin Judkins. 2004. "Partisanship, Trade Policy, and Globalization: Is There a Left-Right Divide on Trade Policy?" *International Studies Quarterly* 48(1):95–119.

Milner, Helen V. and Dustin Tingley. 2011. "Who Supports Global Economic Engagement? The Sources of Preferences in American Foreign Economic Policy." *International Organization* 65(1):37–68.

Mink, Mark and Jakob de Haan. 2005. "Has the Stability and Growth Pact Impeded Political Budget Cycles in the European Union?" CESIFO Working Paper No. 1532.

Moravcsik, Andrew. 1991. "Negotiating the Single European Act: National Interests and Conventional Statecraft in the European Community." *International Organization* 45(1):19–57.

  1993. "Preferences and Power in the European Community: A Liberal Intergovernmentalist Approach." *Journal of Common Market Studies* 31(4):473–534.

  1994. "Why the European Union Strengthens the State: Domestic Politics and International Cooperation." Center for European Studies Working Paper No. 52.

  1997. "Taking Preferences Seriously: A Liberal Theory of International Politics." *International Organization* 51(4):513–553.

  1998. *The Choice for Europe: Social Purposes and State Power from Messina to Maastricht*. Ithaca: Cornell University Press.

  2002. "In Defense of the 'Democratic Deficit': Reassessing Legitimacy in the European Union." *Journal of Common Market Studies* 40(4):603–624.

  2008. "The Myth of Europe's 'Democratic Deficit.'" *Intereconomics* 43(6):331–340.

Moyer, Wayne H. and Tim Josling. 1990. *Agricultural Policy Reform Politics and Process in the EC and the USA*. Ames: Iowa State University Press.

Mueller, Dennis C. 2005. *Public Choice III*. Cambridge: Cambridge University Press.

Müller, Wolfgang C. and Kaare Strøm, eds. 2000. *Coalition Governments in Western Europe*. Oxford: Oxford University Press.

Mylonas, Yiannis. 2012. "Media and the Economic Crisis of the EU: The 'Cultiralization' of a Systemic Crisis and Bild-Zeitung's Framing of Greece." *tripleC: Cognition, Communication, Co-operation* 10(2):646–671.

Nadeau, Richard, Richard G. Niemi, and Antoine Yoshinaka. 2002. "A Cross-national Analysis of Economic Voting: Taking Account of the Political Context Across Time and Nations." *Electoral Studies* 21(3):403–423.

Novak, Stéphanie. 2013. "The Silence of Ministers: Consensus and Blame Avoidance in the Council of the European Union." *Journal of Common Market Studies* 51(6):1091–1107.

Nugent, Neill and Janet Mather. 2006. The United Kingdom: Critical Friend and Awkward Partner? In *The European Union and the Member States*, eds. Eleanor E. Zeff and Ellen B. Pirro. Boulder, CO: Lynne Rienner Publishers, pp. 129–150.

Olsen, Johan P., Alberta Sbragia, and Fritz W. Scharpf. 2002. "Symposium: Governing in Europe: Effective and Democratic?" *Journal of European Public Policy* 7(2):310–324.

Olson, Mancur. 1965. *The Logic of Collective Action. Public Goods and the Theory of Groups*. Cambridge: Harvard University Press.

Oltermann, Philip. 2012. "In Berlin." *London Review of Books* 34(13):25.

Page, Benjamin I. and Robert Y. Shapiro. 1992. *The Rational Public: Fifty Years of Trends in Americans' Policy Preferences*. Chicago: University of Chicago Press.

Patterson, Lee Ann. 1997. "Agricultural Policy Reform in the European Community." *International Organization* 51(1):135–165.

Pedersen, Mogens N. 1979. "The Dynamics of European Party Systems: Changing Patterns of Electoral Volatility." *European Journal of Political Research* 7(1):1–26.

Persson, Torsten and Guido Tabellini. 2002. *Political Economics. Explaining Economic Policy*. Cambridge: MIT Press.

Pervez, Fouad. 2015. "Waiting for Election Season." *The Review of International Organizations* 10(2):265–303.

Plümper, Thomas and Christina J. Schneider. 2007. "Discriminatory EU Membership and the Redistribution of Enlargement Gains." *Journal of Conflict Resolution* 51(4):568–587.

Pollack, Mark A. 1997. "Delegation, Agency, and Agenda Setting in the European Community." *International Organization* 51(1):99–134.

Powell, G. Bingham. 2000. *Elections as Instruments of Democracy: Majoritarian and Proportional Visions*. New Haven: Yale University Press.

  2004a. "The Chain of Responsiveness." *Journal of Democracy* 15(4):91–105.

  2004b. "Political Representation in Comparative Politics." *Annual Review of Political Science* 7:273–296.

Powell, G. Bingham and Guy D. Whitten. 1993. "A Cross-National Analysis of Economic Voting: Taking Account of the Political Context." *American Journal of Political Science* 37(2):391–414.

Proksch, Sven-Oliver and Jonathan B. Slapin. 2006. "Institutions and Coalition Formation: The German Election of 2005." *West European Politics* 29(3):540–559.

  2010. "Position Taking in European Parliament Speeches." *British Journal of Political Science* 40(3):587–611.

Przeworski, Adam, Susan C. Stokes, and Bernard Manin, eds. 1999. *Democracy, Accountability and Representation*. Cambridge: Cambridge University Press.

Przeworski, Adam and James R. Vreeland. 2000. "The Effect of IMF Programs on Economic Growth." *Journal of Development Economics* 62(2):385–421.

Puia, Dana Adriana. 2010. "The Dynamics of Institutional Change and the Case of EU Budgetary Negotiations." PhD diss. University of Pittsburgh.

Putnam, Robert D. 1988. "Diplomacy and Domestic Politics: The Logic of Two-Level Games." *International Organization* 44(3):427–460.

Putnam, Robert D. and Nicholas Bayne. 1984. *Hanging Together: The Seven-Power Summits*. Cambridge: Harvard University Press.

Rauh, Christian. 2016. *A Responsive Technocracy? EU Politicisation and the Consumer Policies of the European Commission*. Colchester: ECPR Press.

Ray, Leonard. 2003. "When Parties Matter: The Conditional Influence of Party Positions on Voter Opinions about European Integration." *Journal of Politics* 65(4):978–994.

Reif, Karlheinz and Hermann Schmitt. 1980. "Nine Second-Order National Elections: A Conceptual Framework for the Analysis of European Election Results." *European Journal of Political Research* 8(1):3–45.

Rickard, Stephanie J. and Teri L. Caraway. 2014. "International Negotiations in the Shadow of National Elections." *International Organization* 68(3): 701–720.

Risse, Thomas, ed. 2015. *European Public Spheres. Politics is Back*. Cambridge: Cambridge University Press.

Rittberger, Berthold. 2007. *Building Europe's Parliament. Democratic Representation Beyond the Nation State*. Oxford: Oxford University Press.

Robertson, David. 1976. *A Theory of Party Competition*. London: Wiley.

Rodden, Jonathan. 2002. "Strength in Numbers? Representation and Redistribution in the European Union." *European Union Politics* 3:151–175.

Rohrschneider, Robert. 2002. "The Democracy Deficit and Mass Support for an EU-Wide Government." *American Journal of Political Science* 46(2): 463–475.

Rohrschneider, Robert and Matthew Loveless. 2010. "Macro Salience: How Economic and Political Contexts Mediate Popular Evaluations of the Democracy Deficit in the European Union." *Journal of Politics* 72(4): 1029–1045.

Rohrschneider, Robert and Stephen Whitefield. 2012. *The Strain of Representation: How Parties Represent Diverse Voters in Western and Eastern Europe*. Oxford: Oxford University Press.

Rose, Richard. 2014. "Responsible Party Government in a World of Interdependence." *West European Politics* 37(2):253–269.

Rosenau, James N. 1961. *Public Opinion and Foreign Policy: An Operational Formulation*. New York: Random House.

Ross, George. 1995. *Jacques Delors and European Integration*. New York: Oxford University Press.

Sartori, Giovanni. 2005. "Party Types, Organization and Functions." *West European Politics* 28(1):5–32.

Sbragia, Alberta M. 1994. From "Nation State" to "Member State": The Evolution of the European Community. In *Europe After Maastricht: American and European Perspectives*, ed. P. M. Lützeler. Providence: Berghahn, pp. 69–87.

Scharpf, Fritz W. 1992. "Europäisches Demokratiedefizit und deutscher Föderalismus." *Staatswissenschaften und Staatspraxis* 3(3):293–306.

1999. *Governing in Europe: Effective and Democratic?* Oxford: Oxford University Press.

2003. "Problem-Solving Effectiveness and Democratic Accountability in the EU." MPIfG Working Paper No. 03/1.

2006. "The Joint-Decision Trap Revisited." *Journal of Common Market Studies* 44(4):845–864.

Schattschneider, E. E. 1960. *"The Semisovereign People: A Realist's View of Democracy in America."* Hinsdale: The Dryden Press.

Schild, Joachim. 2008. "How to Shift the EU's Spending Priorities? The Multiannual Financial Framework 2007–13 in Perspective." *Journal of European Public Policy* 15(4):531–549.

Schimmelfennig, Frank. 2001. "The Community Trap: Liberal Norms, Rhetorical Action, and the Eastern Enlargement of the European Union." *International Organization* 55(1):47–80.

2003. *The EU, NATO and the Integration of Europe: Rules and Rhetoric*. Cambridge: Cambridge University Press.

forthcoming. *Europäische Integration*. Paderborn: Schöningh.

Schmidt, Vivien. 2006. *Democracy in Europe: The EU and National Polities*. Oxford: Oxford University Press.

Schmitt, Hermann, Evi Scholz, Iris Leim, and Meinhard Moschner. 2005. "The Mannheim Eurobarometer Trend File, 1970–2002 [Computer file]." Prepared by Zentralarchiv für Europäische Sozialforschung und Zentrum für Umfragen, Methoden und Analysen.

Schmitt, Hermann and Jacques J. A. Thomassen. 1999. *Political Representation and Legitimacy in the European Union*. Oxford: Oxford University Press.

2000. "Dynamic Representation. The Case of European Integration." *European Union Politics* 1(3):318–339.

Schneider, Christina J. 2007. "Enlargement Processes and Distributional Conflicts: The Politics of Discriminatory Membership in the European Union." *Public Choice* 132(1–2):85–102.

2009. *Conflict, Negotiations, and EU Enlargement*. Cambridge: Cambridge University Press.

2010. "Fighting with One Hand Tied Behind the Back: Political Budget Cycles in the West German States." *Public Choice* 142(1):125–150.

2011. "Weak States and Institutionalized Bargaining Power in International Organizations." *International Studies Quarterly* 55(2):331–355.

2013. "Globalizing Electoral Politics: Political Competence and Distributional Bargaining in the European Union." *World Politics* 65(3):452–490.

2014. "Domestic Politics and the Widening-Deepening Trade-Off in the European Union." *Journal of European Public Policy* 21(5):699–712.

2017. "The Sources of Government Accountability in the European Union. Evidence From a Conjoint Experiment in Germany." Unpublished Working Paper.

Schneider, Christina J. and Branislav L. Slantchev. 2017. "The Domestic Politics of International Cooperation. Germany and the European Debt Crisis." *International Organization* 72(1):1–31.

Schneider, Christina J., Tilko Swalve, and Vera E. Troeger. 2016. "Strategic Budgeteering." Unpublished Working Paper.

Schneider, Christina J. and Jennifer L. Tobin. 2013. "Interest Coalitions and Multilateral Aid Allocation in the European Union." *International Studies Quarterly* 57(1):103–114.

Schneider, Christina J. and Johannes Urpelainen. 2014. "Partisan Heterogeneity and International Cooperation: The Case of the European Development Fund." *Journal of Conflict Resolution* 58(1):120–142.

Schneider, Gerald and Konstantin Baltz. 2004. The Power of Specialization: How Interest Groups Influence EU Legislation. In *The Role of Organized Interest Groups in Policy-Making*, eds. Debora Di Gioacchino, Sergio Ginebri, and Laura Sabani. New York: Palgrave MacMillan, pp. 253–284.

Schneider, Gerald and Lars-Erik Cederman. 1994. "The Change of Tide in Political Cooperation: A Limited Information Model of European Integration." *International Organization* 48(4):633–662.

Schoen, Harald. 2008. "Turkey's Bid for EU Membership, Contrasting Views of Public Opinion, and Vote Choice: Evidence from the 2005 German Federal Election." *Electoral Studies* 27(2):344–355.

Schulz, Heiner and Thomas König. 2000. "Institutional Reform and Decision-Making Efficiency in the European Union." *American Journal of Political Science* 44(4):653–666.

Sen, Amartya K. 1970. *Collective Choice and Social Welfare*. San Francisco: Holden-Day.

Shackleton, Michael. 2000. "The Politics of Codecision." *Journal of Common Market Studies* 38(2):325–342.

Shapley, Lloyd S. and Martin Shubik. 1954. "A Method for Evaluating the Distribution of Power in a Committee System." *American Political Science Review* 48:787–792.

Shi, Min and Jakob Svensson. 2006. "Political Budget Cycles: Do they Differ Across Countries and Why?" *Journal of Public Economics* 90(8-9):1367–1389.

Slapin, Jonathan B. 2008. "Bargaining Power at Europe's Intergovernmental Conferences: Testing Institutional and Intergovernmental Theories." *International Organization* 62(1):131–162.

Smith, Mitchell P. 1997. The Commission Made Me Do It: The European Commission as a Strategic Asset in Domestic Politics. In *At the Heart of the Union: Studies of the European Commission*, ed. Neill Nugent. Basingstoke: Macmillan Press Ltd, 167–186.

Spoon, Jae-Jae and Christopher J. Williams. 2017. "It Takes Two: How Eurosceptic Public Opinion and Party Divisions Influence Party Positions." *West European Politics* 40(4):741–762.

Stasavage, David. 2004. "Open-Door or Closed-Door? Transparency in Domestic and International Bargaining." *International Organization* 58(3):667–703.

2005. "Does Transparency Make a Difference? The Example of the European Council of Ministers." Unpublished Working Paper.

Stimson, James A., Michael B. MacKuen, and Robert S. Erikson. 1995. "Dynamic Representation." *American Political Science Review* 89(3): 543–565.

Stokman, Frans N. and Robert Thomson. 2004. "Winners and Losers in the European Union." *European Union Politics* 5(1):5–23.

Strong, James. 2017. *Public Opinion, Legitimacy and Tony Blair's War in Iraq.* London: Routledge.

Svolik, Milan. 2006. "Lies, Defection, and the Pattern of International Cooperation." *American Journal of Political Science* 50(4):909–925.

Szemlér, Tamás. 2006. "EU Budget Milestones: From Fundamental Systemic Reforms to Organised Chaos." *Papeles del Este* 11:1–20.

Tallberg, Jonas. 2002. "Delegation to Supranational Institutions: Why, How, and with What Consequences?" *West European Politics* 25(1):23–46.

2006. *Leadership and Negotiation in the European Union.* Cambridge: Cambridge University Press.

2008. "Bargaining Power in the European Council." *Journal of Common Market Studies* 46(3):685–708.

Tallberg, Jonas and Karl Magnus Johansson. 2008. "Party Politics in the European Council." *Journal of European Public Policy* 15(8):1222–1242.

Tausanovitch, Chris and Christopher Warshaw. 2014. "Representation in Municipal Government." *American Political Science Review* 108(3):605–641.

Thomassen, Jacques J. A. 1994. Empirical Research into Political Representation. In *Elections at Home and Abroad*, eds. M. Kent Jennings and T. E. Mann. Ann Arbor: University of Michigan Press, pp. 237–264.

1999. Political Communication Between Political Elites and Mass Publics: The Role of Belief Systems. In *Policy Representation in Western Democracies*, eds. Warren E. Miller, Roy Pierce, Jacques J. A. Thomassen, Richard Herrera, Sören Holmberg, Peter Esaisson, and Bernhard Webels. Oxford: Oxford University Press, pp. 33–58.

Thomassen, Jacques J. A. and Hermann Schmitt. 1997. "Policy Representation." *European Journal of Political Research* 32(2):165–184.

Thomson, Robert. 2007. "National Actors in International Organizations: The Case of the European Commission." *Comparative Political Studies* 41(2):169–192.

2011. *Resolving Controversy in the European Union. Legislative Decision-Making Before and After Enlargement.* Cambridge: Cambridge University Press.

Thomson, Robert, Javier Arregui, Dirk Leuffen, Rory Costello, James Cross, Robin Hertz, and Thomas Jensen. 2012. "A New Dataset on Decision-making in the European Union Before and After the 2004 and 2007 Enlargements (DEUII)." *Journal of European Public Policy* 19(4):604–622.

Thomson, Robert and Frans N. Stokman. 2006. Research Design: Measuring Actors' Positions, Saliences and Capabilities. In *The European Union Decides*, eds. Robert Thomson, Frans N. Stokman, Christopher H. Achen, and Thomas König. Cambridge: Cambridge University Press, pp. 25–53.

Thomson, Robert, Frans N. Stokman, Christopher H. Achen, and Thomas König, eds. 2006. *The European Union Decides*. Cambridge: Cambridge University Press.

Tillman, Erik R. 2004. "The European Union at the Ballot Box? European Integration and Voting Behavior in the New Member States." *Comparative Political Studies* 37(5):590–610.

2012. "Support for the Euro, Political Knowledge, and Voting Behavior in the 2001 and 2005 UK General Elections." *European Union Politics* 13(3): 367–389.

Tomz, Mike and Robert Van Houweling. 2008. "Candidate Positioning and Voter Choice." *American Political Science Review* 102(3):303–318.

Toshkov, Dimiter. 2015. "Public Opinion and Policy Output in the European Union: A Lost Relationship." *European Union Politics* 12(2):169–191.

Traber, Denise, Martijn Schoonvelde, Gijs Schumacher, Tanushree Dahiya, and Erik de Vries. 2016. "Issue Avoidance and Blame Attribution in Leader Speeches During the Economic Crisis in Europe." Unpublished Working Paper.

Treib, Oliver. 2014. "The Voter Says No, but Nobody Listens: Causes and Consequences of the Eurosceptic Vote in the 2014 European Elections." *Journal of European Public Policy* 21(10):1541–1554.

Trenz, Hans-Jörg. 2005. *Europa in den Medien: Die Europäische Integration im Spiegel Nationaler Öffentlichkeit*. Frankfurt am Main: Campus.

Tsebelis, George. 1994. "The Power of the European Parliament as Conditional Agenda Setter." *American Political Science Review* 88(1):128–142.

2002. *Veto Players: How Political Institutions Work*. Princeton: Princeton University Press.

Tufte, Edward R. 1978. *Political Control of the Economy*. Princeton: Princeton University Press.

Tzogopoulos, George. 2013. *The Greek Crisis in the Media: Stereotyping in the International Press*. London: Routledge.

van der Brug, Wouter and Cees van der Eijk. 2007. *European Elections and Domestic Politics: Lessons from the Past and Scenarios for the Future*. Notre Dame: University of Notre Dame Press.

van der Brug, Wouter, Cees Van der Eijk, and Mark Franklin. 2007. *The Economy and the Vote: Economic Conditions and Elections in Fifteen Countries*. Cambridge: Cambridge University Press.

van der Eijk, Cees and Mark N. Franklin. 1996. *Choosing Europe? The European Electorate and National Politics in Face of Union*. Ann Arbor: University of Michigan Press.

2004. Potential for Contestation on European Matters at National Elections in Europe. In *European Integration and Political Conflict*, ed. Gary Marks and Marco Steenbergen. Cambridge: Cambridge University Press, pp. 33–50.

van der Eijk, Cees, Mark N. Franklin, and Michael Marsh. 1996. "What Voters Teach Us About Europe-Wide Elections: What Europe-Wide Elections Teach Us About Voters." *Electoral Studies* 15(2):149–166.

Vasilopoulou, Sofia, Daphne Halikiopoulou, and Theofanis Exadaktylos. 2014. "Greece in Crisis: Austerity, Populism and the Politics of Blame." *Journal of Common Market Studies* 52(2):388–402.

Vaubel, Roland. 1986. "A Public Choice Approach to International Organization." *Public Choice* 51(1):39–57.

von Hagen, Jürgen. 2003. "Fiscal Discipline and Growth in Euroland. Experiences with the Stability and Growth Pact." ZEI Working Paper No. B062003.

Vreeland, James R. 1999. "The IMF: Lender of Last Resort or Scapegoat?" Prepared for the Midwest Political Science Association Annual Meeting, Chicago, IL, April 15–17, 1999.

Warntjen, Andreas, Simon Hix, and Christophe Crombez. 2008. "The Party Political Make-Up of the EU Legislative Bodies." *Journal of European Public Policy* 15(8):1243–1253.

Weaver, R. Kent. 1986. "The Politics of Blame Avoidance." *Journal of Public Policy* 6(4):371–398.

Williams, Christopher J. 2016a. "Issuing Reasoned Opinions: The Effect of Public Attitudes Towards the European Union on the Usage of the 'Early Warning System.'" *European Union Politics* 17(3):504–521.

2016b. "Responding through Transposition: Public Euroskepticism and European Policy Implementation." *European Political Science Review* 10(1):51–70.

Williams, Christopher J. and Jae-Jae Spoon. 2015. "Differentiated Party Response: The Effect of Euroskeptic Public Opinion on Party Positions." *European Union Politics* 16(2):176–193.

Wittman, Donald. 1989. "Why Democracies Produce Efficient Results." *The Journal of Political Economy* 97(6):1395–1424.

Wlezien, Christopher. 1995. "The Public as a Thermostat: Dynamics of Preferences for Spending." *American Journal of Political Science* 39(4):981–1000.

Wlezien, Christopher and Stuart N. Soroka. 2011. "Federalism and Public Responsiveness to Policy." *Publius: The Journal of Federalism* 41(1):31–52.

Wratil, Christopher. 2017. "Democratic Responsiveness in the European Union: The Case of the Council." European Union Politics 19(1): 52–74.

Zaum, Dominik. 2013. *Legitimating International Organizations*. Oxford: Oxford University Press.

Zimmer, Christina, Gerald Schneider, and Michael Dobbins. 2005. "The Contested Council: Conflict Dimensions of an Intergovernmental EU Institution." *Political Studies* 53(2):403–422.

Zweifel, Thomas D. 2006. *International Organizations and Democracy*. Boulder, CO: Lynne Rienner.

Index

A10, 147, 148, 158–160, 162, 163, 165, 169, 170, 173, 223, 232
accountability, 1, 2, 4, 5, 9–11, 39, 43, 59, 68, 70, 72, 90, 91, 300, 303–305, 307, 310
acquis communautaire, 30
Act on Financial Stability within the Monetary Union, 290
actor, 31, 35, 37, 55, 57, 62, 63, 150, 151, 190, 219–221, 225, 270, 276, 310
  expansion, 18, 35
  foreign, 1
  institutional, 4
  legislative, 4
  polarization, 18
  supranational, 6, 33, 42, 55, 56, 58, 70, 188, 252, 261, *see also* supranational bureaucrat
AfD, *see* Alternative für Deutschland
Afghanistan, 75
Africa, 75
African Development Fund, 301
age, 73, 75
Agenda 2000, 104, 147, 154, 157–159, 162–164, 172, 173
Alternative für Deutschland, 23, 282
Amsterdam Treaty, *see* Treaty of Amsterdam
analysis, 253, 255, 257, 262
  observational, 7, 9
  qualitative, 9, 11, 14, 145, 218, 268, 269
  quantitative, 9, 12, 14, 95, 112, 145
archival research, 9, 12, 14, 269
Argentina, 280
Association of Southeast Asian Nations, 1
asylum application, 75
asylum seeker, 11, 72, 75
  Definition, 75
Athens, 282, 283, 285, 286
attitude
  diffuse, 9, 18, 32, 36–38, 40, 58, 70, 90, 114, 118, 144, 311
  specific, 9, 37, 38, 57, 58

austerity, 208, 269, 273, 279, 281–283, 285, 286, 288, 293
Austria, 107, 147, 156, 159, 166, 169, 171, 201, 203, 223, 256, 311
average marginal component specific effects, 83

backlash, 67, 105, 290, 300, 304
backlog, 261
Baden-Württemberg, 163
bailout, 11, 14, 23, 72, 74–76, 78, 81, 83–85, 87, 88, 90, 266, 268–270, 273–284, 286, 288–295, 297
Balkenende, Jan Peter, 180
bargaining, 5, 7, 10–12, 15, 25, 32, 42, 48–54, 56, 61–64, 67–70, 72, 77, 78, 85–87, 89–91, 94–96, 99–107, 112–114, 116–118, 120, 126, 127, 133, 135, 141, 143–154, 157, 159, 161, 163–166, 169, 175, 177, 178, 180, 181, 184–186, 190–192, 194–197, 200, 204–207, 209–218, 221–223, 225, 227–229, 232, 235–238, 240, 243, 244, 246–249, 252, 253, 255, 259–268, 276, 285, 288, 297, 303–309, *see also* decision-making
closed door, 2, 3, 11, 15, 16, 53, 54, 58, 59, 63, 66–68, 72, 129, 144, 214, 234, 246, 301, 304, 307, *see also* transparency
collective, 6, 8, 10, 11, 14, 30, 39, 40, 42, 48, 51, 56, 58, 59, 85, 127
competence, 6, 11, 77, 78, 82, 89, 95, 107, 119, 120, 129, 248, 249, *see also* competence
cooperative, 52, 53
delay, *see* strategic delay
failure, 14, 15, 47, 60, 61, 63, 65, 70, 73, 149
informal, 183
legislative, 14, 95, 212, 213, 215, 219, 232, 243–245, 247, 303

Index

leverage, 1, 6, 12, 42, 50, 51, 61, 63, 64, 126, 128, 210
  formal, 7, 10, 11, 13, 48, 50, 53, 56, 58, 64, 69, 70, 96, 113, 114, 117, 127, 150, 226, 229, 235, 236, 240, 244, 246, 247
  informal, 7, 10, 11, 48, 50, 52, 58, 60, 64, 69, 70, 96, 113, 127, 135, 144
  structural, 50, 53, 64, 69, 70, 127, 135, 144, 226, 229, 244
  outcome, 237, 244
  strategy, 13, 62, 65, 145, 205, 211, 214, 266
  success, 11, 14, 42, 47, 60, 67, 70, 72, 82, 87, 91, 94, 95, 190, 201, 211, 213, 215, 218, 237–240, 244, 246, 247, 249, 252, 261, 267, *see also* credit claiming
  unilateral, 6, 10, 13
  zero-sum, 95
Barroso, José Manuel, 164, 182, 183, 186, 198, 201
Bayern, 163, 203
Belgium, 107, 109, 182, 220, 225
Belka, Marek, 195
Berlin, 191, 281
Berlusconi, Silvio, 186
Blair, Tony, 68, 149, 161, 166, 170, 174, 175, 177–184, 186, 187, 189–202, 204–211, 260, 263, 296, 297
blame, 11, 20, 31, 40, 42, 59, 62, 65, 72, 73, 85, 86, 190, 192, 194, 249, 269, 279, 310
blame avoidance, 5, 42, 60, 62, 68, 70, 71, 87, 91, 149, 150, 180, 181, 183, 190, 194, 208, 210, 214, 217, 266, 290, 296, 297, 309, *see also* strategic delay
  definition, 60
blame shifting, 60, 63
blocking minority, 51
bond, 272, 280, 282, 285, 287, 290
  spread, 286
  yield, 272, 283, 285, 287
box plot, 21, 26, 109, 232, 244
Brady, Graham, 185, 199
Brazil, 280
Bretton Woods institutions, 53
Brexit, 3, 100, 103, 104, 311
British rebate, *see* UK budget rebate
Brown, Gordon, 170, 178, 181, 183, 186, 198, 204

Brussels, 2, 3, 101, 170, 177–180, 183, 191, 195, 200, 250, 251, 274, 310, 311
budget, *see* EU budget
budget rebate, *see* UK budget rebate
Bulgaria, 107, 147, 149, 165, 222, 225, 237, 244, 257
Bundesrat, 276, 277, 295, 305
Bundestag, 23, 149, 185, 187, 191, 197, 209, 270, 276, 283, 291, 307
bureaucrat, *see* supranational bureaucrat
business group, *see* interest group

Cameron, David, 205, 250, 266
campaign contribution, *see* financial campaign contribution
CAP, *see* Common Agricultural Policy
CFSP, *see* Common Foreign and Security Policy
Chancellor, 23, 32, 60, 75, 93, 104, 149, 166, 185–187, 189–192, 197, 203, 204, 209, 211, 270, 274–277, 281, 284, 286, 289–291, 294, 296, 297
chancellor of the Exchequer, 170, 178
chef de cabinet, 17
China, 288
Chirac, Jacques, 68, 149, 150, 162, 169, 182–184, 186–194, 198, 200, 202, 204, 205, 207–211
Christlich Demokratische Union, 94, 131, 149, 185–187, 192, 196, 197, 203, 211, 274, 276, 277, 280, 282, 284, 292, 294–297
citizen, 1, 3–5, 8–10, 15, 16, 20, 27, 31, 33, 34, 37, 39, 40, 43, 44, 51, 55, 57–59, 65, 73, 95, 105, 114, 116, 119, 122, 136, 140, 142, 166, 184, 188, 207, 212, 216, 217, 252, 266, 273, 279, 289, 300, 301, 303–305, 307, 309–311
citizenship, 75
civil war, 2
Clausewitz, Carl von, 298
climate change, 220
co-decision procedure, *see* ordinary legislative procedure
Cohesion Fund, 97
Cohn-Bendit, Daniel, 269
Cold War, 147
Commission, *see* European Commission
commitment, 97, 108
Committee of Permanent Representatives, 49
common acquis, *see* acquis communautaire

Common Agricultural Policy, 32, 68, 93, 94, 97, 98, 100, 107–109, 111–113, 116–118, 121, 122, 124, 126, 127, 130, 133, 134, 140, 141, 143–145, 148–150, 154, 157–159, 161–163, 165, 166, 168, 173, 174, 176, 180, 182, 184, 185, 187–202, 204–206, 208–210
Common Foreign and Security Policy, 28, 51, 104, 105
common market, 102
common position, 32, 100, 172, 219, 220
competence, 20, 21, 27, 28, 30–32, 35, 43, 46, 47, 59, 62, 64–69, 77, 78, 82, 86–90, 284
  exclusive, 28, 30
  shared, 28, 30, 32
  supporting, 28
compromise, 49–52, 54, 56, 61, 64, 67, 68, 70, 102, 127, 161, 169, 180, 181, 185–188, 190, 191, 193, 194, 202, 204, 208, 213–217, 220, 222, 223, 225, 228–230, 236–238, 243, 244, 246, 251, 262, 264, 296, 303, 311
  Luxembourg, 260
Conciliation Committee, 55, 100, 101
conflict, 15, 32–34, 38, 40, 102, 133, 146, 152, 154, 157, 158, 165, 230, 237, 253, 256, 263, 264, 300, 311
  distributional, 14, 19, 158, 213
consens procedure, *see* special legislative procedure
consensus, 7, 35, 37, 40, 77
Conservative Party, 131, 161, 170, 175, 176, 178, 180, 183–186, 190, 191, 199, 204, 205, 207, 250, 251, 266
constituent, *see* voter
constituent preference, *see* public preference
Constitutional Treaty, 13, 150, 178, 182, 184, 187, 188, 191
constraining dissensus, 37
consultation procedure, *see* special legislative procedure
cooperation, 3, 5, 9, 14, 16, 18, 19, 64, 129, 131, 181–183, 190, 208, 210, 212, 213, 256, 263, 264, 269, 271, 300
  European, 9, 10, 15, 19, 42, 53, 62, 73
Coreper, *see* Committee of Permanent Representatives
corporate group, *see* interest group
Council of the European Union, 3–6, 8–10, 12–14, 17, 32, 33, 38, 42, 44, 48–56, 58, 59, 61–68, 70, 72, 94, 95, 99, 100, 113, 126–131, 133, 141, 144, 152, 153, 155, 158, 163, 165, 172, 180, 181, 190, 193, 202, 206, 210, 212, 214, 216, 218–220, 222, 224, 226–230, 234, 236, 243, 244, 246–248, 253, 256, 261, 263, 265, 303, 304, 306–309, 311
  Description, 49
  Agriculture, 100
  Economic and Financial Affairs, 49, 96, 152, 282
  General Affairs and External Relations, 49, 96, 152
Council of the European Union, 235
Council Presidency, *see* Presidency
counterfactual, 14, 265, 268, 310
country, 2, 6, 21, 22, 24–26, 50, 51, 64, 66, 72, 95, 98, 102–104, 107, 109, 110, 112–117, 120, 124, 126, 127, 138, 139, 143–145, 150, 156, 158–161, 169, 181, 191, 204, 205, 207, 222, 226, 232, 237, 244, 255, 259, 270, 271, 273, 274, 277–279, 283, 287, 293, 307
cohesion, 139, 168, 170
credit claiming, 6, 7, 13, 38, 42, 47, 59, 60, 63, 68, 71, 72, 82, 87–89, 91, 94, 107, 111, 113, 116, 126, 127, 135, 136, 142, 144, 145, 149, 182, 190, 203, 210, 212, 214, 215, 230, 236, 241, 243, 246, 247, 249, 252, 261, 266, 303, 307, 310
  Definition, 59
  undeserved, 59, 89, 214, 308
credit rating agency, 272, 280, 287, 292
Crimea, 2
Croatia, 107, 147
CSDP, *see* Common Security and Defense Policy
Cyprus, 107, 147, 225
Czech Republic, 107, 147, 225, 244

data, 3, 10, 217, 219, 220, 222, 225, 226, 228, 229, 232, 234, 237, 240
  Comparative Manifesto Project, 129, 131
  DEU II, 13, 215, 218, 222, 224, 230, 234, 237, 253, 257
  EU budget, 12, 102, 107
  EULO, 14, 212
  EUR-Lex, 212, 253
  Eurobarometer, 2–4, 12, 24, 33–35, 175
  European Union Legislative Output Data Set, 253

Index   337

ParlGov, 113
PreLex, 54, 212, 253
VoteWatch Europe, 54
debt crisis, 21, 274, 279, 280, 287
   European, 268, 280
   Eurozone, 3, 35, 60, 158, 276, 288, 292
   global, 274, 279
   Greece, 2, 74, 75, 269, 270, 272,
      274–277, 279, 280, 282, 283, 286,
      290, 292, 294
decision, 1, 6–8, 10, 13, 18, 37, 63, 99,
   100, 122, 127, 136, 229, 234, 256,
   260–264, 267, 270, 272, 276, 288,
   304, 306, 310
decision-making, 15, 32, 42, 49, 51, 142,
   148, 179, 214, 222, 229, 255,
   263–265, *see also* bargaining
   apparatus, 8
   body, 3, 33, 42, 48, 49, 55
   outcome, 6, 12–14, 38, 40, 42, 46–48,
      53, 56, 58–66, 82, 85, 87, 95, 107,
      148, 150, 165, 170, 194, 205, 212,
      214–218, 220, 222, 229, 234, 236,
      237, 239–241, 243, 245–249, 251,
      252, 254, 255, 261, 262, 266–268,
      296, 301–303, 309
   output, 8
   process, 6, 44, 50, 62
   rule, 12, 16, 50, 127, 226
   consensus, 7, 51–53, 56, 58–62, 64, 70,
      100, 126, 144, 204, 210, 216,
      228, 244, *see also* consensus
   double qualified majority, 51
   qualified majority, 50, 51, 62, 64, 70,
      100, 152, 226, 229, 236, 244,
      252, 255, 261, 263
   supermajority, 100, 101
   unanimity, 6, 50, 51, 55, 59, 64, 70,
      152, 202, 226, 229, 236, 244,
      255, 261, 263, 284, 306
delay, *see* strategic delay
delegation, 8, 30, 31, 40, 299–302, 307,
   310
Delors I, 146, 151, 154, 157
Delors II, 146, 151, 157, 162
Delors, Jacques, 175
democracy, 7–10, 15–17, 20, 38, 40, 42,
   43, 175, 294, 299, 301, 304, 305,
   308, 309
   consociational, 305
democratic deficit, 1, 17, 18, 40, 301, 302
democratic legitimacy, 2, 4, 7–9, 15, 16,
   54, 301, 302, 305, 307, 311
   crisis, 1–3, 8, 15, 301, 307, 308, 310
democratic scrutiny, 1, 5, 18, 308

democratization, 2
Denmark, 67, 103, 107, 150, 169, 244
directive, 32, 219, 220, 232, 253, 256,
   262, 263
Doha Round, 308
domestic electoral competition model, *see*
   political economy model
domestic politics, 4, 5, 9, 18, 31, 33,
   35–37, 39, 42, 45, 102, 107, 141,
   142, 150, 207, 209–211, 217, 219,
   222, 245, 265, 267, 269, 299,
   301–304
Dutch Republic, 306

ECB, *see* European Central Bank
economic distress, 2, 119, 122, 124, 185,
   309
economic growth, 28, 138, 139, 141, 147,
   273, 285, 299
economic liberalism, 187, 189
economic liberalization, 184, 208
economy, 20, 24, 27, 46, 69, 74, 75, 98,
   112–114, 117, 119, 124, 139, 159,
   163, 175, 184, 270, 272, 276, 284,
   288, 289, 291, 292, 297, 309
ECSC, *see* European Coal and Steel
   Community
education, 73
EEC, *see* European Economic Community
election, 43, 45, 59, 66–68, 70, 72, 78, 80,
   81, 91, 94–96, 105–107, 111–113,
   115, 116, 118, 120, 122, 124, 126,
   127, 129, 131, 133, 135, 136, 138,
   141, 143–145, 218, 222, 243, 247,
   267–269, 296
   distress, 68, 69, 96, 119, 120, 122, 126,
      135, 141, 143, 185, 190, 204, 215,
      240, 242, 246, 303, 304
   endogenous, 112
   European, 4, 9, 18, 37, 45, 58, 176
   local, 250
   national, 5–7, 9–15, 18, 19, 21, 23–25,
      27, 28, 30, 36, 37, 58, 60, 94,
      111–113, 135, 141, 145, 149, 150,
      162, 180, 181, 183–187, 190–192,
      196, 199, 204, 206–208, 212–219,
      223–225, 227–230, 232, 233,
      235–238, 240–255, 257, 259–263,
      265, 266, 270, 274, 276, 296, 303,
      304, 307
   state, 13, 94, 149, 185, 186, 208, 276,
      277, 280, 281, 289–295, 297
   volatility, 10, 19, 21–23, 25, 39, 48, 149
electoral uncertainty, *see* political
   uncertainty

338   Index

electorate, *see* voter
eligibility, 98, 99, 107, 109, 111, 113, 116, 117, 127, 128, 135, 141, 144, 161, 169, 170, 202
EMU, *see* European Monetary Union
entropy balancing, 73
EPP, *see* European People's Party
Estonia, 107, 147
EU, *see* European Union
EU budget, 12, 14, 15, 60, 73, 93–95, 97–107, 111, 112, 114, 116–118, 120, 126, 129, 133, 135, 144, 146–159, 161–166, 169, 171–174, 176–178, 181, 184–191, 193, 196, 198–213, 215, 244, 245, 247, 249–252
   annual, 12, 93–97, 99, 101, 104, 106, 107, 113, 114, 135, 145, 146, 151, 152, 154, 211, 228, 244, 267, 303
   Description, 96
   contribution, 94, 97, 102–107, 113, 138, 146, 148–151, 153, 156–159, 161, 163–166, 168, 169, 171–174, 179, 185, 188–190, 192, 193, 200, 201, 203, 207, 211, 223, 249, 266
   multiannual, 12, 13, 96–99, 101, 103, 104, 106, 107, 145–155, 157, 158, 163–166, 173, 190, 193, 196, 211, 212, 252, 266, 267, 303, 304
   Description, 96
   receipt, 12, 13, 94–96, 99, 101, 103, 104, 107–109, 111, 112, 114–118, 120, 122, 123, 125–127, 129, 131, 133–139, 141–145, 159, 161, 163–166, 189, 223, 234, 236, 240, 242, 243, 245–247
EU summit, 146, 149, 151, 171, 175, 178, 182–184, 187, 188, 191, 192, 194–196, 200, 201, 206, 249, 274, 282, 283, 288
Eurogroup, 276, 281, 283, 284, 290
Europe, 2, 11, 21, 23, 25, 26, 28, 33, 44, 57, 72, 85, 97, 139, 176, 177, 179, 180, 182, 184–186, 193, 194, 198, 199, 201, 202, 205, 206, 214, 270, 278, 279, 281, 286, 287, 291, 293–296, 298, 311
   Central and Eastern, 13, 25, 51, 64, 94, 104, 109, 111, 117, 147, 149, 165, 169, 171, 179, 194, 198–200, 202, 206, 207, 209, 210, 264
   Mediterranean, 94
   Western, 21, 22, 24
European Agricultural Fund for Rural Development, 97
European Central Bank, 28, 274, 276, 284, 288, 289

European Coal and Steel Community, 2, 17, 299, 302
European Commission, 3, 6, 17, 24, 33, 38, 44, 48, 51, 54–56, 58, 59, 64, 70, 94, 97–101, 107, 146, 148, 151–153, 155, 156, 162, 164–166, 169, 172–178, 180–182, 186, 188, 193, 202, 206, 207, 210, 218–220, 225, 229, 232, 249–253, 266, 269, 271, 275, 283, 284, 297, 304, 308, 309
   Description, 55
European Communities, 2, 17, 30, 33, 34, 93, 175, 275
European Council, 3, 49, 50, 58, 149, 151–153, 158–160, 186, 188, 200, 202, 208, 274, 282
   Description, 49
European Court of Auditors, 107, 138
European Court of First Instance, 54
European Court of Justice, 17, 55
European demos, 16, 58, 304, 306, 311
European Economic Community, 2, 103, 158
European Integration Index, 30
European interest, 6
European Maritime and Fisheries Fund, 97
European Monetary Union, 28, 102
European Parliament, 3, 4, 6, 9, 18, 32, 33, 37, 44, 48–50, 53–56, 58, 59, 70, 99–101, 104, 113, 128, 131, 135, 141, 144, 148, 149, 152, 153, 172, 175, 176, 193, 201, 202, 205, 218–220, 226, 228, 229, 256, 261, 304, 306–309
   Description, 55
European People's Party, 131
European Regional Development Fund, 98
European Republic, 306, 311
European Social Fund, 98
European Structural and Investment Fund, 97, 107–109, 111–113, 116–118, 120, 124, 126–128, 130, 133, 134, 139, 141, 143–145, 185
European Union, 1–12, 14–17, 19, 25, 28, 37, 38, 49, 51, 52, 54, 57, 67, 72, 74–77, 84, 85, 89–94, 96–98, 100–104, 109, 116, 117, 131, 135, 142, 146, 147, 149–152, 155, 156, 158–166, 168–172, 175–177, 179, 186, 188, 189, 191, 194, 212, 213, 222, 230, 247–253, 256, 261, 262, 265, 267, 270, 271, 274, 280, 281, 283, 288–290, 295, 296, 299, 302–311

Index

Eastern enlargement, 147, 148, 158–165, 170, 171, 179, 187, 189, 194, 201, 208, 257, 264
enlargement, 4, 8, 30, 50, 52, 64, 67, 102, 104, 105, 109, 114, 117, 142, 146, 147, 154, 158, 219, 234, 256, 264, 302
membership, 3, 6, 28, 39, 66, 67, 77, 78, 102, 112, 131, 146–148, 150–156, 158–161, 163–166, 168, 170, 171, 173, 175, 179–183, 186–188, 191, 193, 195, 198–200, 203, 206, 207, 210, 212, 218–226, 228, 229, 232, 234, 236, 237, 240, 243, 244, 246, 250–253, 255, 256, 259, 260, 262–266, 269, 270, 274, 293, 297, 303, 304
europeanization, 44
euroscepticism, 23, 36, 37, 40, 70, 90, 103, 131, 175–177, 186, 188, 205, 207, 209, 309
Eurostat, 75, 114, 138, 139, 250, 271, 272, 285
Eurozone, 2, 28, 30, 269–276, 279–283, 285, 287–293, 297
exchange rate, 28, 30, 274
executive, *see* government
experience, *see* political experience
expert, 219, 220, 226, 232, 274, 286, 287, 297

Farage, Nigel, 104, 205, 250
farmer, 93, 94, 97, 98, 102, 113, 116, 140, 143, 161–163, 165, 208, 277
Federal Republic of Germany, *see* Germany
financial aid, *see* bailout
financial campaign contribution, 44
financial contribution, 74, 269, 276, 289, 290, 306
Finland, 25, 107, 147, 193, 201, 256
fiscal policy, 27, 28, 30, 39, 59
foreign policy, 6, 122, 197
France, 13, 17, 22, 46, 53, 93, 94, 102, 103, 107, 109, 149–151, 158, 160, 162, 163, 166, 168, 169, 171, 172, 174, 177, 180, 182–192, 194, 195, 200, 201, 204–210, 220, 222, 223, 232, 237, 244, 259–261, 270, 279, 299
Freie Demokratische Partei, 185, 186, 197, 274, 276, 282, 292, 294
fund, 98, 109, 113, 114, 149, 152, 155
agricultural, 126, 135, 161

structural, 94, 97, 98, 102, 111, 120, 124, 126, 127, 135, 141, 143, 144, 148–150, 152, 154, 157, 160, 161, 163–165, 168–170, 173, 174, 176, 185, 186, 188, 198, 199, 201–203, 206, 207, 209, 210, 274

GDP, *see* gross domestic product
gender, 11, 72, 73, 75, 78, 82
generalized correction mechanism, 174, 180
German Basic Law, 280
German Democratic Republic, 147
Germany, 11, 13–15, 23, 32, 46, 53, 64, 67, 72, 73, 75–78, 90, 93, 94, 102–105, 107, 109, 131, 147, 149, 151, 156, 159, 162, 163, 166, 168, 171, 172, 174, 176–178, 180, 182, 185–192, 194, 195, 197, 203, 204, 206–211, 220, 223, 225, 232, 244, 259–261, 266, 269, 270, 272, 274–286, 288–293, 297, 299, 305, 307
Google Trends, 105
governance, 65, 127, 211, 216, 302, 304, 306, 309, 310
democratic, 8
multilevel, 4, 8
government, 1, 3–19, 21, 23, 25–28, 30–33, 36–40, 42, 44–51, 53, 54, 56, 58–70, 72–75, 77, 89–91, 93–96, 99, 103, 104, 106, 107, 111–113, 115, 116, 118–120, 122, 124–141, 143–145, 150, 151, 161, 163, 168, 170, 172, 174, 175, 177–180, 183–188, 190, 192, 193, 195–197, 199, 201, 203, 205–210, 212–226, 228–230, 232–238, 240–249, 251, 252, 254–257, 259, 261–282, 284–287, 289–310
appointee, 58
approval, 6, 7, 10–12, 23–25, 37, 62, 69, 73, 78, 79, 81, 84, 87, 88, 90, 91, 96, 119, 122, 123, 136–139, 141, 143, 145, 175, 178, 187, 188, 234, 259, 284, 294, 296
coalition, 23–26, 46, 48, 58, 122, 136–138, 141, 149, 197, 209, 274, 276, 277, 297
debt, 30, 270–272, 274, 278, 280, 282, 283, 286, 287, 291, 293, 297
deficit, 27, 28, 30, 66, 67, 97, 270–272, 282, 285, 286, 296
foreign minister, 67

340 Index

government (cont.)
 incumbent, 9, 10, 12, 19, 21, 23, 25, 27, 30, 39, 43, 47, 69, 122, 124, 143, 149, 150, 263, 268, 276, 303
 minister, 3, 4, 6, 33, 49, 58, 96, 129, 274, 275, 283, 285, 286, 288
 minority, 25, 138, 141
 opportunistic, 13
 spending, 101
 subnational, 58, 170, 305
Greece, 11, 14, 72, 74–78, 81, 85, 107, 169, 256, 266, 268–295, 297
Green Party, 185, 197, 295, 296
 European, 269
gridlock, 15, 50, 51, 61, 62, 96, 180
gross domestic product, 30, 64, 98, 101, 103, 109, 114, 116, 117, 138, 139, 147, 166, 168, 170, 171, 174, 270, 271, 273, 285
gross national income, 97, 101, 153, 155–160, 166, 168–172, 176, 177, 188, 199, 201, 203, 210, 250, 306
gross national product, 139, 141, 146, 151, 155, 158, 159

hidden cooperation, 11–15, 42, 56, 66–70, 107, 111, 126, 129, 133, 135, 144, 149, 150, 183, 184, 190, 207, 210, 296, 303, 311
 Definition, 66
High Representative of the Union for Foreign Affairs and Security Policy, 51
Holmes, Kim R., 2
House of Commons, 175, 181, 190, 205, 250, 260
Hungary, 75, 107, 147, 150, 225

ideological affinity, *see* partisan affinity
ideology, 20, 21, 26, 39, 45, 69, 73, 77, 129, 176, 215, 270, 310
 divergence, 129–131, 144, 222, 235, 236, 243, 246, 247, 263
 heterogeneity, 129, 256, 263, 264
IMF, *see* International Monetary Fund
immigration, 23, 37, 51, 72, 75, 76, 84, 105, 186, 189
incompetence, *see* competence
inflation, 28, 30, 138, 278
information obstruction policy, 17
information shortcut, 20, 43
informed consent, 73
institution, 2, 4, 6, 8, 9, 15, 17, 39, 40, 42, 46, 48, 49, 58, 62, 64, 70, 93, 99, 126, 274, 275, 299, 301–304, 307–309, 311

instrumental variable regression, 137
integration
 European, 2, 4, 5, 9, 10, 17, 18, 27, 30, 33–40, 49, 53, 55, 70, 93, 96, 102, 104, 118, 133, 142, 144, 175, 176, 208, 299, 301, 302
 international, 1, 307
 regional, 2
interest group, 1, 5, 19, 20, 27, 32, 33, 40, 43–47, 53, 62, 113, 122, 124, 140, 143, 213–215, 301, 302, 304, 307, 308
 agricultural, 46, 93, 121, 124, 143
 automobile, 46
interest rate, 28
intergovernmental, 3–5, 8–10, 33, 42, 44, 46, 48–50, 53, 56, 62, 300, 303
intergovernmental organization, *see* international organization
internal market, 28, 64
Internal Review Board, 73
international bureaucrat, *see* supranational bureaucrat
International Monetary Fund, 1, 74, 139, 269, 276, 279, 283, 284, 288, 289, 297, 307
international organization, 1, 2, 53, 60, 298, 300, 301, 307, 308
interquartile range, 21
interview, 9, 14, 24, 95, 219, 269, 270, 275, 278, 280, 282, 286, 290, 292
intrinsic competence, *see* competence
investment, 28, 93, 148, 270, 272, 275, 280, 287
IQR, *see* interquartile range
Iraq, 75, 287
Iraq war, 68, 169, 174, 175, 182, 186, 204
IRB, *see* Internal Review Board
Ireland, 107, 110, 220, 244, 280, 287, 288
issue salience, *see* salience
issue-linkage, 53
Italy, 103, 107, 109, 137, 150, 160, 168, 169, 171, 174, 186, 223, 225, 232, 244, 250, 259–261, 279, 280, 286–288

joint decision trap, 96
Juncker, Jean-Claude, 181, 184, 187, 188, 192–195, 199, 203, 281

Kohl, Helmut, 60, 68, 93, 94, 104, 105

Labour Party, 131, 150, 161, 170, 174–176, 178, 180, 181, 183, 185, 186, 189, 205, 206, 208, 296

Index

Lamy, Pascal, 17
Landtag, 276
Latvia, 107, 147, 225
Leave campaign, 104
legislative, 95, 145, 187, 211
  act, 14, 33, 54, 95, 99, 212, 247
  adoption, 14, 55, 56, 153, 253, 255, 257, 259, 261, 264, 265, 296
  body, 4, 49
  instrument, 253
  issue, 13, 219, 220, 224–226, 230, 232–234, 237, 246
  negotiation, 6, 7, 14, 95
  output, 38, 212, 265
  period, 23
  process, 28, 48, 268
  Description, 54
  proposal, 14, 44, 54, 55, 62, 152, 153, 166, 172, 174, 176, 177, 180, 181, 188, 193, 198, 199, 201, 202, 207, 213, 218–220, 226, 227, 230, 232, 234, 237, 240, 252, 253, 255–259, 262, 265, 267, 304
  tide, 14
legitimacy, *see* democratic legitimacy
Lehman bankruptcy, 272, 274, 288
Liberal Democratic Party, 175
Lisbon Treaty, 99, 101, 153, *see* Treaty of Lisbon
Lithuania, 107, 147
loan, 97, 274, 278–280, 283, 284, 291
logit model, 83
lowest common denominator, 96
Luxembourg, 25, 107, 150, 181, 188–190, 192, 193, 196, 198, 199, 202, 225, 244, 260

Maastricht
  criteria, 30
  Treaty, 1, 9, 12, 28, 35, 55, 118, 288, 302
Malta, 107, 147, 225
Marcinkiewicz, Kazimierz, 201, 206
margin of victory, 122
market
  agriculture, 97
  capital, 28, 97
  financial, 2, 272–275, 280–283, 285, 287, 290
media, 5, 17, 36, 43, 49, 62, 75, 177, 192, 222, 249, 269, 277, 284, 286, 289, 292, 295, *see also* newspaper
median voter theorem
  Definition, 45
Mercosur, 1, 307

Merkel, Angela, 23, 75, 149, 187, 189–192, 194, 196–198, 200, 203, 204, 206, 208, 209, 211, 260, 274–278, 280–284, 286, 288–292, 294–297
Mexico, 280
Middle East, 2
Ministry of Commerce, 270
Ministry of Finance, 270
Mitterrand, François, 93, 94
monetary policy, 27, 28, 39, 59
Monnet, Jean, 17, 298, 299, 301
moral hazard, 282, 283
multilevel mixed-effects estimation, 226, 240
multiple issues, 226, 230
Muslim, 75

national budget, 101, 104, 116
National Health Service, 104
national interest, 6, 52, 55, 60, 61, 73, 92, 101, 118, 127, 179, 180, 199, 205, 212, 213, 215, 218, 249, 300, 306–309
national parliament, 24, 38, 138, 186, 277, 281, 283
NATO, *see* North Atlantic Treaty Organization
negotiation, *see* bargaining
Netherlands, 25, 94, 103, 107, 109, 111, 112, 150, 156, 159, 166, 170–172, 174, 180, 187–189, 193–195, 203, 208, 211, 220, 223, 225, 232, 250, 251
newspaper, 17, 35, 53, 177, 206, 213, 219, 249, 250, 278, 282, *see also* media
Nice Treaty, *see* Treaty of Nice
Nordrhein-Westfalen, 149, 163, 185, 208, 276, 277, 280, 281, 288–296
North Africa, 2
North American Free Trade Agreement, 301, 307
North Atlantic Treaty Organization, 1, 147
Norway, 147
nuclear power station, 23

OECD, 283, 288
OLS, *see* ordinary least squares
opinion, 75, 76, 78
  popular, 3, 281
  public, 3, 11, 16, 18–20, 23, 24, 33, 37, 39, 45, 48, 52, 66, 136, 150, 187, 199, 208, 216, 218
opportunistic, 7, 11, 30, 31, 308
opposition, *see* political opposition

ordinary least squares, 36, 83, 257
ordinary legislative procedure, 56, 70, 99, 144, 219, 229, 261
  Description, 55
organized interests, *see* interest group
Osborne, George, 196
outcome affinity, 82
outlier, 21
outside option, 63

Papandreou, George, 270–274, 277, 283
Papantoniou, Yannos, 288
Paris, 2
parochial interest, 1, 102, 299, 300
partisan affinity, 11, 19–21, 23, 39, 45, 67, 72, 77, 78, 81, 82, 84, 85, 87–91
partisan dealignment, 10, 20, 21, 39, 48
party, *see* political party
paymaster, 53, 104
payment, 97
Pedersen index of volatility, 21
performance, 5, 6, 18, 25, 31, 43, 65, 69, 95, 176, 178, 194, 249, 276, 294, 295, 303, 309
permissive consensus, 18, 37
Philippines, 308
PIIGS, 280, 287
placebo test, 228
Poland, 107, 109, 110, 147, 149, 151, 166, 195, 200, 201, 203, 206, 209, 210, 222, 223, 232
polarization, 35
political business cycle, 27, 59, 66, 116
political economy model, 10, 42, 48, 59
political elite, 1, 2, 9, 14, 18, 20, 38–40, 43, 270, 279, 301, 308
political experience, 11, 72, 73, 78, 82, 179
political instability, 186
political knowledge, 83
political opposition, 8, 21, 23, 39, 40, 46, 47, 53, 69, 124, 138, 141, 161, 170, 175, 178, 180, 185, 186, 190, 196, 208, 249, 250, 263, 266, 267, 276, 280, 294, 297, 303, 304, 309
political party, 5, 18–21, 23–25, 27, 31, 36–40, 43–46, 57, 68, 69, 82, 122, 124, 129, 131, 137–139, 141, 149, 170, 175, 176, 178, 196, 197, 203, 205, 209–211, 250, 252, 276, 282, 294, 295, 303, 306, 311
political responsiveness, *see* responsiveness
political uncertainty, 2, 10, 19–21, 39, 47, 48, 119, 124–126, 143, 162, 188, 260, 268

politician, 7, 11, 18–21, 37, 38, 42, 43, 72, 73, 77–91, 102, 106, 250, 274, 278, 282, 292–294, 305, 308–310
politicization, 5–7, 9, 10, 12, 15, 17–19, 30, 35, 37, 38, 40, 43, 45, 48, 70–73, 75, 77, 91, 94, 95, 104, 105, 112, 118, 142, 143, 150, 214, 250, 257, 262, 263, 300, 303, 308–310
  Definition, 18
Politicization Index, 36
poll, *see* survey
popular opinion, 276
population, 3, 21, 44, 51, 64, 73–75, 109, 118, 138, 147, 158, 159, 189, 278, 305, 311
populism, 2, 6, 21, 194, 309, 311
Portugal, 107, 109, 149, 159, 169, 186, 225, 244, 256, 280, 287, 288
position, 23, 32, 33, 36–38, 40, 42, 45, 46, 53, 54, 56–58, 61, 62, 65, 72, 74, 78, 81–91, 147, 149, 150, 153, 161, 164, 165, 168–170, 172, 174, 179, 180, 185, 188, 189, 191, 192, 198, 205, 207, 208, 210, 213–222, 225, 226, 229, 230, 234, 237, 240, 244, 245, 247, 249, 261, 266, 268–270, 282, 289, 294, 296, 297, 309
position affinity, *see* partisan affinity
position defense, 5–7, 10, 11, 13, 15, 42, 61, 62, 66, 68, 70–72, 82, 85–87, 90, 91, 149–151, 212, 214–218, 220–225, 228–230, 233–238, 240–243, 245–249, 251, 261, 263, 266–268, 281, 290, 295, 296, 303
  Definition, 61
position extremity, 68
position taking, 5–7, 10, 11, 42, 50, 61, 62, 68, 70, 71, 83–87, 90, 91, 149, 151, 166, 168, 184, 195, 212, 214–216, 218, 228, 249, 251, 267, 295, 303
  Definition, 61
preference
  popular, 15
  public, 1, 5, 7, 8, 10, 19, 42–45, 56–59, 75–77, 80, 81, 85, 91
preference dimension
  left-right, 18, 36, 38, 57, 58, 129, 131, 133, 144, 216, 218, 256
  pro-anti EU, 58, 104, 131, 132, 144, 175, 176, 179, 216, 218
  see also euroscepticism
Presidency, 50, 180–182, 187, 188, 190, 192, 193, 196, 199, 201, 202, 288

Index 343

prime minister, 25, 26, 60, 102, 166, 178–182, 185, 186, 195, 196, 198, 201, 205, 250, 270, 275, 277, 297
probability sample, 73
Prodi, Romano, 166, 169, 176, 177, 186, 207
public good, 27, 39, 67, 116, 299
public opinion, 175, 192, 278–280, 297, 307, 310
public support, 311

Rüttgers, Jürgen, 292
rating agency, 285
reciprocity, 11, 52, 66, 67, 129, 228
redistribution, 39, 40, 94, 95, 102, 107, 110, 111, 114, 133, 135, 141, 143–146, 152, 153, 165, 211
referendum, 147, 277
  Constitution, 150, 183, 184, 187, 189, 194, 204, 208, 210
  UK exit, 2, 100, 103, 104, 250, 311
refugee, 2, 11, 72, 75, 76, 78, 81, 83–85, 90
  crisis, 2, 23, 72, 76, 100
regime, 38, 66, 90
regulation, 28, 152, 153, 172, 178, 213, 253, 256, 262, 263
representation, 43–45, 48, 49, 55, 57–59, 64, 65, 72, 78, 91, 141, 173, 177, 210, 265, 299–301, 304–306, 308
  proportional, 19, 25, 122
Respondi, 73
responsibility, 24, 25, 60, 98, 176, 219, 279, 282, 290, 292, 300, 304, 309, 311
  Definition, 300
responsible party government, 57
responsiveness, 4, 19, 27, 44, 45, 50, 79, 90, 91, 107, 111, 112, 117–119, 122, 266, 300, 301, 311
  Definition, 6, 56
  chain, 42, 57–59
  domestic, 7, 8, 10, 38, 45, 56
  EU, 8, 10, 15, 18, 58, 62, 92, 302, 304, 307, 308
  governance, 5, 6, 8, 10, 16, 58, 72, 212, 305, 306
  government, 3–13, 15, 19, 21, 25, 30, 31, 37, 39–44, 46–48, 56, 58, 59, 61, 65–73, 77–79, 83, 85, 87, 88, 91, 95, 96, 106, 112, 118, 120, 122, 124–126, 128, 133, 135, 142–145, 149, 150, 183, 184, 206, 207, 211, 213–217, 221–223, 228, 230, 236, 243, 247, 249, 251, 267, 290, 295, 303–305, 307–309
  input & output, 10, 59–62, 95
supranational actors, 4, 57
Romania, 107, 147, 165, 222, 237, 244, 257
Rotating Presidency, *see* Presidency
running scared, 23
Russia, 2

Saarland, 163
Saint Simon, 17, 298
salience, 2, 5, 9, 17, 18, 25, 32, 33, 35, 36, 40, 48, 67, 70, 72, 102, 105, 106, 140, 144, 226, 230, 232–234, 236, 237, 240–242, 246
Schäuble, Wolfgang, 274, 280, 286, 287, 291
Schleswig-Holstein, 185
Schröder, Gerhard, 32, 60, 149, 182, 185–192, 194–198, 203, 204, 206, 208, 209, 211, 260, 263, 276
SEA, *see* Single European Act
SGP, *see* Stability and Growth Pact
shadow of the future, 52
Shapley-Shubik index, 114, 226, 244
shock, 2, 15
side payment, 53, 63, 216, 229
Single European Act, 35, 102, 110, 253
Single European Market, 28, 35, 94
sleeping giant, 17, 18, 20, 33, 40, *see also* slumbering giant
Slovakia, 107, 147, 225, 244
Slovenia, 64, 65, 107, 147
slumbering giant, 20, *see also* sleeping giant
societal interest, 1, 8, 27, 62, 67, 102, 188, 213, 300
Southwest Asia, 75
sovereignty, 1, 6, 19, 30, 32, 146, 299, 300, 304, 306, 307
Sozialdemokratische Partei Deutschlands, 149, 185, 186, 189, 192, 196, 197, 209, 274, 276, 277, 280, 281, 295
Spain, 107, 109–111, 149, 150, 159, 160, 163, 168, 169, 171, 186, 187, 193, 195, 202, 225, 232, 256, 279, 280, 287, 288, 311
special legislative procedure, 56, 152, 219, 256, 261
  Description, 56
spending plan, *see* EU budget
Stability and Growth Pact, 28, 30, 181, 270, 271, 275
State Department, *see* US State Department

Steinbrück, Peer, 274
Steinmeier, Frank-Walter, 274, 281
Stoiber, Edmund, 190
strategic delay, 5, 6, 10, 13–15, 60, 63, 70, 100, 105, 149, 180, 181, 189, 190, 195, 206, 212, 213, 248, 251–255, 258–261, 263–269, 276, 280, 289, 291, 297, 303, 304, 309, *see also* blame avoidance
Straw, Jack, 184, 191
subsidies, 28, 301
  agricultural, 93, 94, 98, 102, 109, 111, 113, 143, 157, 158, 162, 165, 166, 189, 192, 194, 202, 205, 277
Sunday vote question, 24, 72, 78, 80, 124
supranational bureaucrat, 1, 3, 8, 42, 178, 219, 252, 256, 261, 300, 304, 308, 311
survey, 4, 11, 24, 33, 69, 72–75, 77, 83, 136, 187, 192, 267, 268, 276, 277, 279, 288, 291, 294, 297
  experiment, 7, 9, 11, 12, 72–74, 77, 78, 85, 88, 90
  respondent, 11, 24, 33, 72, 74, 76–83, 85, 87, 89–91, 219
Sweden, 75, 103, 107, 147, 156, 159, 166, 170, 171, 174, 188, 193, 203, 220, 225, 256
Switzerland, 147
Syria, 75

Takeover directive, 32
taxpayer, 75, 94, 161, 190, 196, 250, 270, 280, 292, 295
terrorist attack, 2
TEU, *see* Treaty on European Union
TFEU, *see* Treaty on the Functioning of the European Union
Thatcher, Margaret, 60, 102, 170, 175, 176
trade, 27, 28, 139, 168, 206, 288, 300, 301, 308
transparency, 13, 15, 27, 30, 53, 54, 56, 60, 62, 67, 171, 232, 310, 311
Treaty of Amsterdam, 55
Treaty of Lisbon, 49–51, 56
Treaty of Maastricht, *see* Maastricht Treaty
Treaty of Nice, 50, 55
Treaty of Versailles, 299
Treaty on European Union, *see* Maastricht Treaty
Treaty on the Functioning of the EU, 271, 274
Treaty on the Functioning of the European Union, 55, 99, 100, 152, 160
Turkey, 67, 191

UK, *see* United Kingdom
UK budget rebate, 13, 102, 103, 148–150, 156–162, 164, 165, 170–172, 174–186, 189–210, 296
UK Leave campaign, 103
Ukraine crisis, 2, 105
uncertainty, *see* political uncertainty
unemployment, 38, 109, 114, 119–121, 124, 138, 139, 141, 143, 185, 191, 234, 235, 242, 246, 273, 292
United Kingdom, 2, 13, 22, 60, 93, 94, 102–104, 107, 131, 148–151, 156–165, 169–172, 174–210, 220, 223, 225, 232, 244, 249–251, 259, 260, 266, 268, 279, 288, 297, 311
United Kingdom Independence Party, 176, 205, 250, 251
United Nations, 1, 174, 301, 307
United States of America, 8, 20, 79, 139, 169, 174, 179, 182, 194, 200, 206, 274, 278, 305
  House of Representatives, 139, 305
  Senate, 8, 139, 172, 305
  State Department, 2

validity
  external, 73, 88, 89
  internal, 11, 73, 89
value-added tax, 97, 156, 158, 159, 203
Venezuela, 287
Verhofstadt, Guy, 182, 183, 204
veto player, 96
  institutional, 8
veto power, 64, 147, 163, 172, 178, 182, 184, 186, 189, 200–202, 204, 206, 210, 229, 263
vote affinity, 82
vote of confidence, 185, 187
voter, 1, 3, 6–9, 11, 12, 14–21, 25–27, 30–32, 37–40, 42–48, 58, 59, 61, 62, 65–74, 76–82, 84–93, 95, 102, 103, 107, 116, 124, 126, 133–136, 141, 143, 145, 162, 170, 175, 181, 183, 185, 187, 189, 196, 210, 211, 213–218, 222, 240, 247, 249, 251, 261, 266–268, 276–278, 280, 281, 284, 290–293, 295–297, 300, 303–309
  core, 45, 46, 48, 69, 91
  electorally relevant, 5, 6, 42, 46–48, 59, 61, 69, 91, 124, 214–216
  Definition, 45
  median, 45, 46
  opposition, 23, 43, 91, 175, 277, 283, 289
  polarization, 34

reasoning, 20, 91
　　swing, 45, 46, 48, 69, 91, 92, 124–126, 143
　　turnout, 44
　　undecided, 69, 124–126, 143
　　uninformed, 18–20, 43, 72
voter preference, *see* public preference

war of attrition, 267
Warsaw, 206

Westerwelle, Guido, 274, 286
World Bank, 301, 308
World Trade Organization, 1, 53, 301, 307, 308
World War I, 298, 299
World War II, 1, 299, 310
WTO, *see* World Trade Organization

xenophobia, 75